The Batsford Book
of Chess Records

Yakov Damsky

Translated by John Sugden

BATSFORD

First published in the United Kingdom in 2005 by
Batsford
151 Freston Road
London
W10 6TH

An imprint of Anova Books Company Ltd

ISBN-13 9780713489460
ISBN-10 0 7134 8946 4

A CIP catalogue record for this book is available from the
British Library.

10 9 8 7 6 5 4 3 2

Printed and bound by Creative Print and Design (Wales), Ebbw Vale

This book can be ordered direct from the publisher at the website:
www.anovabooks.com, or try your local bookshop

Distributed in the United States and Canada by
Sterling Publishing Co.,
387 Park Avenue South, New York, NY 10016, USA

TO THE BLESSED MEMORY
OF MY DAUGHTER
TATIANA

Contents

Foreword

The idea for this book has accompanied me throughout my chess life – which began when I was a thirteen-year-old schoolboy, in other words impossibly late. No sooner had I learnt the moves of the pieces and the name of the current World Champion than I grew curious to know who the world record holder was – by analogy with other sporting activities that interested me. I remember being astonished to discover that in chess there was no such person....

Years passed. Chess became my favourite recreation, and in due course it was happily linked to my work as a journalist. While managing a programme called 'Four Knights Club' on what was then Central Television, I began seriously collecting facts and putting together a sketch (as you might call it) of those records which *did* after all exist in this ancient game of the mind. Unfortunately the task remained unfinished; Soviet TV programmes on 'intellectual' themes in the 1970s were prone to be whittled down....

More years, and decades, elapsed. Then, half way through the 1980s, a book by the English author Ken Whyld came into my hands. I was positively spellbound by its title – *Chess: The Records*. However, a mere three of its 176 large-size pages proved to be devoted

to records in the sense that interested me, and even those three referred largely to compositions, mathematics in chess, and the like. Apart from that, the contents were those of a high-quality reference book: the names of champions of the principal chess-playing nations, tables of the most important tournaments, some superb photos....

I shared my feelings with my best friend Mikhail Tal. Suddenly he promised to contribute a preface to the book which absolutely had to be written. Alas, the manuscript only took shape long after the day when Tal – himself the holder of several chess records – departed from this world. I continue nonetheless to regard him as the godfather of this book, the like of which has not been seen before in world chess literature. In addition I wish to thank all those who have generously helped in its creation – above all Grandmaster Yuri Averbakh, whose immense erudition helped me out of more than one stalemate situation.

In what specific fields did I look for records, and by what criteria did I decide on the record holders? The criteria were fluid, and it would be naive to expect a work of this kind to be free from inaccuracies or indeed outright errors. The quantity of chess material is too large (or rather, vast!) for that; there is always the likelihood that something has been left out or not given due recognition, something in fact which might not have found its way into the contemporary periodicals or books. Therefore, friends, any amendments you can offer will be gratefully received.

Part One: Games

The shortest and the longest

Everything under this heading ought by definition to be a record, but it isn't always easy to get things straight. For one thing, it will not do to compare games played on a park bench with duels enacted before the eyes of the whole world – in matches for the crown, in the Candidates elimination series, in international tournaments and the championships of the major chess powers. For anything we know, five or six thousand moves may have been played between dawn and dusk by a Mr Hopkins in some suburb of Sydney, in an effort to force mate with knight and bishop against Mr Smith's lone king – but no one but themselves will have heard of this feat, which in any case violates the rules of tournament chess. When we talk about records, we can only work with authenticated data.

The *shortest* game in any World Championship match was the second between Fischer and Spassky at Reykjavik in 1972. After losing the opening game, Fischer simply didn't turn up for the following one – and since he had the white pieces, not even 'one half-move' was carried out on the chessboard. The minute hand of the clock performed its hour-long rotation, the flag fell, and the score became 2:0 to the World Champion.

There was, incidentally, a chance that this record of sorts might be repeated. The sagacious Mikhail Tal, who among other things was a brilliant practical psychologist, had some advice for Spassky and his seconds – Efim Geller, Nikolai Krogius (who was later to gain a doctorate in psychology) and Ivo Nei. Tal urged them not to turn up for the third game; he wanted them to 'return' the point to Fischer, on the principle of 'not taking from the destitute'! After a 'coup' like that, the highly-strung Fischer would probably not have become World Champion, but ... Spassky lost the third game by 'normal' means, and chess history took its course.

In Candidates matches, the shortest game lasted a little longer. In 1983 in the American city of Pasadena, Viktor Korchnoi played 1 d4, and since the Soviet authorities in their ideological obstinacy refused to let Garry Kasparov play on American soil, Korchnoi's half-move took him to the final of the Candidates cycle – just like the Hungarian Grandmaster Zoltan Ribli, who, as it happens, had 'won' his match against ex-World Champion Vasily Smyslov in exactly the same way.

While we are about it, these 'half-moves' were record-breaking in another sense too. As a result of prolonged negotiations it became possible to 'retract' them, and both the matches in question took place after all. This cost the Soviet Union more than 120,000 dollars – a record price for not playing some such move as 1...♘f6!

And finally we will add one other fully official game to our collection. In round 23 of the 1970 Interzonal Tournament at Palma de Mallorca, Fischer's very first move 1 c4 brought him victory because his adversary Oscar Panno refused to start play at 7 o'clock in the evening. Up to that time the sun was still shining on the Mediterranean island, and so, true to his religious convictions, Bobby refused to sit down at the chessboard on that sabbath day of 12 December. The tournament regulations had granted his request in advance, so the Argentine player's stand against the rules brought him a zero in the tournament table.

And now a brief digression, but this too is about a record. A couple of decades later Fischer turned into a rabid, militant anti-Semite. It never even entered the head of the ex-king of chess to write a letter of apology to Panno, let alone to compensate him for the moral and material injury he suffered.

However, a game involving International Master Archil Ebralidze is a worthy rival to Fischer-Panno and even surpasses it on 'bonus points'. One day during the Georgian championship Ebralidze replied to 1 e4 by stopping the clock and signing his scoresheet underneath the words 'Black resigned'. To a perturbed controller, the master explained his decision like this: "Somehow I just don't like my opponent's face today!"

So much for the shortest wins and losses. As for draws ... there is hardly a chessplayer in the world who has never agreed a draw with his opponent prior to the start of play and then gone through the motions with one or two dozen completely harmless moves, before signing the scoresheet and handing it to the controllers.

And yet the score of the game between International Masters William Watson of England and Milan Drasko of Yugoslavia in the Chigorin Memorial at Sochi (1988) is not to be found in any archives, never mind any databases or periodicals. On that day White offered a draw with his first move 1 e4, and Black accepted. As it turned out, this wasn't quite sufficient to leave a trace in the treasure-house of chess annals.

It isn't easy to talk about ultra-short games that were genuinely contested. In theory you can be mated by 1 g4 e6 2 f4 ♛h4!. Haven't we all fallen for this as beginners, only to inflict the Scholar's Mate on the black king at move four of a later game, priding ourselves on our acquired knowledge? There are, however, a great many official confirmations of how short life on the chessboard can be. Here are just a few.

Rigo (Antilles) –
Cooper (Wales)
Nice Olympiad 1974
King's Gambit [E11]

1 e4 e5 2 f4 d5 3 fxe5?? ♛h4+ 4 g3 ♛xe4+ 5 ♔f2 ♝c5+ 0-1

Hartlaub – Rosenbaum
Freiburg 1892
Bishop's Opening [C23]

1 e4 e5 2 ♗c4 ♘c6 3 ♘f3 f6?
4 ♘h4 g5?? 5 ♕h5+ ♔e7 6 ♘f5
mate

Combe (Scotland) –
Hasenfuss (Latvia)
Folkestone Olympiad 1933
English Opening [A43]

1 d4 c5 2 c4 cxd4 3 ♘f3 e5
4 ♘xe5?? ♕a5+ 0-1

Klein (Ecuador) – **Miagmasuren**
(Mongolia)
Leipzig Olympiad 1960
Sicilian Defence [E71]

1 e4 c5 2 ♘f3 ♘c6 3 d4 cxd4
4 ♘xd4 ♘f6 5 ♘c3 d6 6 ♗d3??
♘xd4 0-1

Pfeiffer (West Germany) –
Baltouni (Lebanon)
Leipzig Olympiad 1960
Dutch Defence [D62]

1 d4 d5 2 c4 c6 3 ♘c3 e6 4 e3 f5
5 ♘f3 ♗d6 6 ♘e5 ♘d7? 7 ♕h5+
♔f8?? (instead of 7...g6 8 ♘xg6
♘gf6) 8 ♕f7 mate

The next game is between more
weighty contestants:

Wade (England) –
Kinzel (Austria)
Varna Olympiad 1962
Queen's Pawn Opening [D56]

1 d4 d5 2 ♘c3 ♘f6 3 ♗g5 c6

4 ♗xf6 gxf6 5 e3 e5 6 ♕h5 e4 7 f3!
f5 8 fxe4 fxe4?? 9 ♕e5+ 1-0

Finally, the following game
became known the world over:

Keres – Arlamowski
Szczawno Zdroj 1950
Caro-Kann Defence [B10]

1 e4 c6 2 d4 d5 3 ♘c3 dxe4
4 ♘xe4 ♘d7 5 ♕e2 ♘gf6?? 6 ♘d6
mate!

I should add that Keres got up
from the table after playing his fifth
move and was standing behind his
opponent's back when he saw him
make the suicidal reply. Thereupon
his arm reached out over the
Polish master's shoulder and
carried out the move with the
knight. Perfect gentleman that he
was, the Grandmaster couldn't help
speaking the word that was by no
means obligatory: "Mate!"

What is much more interesting,
though, is that the earlier games
Alekhine-Mohner (Palma de
Mallorca 1938) and Vogt-Lehmann
(Weidenau 1947) ended in exactly
the same way – as did the
later games Kosterin-Lanzias
(Havana Olympiad 1966), Guzden-
Krysztanowski (Elbat 1973),
Nizimura-Marco (Lucerne Olymp-
iad 1982) etc. etc.

Now for the shortest of all. In
over-the-board play –

Djordjević – Kovacević
Bela Crkov 1984
Trompowsky Attack [A45]

1 d4 ♘f6 2 ♗g5 c6 3 e3 ♕a5+
0-1

And by correspondence (!) –

11

Antuanes – Suta
1988
Nimzo-Indian Defence [E30]

1 d4 ♘f6 2 c4 e6 3 ♘c3 ♗b4
4 ♗g5 h6 5 ♗h4 ♕e7 6 e3 d6
7 ♕a4+?! ♘c6 8 d5 exd5 9 cxd5
♕e4!!

Faced with the threats of
10...♗xc3+ and 10...♕xh4, White
can save himself neither with 10
♕b3 ♘a5 nor with 10 ♕d1 ♘xd5;
while after 10 ♗b5 ♗xc3+ 11 bxc3
♕xa4 12 ♗xa4 ♘xd5, his central
pawn is lost. He therefore decided
against prolonging the fight (**0-1**).

As for the *longest* games, there is
clearly little point in reproducing
them here; there wouldn't be many
people with the inexhaustible
patience to play through them. Let
us therefore confine ourselves to
stating the facts as reported in the
chess press. Here goes....

In a tournament in Tampere, the
Swede Thomas Ristoja and the Finn
Michael Nykopp chuckled as they
moved their pieces around for
precisely 300 (!) moves, and we
have ample reason to suppose that
this game is not worth taking
seriously.

By contrast, the following very
long games were a life-and-death
struggle.

At Belgrade in 1989, the game
between the Yugoslavs Ivan Nikolić
and Goran Arsović ended in a draw
on the 269th move. Playing to the
classic time control of forty moves
in two and a half hours and twenty
moves per hour thereafter, they had
spent 20 hours and 15 minutes at
the board and filled up seven
scoresheets each.

In the USA-China match at the
Saloniki Olympiad in 1988, the
game between Seirawan and Xu Jun
ended in stalemate on move 198.

What was the longest game that
had a 'result'? (Actually that
is a misnomer, for a draw is a
result too.) In the 1981 Israeli
championship, Edael Stepak beat
Yakov Mashinan in 193 moves!

And finally, in World Championship matches there has never
been a longer game than the fifth
between **Korchnoi** and **Karpov** at
Baguio in 1978. It was drawn in 124
moves.

60...g6
This piece sacrifice gives Black a
theoretically drawn endgame.
61 ♗d6 ♘f5 (or 61...gxh5 at
once) **62 ♔f4 ♘h4 63 ♔g4 gxh5+**
"This is now forced, as 63...♘f5
64 hxg6 ♘xd6 would fail to 65
♔f4. The move played leads to an

interesting endgame in which Black needs to be exceptionally careful." (Tal)

64 ♔xh4 ♔xd4 65 ♗b8 a5 66 ♗d6 ♔c4 67 ♔xh5 a4 68 ♔xh6 ♔b3 69 b5 ♔c4 70 ♔g5 ♔xb5 71 ♔f5 ♔a6 72 ♔e6 ♔a7

"For the moment the black king won't leave this corner. If White could stalemate it and thus force the b-pawn to advance, he would attain his goal. But bringing this about is beyond his power." (Tal)

73 ♔d7 ♔b7 74 ♗e7 ♔a7 75 ♔c7 ♔a8 76 ♗d6 ♔a7 77 ♔c8 ♔a6 78 ♔b8 b5

"At this point, taking account of the fifty-move rule, there was a sigh of relief in the press centre – the game wouldn't go beyond move 128...." (Tal)

79 ♗b4 ♔b6 80 ♔c8 ♔c6 81 ♔d8 ♔d5

"This ending had been analysed in detail by the Soviet theoretician Rauzer. Korchnoi now strives in vain for over forty moves to overturn Rauzer's verdict that the game should be drawn. I repeat that all the while Black must play with great care; his king is constantly 'on the brink' of the danger zone." (Tal)

82 ♔e7 ♔e5 83 ♔f7 ♔d5 84 ♔f6 ♔d4 85 ♔e6 ♔e4 86 ♗f8 ♔d4 87 d6 ♔e4 88 ♗g7 ♔f4 89 ♔e6

♔f3 90 ♔e5 ♔g4 91 ♗f6 ♔h5

In this position the game was adjourned for the second time. There followed:

92 ♔f5 (sealed) **♔h6 93 ♗d4 ♔h7 94 ♔f6 ♔h6 95 ♗e3+ ♔h5 96 ♔f5 ♔h4 97 ♗d2 ♔g3 98 ♗g5 ♔f3 99 ♗f4 ♔g2 100 ♗d6 ♔f3 101 ♗h2 ♔g2 102 ♗c7 ♔f3 103 ♗d6 ♔e3 104 ♔e5 ♔f3 105 ♔d5 ♔g4 106 ♔c5 ♔f5 107 ♔xb5 ♔e6 108 ♔c6 ♔f6 109 ♔d7 ♔g7 110 ♗e7 ♔g8 111 ♔e6 ♔g7 112 ♗c5 ♔g8 113 ♔f6 ♔h7 114 ♔f7 ♔h8 115 ♗d4+ ♔h7 116 ♗b2 ♔h6 117 ♔g8 ♔g6 118 ♗g7 ♔f5 119 ♔f7 ♔g5 120 ♗b2 ♔h6 121 ♗c1+ ♔h7 122 ♗d2 ♔h8 123 ♗c3+ ♔h7 124 ♗g7 stalemate**

The longest 'decisive' game to occur at the highest level took 102 moves and was played in the Lyon half of the Kasparov-Karpov match in 1990. It was adjourned for the second time in the following position.

Kasparov – Karpov
16th game, World Championship
match 1990

My own comments were published in the Riga magazine *Shakhmaty*:

"White was naturally intent on winning with his extra exchange, but there were two factors hanging over his head like the sword of Damocles. In the first place, before the end of the session he had taken all the remaining time on his own clock, so that he now had to make the next 16 moves in 11 minutes. Still, with the benefit of adjournment analysis, this could hardly count as a serious problem. Running ahead, I will say that Kasparov actually took no more than 5 or 6 minutes to complete the game. But the second point is that White only had 25 moves at his disposal for winning purposes. That's right – a clause in the Laws of Chess which only finds practical application once in a blue moon (as they say) was looming on the horizon. In the 25 moves leading up to this position, there had been no pawn moves or captures.

"This explains why the spectators were treated to a rare spectacle: after the 94th move the World Champion suddenly lifted his eyes to the ceiling and began beating a strange rhythm with his hand in the air, while pensively bending and unbending his fingers. Clearly he was figuring out whether he had enough tempi left to fit into the procrustean bed of the rules.

"Again I will anticipate. Black didn't defend as stubbornly as he could have done, and some of the 25 moves (making up the overall 50-limit) remained unused. But the main subject of lively discussion in the press centre was whether the diagram position lent itself to analysis by a computer. We agreed that it did, and that therefore it was perhaps time to take up an idea of

Fischer's – to play the whole game to a finish without adjourning, just as they had done more than 100 years ago in the very first 'match for the crown' between Steinitz and Zukertort.

"The answer to the riddle came a week later in the shape of a fax to the Lyon press centre, explaining that the position had indeed been given to a computer for analysis – and not just any old computer either, but the World Champion 'Deep Thought', no less. The latter's exertions had produced the following: 89 ♖a7 ♗e4+ 90 ♔c5 ♗g2 91 ♔d4 ♗f3 92 ♔e3 ♗d5 93 ♔f2 ♗e4 94 ♖d7 ♗f5 95 ♖c7 ♗e4 96 ♖c4 ♗d5 97 ♖d4 ♗h1 98 ♖d6 ♔f7 99 ♔e3 ♗g2 100 ♗d4 ♗a8 101 ♗b2 ♗g2 102 ♗c3 ♗a8 103 ♗d4 ♗g2 104 ♔e5 ♗h1 105 ♖b6 ♗g2 106 ♗a1 ♗d5 107 ♗c3 ♗g2 108 ♖a6 ♗f1 109 ♖d6, and White is pretty well back where he started. Nor was that all. The electronic chess champion hit on the right plan only after being shown the first six moves which the 'ordinary' champion had made on resumption. There you are then, colleagues, we can sleep peacefully now. Or can we...?"

Here is how the third playing session proceeded. 'Human' analysis had shown that by making use of *zugzwang* White could after all break through with his king.

89 ♖a7 ♗g4 90 ♔d6 ♗h3 91 ♖a3 ♗g4 92 ♖e3 ♗f5

The first part of the plan is accomplished. The rook has taken up its ideal post, from which it controls all the crucial squares.

93 ♔c7! ♔f7

On 93...♔e7, White wins with 94 ♗d6+ ♔f7 95 ♔d8 ♘g7

96 ♖e7+ ♔g8 97 ♖a7 ♘e6+
98 ♔e7 ♘xg5 99 ♗e5.
94 ♔d8 ♗g4
Nor can Black save himself with
94...♔e6 in view of 95 ♗h2+ ♔d5
96 ♔e7 ♔d4 97 ♖e1 and 98 ♔f7,
followed by a sacrifice on g6.
95 ♗b2! ♗e6
Black also loses with 95...♘f4
96 ♖e7+ ♔f8 (or 96...♔g8 97 ♖e4!)
97 ♗a3!.
96 ♗c3
Zugzwang! The rest is simple.
**96...♗f5 97 ♖e7+ ♔f8 98 ♗e5!
♗d3 99 ♖a7 ♗e4 100 ♖c7 ♗b1
101 ♗d6+ ♔g8 102 ♔e7 1-0**

It would be quite impossible to
find the longest game played by
correspondence. After all, it could
live on (or 'smoulder on'?) for
years, in complete acordance with
the rules – particularly if one
opponent lived, say, in Chile, and
the other in Russia. A letter from
some settlement in the East Siberian
taiga to a foreign destination takes a
month at least. A game to break the
record for duration can nonetheless
be suggested. In 1926 two final-
year students at Aberdeen
University, who afterwards went
their separate ways, began a game
that dragged on for 40 years without
even finishing! One of the
opponents had an extra pawn, but in
Grandmaster Yuri Averbakh's
opinion he would need another ten
years or so to exploit his advantage!
I am afraid that the further course of
this combat is lost in the mists of
time....
The following story is not
dissimilar, though there is a rather
different and surprising twist to it.
In 1921, while they were both in
Europe, the American S.Robertson

from New York and the Australian
G.Keystone from Adelaide had an
argument about a variation of the
French Defence. Since they
couldn't reach agreement, they
decided to settle the matter by a
postal game.
The antagonists parted, and play
began. At first, the moves were sent
by letter. Those from America
travelled via Europe, the Suez
Canal and the Indian Ocean. The
replies made their way over the
boundless expanse of the Pacific,
through the Panama Canal and
across the Caribbean.
After five years of dogged
struggle, the players had only just
entered a complex middlegame.
Then on the American's proposal
they decided to continue by
telegraph; all the telegram expenses
were to be paid by the loser.
A year and a half later the
struggle ended in defeat for
Robertson, who duly reimbursed
the Australian's expenses to the
tune of 6000 dollars. Although
evidently not the longest-lasting
game in chess history, this was the
costliest one in the literal sense of
the word – especially when you
take inflation into account....
As the game of *shortest* duration,
we should probably single out the
following, played by Viswanathan
Anand and Valery Salov in 1991 in
a Paris speed chess tournament.
White contrived to win in
approximately two and a half
minutes.

Anand – Salov
Sicilian Defence [B31]

**1 e4 c5 2 ♘f3 ♘c6 3 ♗b5 g6
4 0-0 ♗g7 5 c3 ♘f6 6 ♖e1 0-0 7 h3**

15

e5 8 d4 cxd4 9 cxd4 exd4 10 e5
♘d5 11 ♗g5 ♕a5 12 ♘a3 a6
13 ♗c4 ♘b6 14 ♗b3 ♘xe5
15 ♘xe5 ♗xe5 16 ♗h6 d6 17 ♗d2
♕c5 18 ♖c1 ♕xc1 19 ♗xc1 ♗d7
20 ♗h6 ♖fe8 21 ♕f3 1-0

And to finish with, here is the shortest game in which the famous fifty-move rule was invoked. It was played in the 14th round of the Rubinstein Memorial Tournament, Polanica Zdroj 1966, between the Pole **Andrej Filipowicz** – International Master, International Arbiter and chief editor of the magazine *Szachy* – and the Yugoslav **Petar Smederavac**.

In the above position, the game was adjourned for the first time.

The above diagram gives the position at the second adjournment.

And here is the position after Black's 70th move. It was only now, in full accordance with the rules (50 moves without a capture or a pawn advance!) that a draw was agreed – although the players might have concluded peace without any regrets at the *start* of that fifty-move sequence. Why they didn't, God only knows....

Observe, too, that during all *seventy* moves there wasn't a single capture. One more record!

Theoretically, according to the mathematicians' calculations, the most protracted game could 'only' last 5949 moves, thanks to the very rule we have been talking about. Thank heaven the likelihood of this actually happening is nil. If the players used the full time allotted under the classical time limit – 2½ hours for the first 40 moves, and one hour for each subsequent 16 – they would spend 596 hours (minus a few minutes) at the chessboard. With a playing session every evening, the game would last 99 days!

Chess history also contains one other exceptional game in which three famous personalities simultaneously 'took a hand' in the full sense of the term. It was played in the Capablanca Memorial in

1965, but just *where* it was played is more difficult to say. The point is that the American authorities prohibited Bobby Fischer from travelling to Cuba in its revolutionary heyday. Consequently, the future World Champion played his game with Vasily Smyslov (just as with everyone else) by telephone from the Manhattan Chess Club in New York.

What, then, is so exceptional about this ordinary encounter between two kings of chess? After all, there have been hundreds of such duels. There was just one thing: thanks to the special method of communication, Smyslov and Fischer each had to have an assistant to receive the opponent's moves and carry them out on the board.

Well, in Havana this was done by José Raoul Capablanca! The son of Chess King number three possessed not only the surname of his great father but his forenames as well. Three champion surnames, involved in their differerent ways in one and the same game – this, you will agree, is no everyday occurrence. And in its way it constitutes a record.

The tournament, incidentally, was won by Smyslov. Fischer and two other contestants finished half a point behind him.

Where is the king going?

In the endgame, when the monarch becomes virtually the chief actor in the drama, everything is clear – he either supports the advance of his own pawn or impedes the pawn movements of his opponent. Exceptionally, he will set up a fortress and hide in it when he needs to save his skin. In the middlegame things are different: as a rule, the more he manages to stick at home, the better it is for him.

And yet even a potentate may have occasion to go for long walks around the whole board. This most often results from a sacrifice to draw him out into the open; he is then left in a 'draught', almost inevitably causing 'inflammation of the lungs' with fatal consequences.

What was the lengthiest procession to a place of execution? A marker was put down by the famous game between the Polish-American player **Edward Lasker** and **Sir George Thomas** (London, 1911).

Placing his queen on e7, Black considered he was safe, for after 11 ♘xf6+ gxf6 the point h7 would be securely defended. White, however, resorted to a characteristic inversion in the order of his moves:

11 ♕xh7+ ♔xh7 12 ♘xf6+ ♔h6 (forced; otherwise mate follows at once) **13 ♘eg4+ ♔g5 14 h4+ ♔f4 15 g3+ ♔f3 16 ♗e2+ ♔g2 17 ♖h2+ ♔g1**, and with two mating moves available, **18 ♔d2** and 18 0-0-0, White chose the former.

Unfortunately this long king march could have been terminated half way. Edward Lasker himself explains this in his book *Chess for Fun and Chess for Blood*. His reasoning before the start of the famous combination is also of interest.

The double attack on h7, veiled only by my knight on e4, suggests, of course, various ways of sacrificing that knight in order to open the line of the bishop. I had five minutes within which to make up my mind. I was sure that this was the decisive moment of the game, because I cannot bring up more fighting forces in less than three moves, and Black threatens to drive me back by ♘b8-c6 or g7-g6 or d7-d6, and then to start operations in the open f-file. Sacrificing my knight on g6, after Black's g-pawn has advanced, would no longer be effective, as bishop or queen can interpose on g7. For all these reasons I must act immediately and drastically.

The knight moves which suggest themselves are 11 ♘d6 and 11 ♘g5. Both I dismissed after a minute's thought, because after 11 ♘g5 g6 12 ♗xg6 hxg6 13 ♘xg6 ♕g7 14 ♘xf8 ♔xf8 no attack is left, and while two pawns and a rook are usually a sufficient equivalent for two minor pieces in an ending, they rarely are in the middle-game, where due to the superior fighting power of two pieces against one the pawns are often regained before long....

The other excursion of the king's knight which had to be considered in the diagram position, 11 ♘d6, proves not playable at all, since after 11...g6 12 ♘xg6 hxg6 13 ♕xg6+ ♕g7 14 ♘xb7 Black will exchange queens, play a7-a5, and then win the knight with ♖a8-a7.

After realizing that the preparation by a knight's move was too slow to make my attack succeed, it occurred to me that I could possibly sacrifice the queen, forcing the king into the line of my bishop, and then discover a check with disastrous effect. I saw right away, not without a flush of excitement, that Black would indeed be checkmate if after 12 ♘xf6+ the king went back to h8: 13 ♘g6 would to the trick. But what if he moved out to h6? Well, a check with my king's knight on g4 would leave him only the square g5 and then my h- and g-pawns could continue the attack. My pawns would control all the black squares and my bishop the white squares to which Black's king might want to flee, so that he would have to approach my camp at f3. Then I could drive him to g2 with the bishop and my rooks would give him the mortal blow. As he would be advancing one rank with each move, I could foresee without any particular difficulty that he must be mate in eight moves....

My own pleasure at this game received quite a jolt another few years later. One fine day I received a letter from a chess club in Australia. The writer said they had analysed my game with Thomas and enjoyed it very much, but he was sorry he had to disappoint me with the information that I could have checkmated my opponent in seven instead of eight moves, unless I had already found this out. He appended the following variations, which I regret to say are really correct:

14 f4+! (This check does it the quickest way! I had not considered it in the game, because I had not seen the nice mate in two which would follow if Black moves 15...♔xf4. Then 15 g3+ ♔f3 would enable mate by 16 0-0, and if instead the king goes back to g5, 16 h4 mates.) 14...♔h4 15 g3+ ♔h3 16 ♗f1+ ♗g2 17 ♘f2 mate.

16 0-0 would also have forced the mate with the knight. Some unaccountable aesthetic predilections most of us have seem to make the mate which actually occurred in the game appear more beautiful.

Lasker refers to the five minutes he had at his disposal; we shall come back to this in the chapter 'Sergeant major's orders'.

I will now hand you over to Alexander Alekhine. In 1930 in the *Deutsche Schachzeitung* he came across a game between two little-known players in an insignificant event – a minor tournament at the German Chess Federation congress in Frankfurt am Main. This is not the sort of game you would expect the World Champion to look at. He not only noticed it, however; he analysed it thoroughly and even devoted a special article to it, under the heading 'A Gem of Combinative Art'.

F.Herrmann – H.Hussong

23...♕xh2+!!

Alekhine commented on this stunning blow as follows:

"The two exclamation marks are not for the queen sacrifice itself (the idea of which has become almost as conventional as, for instance, the popular bishop sacrifices on h7 or f7) but rather for seeing ahead to the study-like finale by which the move is justified. To my knowledge at least, contemporary chess practice can show no sacrifices leading directly to mate which are similar to this one. I even consider this finale worthy to be set beside the best achievements of that unsurpassed master of combination, Anderssen."

24 ♔xh2 ♖h6+ 25 ♔g3 ♘e2+ 26 ♔g4 ♖f4+ 27 ♔g5 ♖h2 28 ♕xf8+ ♔xf8 29 ♘f3

"White had seen everything up to here. In fact, now that Black's main threat of 29...♔f7 etc. has been parried and his rook is under attack, things seem to be turning out very nicely for White. But right now a miracle occurs."

29...h6+ 30 ♔g6 ♔g8

"The reply is forced, in view of the threatened 31...♖f6 mate."

31 ♘xh2

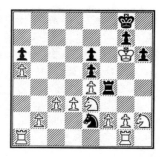

31...♖f5!!

"The essential move to crown the entire sacrificial edifice; despite his enormous preponderance of forces, White cannot cover f4 and g5 at the same time."

0-1

A 'pure' and extremely pretty problem-like mate would occur in the event of 32 exf5 ♘f4.

The character and length of the king's journey in that game are called to mind by the following one.

Cifuentes – Zviagintsev
Wijk aan Zee 1995

24...♘xf2! 25 ♔xf2 ♖xe3! 26 ♗xe3

The lesser evil was 26 ♔xe3 ♘g4+ 27 ♔d2 ♘xh6 28 ♔c1, even though after 28...♕e7 Black would have more than enough compensation for the exchange.

26...♘g4+ 27 ♔f3 ♘xh2+ 28 ♔f2 ♘g4+ 29 ♔f3 ♕e6!

Pretty – and very strong.

30 ♗f4?!

The only way to carry on the fight was the paradoxical 30 ♗c1!. Then on 30...c4!, White has 31 ♕e4 (not 31 ♘f4 ♘h2+ 32 ♔f2 ♗c5+) 31...♕xe4+ 32 ♔xe4 ♘f2+ 33 ♔d4. You will agree, though, that over-the-board, and with time trouble approaching too, players are likely to avoid that kind of retreat.

30...♖e8!

Things aren't so clear after either 30...♗xf4 31 ♕e4! or 30...♗xd5+ 31 ♖xd5 ♕xd5+ 32 ♕e4. Now Black is ready with a concluding combination of rare elegance.

31 ♕c4

Defending against 31...♗xd5+, which this time would be lethal.

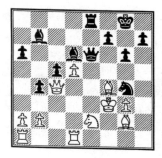

**31...♕e3+! 32 ♗xe3 ♖xe3+
33 ♔xg4 ♗c8+ 34 ♔g5 h6+!
35 ♔xh6 ♖e5**

With an extra queen and rook (!), White is only able to prevent the black rook from giving mate on h5. Against mate on f8 with the bishop, he is powerless.

In a game **Utkin – Grantz**, played by correspondence in 1971, the black king loitered around the open board for even longer.

Alekhine's Defence [B04]

**1 e4 ♘f6 2 e5 ♘d5 3 d4 d6 4 ♘f3
dxe5 5 ♘xe5 ♘d7 6 ♘xf7! ♔xf7
7 ♕h5+ ♔e6 8 g3 ♘7f6 9 ♗h3+
♔d6 10 ♕e5+ ♔c6 11 ♗g2 b5
12 a4! b4 13 c4 bxc3 14 bxc3 ♗a6
15 ♘d2 e6 16 c4 ♗d6 17 ♕xe6**

Black now continued with **17...♖b8 18 0-0 ♕g8 19 cxd5+**

♔b7 20 ♖e1 ♔a8, and lost after **21 ♗a3**. Although his king has found cover, he is two pawns down and his pieces are disunited.

The king march would have established a record after the sharper 17...♖e8 (Black has nothing to lose!) 18 cxd5+ ♔b6 19 a5+ ♔b5 20 ♗f1+ ♔b4 21 ♗a3+ ♔c3 22 ♖c1+ ♔xd4 23 ♘f3 mate. But then, in the quiet of your study, it is no problem to work this variation out, and Black preferred to lose more prosaically rather than be mated in the centre of the board.

The longest journey to execution that actually occurred in a game was in **Stefanov – Andreev**, USSR 1975.

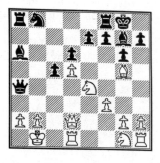

Here Black carried out the forced sequence **14...♕xa2+! 15 ♔xa2 ♗d3+ 16 ♔b3 c4+ 17 ♔b4 ♘a6+ 18 ♔b5 ♖fb8+ 19 ♔c6 ♖c8+ 20 ♔b7 ♖c7+! 21 ♔xa8 ♗d4**, and White resigned, since the inevitable and very pretty mate can only be put off by one move.

I am afraid that Mikhail Tal, the creator of hundreds of explosive attacks, referred to such combinations as 'playing to the gallery', in other words to that part of the audience which rates high-sounding rhetoric, thrills and tear-jerking emotions above the genuine skill of the actors.

The point is that in the diagram position Black could perfectly well have achieved his aim by the much more prosaic 14...♗d3+ 15 ♔c1 (capturing the bishop allows mate in two) 15...♕xa2. White could then resign with a clear conscience, if only because after 16 ♕f2 (the only move) 16...♕c4+ (*not* the only move) 17 ♔d2, Black has 17...♕xd5, or 17...♖a2, or even 17...♗xb2.

But then, beauty in chess is another story. From the point of view of setting up a record of sorts, Black's play in the above game was perfectly in order.

The black king too has been known to take an equally long trip.

Botvinnik – Chekhover
Moscow 1935

By sacrificing his knights White has already forced the enemy ruler to shuffle around, though without yet leaving his own camp. There now followed:

26 ♕xe6+ ♔h8 27 ♕h3+ ♔g8 28 ♗f5 ♘f8

Black is compelled to cover the point e6, but this leads to the irreparable weakening of f6.

29 ♗e6+ ♘xe6 30 ♕xe6+ ♔h8 31 ♕h3+ ♔g8 32 ♖xf6

Now the black king is forced to set out on a long journey which cannot end happily.

32...♗xf6 33 ♕h7+ ♔f8 34 ♖e1 ♗e5 35 ♕h8+ ♔e7 36 ♕xg7+ ♔d6 37 ♕xe5+ ♔d7 38 ♕f5+ ♔c6 39 d5+ ♔c5 40 ♗a3+ ♔xc4 41 ♕e4+ ♔c3 42 ♗b4+ ♔b2 43 ♕b1 mate

A veritable round-the-world trip was accomplished by the black king in the game **Veikas – Abolins**, Latvian Correspondence Championship 1989-90.

18 ♖xf6!
This exchange sacrifice is forced, but Black is none the better off for that – his position now falls apart. Of course 18 cxd4 is no good in view of 18...♘c5!, when White is the one who loses out.

18...♘c5
If 18...gxf6 at once, then 19 ♘h5.

19 ♕f3 gxf6 20 cxd4 ♕b5 21 ♗c3 ♖ac8 22 ♕g4+ ♔h8 23 ♕f5 ♖e6 24 ♘h5!
White isn't satisfied with gaining material by 24 dxc5 ♕xc5+ 25 ♕xc5, when exploiting his advantage would be a lengthy process.

24...♕c4 25 ♘xf6 ♔g7 26 ♖f1 ♕xc3 27 ♕xh7+ ♔f8 28 ♘d7+ ♔e8 29 ♕xf7+ ♔d8 30 ♘xc5 ♖xc5

31 dxc5

A quicker method was 31 ♕xe6 ♕xd4+ 32 ♔h1.

31...♕xc5+ 32 ♔h1 ♖e7 33 ♕f3 b5 34 h3 ♔c7 35 ♖d1 ♖e5 36 ♕f4 ♔b6 37 ♕f6+ ♔a5 38 ♕d8+ ♔a4 39 ♖d4+ ♔b3 40 ♖b4+ ♔c2 41 ♕g8! ♔d2 42 ♖b2+ ♔d3 43 ♕g3+ 1-0 Black resigned without waiting for the final woeful outcome of his king's globetrotting.

But sometimes it is quite other business that prompts the king to set off. Grandmaster Saviely Tartakower, for many years the leader among chess journalists, spoke of this in picturesque terms: "The monarch must be relieved of worry at all times! However, on occasion he will wade through the tangle of pieces like a sleepwalker and settle the outcome of the battle. Such attempts to use the king as a 'strong piece' in the very middlegame are not always successful. But there are occasions when the leader of the army assumes the role of a pitiless executioner. With a terrible laugh, he appears like a spectre before the startled hostile ruler!"

It was just such a spectre that confronted the black king in the game **Geller-Tal**, Moscow 1975 (Alekhine Memorial Tournament).

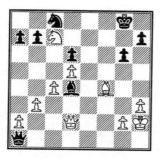

So far White has won a pawn, and objectively speaking he should eventually win the game – although the position is still extremely sharp. I give the continuation with Geller's comments.

30 ♕e2

An inaccuracy which makes victory more difficult. White could have won at once with 30 ♕c1! ♕xa2 31 ♕e1, and the black king can no longer shelter from the mating attack. Yet 'every cloud has a silver lining' – without this inaccuracy the white king's marathon run from h2 to f8 (!) could not have occurred.

30...♘e7!

An excellent practical chance and an exceptionally cunning trap!

31 ♘b5

White saw that after 31 ♕xe7 (the intermediate 31 ♕e6+ ♔h8 doesn't alter matters) 31...♕g1+ 32 ♔g3 ♕f2+ 33 ♔g4 ♕xg2+ 34 ♗g3 h5+ 35 ♔h4 ♕e4+!! 36 ♕xe4 he would fall victim to a problem-like mate by his opponent's sole remaining piece: 36...♗f6 mate!

31...♗g1+

He could have given White more trouble by 31...♕g1+ 32 ♔g3 ♘f5+ 33 ♔f3 ♗f6, with great complications. To be fair, though, it must be said that both players were already short of time.

32 ♔g3 ♘f5+ 33 ♔f3 ♘h4+

A rather better move was 33...a6, to which White would reply 34 g4.

34 ♔g4 ♘f5 35 ♕e8+ ♔g7 36 ♕d7+ ♔h8 37 ♘xd6!

Precise calculation leads to a win by force, although White had only seconds left for it.

37...♛d1+ 38 ♔g5 ♛h5+ 39 ♔f6 ♝d4+ 40 ♔e6 ♞g7+ 41 ♔f7 g5+

Time trouble is over, and Black resigned: after 42 ♔f8 his checks run out and he has no defence: 42...h6 43 ♝e5 ♝xe5 44 ♞f7+ ♔h7 45 ♞xe5.

0-1

Under fire from a sharp middlegame counter-attack, the white king literally forced its way through the ranks of its own and the opponent's pieces, deep into the enemy rear – and came within handshaking distance of its black colleague. I don't recall another such king march in the whole of my rich tournament career.

In the following romantic encounter, the white king took a twelve-move stroll (albeit mainly within its own half of the board) in order to save itself – but also also in pursuit of eventual victory.

Chigorin – Caro
Vienna 1898
Vienna Game [C29]

1 e4 e5 2 ♞c3 ♞f6 3 f4 d5 4 d3 ♝b4 5 fxe5 ♞xe4 6 dxe4 ♛h4+ 7 ♔e2

The compulsory start of the journey.

7...♝xc3 8 bxc3 ♝g4+ 9 ♞f3 dxe4 10 ♛d4 ♝h5 11 ♔e3 (the only move) 11...♝xf3 12 ♝b5+ c6 13 gxf3 ♛h6+ 14 ♔xe4 ♛g6+ 15 ♔e3 cxb5 16 ♝a3

This is the whole point. The black king, sitting at 'home', is also in danger.

16...♞c6 17 ♛d5 ♛xc2 18 ♜ac1 ♛f5 19 ♜he1 ♜d8 20 ♛xb5 a6 21 ♛b1 ♛g5+ 22 f4 ♛g2 23 ♝d6 ♛h3+ 24 ♔e4 f5+ 25 ♔d5

True heroes always travel the world.

25...♛g2+ 26 ♔c4 b5+ 27 ♔d3 ♛f3+ 28 ♔c2 ♛f2+ 29 ♔b3 ♜c8

"After 29...♞a5+ 30 ♔b4! ♜c8, Black draws if White takes the knight (31 ♔xa5 ♜c4 32 ♝b4 ♛a7 33 ♛xf5 ♛c7+ 34 ♔xa6 ♛c6+! 35 ♔a5 ♛a8+ 36 ♔xb5 ♛c6+ etc.). However, if White defends with 31 ♜c2! ♜c4+ 32 ♔a3 ♛xf4 33 ♛d1, the course of the game is hardly altered. For instance, 33...♜a4+ 34 ♔b2 ♛c4 can be met by 35 ♔b1 ♛e6 (otherwise e5-e6) 36 ♛f3 or 36 ♝b4! etc." (Chigorin)

30 ♜c2 ♛xf4 31 ♔b2 ♞a5 32 ♔a1

The white king's odyssey is concluded; for its black counterpart, hard times begin.

32...♛c4 33 e6! ♞c6 34 ♛d1 h5 35 ♜g1 ♜h7 36 ♜xg7! **1-0**

A familiar chess paradox: one ruler survives a barrage of checks, the other perishes without leaving his official residence. This would seem to have been the longest king march of all.

The unique feature of the following game is that after going most of the way towards the scaffold, the king's final step leads – onto the victor's podium.

Hansen – Peicheva
Copenhagen Open Championship,
1989

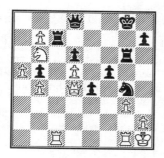

Strategically White has a won
position, but Black resourcefully
searches for counter-chances.

**33...♖h6! 34 ♖ge1 ♘xh2!
35 ♔g2 ♘f3 36 ♕e3 ♖h2+ 37 ♔f1
♘xe1**

After 37...♖xh2+ 38 ♔e2 ♖xe1+
39 ♖xe1 ♖c2+ 40 ♔d1 ♖d2+
41 ♕xd2 ♘xd2 42 ♘d7, White
wins.

**38 ♕g5+! ♕xg5 39 b8=♕+ ♔g7
40 ♖xc7+ ♔h6 41 ♕f8+ ♔h5
42 ♖xh7+ ♔g4 43 ♖g7??**

Having made the black king 'run
the gauntlet', White suddenly
changes tack. Instead of the simple
43 ♖xh2 ♕xg3 44 ♕h6, forcing
instant capitulation, he decides to
bite the enemy queen – and
suddenly the black king is
transformed from the victim into
the executioner!

43...♔f3!!

"After this move," Hansen writes,
"I felt as if I had fallen headlong
into a quarry." White can take either
the queen or the knight – and be
mated.

44 ♔g1 ♕h5 0-1

The more queens, the merrier

It goes without saying that if you
acquire a second queen this
generally ends the fight, unless of
course your opponent manages to
do the same. If he does, some
extremely complicated play will
ensue, offering plenty of excitement
to the contestants themselves, the
spectators and anyone looking at
the game afterwards.

For the record number of queens
in a game, it is customary to look to
a score supplied by a certain pair of
Australians, **Sumpter** and **King**, in
1965. For more than a third of a
century it has kept appearing in
various magazines and popular
chess books. In the chess world
there are quite a few people with the
royal surname, but the first-
mentioned of the two opponents is
unknown to anyone. At bottom I
have an extremely strong suspicion
that this game never actually took
place anywhere. Both players
accumulate their queens in a
manner that is just too deliberate
and clearly not the most essential
for victory.

**1 e4 c5 2 ♘f3 ♘c6 3 d4 cxd4
4 ♘xd4 e6 5 ♘c3 ♕c7 6 ♗e2 a6
7 0-0 b5 8 ♔h1 ♘f6 9 f4 b4 10 e5
bxc3 11 exf6 cxb2**

Why not 11...gxf6, with at least
an equal game?

12 fxg7 bxa1=♕

Among other things, the
elementary 12...♗xg7 13 ♗xb2
♕b6 gives Black a material plus –
even though the position would still
remain sharp after the forced
continuation 14 ♘xc6 ♗xb2
15 ♘e5 ♗xa1 16 ♕xa1 ♖f8.

13 gxh8=♕ ♕xa2

Not so much defending against the threatened ♗c1-a3 as clearing the path of the a6-pawn. After 13...♕xd4 Black would have the pleasanter game.

14 ♕xh7 a5 15 h4 a4 16 h5 a3 17 h6 ♕b1 18 ♕g8 a2 19 h7 a1=♕ 20 h8=♕ ♕b4 21 ♗e3 ♘xd4 22 ♗xd4 ♕aa3 23 ♗h5 d5 24 f5 ♗a6 25 fxe6 0-0-0 26 ♖xf7 ♕ca5 27 c3 ♕d6 28 ♗g4 ♖e8 29 e7+ ♔b8 30 exf8=♕, and after the birth of the seventh (!) queen – with all of them still on the board – Black resigned (**1-0**).

The best known of all 'multiple queen' games is the eleventh encounter between **Capablanca** and **Alekhine** from their World Championship match of 1927. Alekhine stated candidly:

> In my opinion this game has been praised too much, the whole world over. It was doubtless very exciting both for the players – who were continuously short of time – and the public. But its final part represents a true comedy of errors in which my opponent several times missed a draw and I missed about the same number of winning opportunities.

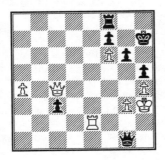

To us, however, the game is of interest from quite a different standpoint. (The following notes are Alekhine's.)

58...♕f1+?

For the second time Black misses an easy win!

The right sequence (which I actually intended when I played my 57th move) was 58...♕h1+ 59 ♖h2 ♕f3!, after which White could not play 60 ♖c2 because of 60...♕f5+; and he would be helpless against the threat 60...♕xf6 etc. (If 60 ♕f4, then 60...♕d1! etc.)

59 ♔h2 ♕xf6 60 a5?

Instead of securing the draw by 60 ♖c2 ♖e8 61 ♔g2 (threatening either 62 ♖xc3 or 62 ♖f2) Capablanca commits another error and should now lose instantly.

60...♖d8?

An immediate decision could be obtained by 60...♕f1! 61 ♕e4 ♖d8 (or 61...♖b8). After the text move the win should become again quite a problem.

61 a6?

After 61 ♔g2 Black could only obtain a queen ending with three pawns against two which, with the right defence, should most probably end in a draw: 61...♔g7 62 a6 ♖d1 63 ♖f2 ♖d2 64 ♖xd2 (but not 64 ♕c5 on account of 64...♖xf2+ 65 ♕xf2 ♕c6+ 66 ♕f3 ♕xf3+ 67 ♔xf3 c2 68 a7 c1=♕ 69 a8=♕ ♕h1+) 64...cxd2 65 ♕d5! ♕b2 6 ♔h3 ♕c2 67 a7 ♕f5+ 68 ♕xf5 gxf5 69 a8=♕ d1=♕. Now at last, it is the end!

61...♕f1! 62 ♕e4 ♖d2 63 ♖xd2 cxd2 64 a7 d1=♕ 65 a8=♕ ♕g1+ 66 ♔h3 ♕df1+ 0-1

If now 67 ♕g2 then 67...♕h1 mate.

In that game, as is almost always the case, the second queens for White and Black appeared on the board within the space of two half-moves. Fairly recently, though, in the Efim Geller Memorial Tournament (Moscow, 2001), the game **Selivanov – Kotsur** saw the queening of *three* pawns within a two-move interval!

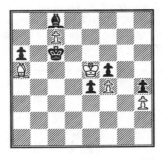

58 **♗e1 ♔c5!** 59 **♗xh4 a5** 60 **♗f2+ ♔c4** 61 **h4 a4** 62 **h5 a3** 63 **h6 a2** 64 **♗d4 e3** 65 **h7 e2** 66 **h8=♕ e1=♕** 67 **♔f6 a1=♕!** 0-1

Two new queens also appeared on successive moves in the game **R.Williams – L.Ginzburg**, New York 1983. But they were both of the same colour!

30...b3! 31 **exf6 b2** 32 **f7+ ♔xf7** (not 32...♔f8?? 33 ♖e1! and it is White who wins) 33 **♖1a7+ ♘d7!** 34 **♕e6+ ♔f8** 35 **♕xd6+ ♔g8** 36 **h3 c1=♕+** 37 **♔h2 b1=♕**

Three black queens against a single white one – this distribution of forces is probably a record.

38 ♖xd7 ♕xd7

When you've got so many queens, why be sparing with them?

39 ♖xb8+ ♕xb8 40 **♕xb8+ ♕cc8** 0-1

In the following game there were two extra queens on the board at the same time:

Dely – F.Portisch
Budapest 1967

Utilizing the various pins, White gives himself an irresistible pair of passed pawns virtually by force.

22 b4 ♕a6 23 **♗xg4 hxg4** 24 **bxc5 ♕xe2** 25 **♖e1 ♕c4** 26 **c6 f5** 27 **♖c1 ♕e2** 28 **♕b3 f4** 29 **♗f2 ♕xe4** 30 **c7 ♖f8** 31 **d6+ ♔h7** 32 **d7 fxg3** 33 **♕xg3 ♖xf2** 34 **d8=♕ ♖f8** 35 **c8=♕** 1-0

As many as five of the strongest type of piece have been known to take part in an active struggle.

Alekhine – NN
Moscow 1915
French Defence [C12]

**1 e4 e6 2 d4 d5 3 ♘c3 ♘f6
4 ♗g5 ♗b4 5 e5 h6 6 exf6 hxg5
7 fxg7 ♖g8 8 h4 gxh4 9 ♕g4 ♗e7**

Better 9...♕f6!. One white pawn
is already close to the rank that it
dreams of. But for the moment it is
stuck fast, and it doesn't look as if
will be able to take that final step in
a hurry. Its companion hastens to its
aid....

10 g3 c5 11 gxh4 cxd4 (11...
♗f6!) **12 h5 dxc3 13 h6 cxb2
14 ♖b1 ♕a5+ 15 ♔e2 ♕xa2 16 h7**

It's time to go ahead with the
decisive assault – without delay!

**16...♕xb1 17 hxg8=♕+ ♔d7
18 ♕xf7 ♕xc2+ 19 ♔f3 ♘c6**

White already has a queen for a
bishop, but the struggle continues.

**20 ♕gxe6+ ♔c7 21 ♕f4+ ♔b6
22 ♕ee3+ ♔c5 (22...d4 23 ♗d3)
23 g8=♕ b1=♕**

"In this extraordinary position
White won by a *coup de repos*:
24 ♖h6!! (threatening 25 ♕d8
mate), for if now 24...♕xf1 then
25 ♕b4+ ♕b5 26 ♕d8+ ♔a6
27 ♕ea3+ and mates in two moves.
This position is certainly unique of
its kind!" (Alekhine)

Well, at that time he may have
been right. However, in the first
place, there is some reason to
suppose that all this is just a
possible variation discovered in
analysis. And in the second place –
time passes....

The position in the next diagram
arose in a game between **Zoran
Mackić** and **Andrei Maksimenko**
in the second division of the 1994
Yugoslav Club Championship. At
first sight, the major piece endgame
promised nothing extraordinary.

After 43 ♕xd4 ♕e2 White would
keep an advantage, but the position
would remain sharp and contain
plenty of drawing potential.
Instead he overreached himself,
overlooking his opponent's 45th
move.

43 ♕a5 d3 44 a7 d2 45 a8=♕ e2!

The immediate birth of a new
queen would lose; a brief
postponement brings victory.

46 ♖f6

The more aggressive 46 ♖f8
wouldn't save White in view of
46...d1=♕+! 47 ♔a2 ♕e6+ (but not
the 'greedy' 47...e1=♕ 48 ♖h8+)
48 ♔a3 ♕a1+.

**46...d1=♕+ 47 ♔a2 e1=♕
48 ♖xh6+ ♔xh6 49 ♕h8+ ♔g6
50 ♕a6+ ♔f7 51 ♕b7+ ♕dd7 0-1**

Belov – Prokhorov
Cheliabinsk 1991

White has clearly obtained more out of this King's Indian battle than his opponent, even though he has lost the 'key defender' of his dark squares.

26 ♗xa6 bxa6 27 ♘xa6 ♖b7 28 ♖c7 ♕g5!? (the best practical chance) **29 h4?!**

Why such refinements? Instead 29 ♔f1 was safer.

29...♖xc7 30 ♘xc7 ♕xh4 31 b7 ♘h5 32 b8=♕ ♘g3

White has an extra queen, but some problems to go with it.

33 ♕c4 ♕h1+ 34 ♔f2 ♕h4 35 ♔g1

Repeating moves to gain time – a familiar device when short on the clock.

35...♕h1+ 36 ♔f2 ♕h4 37 ♔g1 ♕h1+ 38 ♔f2 ♕h4

Why Black didn't claim a draw here, he alone knows.

39 ♕b6 (a loss of tempo in time trouble) **39...♗e7 40 ♘f1** (he could have played this last move) **40...♕h1 41 ♘d2 ♕h4 42 ♔e1 ♕h1+ 43 ♘f1 ♗h4 44 ♔d2 ♕xg2+ 45 ♔c3 ♘e2+ 46 ♔b2 ♘c1+ 47 ♔xc1 ♕xf3 48 ♘e6 ♕a3+ 49 ♔d2** (49 ♕b2 is more 'solid') **49...♗e7 50 ♕cb3 ♕a8 51 ♕c7 ♗e8 52 a3 ♕a6 53 ♕cc4 ♕a7**

54 ♕f3 ♗h4 55 ♕h3 (with the transparent idea of 55...♗f2 56 ♘g5+) **55...g5 56 ♘d8 ♗d7 57 ♕hc3 ♖g7 58 ♘c6 ♕g1 59 ♔c2 g4 60 ♘b8 ♗e8 61 ♘d2 ♗g6 62 ♕c8 ♕g2 63 ♘d7 ♗e7 64 ♘xe5 dxe5 65 ♕xe5 ♗xa3 66 ♕cc3 ♗f8 67 d6 f3 68 d7 f2 69 d8=♕ f1=♕**

70 ♕de7 ♕f7 71 ♕xf7 ♗xf7 72 ♕f5+ ♔g8 73 ♕fc8 ♕f2 74 ♕b4 ♗g6 75 ♕bc4+ ♔h7 76 ♕xg4 ♗d6 77 ♕ce6 ♗b4 78 ♕d5 ♖c7+ 79 ♔d1 ♗xd2 80 ♕xd2 ♕f1+ 81 ♕e1 ♖c1+ 82 ♔xc1 ♕xe1+ 0-1

All correctly done; a stud of queens has to be managed skilfully.

In a curious way the game **Tal – Cirić**, Sarajevo 1966, was probably a record-breaking one in this field. Black acquired a new queen ... and resigned!

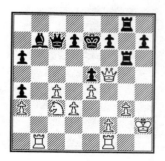

24 ♖xb7! ♕xb7 25 ♖b1 ♕c8
26 ♕xe5+ ♖e6 27 ♘d5+ ♔f8
28 ♕f4 ♔g7 29 ♔g2!

Clearing a new avenue of attack;
it becomes clear that the black king
won't find peace on h8.

29...♕c5 30 ♖h1 ♕xa3 (the only
counter-chance) 31 ♕g5+ ♔f8
32 ♕e3 ♕d6 33 ♖xh7 a3 34 ♖h1
♖e5 35 d4 ♖xd5 36 exd5 ♕b4
37 c5 a2 38 ♕e5! ♕b1 39 ♖h8!
a1=♕

Capturing the rook would allow
mate in three.

40 ♕d6+ 1-0

And of course, a sacrifice of the
strongest piece is always something
out of the ordinary. The sacrifice is
usually accepted out of necessity,
but sometimes the defending side
declines the Trojan horse and then
... the offer is renewed! The queen
is either left under attack or keeps
looking for new possibilities to die
the death of the valiant. In this
department a peculiar record was
established by two different games
in which the queen offered its head
to the executioner four times. One
of these encounters has become a
classic textbook example of the
deflection theme.

Adams – Torre
New Orleans 1920

18 ♕g4!!

The pressure of the rooks on the
file is intensified to the utmost by a
diagonal blow from the queen! One
of the defenders is drawn away
from the e8-point, in other words
White is disrupting the co-
ordination of his opponent's pieces.
What makes an even more powerful
impression is the fact that the white
queen is only just beginning its
sacrificial epic.

18...♕b5

For the moment the square e8
remains defended; furthermore
Black is ready to carry out a
diversionary sacrifice of his own
with 19...♕xe2!, enabling his
rook on c8 to penetrate to the first
rank.

19 ♕c4!!

If the queen isn't deflected from
e8, perhaps the rook will be?

19...♕d7 20 ♕c7!!

The same idea, but executed in
the most vivid way possible.

20...♕b5 21 a4!!

It still wasn't too late for White to
lose with 21 ♕xb7?? ♕xe2!.

21...♕xa4 22 ♖e4! ♕b5
33 ♕xb7

Black resigned, as his queen no
longer has the power to control e8.

1-0

Geller – Smyslov
Candidates match,
Moscow 1965

White's offensive in the f-file has
begun to look menacing, but Black
has just obtained a material plus by
capturing a knight on e4 and is
hoping that the attack on the queen
will gain him some time for
defence. Alas...

25 fxg6! f6

Naturally the queen can't be captured by 25...♖xf4 in view of 26 gxh7 mate. In the event of 25...♕xg6 26 ♕xf7+ ♕xf7 27 ♖xf7, Black could only avert mate with big material losses: 27...♗g7 28 ♖xg7+ ♔h8 29 ♖xb7 ♘xb7 30 ♗xe4.

26 ♕g5!

The second queen sacrifice is not motivated by a quest for beauty; it is a means to an end. In face of the threat of 27 g7, Black's reply is forced.

26...♕d7 27 ♔g1!

Accuracy is required to finish the game in the quickest way possible. After the immediate 27 ♖xf6 ♗xf6 28 ♕xf6 hxg6 29 ♕xg6+ ♔h8 30 ♗g5 ♖4e6 31 ♗f6+ Black plays 31...♖xf6, whereupon 32 ♖xf6 brings about mate – to the *white* king – by means of 32...♖e1+. Black now has no useful moves, while the white queen is invulnerable as before.

27...♗g7 28 ♖xf6 ♖g4

Now 28...♗xf6 would lead to the variation in the last note, only without the mate at the end.

29 gxh7+ ♔h8 30 ♗xg7+ ♕xg7 31 ♕xg4

The fourth and final queen sacrifice.

1-0

A heavy piece stepping lightly

So many epithets have been attached to the rook! Officially, like the queen, it is a 'major' or 'heavy' piece. In practice, more often than not, two rooks are *stronger* than a queen. In unofficial terms the rook is a long-range piece which, with its fire-power on an open file, can positively shatter the normal life of the enemy forces in their own camp. On breaking through to the so-called 'glutton's rank' – the seventh, that is – one or two rooks will decimate pawns and threaten no end of trouble to the hostile king. Of the endgame with the board half empty, there is no need to speak.

In the middlegame, the rook is inclined to sluggishness, for all its potential power; it is reluctant to move forward except in the case of a breakthrough. Yet here is an exception which perhaps represents a record.

Karpov – Hort
Moscow 1971
Sicilian Defence [B81]

1 e4 c5 2 ♘f3 d6 3 d4 cxd4 4 ♘xd4 ♘f6 5 ♘c3 e6 6 g4 ♘c6 7 g5 ♘d7 8 ♗e3 a6 9 f4 ♗e7 10 ♖g1 ♘xd4 11 ♕xd4 e5 12 ♕d2 exf4 13 ♗xf4 ♘e5 14 ♗e2 ♗e6 15 ♘d5!

This active move is the only one to promise White an opening advantage. Black would answer 15 0-0-0 with 15...♕a5!, after which he has an excellent position with prospects of attack.

15...♗xd5 16 exd5!

With this capture Karpov not only cramps his opponent's forces but also increases the activity of his light-squared bishop. Admittedly he would also retain a distinct advantage after 16 ♕xd5, but then his e4-pawn would need defending.

16...♘g6 17 ♗e3 h6!?

White has a space advantage, hence Black's wish to obtain counterplay even by risky means is easy to understand. Now the nature of the position abruptly changes. The pieces on both sides obtain wide scope for action on the open files and diagonals.

18 gxh6 ♗h4+ 19 ♔d1 gxh6 20 ♗xh6 ♗f6 21 c3 ♗e5

It looks as if Black has regrouped his forces successfully and created the unpleasant threat of 22...♕h4. However...

22 ♖g4!

This difficult move not only parries the threat but also activates the rook. The astonishing manoeuvres of this piece are going to wreck all Black's plans.

22...♕f6

Karpov considers that 22...♗xh2, which at least restores material equality, would have been more tenacious.

23 h4!

The sickly white pawn suddenly becomes a terrible force.

23...♕f5 24 ♖b4! ♗f6 25 h5

Of course not 25 ♖xb7?? on account of 25...♖xh6 26 ♖xh6 ♕xd5+.

25...♘e7

Not 25...♘e5?, which loses a piece at once to 26 ♖f4.

26 ♖f4 ♕e5 27 ♖f3

"A rook is often such a cumbersome piece, but in this position it performs miracles of manoeuvrability. It sets up one threat after another, and proves its worth not only in attack but in defence too. Thus, Black now gains nothing from 27...♕xh5 28 ♖xf6 ♕h1+ 29 ♗f1 (the rook is protecting both bishops) 29...♘g8 30 ♕e1+, and White wins. (Karpov).

27...♘xd5 28 ♖d3 ♖xh6

If 28...♘e7, then 29 ♗f4 is decisive.

29 ♖xd5 ♕e4

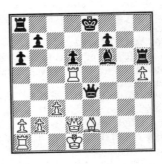

30 ♖d3!

Amazing energy! Truly, songs could be composed in praise of this white rook! From move 22 onwards, Karpov has virtually been playing with this piece alone, notwithstanding the large quantity of forces on the board! In the present game the rook has literally tried its hand at every 'profession'. First it was active in the g-file, then it set to work on the fourth rank; then another change of scene took it to the d-file. As the final gesture before the curtain comes down, the irrepressible rook modestly retraces its steps and fixes its eyes on the e-file; if Black plays 30...♖h8, White wins with 31 ♖e3.

30...♕h1+ 31 ♔c2 ♕xa1 32 ♕xh6 ♗e5 33 ♕g5

Now the black king has nowhere to go. In this hopeless position Hort overstepped the time limit. **(0-1)** This superb game was awarded a special prize by the tournament organizers. In the Yugoslav *Informator*, it was singled out as the best achievement of 1971.

And where will you plant your hooves?

Where will you gallop,
charger proud,
Where next your plunging hoofbeats settle?

Pushkin

How can you go all the way round the chessboard with a knight, landing on each square? This popular puzzle has a precise mathematical solution – more than one, indeed – but it never has been and never will be carried out during an actual game.

For all its 'hobbling' gait – a far cry from the long-ranging bishops! – a knight on a relatively empty battlefield is sometimes capable of lengthy and intricate manoeuvres. In the middlegame, the record journey for a knight probably took place in the following encounter, from the first round of the Euwe Memorial Tournament.

Topalov – Kasparov
Amsterdam 1996
Sicilian Defence [B86]

1 e4 c5 2 ♘f3 d6 3 d4 cxd4 4 ♘xd4 ♘f6 5 ♘c3 a6 6 ♗c4 e6 7 ♗b3 ♘bd7 8 f4 ♘c5 9 0-0 ♘cxe4 10 ♘xe4 ♘xe4 11 f5 e5 12 ♕h5 ♕e7 (not 12...♕c7? 13 ♘e6) 13 ♕f3 ♘c5 14 ♘c6!

Simply a strong move – in itself there is nothing record-breaking about it. In the Sicilian Defence this jump, if not typical, is by no means unique – just look at some games by Geller, Kholmov and others besides. The unique sprightliness of this knight will appear later.

14...♕c7 15 ♗d5

Seizing firm control of the long white diagonal and again indirectly defending the impudent knight. White definitely has full compensation for his pawn.

15...a5?

Cutting off the intruder's retreat. A more natural move might seem to be 15...♗d7, but then after 16 ♘b4! White already threatens 17 ♗xf7+ ♔xf7 18 ♘d5 ♕c6 19 ♕h5+ ♔g8 20 f6 with a direct attack on the king.

16 ♗g5!

Preparing something incredible.

16...♖a6? 17 ♘d8!

The point f7 is now attacked from the rear, and it is time for epithets like 'daring', 'dashing' and 'imperious' to be applied to the white knight. A march like this, from a stopping place (not a station, by any means!) into the very centre of the Black camp is something never seen before in chess history.

17...f6 18 ♘f7 (one more step!) **18...♖g8 19 ♗e3 g6 20 ♘g5** (and another!) **20...♖g7 21 fxg6 ♖xg6**

The position after 21...hxg6 22 ♕xf6 could hardly have been to the World Champion's liking.

22 ♗f7+ ♕xf7 23 ♘xf7

By capturing the queen, the knight concludes its glorious march along the route g1-f3-d4-c6-d8-f7-g5-f7. It dies a valiant death, guaranteeing White a victory that in many ways was sensational **(1-0)**.

An equally lengthy dance is sometimes performed by the white queen's knight in the closed systems of the Ruy Lopez, before it sacrifices itself somewhere around f5 or h5. You will agree, though: taking one step across the boundary line is one thing; paying a visit to the black queen's apartments is quite another!

Nonetheless, an even longer and more intricate knight's tour has been seen, and it is no less spectacular and effective.

Tal – Hjartarson
Reykjavik 1987
Ruy Lopez [E49]

1 e4 e5 2 ♘f3 ♘c6 3 ♗b5 a6 4 ♗a4 ♘f6 5 0-0 ♗e7 6 ♖e1 b5 7 ♗b3 0-0 8 c3 d6 9 h3 ♘a5 10 ♗c2 c5 11 d4 ♕c7 12 ♘bd2 ♗d7 13 ♘f1 cxd4 14 cxd4 ♖ac8 15 ♘e3 ♘c6 16 d5 ♘b4 17 ♗b1 a5 18 a3 ♘a6 19 b4

The game is still following theory! The white pawn is immune: after 19...axb4 20 axb4 ♘xb4 21 ♗d2, Black loses a piece. Another bad line is 19...♕c3 20 ♖a2 axb4 21 ♖c2! ♕b3 22 ♖xc8 ♕xb1 23 ♖xf8+ ♔xf8 24 ♘d2 ♕d3 25 ♘c2!, and strictly speaking Black can resign.

19...g6 20 ♗d2 axb4 21 axb4 ♕b7 22 ♗d3

Original play begins only from this point; White's natural move is linked to a highly unconventional idea.

22...♘c7 23 ♘c2!?

The knight heads towards the very opposite side of the board. For the moment it isn't even particularly easy to see where exactly it is going.

23...♘h5 24 ♗e3 ♖a8 25 ♕d2 ♖xa1

The alternative was counterplay on the other wing with 25...f5, against which White could choose 26 exf5 gxf5 27 ♗g5 or 27 ♗h6. Then 27...♖xa1 could be answered by 28 ♖xa1, leaving the knight on c2 ready to fulfil its straightforward 'Ruy Lopez' duties – advancing to storm the black king's position.

26 ♘xa1!?

White's aim is now a little clearer. Instead of further simplification, he continues his knight manoeuvre; its destination is none other than c6.

26...f5 27 ♗h6 ♘g7

Forced, since on 27...♖a8 White would continue 28 exf5 (but not 28 ♘b3 fxe4 29 ♗xe4 ♘f6 30 ♘a5 ♘xe4! and 31...♕xd5), and if 28...gxf5 then 29 ♘xe5! dxe5 30 d6, with threats aimed principally at the enemy king.

28 ♘b3 f4 29 ♘a5 ♕b6 30 ♖c1

"Incidentally a small trap; if

Black plays 30...♖c8, then simply 31 ♕c2 or 31 ♕c3 follows, and after the forced withdrawal of the knight from c7 White will sacrifice his queen, eliminating his opponent's only good piece – the bishop on d7." (Tal)

30...♖a8

"In this position I couldn't find a way to exploit my advantage by technical means. The laws of strategy suggest that an exchange of light-squared bishops would be very much in White's favour. But this, as they say, is easier said than done. If the bishop leaves d3 Black can play ♘g7-h5, and then if ♘f3-h2, the possibility of the knight jumping to g3 crops up. In any case White would be weakening d4....

"Therefore without advertising too much of my plans, I decided to play on the queenside but not to forget about the kingside either. The bishop on h6 might after all come in useful." (Tal)

31 ♕c2 ♘ce8 32 ♕b3

Threatening to strike at e5 if an opportunity arises.

32...♗f6 33 ♘c6 ♘h5!

Black isn't frightened by imaginary dangers such as 34 ♘fxe5 dxe5 35 d6+ ♔h8 36 ♕f7, since instead he can reply 34...♗xe5! 35 ♘xe5 dxe5 36 d6+ ♔h8 37 ♕d5 ♕xd6! 38 ♕xa8 ♕xd3 39 ♕d8 ♕d6, after which he has nothing to fear.

"At this stage the outline of a combination began to take shape in my mind – a very abstract outline for the moment...." (Tal)

34 ♕b2

This might seem to be pure prophylaxis. White defends the f2-point with the idea of ♔g1-h1 and ♘f3-h2.

34...♗g7 35 ♗xg7 ♔xg7

This is not only natural – you might even say it was almost forced, since 35...♘hxg7 is passive while 35...♘exg7 loses a pawn to 36 ♕e2. However...

"Now the scheme which began by being very, very hazy acquires fully concrete features. It's like a composed study: White to play and win. But I think that finding the solution without moving the pieces on the board is very complicated. Thus, 36 ♘fxe5 dxe5 37 ♘xe5 doesn't work on account of 37...♕f6. Instead, the blow is struck from the other side." (Tal)

36 ♖c5!! ♕a6!

Obviously 36...dxc5 37 ♘fxe5 ♔g8 38 ♘xd7 ♕a6 39 bxc5 would be bad for Black; while after 36...♘c7, the sacrifice 37 ♘fxe5 is playable. Instead Black produces a counter-stroke threatening 37...♕a1+. This had to be foreseen by White – and it was.

37 ♖xb5 ♘c7

"This is the main line of the combination, but another variation is also interesting. It involves a preliminary 37...♗xc6 38 dxc6, and only now 38...♘c7. Then 39 ♖b7 is bad on account of 39...♕xc6, while 39 ♖d5 is met by 39...♕a1+

40 ♕xa1 ♖xa1+ 41 ♔h2 ♘xd5 42 exd5 ♘f6 and the pawns aren't going anywhere, because the black rook is in the right place – behind them.

"There remain two other moves with the white rook – 39 ♖b8 or 39 ♖a5. If Black replies 39...♕xd3, they come to the same thing: 40 ♖xa8 ♘xa8 41 ♕a1 ♘c7 42 ♕a7. This is very simple, but unfortunately after 39 ♖b8 Black can once again content himself with 39...♕xc6, since 40 b5 fails to 40...♖xb8.

"Nonetheless there *is* a way to win, namely 39 ♖a5 ♕xc6 40 ♘xe5 dxe5 41 ♕xe5+ followed by 42 ♖c5, preserving enough advantage for victory.

"But this, I repeat, is a sub-variation. Now back to the game. The white knight has already demonstrated its energy by reaching its present post on c6, but its biography is not yet finished...." (Tal)

38 ♖b8

Taking the back rank away from the black king.

38...♕xd3 39 ♘cxe5! ♕d1+

The only move. Black loses with 39...dxe5 40 ♕xe5+ ♔h6 (or 40...♘f6 41 ♕e7+ ♔h6 42 ♕f8+ ♔h5 43 ♕xf6) 41 ♕g5+ ♔g7 42 ♕e7+ ♔h6 43 ♕f8+ and mate in two.

40 ♔h2 ♖a1

Capturing the knight is impossible for the same reasons as before, while after 40...♕a1 41 ♕xa1 ♖xa1 42 ♘xd7 White has a winning advantage. Now, however, who will checkmate first?

41 ♘g4+

The knight takes the correct route; on 41 ♘xd7+ ♔h6, Black would win.

41...♔f7 42 ♘h6+!

A different check, with the other knight – 42 ♘g5+? – would lose after Black's forced king move.

42...♔e7 43 ♘g8+

"Of course White could impress the 'gallery' by playing first 43 ♕g7+ ♘xg7, and then 44 ♘g8+ ♔f7 45 ♘g5 mate, but this would show little regard for the opponent – or for that fearless knight which, by running right the way round the board and never once missing its way, has made a decisive contribution to the success of the whole army." (Tal)

Yes indeed, the march ♘b1-d2-f1-e3-c2-a1-b3-a5-c6-e5-g4-h6-g8 is most imposing.

Black resigned in view of 43...♔f7 44 ♘g5 mate.

1-0

I would not venture to state or even suggest that the knights' dance in the following game represents a record, but it cannot be disputed that the white knights play the decisive role.

Hausner – Andrzejewski
Lodz 1984
Catalan System [E00]

1 d4 ♘f6 2 ♘f3 e6 3 c4 d5 4 g3 c5 5 cxd5 ♘xd5 6 ♗g2 cxd4 7 ♘xd4 ♗b4+ 8 ♗d2 ♕b6 9 ♗xb4 ♘xb4 10 0-0 0-0 11 ♘c3 ♘4c6 12 ♘b3 ♘d7 13 ♕d6 ♘de5 14 ♖fd1 ♖d8 15 ♕c5 ♗d7 16 ♘e4 ♕a6 17 ♘d4 ♘g6 18 ♘b5 b6 19 ♕h5 ♕a5 20 ♘ed6 ♖ab8

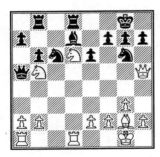

21 ♘b7!

This ninth move with a white knight (and people still teach you that you shouldn't keep moving the same piece) brings an immediate win.

21...♖xb7   22   ♗xc6   ♗xc6 23   ♖xd8+   ♘f8   24   ♖c1   ♖d7 25 ♖xf8+ ♔xf8 26 ♖xc6

Black now resigned. *His* knights too performed quite a dance in this game, but to much less effect.

1-0

All the same, the knight is not by nature an especially 'lively' piece, and according to all the canons of chess strategy the knights have to be developed as early as possible. The *latest* development of a knight (in this case the queen's knight) was seen in the well-known game Anand-Karpov, Las Palmas 1996. It was only on move 29 that the ex-World Champion played ♘b8-c6, only to lose on time on move 35. All the games of that super-tournament were widely publicized, so there is clearly no need to reproduce the score here.

But how long can an attacked piece survive on the board? The record for 'longevity' under such conditions was probably achieved by a knight (of course!) in the game

Beliavsky – Lobron, Dortmund 1995. (The notes are Beliavsky's.)

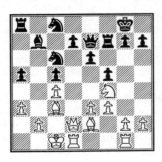

18...♘b4?

Pretty, but White doesn't have to capture. A stronger move was 18...♘b6 with the idea of 19...♘a4.

19 ♔b1

Not 19 axb4? axb4 20 ♗e5, on account of 20...d6 21 ♗xd6 b3 22 ♔b1 ♗e4+! 23 fxe4 ♕a7 etc.

19...e5 20 ♘d5 ♗xd5 21 cxd5 ♘b6 22 e4 d6 23 ♖gf1 ♕e8

Intending a raid with the queen along the route e8-a4-b3-a2.

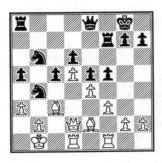

24 f4!

Played not so much in order to attack as to defend against the black queen's incursion.

24...exf4 25 ♖xf4 ♕a4?

Firing a blank; he had to decide on 25...fxe4.

26 ♖f3

Now 26...♕b3 can be met by 27 ♗xb4.

26...♖e8 27 ♖df1 ♖xe4 28 ♖xf5 ♖xf5 29 ♖xf5 ♕e8

Black has to go back in view of the threatened 30 ♕g5. If he persists with 29...♕b3, White wins by 30 axb4 ♘a4 (or 30...axb4 31 ♕g5) 31 ♗xg7.

30 ♕g5 ♖e7 31 axb4

Now the time for the 'forgotten' knight has come. It's amusing how the poor thing has been *en prise* for as long as 13 moves before being put out of its misery.

31...axb4

32 ♗b5! ♖e1+

Banking on a time-trouble miracle; if instead he tries 32...♕d8, he runs into 33 ♗f6.

33 ♗xe1 ♕xe1+ 34 ♔a2 b3+ 35 ♔xb3 c4+ 36 ♔a2?!

Lobron wasn't that far wrong. Short of time, I miss the decisive 36 ♗xc4 ♕d1+ 37 ♔c3 ♘a4+ 38 ♔b4.

36...♕a5+ 37 ♔b1 ♕e1+ 38 ♔a2 ♕a5+ 39 ♔b1 ♕e1+ 40 ♕c1?!

White could escape the perpetual check by 40 ♔c2 ♕e2+ 41 ♔c3 ♕d3+ (or 41...♕e1+ 42 ♕d2) 42 ♔b4.

40...♕e4+ 41 ♔a2 ♕xf5 42 ♕e3!

Black appears to have emerged from the time-scramble without losses, but now he will have to exchange queens, and both types of endgame that may result are lost for him.

42...♘xd5

Black prefers to maintain material equality. By going into a minor piece ending with 42...♘d7 43 ♕e6+ ♕xe6 44 dxe6 ♘f6, he would lose a pawn but could resist for much longer: 45 ♗xc4 ♔f8 46 ♗b5 ♔e7 47 ♗d7 ♔d8 48 ♔a3 ♔c7 49 ♔a4 ♘d5 (or 49...♘g4 50 b4 ♘xh2 51 b5 ♘g4 52 ♔a5 ♘e5 53 b6+ ♔b7 54 e7) 50 ♔a5 ♔b7 51 b4 ♘e7 52 b5 ♔a7 53 ♗c6 ♘c8 54 b6+ ♔b8 55 b7 ♘e7 56 ♔b6 d5 57 ♗b5 d4 58 ♗d3 h6 59 h4.

43 ♕e8+ ♕f8 44 ♕e6+ ♕f7 45 ♕xf7+ ♔xf7 46 ♗xc4 ♔e6 47 b4 ♔e5 48 ♗xd5 ♔xd5 49 ♔b3 ♔d4 50 ♔a4 d5 51 b5 ♔c5 52 ♔a5! 1-0

Both sides queen a pawn, but after 52...d4 53 b6 ♔c6 54 ♔a6 d3 55 b7 d2 56 b8=♕ d1=♕ 57 ♕c8+ ♔d5 58 ♕d8+ the black queen is lost.

Slow and steady

In the career of any pawn on the chessboard, the highest ambition is to take 5 or 6 steps forward and be promoted to a queen. On the way the pawn will often manage to 'eat' a couple or even a trio of hostile fighting units, thereby switching files of course, and sometimes increasing the spectacular effect of its advance. There are countless examples of this, and establishing a record pawn march is practically impossible. Nonetheless, chess history can point incontrovertibly to some record-breaking actions with pawns – not just one pawn, but all of them together!

Marshall – Rogosin
New York 1940
Sicilian Defence [B20]

1 e4 c5 2 b4 cxb4 3 a3 ♘c6 4 axb4 ♘f6? 5 b5 ♘d4 6 c3 ♘e6 7 e5 ♘d5 8 c4 ♘df4 9 g3 ♘g6 10 f4 ♘gxf4 11 gxf4 ♘xf4 12 d4 ♘g6 13 h4 e6 14 h5

Having made 14 (!) pawn moves running, White has an extra piece and a won position. A record achievement by 'infantry' unsupported (except from a distance) by either 'tanks' or 'artillery'.

The rest, strictly speaking, isn't all that important; the pawns have done their job.

14...♗b4+ 15 ♗d2 ♗xd2+ 16 ♘xd2 ♘e7 17 ♘e4 ♘f5 18 h6 g6 19 ♘f6+ ♔f8 20 ♘f3 d6 21 ♘g5 dxe5 22 dxe5 ♕xd1+ 23 ♖xd1 ♔e7 24 ♖h3 b6 25 ♗g2 ♖b8 26 ♘gxh7

Black resigned; his king is in a mating net, and White isn't far off making a new queen.

1-0

But in that game it all happened in the opening. Who would have imagined that in **Ibragimov – Filipov**, Linares (open) 1997, the

pawns would make thirteen moves (or more precisely half-moves) in a row, while the pieces of both colours would watch their hand-to-hand fight 'from the sidelines'? (The notes are by V.Bagirov.)

17...f5 18 f3

If White plays 18 e3?, then 18...f4! follows with terrible effect.

18...b5 19 e3?!

A relatively better line was 19 b4 cxb4 20 axb4 ♖fc8 21 ♗d2 a4, though Black's advantage would still be considerable.

19...b4! 20 exd4 bxc3 21 dxc5 f4!

Clearing the way to f3 for the queen.

22 g4 e4!

Now an avenue is cleared for the bishop.

23 dxe4 c2!

Successfully concluding the 'psychological warfare'.

24 ♕xc2 ♗d4+ 25 ♖f2 ♕xf3 0-1

In the 16th game of the 4th match between **McDonnell** and **La Bourdonnais**, Black's plan culminated in a record triumph for the pawns.

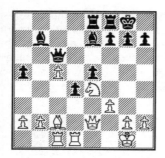

There is no doubt about Black's advantage thanks to his strong pawn centre, but he needs to make it mobile – and doesn't shrink from material losses in order to do so.

20...f5! 21 ♕c4+ ♔h8 22 ♗a4 ♕h6 23 ♗xe8 fxe4 24 c6 exf3! 25 ♖c2 (White is mated in 6 moves in the event of 25 cxb4 ♕e3+) **25...♕e3+ 26 ♔h1 ♗c8 27 ♗d7 f2**

So far, the direct threats (28...♕e1+ 29 ♕f1 ♕xd1 30 ♕xd1 f1=♕+) are being created solely by this passed pawn which has followed a truly breathtaking career in a short space of time. Its comrades, rooted to the spot, seem left in the background.

28 ♖f1

Not 28 ♕f1 on account of 28...♗a6!.

28...d3 29 ♖c3 ♗xd7 30 cxd7 e4

Now it seems that the passed pawn trio has started singing in unison!

31 ♕c8 ♗d8 32 ♕c4 ♕e1 33 ♖c1 d2! 34 ♕c5 ♖g8 35 ♖d1 e3! 36 ♕c3 ♕xd1 37 ♖xd1 e2! 0-1

Strong, original and beautiful. It would have made André Danican Philidor happy.

However, even without queening, a pawn is capable of striking the decisive blow. In the centre of the board in the middlegame, this is an extremely rare event! To be sure,

the pawn has to be grateful to the pieces for driving the enemy king into its sphere of influence.

Morozevich – Chernin
Moscow 1995

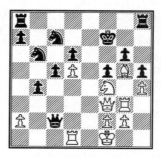

27 ♘xg6 ♔xg6 28 ♗h6+ ♔f6 (taking the bishop leads to mate) **29 ♕xh5 ♖ag8 30 ♗g5+ ♔e5 31 ♖e3+ ♕e4 32 f4 mate!**

But then, pawn moves which were *not* made may also establish a record.

In the immortal novel *The Twelve Chairs* by Ilya Ilf and Evgeny Petrov, the hero Ostap Bender knew full well that no harm could come of playing e2-e4 on his first move. Indeed, in the Romantic epoch of chess, virtually all games started like that, and to this day the opening with the king's pawn has not in any way been discredited.

You could hardly have suspected **Mikhail Tal**, the eighth World Champion, of not knowing this. And yet in his game with **Anatoly Karpov**, later to be Champion number twelve, in the Alekhine Memorial tournament (Moscow 1971), Tal's e-pawn remained on e2 for a record 105 moves (!), before the players agreed a draw in this position:

40

A notable point is that one other record (or more exactly an anti-record) is bound up with this game. The entire chess world knew about Tal's phenomenal memory. He could reproduce thousands of games on a chessboard or simply dictate them to you. They certainly weren't just his own games – they were from all periods. Yet he slipped up when telling of his chess relationship with Karpov in the volume *Karpov: Selected Games 1969-1977*. (The book was published in Moscow in 1978, as part of the famous series in black covers: 'Outstanding Chessplayers of the World'.) Tal stated that in the above game he played e2-e4 on the 101st move, "just for fun". Perhaps he had merely *wanted* to do so, against the demands of the position. Who knows? We can no longer obtain an answer.

No one ever saw further

This is about combinations. We will keep away from the purely theoretical and even somewhat abstract argument about what defines their essence; in the 1950s the topic was debated by World Champion Botvinnik, Grandmasters Levenfish and Bondarevsky, and other chess authorities. But taking a combination as a unified whole – from the initial sacrifice to the point where the situation is cleared up – we can try to find out which one was calculated the furthest ahead.

On this subject, generally speaking, the creators of combinations have not given us too much information. All the same, there is every reason to suppose that a majority – indeed the overwhelming majority – of combinative attacks stretching over many moves were *not* calculated right to the end, and indeed were mostly undertaken intuitively.

This example has become a classic:

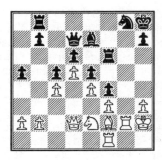

The position arose in the game **Averbakh – Kotov** from the Candidates Tournament in Switzerland, 1953. At this point Black sacrificed his queen; in general terms he had no doubt about the correctness of the sacrifice, but he didn't by any means work it all out to the end.

41

30...♕xh3+ 31 ♔xh3 ♖h6+ 32 ♔g4 ♘f6+ 33 ♔f5 ♘d7

"If the queen sacrifice had been 'precisely calculated', Kotov would have preferred the move indicated afterwards by Stahlberg: 33...♘g4, making ♖g2-g5 impossible. White would then have to accept colossal losses to avert the mate threat." (Bronstein)

34 ♖g5 ♖f8+ 35 ♔g4 ♘f6+ 36 ♔f5 ♘g8+ 37 ♔g4 ♘f6+

Black repeats the position to get through his time trouble and ... adjourn the game. In the quiet of private study, the combination can be analysed and calculated 'up to mate'.

38 ♔f5 ♘xd5+ 39 ♔g4 ♘f6+ 40 ♔f5 ♘g8+ 41 ♔g4 ♗xg5 42 ♔xg5 ♖f7 43 ♗h4 ♖g6+ 44 ♔h5 ♖fg7 45 ♗g5 ♖xg5+ 46 ♔h4 ♘f6 47 ♘g3 ♖xg3 48 ♕xd6 ♖3g6 49 ♕b8+ ♖g8 0-1

As we see, the combination that brought Kotov the first brilliancy prize and attracted an enthusiastic chess press ('once in 100 years', 'unique', 'a magnificent queen sacrifice', etc.) was in fact by no means calculated all that deeply.

In our next example the winner went further down the path. The game between **José Raoul Capablanca** and **Osip Bernstein** received the first brilliancy prize in the great tournament at St Petersburg in 1914. In the diagram position, after giving up a piece for three pawns, White had the opportunity to capture a fourth one without breaking off his attack on the king, but he preferred a different continuation.

21 ♗h4!

"In my opinion the finest move of the game, but the commentators all failed to appreciate it. Before discovering it, I examined a whole host of combinations involving a total of at least 100 moves. The combination in the game is one of them, and I had to study it all the way to the end before deciding on this move. Otherwise I would simply have continued 21 ♘xe5." (Capablanca)

21...♕d7 22 ♘xc8! ♕xc6 23 ♕d8+

Here White could have reached his goal more quickly, and in no less beautiful a manner than the game continuation. After 23 ♗e7+, Black perishes whatever he plays:

(a) 23...♔e8 24 ♕d8+ ♔f7 25 ♘g5+ ♔g6 26 ♕xh8 ♘f6 27 ♗xf6 ♕xf6 28 h4!, and on 28...h6 or 28...♕xg5 (with the idea of 29...♖xc8), White has the decisive 29 ♕e8+.

(b) 23...♔f7 24 ♘g5+ ♔g6 25 ♕xg4 ♕xc8 26 ♘e6+ ♔f7 27 ♕xg7+ ♔xe6 28 ♖d1! with mate on d6 or f6.

Evidently Capablanca was simply sticking to the variation he had worked out in advance.

23...♕e8

23...♔f7 would lose the queen to 24 ♘d6+.

24 ♗e7+ ♔f7 25 ♘d6+ ♔g6 26 ♘h4+ ♔h5

26...♔h6 allows mate in three: 27 ♘df5+ ♔h5 28 ♘g3+ (interestingly, in his notes to the game Capablanca himself only gives 28 ♘xg7+ ♔h6 29 ♘hf5+ ♔g6 30 ♕d6+ with mate to follow) 28...♔h6 29 ♗g5 mate.

27 ♘xe8 ♖xd8

The agony couldn't have been prolonged by 27...♖xe8 28 ♕d1 ♖xe7 29 h3, when 29...g6 is met by 30 ♕xg4+ ♔h6 31 ♘f5+ gxf5 32 ♕h4+.

28 ♘xg7 ♔h6 29 ♘gf5+ ♔h5 30 h3!

"The culminating move of the combination that began with 21 ♗h4. White is still threatening mate, and the best way for Black to avoid it is to give up all his material advantage and remain three pawns down. I believe this combination is of record-breaking length, and if you take into account how many pieces participated in it, as well as the quantity of variations and complexities, it will be hard to find its equal. The position reached by this last move is more akin to a study than to a game that was actually played. It appeals to my artistic taste, since it embodies the logical and analytic perfection which I consider essential to a masterpiece." It must be said that the future World Champion's commentary is not remarkable for its modesty.

30...♘c8 31 hxg4+ ♔xg4 32 ♗xd8 ♖xd8 33 g3 ♖d2 34 ♔g2 ♖e2

This is more stubborn than 34...♖xa2 35 ♘f3, when 35...♗b8 allows 36 ♖h1 and mate.

35 a4 ♘b6 36 ♘e3+ ♔h6 37 a5 ♘d7 38 ♘hf5 ♘f6 39 b5 ♗d4 40 ♔f3 ♖a2 41 a6 ♗a7 42 ♖c1 ♖b2 43 g4+ ♔g5 44 ♖c7 ♖xf2+ 45 ♔xf2 ♘xg4+ 46 ♔f3 1-0

In all its genuine beauty, Capablanca's combination lasted ten moves. Well then, should we agree with the young Cuban's self-assessment as a record holder? I am afraid not. The absolute record should be credited to Alexander Alekhine. He played the following game against the Czechoslovak Master Karel Treybal while on his way to the throne. From the diagram position, Alekhine's combination – by his own account – was calculated 20 moves ahead! (I reproduce his notes.)

Treybal – Alekhine
Pistyan 1922

31...♕b5!

The only move to win. It threatens both 32...♖xf5 and 32...d2! followed by 33...c3. If White plays 32 ♔g2, then 32...♗a5! and 33...♖d8 would also win without difficulty.

32 f6 d2! 33 ♕f4!

Anticipating the continuation 33...dxc1=♕ 34 ♖xc1 ♖c8 35 ♕g4! with drawing chances, since the square h1 is not of the same colour as the bishop.

By the ensuing combination, *the longest which I have ever undertaken*, Black avoids this doubtful variation and secures a winning pawn-ending.

33...♕d7+! 34 ♔g2 d1=♕ 35 ♖xd1 ♕xd1 36 ♕xc4+ ♖f7 37 ♕xb4 ♕xc1 38 ♕b8+ ♖f8 39 f7+!

The key-move of a variation enabling White to recover his rook. As we shall see shortly, Black's winning manoeuvre initiated by 33...♕d7+! comprises no less than 20 moves!

39...♔xf7 40 ♕b3+?

It is astonishing that a master of the strength of Dr Treybal, so conspicuously endowed with the imaginative sense, should not have perceived 40 g6+!, the only logical continuation.

Black could not have answered it by 40...♔g8, on account of 41 gxh7+; nor by 40...hxg6 for in that case White would have forced a draw by perpetual check, e.g. 41 ♕b3+ ♔f6 42 ♕f3+ ♔e7 43 ♕a3+ ♔e8 44 ♕a4+! ♔d8 45 ♕a8+ ♔e7 46 ♕a3+ ♔f7 47 ♕b3+ etc.

The only move to win was consequently 40...♔xg6!, leading to the forced continuation 41 ♕xf8 ♕xb2+ 42 ♔g3 ♕c3+ 43 ♔g2 ♕d2+ 44 ♔g3 ♕e3+ 45 ♔g2 ♕e4+ 46 ♔g3 ♕e5+ 47 ♔g2 ♔h5!

48 ♕f3+ ♔xh4 49 ♕h3+ ♔g5 50 ♕xh7 ♕e2+ 51 ♔g3 (or 51 ♔g1) 51...♕g4+ followed by 52...♕f5+ or 52...♕h5+, and Black wins by forcing exchange of queens next move.

40...♔g6!

And White can only give a few harmless checks, e.g. 41 ♕e6+ ♔h5 42 ♕e2+ ♔xh4! and wins.

0-1

Some doubts remain, however. This game was both played and annotated at a time when the great player had set himself a precise goal: to gain the World Championship title. Alekhine perfectly well understood how loudly his name would have to be trumpeted if a match with José Raoul Capablanca was to emerge from the realm of hypothesis into reality. He was doing everything in his power to build up his uncommon chess image. He was indeed extraordinary and brilliant, but this had to be made known, it had to be brought home to people who played chess weakly but possessed more money. Hence Alekhine's blindfold displays that so impressed the neophytes, hence his tours round most of the globe – and, possibly, some exaggerations in his commentaries. Assuredly, his phenomenal intuition and amazing ability to grasp all the nuances of a position will have told Alekhine (who in Lasker's words "grew out of combinations") that the line he chose gave chances of success. But at what stage, at which move, did this become clear? Should not Alekhine's 'confession' of his incredible depth of calculation be viewed as one more detail in the requisite image of a man worthy to challenge for the crown?

Still, as we know, suspicions are not proof; and Alekhine's words about his 20-move combination are what we have before us.

There is no reason to doubt the sincerity of the 13th World Champion who stated after the following game that in the diagram position he had calculated an 18-move variation for the first time in his life!

Kasparov – Topalov
Wijk aan Zee 1999

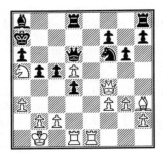

24 ⊒xd4?!

In his obvious enthusiasm, Kasparov called this the best game of his life on the basis of the sacrifice undertaken here and the exceedingly long calculation. Alas! The alternative 24 ♘c6+ ♗xc6 25 ♕xd6 ⊒xd6 26 dxc6 ♔b6 27 ⊒e7 ♔xc6 28 ⊒de1!, threatening 29 ⊒a7 ♔b6 30 ⊒ee7, would have given him at least a draw, whereas in the actual game he could have landed in difficulties.

24...cxd4?

This is just what White was counting on, and yet after 24...♔b6! 25 ♘b3 g5 (25...♗xd5 isn't bad either; Black has the better ending

after 26 ♕xd6 ⊒xd6 27 ⊒d2 ⊒hd8 28 ⊒ed1 c4 29 ♘c1 ♔c7) 26 ♕d2 g4 27 ⊒xg4 ♘xg4 Black's game is somewhat pleasanter.

Now everything runs on oiled wheels for White.

25 ⊒e7+ ♔b6

Not 25...♕xe7? 26 ♕xd4+ ♔b8 27 ♕b6+ ♗b7 28 ♘c6+, or 25...♔b8 26 ♕xd4 ♘d7 27 ♗xd7! ♗xd5 28 c4! ♕xe7 29 ♕b6+ ♔a8 30 ♕xa6+ ♔b8 31 ♕b6+ ♔a8 32 ♗c6+.

26 ♕xd4+ ♔xa5 27 b4+ ♔a4 28 ♕c3 (threatening mate on b3) **28...♕xd5 29 ⊒a7! ♗b7**

On 29...⊒d6 White wins by 30 ♔b2, as there is no defence against ♕c3-b3+.

30 ⊒xb7 ♕c4?!

After this Black loses by force. At first it was thought that he could have drawn by 30...⊒he8!? 31 ⊒b6 ⊒a8, but afterwards the following line was discovered: 32 ♗f1! (not 32 ♗e6 ⊒xe6 33 ⊒xe6 ♕c4 34 ♕xc4 bxc4 35 ⊒xf6 ♔xa3) 32...⊒e1+ (or 32...♘d7 33 ⊒d6! ⊒e1+ 34 ♔b2 ♕e5 35 ⊒d4) 33 ♕xe1 ♘d7 34 ⊒b7! ♘e5 (or 34...♕xb7 35 ♕d1! ♔xa3 36 c3, threatening ♕d1-c1+) 35 ♕c3 ♕xf3 36 ♗d3 ♕d5 37 ♗e4 ♕c4 38 ♕xe5, and White wins after all.

31 ♕xf6 ♔xa3

31...⊒d1+ 32 ♔b2 ♕d4+ 33 ♕xd4 ⊒xd4 34 ⊒xf7 is also hopeless for Black.

32 ♕xa6+ ♔xb4 33 c3+! ♔xc3 34 ♕a1+ ♔d2 35 ♕b2+ ♔d1 36 ♗f1+

Elegantly concluding the fight. Of course Black can't take the bishop in view of 37 ♕c2+ ♔e1 38 ⊒e7+.

36...⊒d2 37 ⊒d7! ⊒xd7 38 ♗xc4 bxc4 39 ♕xh8 ⊒d3 40 ♕a8 c3

**41 ♕a4+ ♔e1 42 f4 f5 43 ♔c1 ♖d2
44 ♕a7 1-0**

You decide then, dear readers – which combination, which lengthy calculation, should be regarded as the record, taking account of all circumstances in this chapter?

Fall of the Giants

No, I am not about to speak of upheavals in the chess realm, the toppling of kings of chess, astounding failures by World Champions. My topic here is the refutation of those brilliant combinations which all lovers of chess art have admired for years, decades, centuries. Among chess composers there is a melancholy joke that "all studies can be divided into those which have been refuted and those which are going to be." Practice, that touchstone of truth, has shown that the same joke probably extends to what is most sublime in chess, to its Song of Songs, to what makes this sport with its elements of science into an artistic phenomenon also, a sphere where genuine Beauty resides.

At all events there is nothing in the universe more powerful, or more just, than Time. It alone revises the meaning of events, alters the scale of human personalities, separates the wheat from the chaff, overturns ideas and attainments which seemed unshakeable.

In this respect chess is no exception.

Adolf Anderssen's brilliant attacks in the 'Immortal' and 'Evergreen' games have already been refuted....

Defences have been found against many brilliant tactical strokes brought off not only by Mikhail Tal but also by Alexander Alekhine who "grew out of combinations"....

As to the fantastic conception in Kholmov-Bronstein from the 1964 Soviet Championship, it was eventually established that if his opponent had defended ideally, White could have extracted nothing more from his combination than some winning chances in the endgame....

And so on, and so forth.

Which refutation of a famous performance should be viewed as the record? As always there is no unequivocal, arithmetically precise answer. And yet the record to end all records for refutations applies to a completely different game which is nowhere near so famous, indeed practically forgotten. It was played in 1906 between **Josef Krejcik** and **Adolf Schwarz**, in a perfectly ordinary tournament in Austria. Incidentally this last-round defeat deprived the old master of first prize; in fact the game proved to be the last of Schwarz's life.

31 ♘xc6+ ♔c7 32 ♕e7+ ♔b6

At this point the simple 33 ♕xb7+ ♔xb7 34 ♗f3 would have won the game. Since the c-pawn at present is 'poisoned' (34...♘xc4 35 ♘e5+), White picks up the d-pawn, which guarantees the win even if the knights are exchanged and the opposite bishops remain!

Instead White played a combination which was rewarded with a brilliancy prize.

33 c5+ ♔a6 34 ♗c8(??)

It still wasn't too late to exchange queens and play to win the endgame.

34...♕xc8 35 ♕a7+ ♔b5 36 ♕b6+ ♔c4 37 ♕b4+ ♔d5 38 ♘e7+, and Black resigned as he loses his queen (**1-0**).

Unfortunately the prize was awarded for an *anti*-brilliancy. But the unique thing about it is that the truth was ascertained by Krejcik himself a full fifty years later! He published an analysis which totally demolished the plan and decision he had implemented in the game. For in the position where Black resigned, he could have *won* by force, as follows: 38...♔e4 39 ♘xc8 f3+ 40 ♔f2 (the only square; otherwise the white queen is lost) 40...♗h4+ 41 ♔g1 f2+ 42 ♔h2 f1=♕ 43 ♘d6+ ♔e5 44 ♘f7+ ♔f5 45 ♘d6+ ♔g6, and White has the choice between resigning (since he is a piece down) or being mated in three moves by 46 ♕b7 ♕f2+ 47 ♔h1 ♕e1+ 48 ♔h2 ♗g3.

No other comparable case is known to chess history. But a thought occurs to me: wasn't that brilliant chess writer Krejcik setting up an extra record for gentlemanly conduct when he 'returned' his prize (albeit only morally) after keeping it for half a century?

Better late than never

Even chess novices know that at the start of the game the king is the weakest piece, and they are always advised by their teachers to castle as quickly as they can. In the first place there are safety reasons; kings left stuck in the centre have been overwhelmed by deadly attacks in countless games. Secondly, his Majesty has to be prevented from getting under the feet of his own subjects – in particular, from blocking the connection between his rooks.

But then there is no rule without exceptions, and the record for late castling keeps on being broken. Here are the results.

(1) The game in which *both sides* castled latest was the following. White castles on move 24, Black on move 36.

Yates – Alekhine
San Remo 1930
Ruy Lopez [C71]

1 e4 e5 2 ♘f3 ♘c6 3 ♗b5 a6 4 ♗a4 d6 5 ♘c3 ♗d7 6 d3 g6 7 ♘d5 b5 8 ♗b3 ♘a5 9 ♗g5 f6 10 ♗d2 c6 11 ♘e3 ♘xb3 12 axb3 ♘h6 13 b4 f5 14 ♕e2 ♘f7 15 ♘f1 ♕e7 16 ♘g3 f4 17 ♘f1 g5 18 ♗c3 h5 19 ♘3d2 ♗g4 20 f3 ♗e6 21 d4 ♗g7 22 ♕d3 exd4 23 ♗xd4 ♘e5 24 ♕e2

24...0-0 25 h3 c5 26 ♗c3 cxb4 27 ♗xb4 ♘c6 28 ♗c3 ♗xc3 29 bxc3 ♕f6 30 e5 ♘xe5 31 ♘e4 ♕e7 32 ♘fd2 ♗c4 33 ♘xc4 ♘xc4 34 ♖d1 ♕e5 35 ♕d3 ♖f5

36 0-0 d5 37 ♕xd5+ ♕xd5 38 ♖xd5 ♖xd5 39 ♘f6+ ♔f7 40 ♘xd5 ♖d8 41 ♘b4 ♖d2 42 ♖a1 a5 43 ♘c6 ♖xc2 44 ♘xa5 ♘e3 45 ♖b1 ♖xg2+ 46 ♔h1 ♖g3 47 ♘c6 ♖xh3+, and the World Champion won on the 66th move (0-1).

(2) The latest instance of *kingside castling by White* was move 46 of this game:

Bobotsov – Ivkov
Wijk aan Zee 1966
King's Indian Defence [E84]

1 d4 ♘f6 2 c4 g6 3 ♘c3 ♗g7 4 e4 d6 5 f3 0-0 6 ♗e3 ♘c6 7 ♘ge2 a6

8 ♕d2 ♖b8 9 ♘c1 e5 10 d5 ♘d4 11 ♘b3 ♘xb3 12 axb3 c5 13 b4 cxb4 14 ♘a4 b5 15 cxb5 axb5 16 ♕xb4 ♘e8 17 ♘c3 ♗h6 18 ♗f2 ♕g5 19 ♖d1 ♗d7 20 h4 ♕e7 21 g4 ♘c7 22 g5 ♗g7 23 ♗e2 f6 24 ♗e3 fxg5 25 hxg5 ♖a8 26 ♖c1 ♘a6 27 ♕b3 ♘c5 28 ♕c2 b4 29 ♘d1 ♗a4 30 ♕d2 ♘b3 31 ♕xb4 ♘xc1 32 ♗xc1 ♗xd1 33 ♗xd1 ♖a1 34 ♕c3 ♕b7 35 b4 ♖b1 36 ♗d2 ♖c8 37 ♕d3 ♖b2 38 ♕a3 ♖b1 39 ♕a2 ♖xb4 40 ♗xb4 ♕xb4+ 41 ♕d2 ♕b6 42 ♕f2 ♕a5+ 43 ♕d2 ♕a7 44 ♕f2 ♕a3 45 ♕d2 ♖b8

46 0-0 ♖b2 47 ♗c2 ♗f8 48 ♖f2 ♗e7 49 ♔g2 ♗d8 50 f4 ♗b6 51 ♖f3 ♗a5 52 ♕f2 ♕c5 53 fxe5 ♕xf2+ 54 ♖xf2 dxe5 55 ♔h3 ½-½

(3) The game in which *Black* delayed longest before bringing his king to safety was Suterbuck-Van der Heiden, from the 1981 Dutch Championship.

Compared with such monstrosities, Kasparov's castling move in the next example may seem trivially early; it occurs as soon as move thirty! But in reply to it, White resigned – a record-breaking effect of the move 0-0!

Timman – Kasparov
2nd match game,
Prague 1998

14...♛d5!!

After this, it is White's minor pieces, not Black's, that start to feel shaky.

15 ♗f3 ♞e4 16 ♞xc6 ♖xc6 17 ♞d2 f5 18 ♖e1 d3!

Preventing the white rook from coming into play.

19 ♞xb3 e5! 20 ♗d2 ♖b6 21 ♗xe4 fxe4 22 ♞c1 ♖xb2 23 ♗c3 d2

The most energetic.

24 ♖f1

After 24 ♗xb2 dxe1=♛+ 25 ♛xe1 ♗b4! the white queen is trapped!

24...♗xf1 25 ♗xb2 ♗c4 26 ♞e2 ♗b3 27 ♞c3 ♗xd1 28 ♞xd5 ♗b3 29 ♞c3 ♗b4 30 ♞d1 0-0

Now White can't stop the black rook from penetrating.

0-1

(4) In a game from Lone Pine 1976, there were only 8 fighting units left on the board when White, threatened with mate, *castled long* on move forty!

Pupols – Mayers

40 0-0-0 ♖a2 41 ♖e1+ ♚d7 42 a7 ♖a8 43 ♖f7+ ♚d6 44 ♖ee7 ♖c8+ 45 ♚d1 ♖c5 46 ♖d7+ ♚e6 47 ♖h7 ♖ca5 48 ♚e1 ♖5a4 49 ♚f1 ♖a1+ 50 ♚g2 ♖4a3 51 ♖he7+ ♚f6 52 ♖b7 ♖3a2 53 ♖h7 ♚e6 54 ♖b6+ ♚d5 55 ♖h5+ ♚c4 56 ♖b7 ♖xa7 57 ♖xa7 ♖xa7 58 ♖e5 ♚d4 59 f4 ♖g7+ 60 ♚f3 ♖g1 61 ♖e8 ♚d5 62 f5 ♚d6 63 ♚f4 ♚d7 64 ♖e2 ♖g8 65 ♖a2 ♚e7, and peace was signed on the 76th move (½-½).

(5) *Black* castled queenside even later – on move 43 – in Popović-Ivanov, New York 1983. In the following example he did so a little earlier, but the position was well into the endgame stage; moreover the effect was almost the same as in the Kasparov game....

Sznapik – Adamski
Polish Championship 1973
Sicilian Defence [B82]

1 e4 c5 2 ♞f3 e6 3 d4 cxd4 4 ♞xd4 ♞f6 5 ♞c3 d6 6 ♗e3 a6 7 f4 b5 8 ♛f3 ♗b7 9 ♗d3 ♞bd7 10 g4 b4 11 ♞ce2 e5 12 ♞f5 g6 13 ♞fg3 exf4 14 ♗xf4 h5 15 gxh5

♘xh5 16 ♘xh5 ♖xh5 17 ♗g3 ♗g7
18 ♖f1 ♕f6 19 ♗xd6 ♕xf3
20 ♖xf3 ♗xb2 21 ♖b1 ♗e5
22 ♖xb4 ♗xd6 23 ♖xb7 ♘e5
24 ♖f6 ♗e7 25 ♖f2 ♗c5 26 ♖g2
♘f3+ 27 ♔d1 ♖xh2 28 ♖xh2
♘xh2 29 ♘f4 ♘g4 30 ♘d5 ♘e3+
31 ♘xe3 ♗xe3

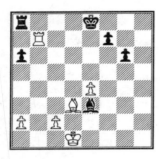

32 ♗c4??

In the fifth hour of play it's easy to forget that Black still has the right to castle.

32...0-0-0+

Objectively speaking, White could have stopped the clock (if 33 ♗d5 then 33...♖xd5+), but he played on out of inertia.

33 ♔e2 ♔xb7 34 ♔xe3 f6 35 ♔f4 ♖d7 36 ♗d3 ♖e7 37 ♗c4 ♔b6 38 ♗g8 ♔c5 39 c3 a5 40 ♗b3 ♔d6 41 ♗g8 ♖c7 42 c4 ♖g7 43 ♗d5 ♖e7 44 ♔e3 ♔c5 45 ♔d3 ♖h7 0-1

And to conclude, here is one more story which in its way constitutes a record.

Kindermann – Korchnoi
Central European Zonal
Tournament, Ptuj 1995

The position is double-edged and full of life. Black's attack in the h-file has clearly come to a dead end, and Korchnoi quite rightly decided to attend to his own king's safety. Better late than never; and anyway the players had just 10 minutes left each.

He therefore played **26...0-0!**. The game ended in a furious time scramble; no one kept the score, and both flags dropped within a second of each other when 49 moves had already been played. Under the arbiter's supervision the players began reconstructing the game; as they did so, the secretary of the tournament committee entered the moves into a computer. All of a sudden the computer refused to accept Black's castling move! Why? For a very simple reason. The play leading to the diagram position went like this:

Caro-Kann Defence [B12]

1 e4 c6 2 d4 d5 3 e5 c5 4 dxc5 e6
Going over to a French set-up with a tempo less.

5 ♗e3 ♘d7 6 ♗b5 ♕c7 7 ♘f3 ♗xc5 8 ♗xc5 ♕xc5 9 ♘c3 ♘e7 10 0-0 a6 11 ♗d3 h6 12 ♖e1 ♘c6 13 ♕d2 g5!?

Attack is the best means of defence.

14 h3 ♖g8 15 a3 ♕f8 16 g4 h5

17 ♕e3 ♕h6 18 ♗f1 hxg4 19 hxg4 b6 20 ♗g2 ♗b7 21 ♘a4 ♖h8 22 ♘xb6 ♘cxe5 23 ♘xd7 ♘xd7 24 ♖ad1 ♖c8 25 ♕a7 ♖c7 26 ♖d3

At this point the second prize winner made an illegal move, and the tournament victor didn't notice! They both appeared shaken when the arbiter told them to resume the game from Black's 26th move. A solution was found when, on Korchnoi's proposal, peace was immediately concluded (½-½).

So many checks

"As long as I keep checking I've got nothing to be afraid of." That was what we boys were once told by an older school friend, who obviously had it from someone else. And he was absolutely right, just on condition that the attacks pestering the enemy king never come to an end.

Yes, perpetual check is the lifeline that our wise predecessors perceptively incorporated into chess. It's as if they wanted to reward the boldness of a dashing attacker who doesn't shrink from sacrifices, by giving him the right to avoid loss through constantly checking the king. In practice the fight usually ends very quickly once the mechanism of perpetual check intervenes. The following game, however, contains a series of checks of record length.

Westerinen – Keres
Match Finland v Estonia,
Tallinn 1969
Ruy Lopez [C72]

1 e4 ♘c6(?!)
One of the best chessplayers on the planet had obviously decided to

tease his young colleague whom he had easily beaten the previous day. Still, Markku Heikki Julius Westerinen had won the Finnish Championship three times and gained a couple of first places in international tournaments; in those years he was clearly assuming the leadership of Scandinavian chess. In this position he steers clear of the unfamiliar play arising from the tempting (and strongest!) move 2 d4.

2 ♘f3 e5 3 ♗b5 a6 4 ♗a4 d6 5 0-0 ♗d7 6 c3 ♘ge7 7 d4 ♘g6 8 ♗e3
Solid, safe ... and unaggressive.

8...♗e7 9 ♘bd2 0-0 10 ♗c2 exd4 11 ♘xd4?! ♘xd4 12 cxd4 ♗b5!? 13 ♖e1 ♗g5

White's 'restrained' strategy has allowed Black full equality, and Keres later succumbs to temptation and overreaches. For the moment, though, he holds the initiative.

14 ♘f3 ♗xe3 15 ♖xe3 c5 16 ♖c1 ♖c8 17 ♖c3 ♘f4 18 ♖e3 ♕f6 19 e5 ♕h6 20 ♔h1 dxe5 21 dxc5!? ♖fd8 22 ♕e1 ♗c6 23 ♖d1 ♕h5 24 ♖xd8+ ♖xd8 25 ♖xe5 ♕g4 26 ♖g5 ♕e6 27 ♕c3 g6 28 ♗b3 ♗xf3 29 gxf3 ♕e2 30 ♕e3 ♕d2 31 ♖g4! ♘h5 32 ♕e7 ♖d7 33 ♕e8+ ♔g7 34 ♕e5+ ♔g8 35 ♕xh5 ♕xf2 36 ♕h3 ♖e7 37 ♖g1 ♖e1 38 ♖xe1 ♕xe1+

Black's hopes rest on the sidelined white queen and, naturally, the possibility of endlessly persecuting the king.

39 ♔g2 ♕e2+ 40 ♔g3 ♕e1+ 41 ♔g2 ♕e2+ 42 ♔g1 ♕e3+ 43 ♔f1 ♕d3+ 44 ♔e1 ♕e3+ 45 ♔d1 ♕d3+ 46 ♔c1 ♕e3+ 47 ♔b1 ♕e1+ 48 ♔c2 ♕e2+ 49 ♔c3 ♕e3+ 50 ♔c4 ♕e2+ 51 ♔d5 ♕d2+ 52 ♔e5 ♕xb2+ 53 ♔d6 ♕d4+ 54 ♔c7 ♕xc5+ 55 ♔xb7 56 ♔a7 ♕c5+ 57 ♔xa6 ♕c6+ 58 ♔a7 ♕c7+ 59 ♔a8 ♕c6+ 60 ♔b8 ♕b6+ 61 ♔c8 ♕c6+ 62 ♔d8 ♕b6+

White was hoping for 62...♕d6+ 63 ♕d7, when there could follow (e.g.) 63...♕b8+ 64 ♔c8 ♕d6+ 65 ♔e8 ♕e5+ 66 ♔d7+ ♔g7 67 ♕c4 ♕f5+ 68 ♔c7 ♕xf3 69 ♕xf7+.

63 ♔d7 ♕b7+ 64 ♔d6 ♕b4+ 65 ♔c6 ♕c3+ 66 ♔b5 ♕e5+ 67 ♔c4 ♕e2+ 68 ♔b4 ♕e7+ 69 ♔c4 ♕e2+ 70 ♔d4 ♕d2+ 71 ♔e4 ♕e2+ 72 ♔f4 ♕d2+ 73 ♔e5 ♕e3+ 74 ♔d6 ♕d4+ 75 ♗d5 ♕b4+ 76 ♔d7

After going all round the board and being checked 38 times in a row, the white king obtains a minute's breathing space – but no more than that.

76...♕d4

The defender (the bishop) needs defending itself, and everything starts all over again.

77 ♔c6 ♕a4+ 78 ♔c5 ♕a5+ 79 ♔c4 ♕xa2+ 80 ♔d4 ♕d2+ 81 ♔e5 ♕b2+ 82 ♔d6 ♕b4+ ½-½

Unrealized advantage

The most difficult thing in chess is to win a won position. This aphorism has found confirmation in tens of thousands of games – and continues to do so! Therefore looking for the record in the field of unrealized advantages is a thankless and unpromising task. You might, of course, see a record in that match game on the highest level in which the reigning World Champion, Mikhail Botvinnik, picked up an extra rook against his challenger David Bronstein when scarcely out of the opening – only to end up sharing the point with his opponent. Or again there are similar situations in games that are *not* on such a high level. Or....

Well, taking up this last 'or', I *would* like to present a couple of contenders for the record in this field.

Within the space of ten years, starting from the first post-war international tournament at Groningen in 1946, the Argentine Grandmaster Miguel Najdorf and the Soviet Grandmaster Alexander Kotov faced each other seven times, mainly in Interzonal and Candidates Tournaments. One of these games was won by Najdorf. The rest all ended in draws, despite the fact that the Argentinian was one or two pawns up in every game – even, on one occasion, in a king-and-pawn ending! Through some sort of mystical influence, the ball just refused to land in the goal!

Perhaps for that reason, in the following position Najdorf *declined* to win his fourteenth (!) pawn against the same opponent.

Najdorf – Kotov
Mar del Plata 1957

Instead of playing 21 ♗xd5 ♕xd5 22 ♗xf6 ♗xf6 23 ♕xh7+ ♔f8 24 ♕h5 ♗xe5 25 dxe5, White continued with his attack, perceiving that f7 was a weak point as well as h7.

21 ♗d1!

A manoeuvre of which only a great master was capable.

21...♕a5 22 ♗h5 ♖ed8

After 22...♘xh5 23 ♕xh5 Black can't defend against both mate threats. On 22...♖f8, White has a choice of ways to win: the 'prosaic' 23 ♗xf6 ♗xf6 24 ♗xf7+ ♖xf7 25 ♕xh7+, or the spectacular 23 ♗g6.

23 ♗xf7+ ♔f8 24 ♗h6!

The black king is at the mercy of the hostile pieces. The immediate threat is fairly transparent: 25 ♗xg7+ ♔xg7 26 ♕h6+ ♔h8 27 ♘g6 mate.

24...♘e8 25 ♕f4

Again threatening mate in three: 26 ♗xg7+ ♘xg7 26 ♘g6+! hxg6 27 ♖h8 mate.

25...♗f6 26 ♗xg7+ ♔e7

Or 26...♗xg7 27 ♗xe8+.

27 ♗xe8 ♗xg7 28 ♖xh7 1-0

That was probably the best achievement in the encounters between these two Grandmasters. The following case has no parallels in chess history. On 10 May 1949, David Bronstein acquired four extra knights (!), but they all proved redundant!

This occurred on the day for adjournment sessions in the Moscow-Budapest match. First the arbiters set up the position in **Bronstein – Barcza**:

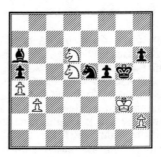

The paucity of material (especially pawns) increases the likelihood of a draw, but White has some advantage nonetheless.

41...♘c6

With his sealed move Black stops his opponent from immediately turning the a4-pawn into a passed pawn.

42 h4+ ♔g6 43 ♔f4 ♗d3 44 ♘b7 ♗c2 45 ♘c5 ♘d4 46 b4 axb4 47 ♘xb4 ♗xa4!

Black at once heads for a type of endgame well known to theory.

48 ♘xa4 ♔h5 49 ♘d3 ♔xh4

Strictly speaking, a halt could have been called at this point.

50 ♘c3 ♘e6+ 51 ♔xf5 ♘g7+ 52 ♔g6 ♘e8 53 ♘e4 ♔g4 54 ♔xh6 ♘f6 55 ♘xf6+, and the two knights can't mate the enemy king (½-½).

After a brief fifteen-minute break, the players in the game **Benko – Bronstein** sat down for their third resumption.

89 ♘e4 ♘g4 90 ♔d2 ♘e5 91 ♔e3 ♘c4+ 92 ♔d4 ♘a3 93 ♔d3 ♘b5 94 ♔d2 ♘d4 95 ♔d3 ♘e6 96 ♔e3 ♘c7 97 ♔d3 ♘d5 98 ♔c2 ♘e3+ 99 ♔c3 ♘f5 100 ♔d2 ♘g3

Having cantered round half the board, the black knight expels its opposite number from the key square – so the pawn can now advance to queen.

101 ♘f6 f2 102 ♘g4 f1=♘+

Sadly, given the threat of a fork on e3, Black can only promote to a knight.

103 ♔c3 ♔f3 104 ♘h2+ ♘xh2

Again it's impossible to make anything of the two extra knights (½-½). A record day? It evidently was!

A record that will not be beaten

Chess adjournments were a twentieth-century phenomenon. They were more or less introduced in that century, and were virtually consigned to history by the time it closed. With the appearance of chess computer programs playing at Grandmaster strength, adjourning a game no longer made sense. This meant there would be no more sleepless nights spent studying adjourned positions, but at the same time, unfortunately, the art of analysis – endgame analysis especially – went into decline. Professor Mikhail Botvinnik, himself one of the first to set about creating an 'electronic Grand-master', spoke many times about the pernicious consequences of the new time control which leaves no place for adjournment; but the progress of artificial intelligence has given chessplayers no other choice.

And yet one glaring injustice has also been eliminated. For all the preparatory work that he might have done with his coaches, a player at the chessboard was nonetheless fighting on his own. Resuming after adjournment, however, he might have a full 'conclave' behind him. And much depended on *who* had been assisting him in his adjournment analysis. That same Mikhail Botvinnik 'confessed' in print that the entire Soviet squad – a tremendous powerhouse – had helped him to save his difficult adjourned position against Bobby Fischer in the 1962 Olympiad in Bulgaria. The all-night vigil of the titans paid off. Naturally the American Grandmaster couldn't count on helpers of such calibre.

Today, even a mention of envelopes with sealed moves (secret or disclosed) has disappeared from the FIDE rules. Hence the record number of adjournments in one contest can no longer be either equalled or surpassed.

That record belongs, perhaps, to the Soviet-American Grandmaster Anatoly Lein. In 1967, in the traditional Chigorin Memorial at Sochi, he adjourned eight (!) games out of his first ten, and another three of the remaining five. Some of his adjourned games were resumed two or three times; his duel with Grandmaster Vladimir Simagin ended in a draw on the 93rd move. This developed into a nightmare for the arbiters and of course for Lein himself, who played below par as a result being so cruelly overtaxed.

"I'm gutted. This is my worst disaster in five years," said Anatoly after the final round. He had scored 7 points and shared 8th-10th places. But what else can you expect when you've been spending your nights in analysis before regularly 'serving your time' in the extra two-hour adjournment session in the morning, and then playing the next fve-hour round in the evening?

Something similar but even more uncanny happened to one of the prizewinners in the 1980/81 USSR Championship at Vilnius. Eleven of Grandmaster Artur Yusupov's games lasted to the adjournment. In an 18-player contest this is by no means a record, but after the penultimate round he still had five of them to play off! And the point was that if the results went his way, the young Muscovite would be national champion!

At that time the regulations for major tournaments stipulated that one day had to be set aside for adjournments before the last round. On that day, as ill luck would have it, only one of the contestants queueing up to play Artur could be crossed off the list. This was Smbat Lputian, later to be the leader of Armenian chess but at that time barely above junior age and an outsider. Once Lputian had earned his half point, Yusupov spent all the rest of the adjournment session in a

battle with Alexander Beliavsky which dragged on to the 91st move, only to be adjourned *again*!

The controllers could only pray to the Almighty and thank him for one thing: before the final round, according to the tournament rules, there was also to be one more rest day. Of course they promptly transformed it into an adjournment day, and after attending a morning reception with the mayor of Vilnius, the four contestants in question went to the 'reception' laid on by Yusupov. Against Grandmaster Vasiukov, Artur had a noticeably better position, but with the board still full of fighting units (nothing had been exchanged except a pawn and a minor piece on each side) he realized that the only solution was to agree a draw. He then defeated Grandmaster Kupreichik, saved a somewhat inferior rook endgame against Grandmaster Tseshkovsky and ... continued the duel broken off the previous day.

Beliavsky – Yusupov

Alas, all efforts to exploit the extra pawn came to nothing. Peace was signed after White's 113th move and 14 hours 7 minutes of confrontation.

The upshot was that Yusupov moved half a point ahead of four pursuers all at once. Utterly exhausted, however, he lost his game with White in the final round without a murmur, and only received a bronze medal.

What adjourned game had the most resumptions? Theoretically this means the longest game in which the players sat down to face each other the greatest number of times. The most notable game under this heading was the one between Grandmaster Efim Geller and the Yugoslav master Jovan Sofrevski in the traditional and very strong 'Tournament of Solidarity', Skopje 1968.

It was begun in the 10th round and adjourned daily, finishing only after round sixteen! In the seventh (!) adjournment session, after 154 moves and nearly 20 hours of struggle, the players agreed a draw. The older player, Geller (who was in the running for first place and playing for a win in every game) had had the better chances in a rook ending but couldn't convert them into a win.

A game by correspondence was once adjourned, or interrupted, for a reason that was completely unusual and therefore constituted a record (if the expression can be used in this context). The players were an inhabitant of the little English town of Burntwood named John Walker (any connection with the well-known whisky brand is coincidental) and Claude Bloodgood from the American state of Virginia. The game came to a halt because ... the American escaped from Powhattan jail, where as prisoner number 99432 he was serving a life sentence.

After he was captured and put back behind bars, the game was resumed. Around fifty postal exchanges followed. Then finally, the English chess enthusiast with paralysed legs received permission from the then American President, Bill Clinton, to visit the prison and play the odd few games over-the-board against his old friend.

When two do the same...

The above words are by the famous author of the famous books *Thirteen Children of Caissa* and *The Chess Muse's Good and Naughty Children* – The Austrian Professor Josef Krejcik. His wise and well-known saying continues: "it doesn't lead to the same thing." Applied to chess, this comes across with particular force when one opponent, playing Black, copies White's moves (or more succinctly 'apes' him), usually out of huge naivety.

At one time our chess predecessors were very much preoccupied by this scenario. The great composer Sam Loyd turned his attention to it, as did the inventor of the Traxler Attack (or Wilkes-Barre Variation) in the Two Knights Defence. Krejcik himself devised some possible symmetrical games in various openings. In the Queen's Gambit, for instance, this was how he 'punished' Black for aping his opponent:

1 d4 d5 2 ♘f3 ♘f6 3 c4 c5 4 ♗g5 ♗g4 5 e3 e6 6 ♘c3 ♘c6 7 ♗e2 ♗e7 8 0-0 0-0 9 ♗xf6 ♗xf3 10 ♗xg7 ♗xg2 11 ♗xf8 ♗xf1 12 ♗xe7 ♗xe2 13 ♗xd8 ♗xd1 14 cxd5 cxd4 15 dxc6 dxc3

**16 cxb7 cxb2 17 bxa8=♕ bxa1=♕
18 ♗f6 mate!**

Plenty of beginners' games have opened 1 e4 e5 2 ♘f3 ♘f6 3 ♘xe5 ♘xe4? 4 ♕e2, and strictly speaking Black can resign, since in the worst case he loses his queen (4...♘f6 5 ♘c6+), while in the best possible case he is left a pawn down in a bad position (4...♕e7 5 ♕xe4 d6 5 d4 etc.).

However, the Krejcik game and some others in his book are artificial constructs. Among games that actually occurred, the following case of prolonged symmetry remained unequalled for a long time:

**Georg Rotlewi –
Mikhail Eliashov**
St Petersburg 1909
Four Knights Game [C49]

**1 e4 e5 2 ♘f3 ♘f6 3 ♘c3 ♘c6
4 ♗b5 ♗b4 5 0-0 0-0 6 d3 d6
7 ♗xc6(!?) ♗xc3(!?) 8 ♗xb7
♗xb2 9 ♗xa8 ♗xa1 10 ♗g5 ♗g4
11 ♕xa1(!?) ♕xa8 12 ♗xf6 ♗xf3
13 ♗xg7 ♗xg2 14 ♗xf8 ♗xf1
15 ♕xf1 ♕xf8 16 ♕g2+ ♕g7 ½-½**
In this game too, however, the opponents were probably not playing seriously but amusing themseves and their most honourable spectators. It was the last round of the amateur tournament in the international Chigorin Memorial congress, and this draw assured Rotlewi of second place behind Alekhine, while Eliashov at best would take undivided fourth place instead of sharing 4th-6th. The playing strength of both Rotlewi (who was fated to

die young) and his opponent was not normally to be laughed at, and in a serious encounter White would hardly have missed the intermediate 13 ♗xe5! ♗xe4 (otherwise Black is left a pawn down) 14 ♗xg7 ♗xg2 15 ♗xf8, when Black has no time for the symmetrical 15...♗xf1 on account of mate.

The current record for symmetry belongs to the masters who played the following game in 1969 in Bulgaria.

Efim Stoliar – Janusz Szukszta
English Opening [A36]

**1 c4 g6 2 ♘c3 ♗g7 3 g3 c5
4 ♗g2 ♘c6**
In the book *Inexhaustible Chess* by Karpov and Gik, these moves appeared in a different order, as if the copying had begun from the first minute of the game. Why was that? As from now, the position *is* symmetrical and will remain so – except for one moment at the seventh move.

**5 a3 a6 6 ♖b1 ♖b8 7 b4 cxb4
8 axb4 b5 9 cxb5 axb5 10 ♘h3
♘h6 11 0-0 0-0 12 d4 d5 13 ♗xh6
♗xh3 14 ♗xg7 ♗xg2 15 ♗xf8
♗xf1 16 ♗xe7 ♗xe2 17 ♗xd8
♗xd1 18 ♗c7 ♗c2 19 ♖b2 ♖b7**

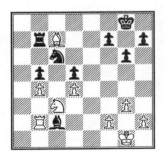

The unintentional record is established.

20 ♗e5

Now Black can't continue with 20...♗e4, since after 21 ♘xe4 ♘xe5 White has the intermediate 22 ♘f6+ and then 23 dxe5.

Therefore:

20...♘xe5 21 dxe5 d4 22 ♖xc2 ♖c7 23 ♔f1 g5 24 ♔e2 dxc3 25 ♔d3 ♖c4 26 ♖xc3 ♖xb4 27 ♖c7

Since the balance has been maintained, a draw was agreed at this point (½-½).

Part Two: People

Chess life histories

The experience of nearly two hundred years has given us a picture of the typical life-story of the kind of chessplayer who is noticed, singled out, revered. Fame at a fairly early stage is followed by quite a swift rise to the top and then a slow decline along a very gentle slope, lasting for 30, 40 or 50 years. Such is the standard pattern for the most brilliant careers, but exceptions do of course occur, and those which can claim record status are the ones we are going to discuss.

Meteors

This is a word we quite often apply to many an outstanding player, without thinking much about its meaning. "Morphy flashed like a meteor in the chess firmament" – "Sultan Khan came and went like a meteor." Undoubtedly the chess chapter in these players' biographies might have been much longer than it was. And yet the great American's absolute superiority over his cowed contemporaries was displayed to the world for a full 8 years; and the enigmatic illiterate Indian kept defeating his most illustrious opponents for just that same amount of time. There *were*, however, some high-class masters whose fortunes truly resembled meteorites....

As the first of these we should name the stunningly handsome Rudolf Charousek – delicate features, sloping eyebrows, a dandy's moustache in the style of the urban (not the country) aristocracy. And his play was like that too: artistic, carefree, imaginative. After two or three years playing with Czech and Hungarian masters, he took part in four international tournaments. Only four – but this didn't stop Lasker from seeing him as one of the probable challengers in a match for the world chess crown, while Chigorin pronounced him "the most capable of all the young players". Nor was this unfounded; in his very first 'prominent' tournament Charousek inflicted defeat on the first prize winner, World Champion Emanuel Lasker. He also had occasion to beat Maroczy, Janowski and Chigorin – and how!

Charousek – Chigorin
Budapest 1896
King's Gambit [C33]

1 e4 e5 2 f4 exf4 3 ♗c4 ♘c6 4 d4 ♘f6 5 e5 d5 6 ♗b3 ♗g4 7 ♕d3 ♘h5 8 ♘h3 ♘b4 9 ♕c3 ♘a6 10 0-0 ♗e2 11 ♗a4+ c6 12 ♗xc6+ bxc6 13 ♕xc6+ ♔e7 14 ♘xf4

♘xf4 15 ♗xf4 h6 16 ♘c3 ♗c4

17 e6! ♖c8 18 ♗c7!! fxe6
19 ♗xd8+ ♖xd8 20 ♕b7+ ♖d7
21 ♖f7+ ♔xf7 22 ♕xd7+ ♗e7
23 ♖e1 ♖e8 24 b3 ♔f8 25 bxc4 1-0

This game has never before appeared in a Russian or Soviet publication.

Charousek's international chess life lasted a mere two years and one month. During that time, he finished 12th at Nuremberg 1896; shared first and second places at Budapest, 100 days later in the same year (losing the play-off match against Chigorin); won quite a strong tournament in Berlin in 1897; and shared 2nd-4th places (equal with Chigorin, behind Steinitz) at Cologne in 1898. However, his passion for the game was evidently so insatiable that simultaneously with his international appearances he took part in an Austro-Hungarian correspondence tournament, sharing victory with Maroczy. He defeated the latter in a match-tournament of four Austro-Hungarian masters.

After 19 August 1898, Rudolf Charousek never again sat down to play in a chess contest; at that time there was no cure for tuberculosis of the lungs. Less than two years later, he was no more; he died at the age of 27 years 7 months.

Carlos Torre Repetto swept across the chess sky even faster, although afterwards he lived quite a long life – and was even awarded the Internationational Grandmaster title in his 73rd year, on the basis of his past achievements. His round of international events was compressed into rather less than six months of the year 1925, and the greater part of that time was spent at home in Mexico. Two years earlier he had set out from his native town of Merida to visit the USA, where he promptly won a double-round tournament against seven American opponents. This time – he came first in the Eastern States Championship in New York, then made the leisurely Atlantic crossing as a second-class passenger on a liner. He took with him an opening variation he had worked out, which was later to be named after him: 1 d4 ♘f6 2 ♘f3 e6 3 ♗g5. He was also accompanied by the more than flattering judgement of the wise Lasker: "Torre's first steps are the very kind which future World Champions take."

The first tournament of his trip, in Baden-Baden, saw Carlos finish in tenth place. Exactly a week later he went into battle at Marienbad (present-day Marianske Lazne) and eventually shared third and fourth places with Marshall, a point behind Nimzowitsch and Rubinstein but ahead of Réti, Tartakower, Spielmann, Grünfeld, Sämisch and others. Not a bad line-up, was it? But even old hands can make mistakes:

Grünfeld – Torre
Dutch Defence [A90]

1 d4 e6 2 ♘f3 f5 3 g3 ♘f6 4 ♗g2
d5 5 0-0 ♗d6 6 c4 c6 7 ♕c2 0-0
8 b3 ♘e4 9 ♗b2?!
Why doesn't White play the
move he has prepared, 10 ♗a3,
reducing Black's chances of a
kingside attack?
9...♘d7 10 ♘e5? (10 ♘c3 is
simply essential) 10...♕f6 11 f3
♘xe5 12 dxe5??
By far the lesser evil was 12 fxe4
♘g4 13 e5 ♕h6 14 h3 ♘e3 15 ♕d3
♘xf1 16 exd6 ♘e3 17 ♗c1 f4
18 gxf4 ♘f5 19 c5.
12...♗c5+ 13 ♔h1 ♘xg3+ 0-1
There was no other humiliation
like this in Ernst Grünfeld's
distinguished chess career!

Torre then returned to Mexico,
but in the autumn he set off again on
an even longer journey. Valerian
Eremeev, one of the organizers of
the first Moscow international
tournament, recollects the following:
"The youngest participant was
Carlos Torre, the envoy from far-off
Mexico. He completed his 21st year
while in Moscow.
"Everything about this young
man was unusual. Small in stature,
with large horn-rimmed spectacles
on his attractive face, Torre made a
most congenial impression. He was
extremely courteous, diffident and
shy. Possessing some special kind
of charm, Torre became the
Muscovites' favourite from the very
first days, and his games always had
a large audience.
"The way he came to Moscow
was also unusual. On the day when
Torre was due to arrive, there was a

hard frost in the city *[it was 9
November]*, and I therefore asked
N.V.Krylenko *[deputy People's
Justice Comissar]* for permission to
use his covered automobile. The
point is that 'Intourist' with its
comfortable vehicles did not yet
exist in 1925, nor were there any
taxis in Moscow, so the tournament
organizing committee had to use
specially hired cars which for some
reason were all open. As it turned
out, my precautions were not
superfluous. The onlookers were all
astounded when Carlos Torre
stepped out of the railway carriage
wearing only a suit, without an
overcoat or even anything on his
head. Greatly embarrassed, he
explained that in his homeland
Mexico it was very warm at that
time, and it hadn't at all occurred to
him that in Russia there would be
snow and so much cold.
"Quickly seating Torre in the car,
I took him to his hotel and from
there I telephoned to tell Krylenko
everything. He asked me to take
Torre straight to the best store and
buy him a fur-lined coat and a hat.
This I did. Torre was delighted.
"Mild-mannered in his life,
Carlos Torre transformed himself
into a fearsome opponent at the
chessboard. In the first round he had
the bye, but in the second he set off
on his triumphal march. From the
first ten games he scored 7½ points,
and his name began to be
mentioned among the likely
contenders for first prize. However,
in the remaining rounds the sheer
physical strain proved too much for
him, and he only scored another
4½. Finishing the tournament with
12 points out of a possible 20, he
shared 5th and 6th prizes with

Tartakower. For a young player this in itself was a success, especially as he had played a number of beautiful games. He had beaten Lasker brilliantly and drawn with Capablanca.

"I shall never forget how exuberantly Torre reacted to his win against Lasker. He seized his opponent's outstretched hand with both of his, and quickly said a few joyful words to him. The spectators launched into a full-scale ovation, and it took the controllers a long time to quieten the fans of the likeable Mexican."

The admirers of the young talent had something to rejoice about. The 'see-saw' device had never before been executed in such a high-level tournament, let alone against the ex-World Champion himself.

Torre – Lasker

It looks as if White's kingside attack has landed in a blind alley and his bishop is doomed, but Torre discovers some extra resources which allow him to emerge unscathed.

23 ♘c4! ♕d5
We will not dwell on Lasker's frame of mind at this moment. Against all the normal practice for competitive events, a telegram had just been brought to him in the tournament arena. It announced that a play written by him and his brother had been accepted for performance in a prestigious German theatre. It was noticeable that his thoughts were already in the *Berliner Theater* amongst the characters called into being by his imagination, wisdom and skill. But this is no excuse for Lasker the chessplayer. The capture 23...hxg5 24 ♘xd6 would have led to a roughly equal ending. However, the move actually played does not yet lose.

24 ♘e3 ♕b5?
But this *is* the end. After 24...♕xd4 25 ♗xh6 ♘g6, there would still be everything to play for.
25 ♗f6!!

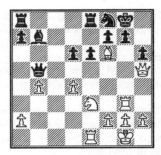

25...♕xh5 26 ♖xg7+ ♔h8 27 ♖xf7+ ♔g8 28 ♖g7+ ♔h8 29 ♖xb7+ ♔g8 30 ♖g7+ ♔h8 31 ♖g5+ ♔h7 32 ♖xh5 ♔g6 33 ♖h3 ♔xf6 34 ♖xh6+, and there was really no need for Black to prolong his resistance until the 43rd move **(1-0)**.

After this triumph came quite a strong American masters' tournament in Chicago the following year. (Marshall was first; Torre finished half a point behind, together with Maroczy who lived in the USA for a short time. In the same event the future Grandmaster Kashdan made a sucessful début on the national scene.) And that was all!

The solitary sequel was a two-game mini-match in 1934 between Torre and Fine, who was acquiring formidable strength as a player. You may recall the words which a writer once put into the mouth of a Carlos: "We may fall ill, die or take leave of our senses." The first part of this utterance affected Torre when he was 22 years old.

Half a century later the chess world remembered him by granting him the International Grandmaster title. In this connection, unfortunately, Carlos set up another forlorn record or anti-record: his life in the family of Grandmasters lasted only 136 days.

There was one other chessplayer, a female one, who made herself the subject of talk for a brief moment before vanishing forever from the sight of all lovers of the Noble Game. To introduce the topic, here is an extract from a book by Vladas Mikenas, International Master and Arbiter, who had defeated Alekhine and Botvinnik, Bogoljubow and Keres, Bronstein, Flohr (at the height of his powers), and many other celebrities.

"I often recall my game with Sultan Khan during the 'Tournament of Nations' at Folkestone in 1933. The young 27-year-old Indian with a white turban on his head came to the board accompanied by an extremely beautiful young woman. They sat down at the table side by side. She looked at me, smiled, and lowered the little Latvian flag, by which I understood her to mean that I was sure to lose. I ticked her off with my finger. At that moment Alekhine came up. He whispered something to Sultan Khan, and they both smiled.

"Play began. With his arms crossed in front of his chest and his intensive gaze fixed on the board, Sultan Khan sat motionless. The beautiful woman wrote down the moves. I confess I couldn't play calmly – she had enchanted me. And yet just like Sultan Khan, she was only looking with lowered eyes at the chessboard."

Who was this companion of the enigmatic Indian, that 'natural talent' whose total ignorance of theory (he was illiterate!) had not prevented him from beating Capablanca, Flohr and Bogoljubow? She was called Fatima, and it was under that name, without a surname, that she twice participated in the British Ladies' Championship. In 1932 she had little success, finishing down in 12th place. Next year she did excellently and became Champion. And yet at the same time as playing, she was writing down the games of her teacher. Admittedly this word sounds strange when applied to a man who a mere three years earlier had switched from the slow-moving Indian chess (a close relative of *shatranj*) to the modern European game, mastering it by the sheer strength of his talent. Presumably he was Fatima's lover as well; at any rate Fatima soon left England together with Sultan Khan, and disappeared forever – more or less like him – from the world of chess.

In justice it must be said that when Fatima took part — victoriously! — in the championships of the island, it was in the absence of Vera Menchik who had no equals in the world. Moreover Fatima's play was not first-rate by present-day standards, though it was adequate to win — particularly since her opponents played much worse!

Fatima – Wheelwright
Hastings 1933

1 d4 ♘f6 2 c4 g6 3 ♘f3 ♗g7 4 ♗f4 d6 5 e3 0-0 6 h3 ♘h5 7 ♗h2 f5 8 ♗d3 ♘c6 9 ♘c3 ♘f6 10 a3 e6 11 ♖c1 ♕e7 12 0-0 e5 13 dxe5 dxe5 (13...♘xe5!?) 14 ♗e2 ♔h8 (14...e4!?) 15 ♘d5 ♘xd5 16 cxd5 ♘d8 17 b4 ♕d6 18 ♕b3!? ♗d7? (18...c6!?) 19 ♕c3 f4 20 ♕xc7 ♕xd5? 21 ♖fd1 ♕a2 22 ♖xd7 ♕xe2 23 ♖xg7 ♘e6 24 ♖xh7+ ♔g8 25 ♕xe5!? (simplest) 25...♔xh7 26 ♕xe6 ♕b2 27 ♖c7+ ♔h8 28 ♗xf4 ♖xf4 29 exf4 ♕a1+ 30 ♔h2 1-0

Ascending the heights

History knows of quite a few cases where a completely unknown or at best little-known chessplayer has risen with dramatic speed to become a star of the first magnitude. Every time, this ascent has been the object of general astonishment, gossip, reverence, and also – it must be said – envy on the part of those who could only dream of doing likewise.

Which of these favourites of Caissa was the most successful of all? Here once again we have a fairly rhetorical question. 'You pays your money and you takes your choice....'

However, if the phenomenon of scaling the heights is considered from the point of view of a player's age, the matter is more or less clear. Within the space of three or four years, a fifth-category player who had received knight odds in skittles games rose to be the strongest player in Russia – by no means the least of the chess powers – and moreover he was getting on for thirty at the time. This was Mikhail Chigorin. No one joined the family of the world's leading chessplayers as late as he did.

The *youngest* player to break into the élite at one jump was the future eleventh World Champion, Bobby Fischer. In 1957, at the age of fourteen, he won three (!) US Championships: the Junior Championship, the overall Championship for adults, and the US Open.

On the subject of rapid ascent, we are used to speaking of Mikhail Tal's rise to the top as though it were unparalleled. In 1957 he was still only a master; by 1960, he was Chess King. However ... in 1955, at the age of nineteen, he had already won a USSR Championship Semi-Final, a tournament unsurpassed in strength by most international contests. After that, he had shared 5th-7th places in the Championship itself, beating a number of Grandmasters and scoring several beautiful wins. Then before reaching the chess throne, he won gold medals – back-to-back! – in the next two national Championships, as well as registering the best overall score in the Munich Olympiad and winning a major tournament in Zurich. David Bronstein too had similar successes to his credit as a master, before winning the first-ever Interzonal Tournament at Saltsjöbaden in 1948. These case histories, then, were rather like an aeroplane, picking up speed along the runway before taking off and steeply ascending.

But who were the players who rose in the chess world like a rocket? In chronological order, the first we should name is Harry Nelson Pillsbury (we have mentioned his great contemporary Morphy already). True, Pillsbury was well known as a player in the USA. He appeared regularly in the newspapers, and had won the Manhattan Chess Cub championship. Yet it never entered anyone's head that in his very first international tournament, Hastings 1895 – where virtually all the world's top masters were assembled – the winner would be none other than Pillsbury! Among those he left behind him were the World Champion and ex-Champion Lasker and Steinitz, as well as giants such as Chigorin and Tarrasch. The latter wrote in the magazine *Frankfurter Schachblatt:* "His success is all the more amazing since he was taking part in a major tournament for the first time. Pillsbury is a brilliant player and his games are full of profound ideas; he regards Steinitz as his teacher. Undoubtedly he will always occupy if not the first then certainly a distinguished place among the great masters of our wonderful game."

Alas, the venerable Siegbert spoke prophetically. "If not the

first", he said. Well, Pillsbury was to play in 12 more tournaments but never again (!) won first prize. (He shared first and second places at Vienna 1898 and again at Munich 1900, but lost both play-off matches – the first against Tarrasch, the second against Schlechter.)

But then Tarrasch was also right in the second part of his assessment. He had personally experienced the power of his 23-year-old opponent who had been all of sixteen when he first discovered how a knight moves.

Pillsbury – Tarrasch
Hastings 1895

Each player is attacking on his own wing....

38 ♘g4 ♗xb3 39 ♖g2 ♔h8
40 gxf6 gxf6 41 ♘xb3 ♖xb3
42 ♘h6 ♖g7 43 ♖xg7 ♔xg7
44 ♕g3+! ♔xh6 45 ♔h1!! ♕d5
46 ♖g1 ♕xf5 47 ♕h4+ ♕h5
48 ♕f4+ ♕g5 49 ♖xg5 fxg5
50 ♕d6+ ♔h5 51 ♕xd7

Threatening a check on f7 followed by capturing the rook – alternatively mate on h7. After the 'positional' 51...♖b1+ 52 ♔g2 ♖b2+ 53 ♔g3 ♔h6 54 ♕e6+ ♔g7 55 ♕xe4 c2 56 ♕b7+ ♔g6 57 ♕c6+ ♔h5 58 d5, White would eventually win. Instead Tarrasch tries his luck with:

51...c2

Perhaps Pillsbury will play 52 ♕f7+ after all...?

52 ♕xh7 mate

It was with less *éclat* but almost equally good results that Osip Bernstein arrived on the chess scene. He was a Russian subject – but on account of his origins, the laws of the Empire virtually excluded him from obtaining higher education in his homeland; hence at 19 he went to study at the Unversity of Berlin. In the space of a year he transformed himself from an artless chess amateur who had never played a single serious game, into one of the best players in the chess club of the German capital. In 1902, aged 22 years, the young man was admitted to the main secondary tournament at the annual congress of the German Chess Federation, held in Hanover. He not only finished second in his event but drew a match with Wolf, one of the prizewinners in the master tournament. For this Bernstein received the master title and was invited to the third All-Russian Tournament, held in his native Kiev in 1903. It was there that he and some other newcomers – the future Grandmaster Akiba Rubinstein and the future Russian Champion Georg Salwe – gave Chigorin, the undisputed leader of Russian chess, a real run for his money. Chigorin still succeeded in winning the contest, but it was not like his previous strolls to victory. Though he finished a point ahead of Bernstein, he lost their individual encounter in truly comical fashion.

Bernstein – Chigorin
King's Gambit [C30]

1 e4 e5 2 f4 ♘f6 3 fxe5 ♘xe4 4 ♘f3 ♘g5 5 c3 ♘xf3+ 6 ♕xf3 ♕g5 7 ♗e2! ♕xe5 8 0-0 ♕e7 9 d4 c6 10 ♕g3 d5 11 ♗g5, and Black resigned as he is bound to lose material (**1-0**).

Naturally, the rise of the player destined to be World Champion number three was on course for the summit from the outset. "A sensational event occurred in America. A player in his 21st year and unknown to the chess world, José Raoul Capablanca, challenged the famous Marshall to a match and crushed him brilliantly with the score of +8 -1 =14 (just as Tarrasch and Lasker had defeated him a few years before). There was lively discussion of this event in the chess periodicals. Some had no hesitation in acknowledging Capablanca as a rising star. Others took rather a sceptical view of his victory, as they knew how uneven Marshall's play could be. They all, however, expressed the wish to see Capablanca play in a great European tournament." That was how N.Grekov, in his *History of Chess Contests*, described the first stage of Capablanca's ascent.

Two years later Capablanca was able to come to Europe for the famous tournament at San Sebastian in 1911. It was intended for players who had won several prizes in international competitions during the foregoing decade, but an exception was made for Capa. Only the World Champion Lasker was absent; all the other leading lights were outperformed by the 'new boy', who in addition received the brilliancy prize for his game against Bernstein; the latter, incidentally, had objected to Capablanca's participation in the tournament.

Capablanca – Bernstein

By sacrificing two pawns White has deflected the black queen from the defence of the kingside. He now breaks the enemy position open.

28 ♘fxg7! ♘c5?

Tantamount to capitulation. He should have given White some complicated tactical problems to solve in the variation 28...♖d8!? (as Capablanca indicated, 28...♘xg7 would lose to 29 ♘f6+ ♔g6 30 ♘xd7, threatening 31 f5!+ ♔h7 32 ♘f6 mate; Black can defend with 30...f6!, but then White has 31 e5 ♔f7 32 ♘xf6 ♖e7 33 ♘e4) 29 f5 ♘f8 30 e5!, and now:

(a) 30...♕xe5 31 ♕d2! ♕b5 32 ♕b2 ♖g8 33 ♘f6+ ♔xg7 34 ♘xd7+ ♔h7 35 ♘f6+ ♔h8 36 ♖e7.

(b) 30...♖g8 31 e6 fxe6 32 fxe6 ♘xe6 33 ♕e4+! ♔h8 34 ♘xe6 ♕xh5 35 ♖g2.

29 ♘xe8 ♗xe8 30 ♕c3 f6 31 ♘xf6+ ♔g6 32 ♘h5 ♖g8 33 f5+ ♔g5 34 ♕e3+ ♔h4 35 ♕g3+ ♔g5 34 h4 mate

No ordinary finish!

In the same category as these figures of world renown, strange though it may seem, there is a chessplayer of decidedly minor stature who is almost entirely forgotten. Or perhaps not; in 1985, on someone's proposal, FIDE suddenly remembered the 83-year-old Mario Monticelli and awarded him the Grandmaster title – on the strength of his one and only success, in Budapest, way back in 1926. But what a success it was! A mere national master from a rather minor chessplaying country, Monticelli was making his début on the international scene only because of a decision taken by the young International Chess Federation at its third congress. Organizing both individual and team competitions, FIDE pursued a policy of equal distribution, issuing invitations not only to distinguished Grandmasters but also to 'non-professional chessplayers'.

Thus it was that Monticelli found himself together with four other 'dark horses' in a master tournament featuring Rubinstein, Grünfeld, Réti, Tartakower, Colle.... Of these, only Grünfeld kept pace with the newcomer. True, Monticelli lost three games, rather a lot for a first prize winner, but he also scored the greatest number of victories.

This result was highly promising for the young Italian. Sure enough, organizers began inviting him to top-class tournaments. The results, however, were as follows:

Budapest 1929: 11th place out of 14 participants.

San Remo 1930: 14th out of 16.

Syracuse (USA) 1934: 8th out of 15.

Admittedly Monticelli shared 4th-5th places at Barcelona 1929 and even 1st-2nd at Milan 1938, a tournament of wholly average composition. There were three victories in Italian championships; but Monticelli's 'rocket' never reached the zenith.

It was something completely different that halted the rise of two players still very young by the standards of their time, whose indisputable talent promised much – perhaps even the maximum attainable in chess. We will come to them next.

Ascent cut short

Four-year-old children live in a world of their own. They make up new words, follow the doings of adults, and judge them by their own standards. All this was true of Klaus Junge too. But he could also read and write; and there was also the two-week-long voyage across the endless ocean which changed with every hour, all the way from Chile where he was born, to Germany; and he was also constantly watching his father, the champion of the country, in play. At the age of 12 he himself was to play his first game with clocks at the Hamburg chess club, unaware that by the end of the 20th century people would be calling him Germany's greatest chess talent after Lasker. And I need hardly remind you of the names of players who were German: Tarrasch and Sämisch, Bogoljubow (by nationality), Schlechter, Spielmann, Mieses, Teichmann, Unzicker (the same age as Junge)....

Junge – Proti
Germany 1937

White very confidently increases his positional plus.

18 Rad1 c6 19 Ne1 Wd7 20 Nc2 Rfd8

A typical move with 'the wrong rook'. He shouldn't have left the point f7 undefended.

21 Ne3 Nf8 22 f4 Nfg6

Black is waiting – but for what?

23 f5 exf5 24 Nxf5 Nxf5 25 Rxf5 Ne7

On 25...Rf8, White would break through in the centre.

26 Rxf7! Kxf7 27 e6+! Wxe6 28 Rf1+ Wf6 29 Rxf6+ and Black was mated on the 42nd move **(1-0)**.

Nothing remarkable, you may say? Yes and no. For one thing, White's play makes such an impression of lucid purity. And for another thing, don't forget that he had no teachers, clubs or opportunities to work together with older players. All these things came only after the above game, indeed not until after the fifteen-year-old Junge had already made his breakthrough and obtained the right to play in a master tournament. In the course of 1941 he came first in four events, either on his own or sharing the top two places with, for instance, the renowned Sämisch.

At the end of the year, after winning the German Championship, he made his entry into the highest chess society of the Third Reich. This occurred at a tournament in Krakow, where almost all the strongest players from the countries conquered by Hitler were taking part. Some of them sympathized with the ideas of Nazism, others were decidedly opposed, some were secretly aiding the resistance. The youthful Junge had no heart for either the war or the 'national' dream of world domination; for this we have the testimony of International Master Karel Opočensky, who harboured Julius Fučik – a hero of the Czech anti-Fascist movement – in his own home.

What could be more memorable than your first game with World Champion Alekhine? One thing, perhaps – your first *win* against him, against Alekhine the legendary and mighty....

Alekhine – Junge
Salzburg 1942

24...b5!
This queenside counter-stroke allows Black to seize the initiative.
25 cxb5 ♗d5! 26 ♖xd5

On 26 ♕a3, the continuation could be 26...♘c4 27 ♖ac1! ♕xg3 28 ♗xc4 ♕e5 29 ♗d4 ♕g5 30 ♗xf6 ♘xf6 31 ♗xd5 ♘xd5 32 ♕b3 ♘e3 and wins.
26...exd5 27 ♖c1
After 27 b6 ♕b7, Black can answer 28 ♖c1 with 28...d4 29 ♖c7 ♕b8, or 28 ♖d1 with 28...♘c4 29 ♗xc4 dxc4 30 ♕c2 ♕c6.
27...♘c4! 28 ♗xc4 dxc4 29 ♖xc4 ♕e5
This move creates several threats: 30...♕a1+, 30...♖xa4 or 30...♕xb5.
30 ♘c5 ♘b6 31 ♖c1 ♘d5 32 ♘ge4 ♘xe3 33 ♕xe3 ♖a1!
The young German player's technique is up to the task of realizing his advantage!
34 ♖f1 ♖d8!
The threat is 35...♖xf1+ 36 ♔xf1 ♕a1+ 37 ♔e2 ♕d1+ 38 ♔f2 ♗d4 and wins.
35 ♘xf6+ ♕xf6 36 b6 ♖xf1+ 37 ♔xf1 ♕xb6 38 ♕e4 ♕b5+ 39 ♔f2 ♖e8 40 ♕d4 ♕b6!
Again a highly competent decision from the technical viewpoint. The threat of Black's next move forces an exchange of queens.
41 ♘b3 ♖b8 42 ♕xb6 ♖xb6 43 g4 ♖xb4, and Black converted his material advantage into a win on the 69th move (**0-1**).

In between these tournaments and afterwards – all through 1942 – Junge hardly stood up from the chess table. It was as if he foresaw his own fate and couldn't play enough. Seventy games in a year was a lot for those times. And what games! Incidentally, in the opening of the following one (and some others too), the 18-year-old German master played that very variation of the Queen's Gambit which was later to be named after Botvinnik. At the end of the century there was even a fairly lengthy argument as to who was the author of this system and whose name it ought to carry.

Lehmann – Junge
Rostock 1942
Slav Defence [D44]

1 d4 d5 2 c4 e6 3 ♘c3 c6 4 ♘f3 ♘f6 5 ♗g5 dxc4 6 e4 b5 7 e5 h6 8 ♗h4 g5 9 ♘xg5 hxg5 10 ♗xg5 ♘bd7 11 ♕f3 ♗b7 12 ♗e2 ♖g8 13 h4 ♕b6

Not 13...♖xg5? 14 hxg5 ♘d5 15 ♖h7 ♕e7 16 g6!.

14 exf6 c5 15 d5 b4 16 ♗xc4! bxc3 17 dxe6!!

White's queen can't be taken, as a new one would appear on g8, eliminating the black rook in the process.

17...cxb2 18 ♖b1 ♖xg5

18...♕xe6+ is adequately met by 19 ♗xe6 ♗xf3 20 ♗xd7+ ♔xd7 21 gxf3.

19 exd7+ ♔d8

Of course not 19...♔xd7? on account of 20 ♕d3+ followed by 21 hxg5.

20 ♕c3 ♖xg2 21 ♖xb2 ♕c7!

It's essential to guard the a5-d8 diagonal. Instead 21...♕c6 would be answered by 22 ♕a5+ ♕c7 (or 22...♔xd7 23 ♗b5) 23 ♕xc7+ ♔xc7 24 ♖xb7+ ♔xb7 25 ♗d5+, winning.

22 ♖h3?

Of course 22 ♖e2! was stronger and would have set Black some problems.

22...♖g1+ 23 ♔e2

23...♗g2!!

Black's concluding attack begins with this difficult move. The following events unfold by force.

24 ♖g3

On 24 ♖e3, Black wins with 24...♗f1+ 25 ♔d2 ♗h6.

24...♗f1+ 25 ♔d1 ♕d6+ 26 ♖d2

On 26 ♔c2, the continuation would be 26...♖xg3 27 fxg3 ♗xc4 28 ♕xc4 ♗h6.

26...♕xg3!! 27 fxg3 ♗d3 mate

Junge's results from this string of tournaments (I repeat he was 18 years old!) made an impact. Judge for yourself:

Krakow 1941: fourth behind Alekhine, Sämisch and Bogoljubow.

Dresden 1942: first.

Rostock 1942: second place, after only accidentally missing victory.

Salzburg 1942: in this championship of 'New Europe' the ex-World Champion Max Euwe declined to take part, and his place was given to Junge – the sole mere master among eleven 'greats'. In the end he shared 3rd and 4th places with Sämisch, behind Alekhine and Keres. Bogoljubow and all the rest were left behind.

Munich 1942: in Junge's estimation, a collapse. He was 8th

70

out of 12 contestants. In the *Frankfurter Zeitung* Alekhine wrote:

"Junge's fortunes in Munich, so different from Salzburg, were decided almost without any play. In the very first round he lost a game he could easily have drawn, against Roháček; then a couple of days later he messed up another clearly drawn position and was forced to resign against Napolitano. In a contest of relatively short duration, such blunders are irreparable, and this time Junge didn't manage to break into the ranks of the prizewinners. His talent showed in his fine games with Foltys *[featuring active defence]* and Rellstab *[in the latter game, the strategic and tactical factors combined in a way that recalled Junge's win over Alekhine at Salzburg]*. However, his lack of international practice prevented him from playing up to his strength." Ah yes, these things happen....

Warsaw 1942: surpassed only by Alekhine, Junge finished ahead of both Bogoljubow and Sämisch among others.

Dresden 1942: second place.

Prague 1942: on the eve of the tournament, Alekhine gave an interview in which he considered his chief rival to be "Klaus Junge – it goes without saying. This young man is extraordinarily talented and is also helped by his good fortune and his uncommon endgame technique. He shows precise thought and a mathematical cast of mind, notwithstanding the handicap of youth."

There is no reason to dispute Alekhine's judgements as far as they relate purely to chess, but 'good fortune' is another question.

One day a young general was recommended to Napoleon – no ordinary warlord – for top-level service. They said he was both a strategist and a brave man. To which the emperor retorted, "That's all very well, but is he lucky?" In both war and chess, to have 'jam' (as players themselves put it) never comes amiss. Suvorov too, who defeated Napoleon's best pupils in the Alpine campaign, spoke very precisely on the subject of luck.

It was past the 20th of December when the Prague tournament ended – in a victory shared between Alekhine and Junge.

After Prague, there were only some games in three master tournaments by correspondence. Drafted into the army on 1 January 1943, Junge departed from big-time chess. More precisely, he was dragged away from it by force. His thinking continued to be original. In hospital he wrote an article on 'Chess by Correspondence and over the Board', which I believe to be the first attempt in world chess literature to investigate and compare these two forms of the game.

It so happened that although resident in Hamburg, he had hardly ever had occasion to play chess in north-west Germany. And yet it was there that Klaus Junge, Lieutenant of the *Wehrmacht*, was killed by a shell from the western allies. In his map case there was an analysis of an interesting endgame. There was no great battle in the Lüneberg area; the war was simply going on. And there were only 21 days left before it ended....

A year and a half before, with the Second World War still raging,

Mark Stolberg, a private in the Red Army who was just as incredibly thin as Klaus, was felled by a German bullet. He was even younger than Junge – being only in his twenty-first year – but he had spent just as much time in the arena of top-class chess: around a year and a half. Or perhaps a little longer, if you count the All-Union tournament of candidates for the master title in 1939. There the seventeen-year-old from Rostov, the youngest participant, conducted his games with such inexhaustible imagination, resourcefulness and obvious combinative talent that David Bronstein, that most independent-minded proclaimer of chess paradoxes, could later assert: "Our generation had its own Tal." He was referring to Stolberg.

The writer Isaac Yudovich had this to say about him:

"In June 1941 the USSR Championship semi-final was in progress in Rostov. The soldier Stolberg was among those taking part. At that time I was the Rostov correspondent for *64*, and well I remember that there were always people crowding round his table. Nor was this was just because they were supporting a player from their own city. Mark played with passion, and frequently amazed them with his breathtaking combinations.

"In one game he ended up in a difficult position. The commentators all considered Mark to be lost. On the following day the game was resumed after adjournment. Everyone thought Stolberg would resign it without a fight. Yet he imperturbably turned up at the board, and after one move which at first sight looked unremarkable,

he suddenly sacrificed a rook, and then his queen too. His opponent thought for a long time with dark forebodings. Declining the sacrifice would be even worse than accepting it. In the end Stolberg gave up a knight into the bargain. Now the enemy king was trapped, and faced with unavoidable mate his opponent resigned. Loud applause broke out in the playing hall, while Stolberg, both elated and embarrassed, remained at his table and blushed at this unaccustomed homage."

Alas, this mind-bending adjournment session took place on June the twentieth. Within little more than twenty-four hours, the nation of 193 millions saw the start of the Great Fatherland War. After one more day, play ceased in all four of the semi-final groups for the 13th USSR Championship; the 14-player tournaments had barely passed the half-way stage. The game scores, with rare exceptions, have been lost; it will evidently not be possible to reconstruct Stolberg's unique finish. He himself had been playing in Red Army uniform (he was called up for military service straight after leaving school, literally three weeks before war started), and now joined his combat unit. He fought as an ungainly, wholly unmilitary soldier near Rostov and perished in 1943 near Novorossiysk.

Another ascent cut short, another great loss for chess. This is clear from his games; they are practically unknown to either amateurs or professionals, and yet anyone who has absorbed the the culture of our ancient game, and has the merest inkling of the state of chess in the USSR at that time, can justly evaluate Stolberg's performance in the last pre-war national championship. Only two players of the generation born in the early 1920s – the 19-year old Smyslov and the 18-year-old Stolberg – had gained admittance to a field which was strengthened by representatives from Estonia, Latvia and Lithuania: Grandmaster Paul Keres, Vladimirs Petrovs and the master Vladas Mikenas. In this tremendous contest, the clear favourite Botvinnik suffered four defeats (!), and 18th-19th places (out of 20) were occupied by Grandmasters Kotov and Levenfish (numbers 3 and 2 respectively in the Soviet Grandmaster list). In all, six holders of the highest chess title were participating. Given his youth, Stolberg couldn't play a leading role, but he didn't at all disgrace himself and kept his banner aloft (finishing 13th-16th). Against the titled players, he scored a couple of points although losing out overall.

Stolberg – Konstantinopolsky
USSR Championship, Moscow
1940

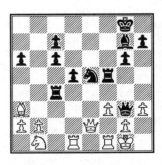

An extra pawn and a position that looks menacing – what more does Black need, to be completely happy? Perhaps more free squares for his queen and queen's rook?

23 ♘d2 ♖h4
Ah, Black is fired up for the attack. Of course, 23...♖a4 was safer.

24 ♖f2! h6
In attending to his own king Black loses a crucial tempo; his opponent's pieces now become astonishingly active.

25 ♗e7 ♖d4 26 ♗c5 ♖d3
(repeating moves would go very much against the grain) **27 ♗e3!**
Now the black queen is short of space.

27...d4 28 ♘e4 ♖xd1+ 29 ♕xd1 ♕h4 30 ♗xd4 ♕d8 31 ♕b3+ ♔h7 32 ♗c3
White's advantage is beyond doubt and he exploits it with precision.

32...♕d5 33 ♖d2 ♕xb3 34 axb3 ♖f7 35 ♘c5 a5 36 ♗xa5 g5 37 ♗c3 ♔g6 38 ♘e6 ♗f6 39 ♘d8 ♗xd8 40 ♖xd8 ♘d7 41 ♖e8 ♔h7 42 ♖e6 ♘b8 43 b4 ♖d7 44 ♔f2 ♖d6 45 ♖d7+ ♔g6 46 g4 h5 47 ♖g7+ ♔h6 48 ♖g8 ♘d7 49 ♖h8+ ♔g6 50 gxh5+ ♔f5 51 ♖h7 ♘e5 52 ♖e7 ♘d3+ 53 ♔e3 ♖h6 54 ♔xd3 ♖xh5 55 ♖f7+ ♔e6 56 ♖f6+ ♔d7 57 ♗d2 ♖xh3 58 ♗xg5 ♖g3 59 ♗d2 0-1

Black's last ten moves or so can be explained only by the highly experienced master's vexation, both at the reversal of fortunes in the game and at the sheer 'implacability' of the newcomer – this "master of a few days' standing".

Between obtaining the master title in 1939 (in the company of I.Boleslavsky and S.Zhukhovitsky) and playing in his only USSR Championship in 1940, Stolberg conducted a number of dashing attacks which looked easy on the surface, as well as some endgames of unusual intricacy for a player of his years.

Stolberg – Golovko
Rostov on Don 1940
Danish Gambit [C21]
(notes by Yuri Averbakh)

1 e4 e5 2 d4 exd4 3 c3 dxc3 4 ♗c4 cxb2 5 ♗xb2 d5
In the book *Sovremenny debyut* ('The Modern Opening'), published in 1940, this move is given a question mark.
6 exd5 ♘f6 7 ♘f3 ♗b4+ 8 ♘bd2 0-0 9 0-0 b5 10 ♗d3 ♕xd5

With his two extra pawns Black seems to have no fears for the future, but White's next move shows that the reality is different.
11 ♕b1! ♗b7 12 ♗xf6 ♗xd2 13 ♗xh7+ ♔h8 14 ♗b2 ♗f4 15 ♖d1 ♗xh2+
This attempt to solve his problems combinatively meets with an acute refutation. However, White also has a strong attack after 15...♕h5 16 ♗e4!.
16 ♔xh2 ♕h5+ 17 ♔g3 f5
Now on 18 ♖h1 Black intended 18...f4 mate, but...

18 ♗xf5! ♕xf5 19 ♕xf5 1-0
After 19...♖xf5 20 ♖d8+ ♔h7 21 ♖h1+ ♔g6 22 ♘h4+ the game is over.

Alexander Evenson, a young player from Kiev, was clearly not surpassed in talent by these chess meteorites (or stars?). After distinguishing himself in local events at the age of 16-18, he performed sensationally in the 1913 All-Russian amateur tournament, where he 'chivalrously' conceded just half a point to the opposition! Naturally he was awarded the master title and a place in the All-Russian Master Tournament which started only five days later. In that contest, where the right to enter the St Petersburg 'Tournament of Champions' in 1914 was at stake, the severely inexperienced Evenson fared less well, finishing only in 9th place (the winners were Alekhine and Nimzowitsch). Yet you can only marvel at how highly the future World Champions Alekhine and Capablanca rated his gifts.

After that famous St Petersburg tournament, incidentally, one of the first international lightning contests was held. Evenson was admitted to it and finished above both Lasker and Alekhine as well as other top Grandmasters; he was outdone by Capablanca alone. At the very start of the First World War he came first in a match-tournament comprising Kiev's four strongest players (one of them was none other than Efim Bogoljubow). At the height of the war Evenson put up a meritorious showing in some demonstration games with Alekhine. And that, sadly, was all! He accepted the 1917 revolution without reservation; a lawyer by training, he served on a military tribunal and was shot in 1919 by General Denikin's forces after their occupation of Kiev. Who knows how far he would have risen in chess if there were no wars or revolutions in this world....

One other figure, clearly less significant but wholly enigmatic, who went down in chess history – or rather, made a fleeting appearance there – was the Tahitian Omai. He had been taken from his native island in the 1770s by the legendary English sailor and discoverer Captain Cook. Ending up in France, he somehow or other found himself at a chessboard facing the Italian linguist Baretti, a friend of Philidor himself and quite a strong player for those times. The native talent of the illiterate islander overcame the man of learning who was well acquainted with the elements of Philidor's theory! Naturally, neither the game, nor any information on what became of Omai, has been preserved.

* * *

In present-day chess, a completely sudden rise and a dazzling début are becoming practically impossible. At the 1992 Manila Olympiad, for instance, the overall best result was achieved by the 17-year-old Vladimir Kramnik, a mere national master (!) at the time; but impressive as this was, it was preceded by victories in the European and World Junior Championships and a share of first place in the the adult Championship of the RSFSR. And when Kramnik scaled the chess Olympus in his victorious match with Garry Kasparov in London in the autumn of 2000, he had dozens of major tournaments and super-tournaments behind him. The same can also be said of Viswanathan Anand and of the older stars Kasparov and Anatoly Karpov. The time when a youthful chessplayer would gather strength and skill at home in his own kitchen (so to speak) has passed into history. Not only has the Internet become the Supreme Being; the chess life of the planet is now unified, so that the burgeoning of any talent is immediately visible to the whole world. It seems likely, then, that the heroes of this chapter are the *definitive* record holders in the domain of swift and unexpected ascent – unless perhaps the Lord sees fit to defy the new realities and intervene in his own way....

Postscript: These lines had been written for less than half a year when Ruslan Ponomariov, at one time the youngest Grandmaster on the planet, became World Champion at eighteen! True, this was the FIDE version of the Championship, with the newly fashionable fast time control; true, Kasparov and Kramnik were absent. Even so, on Ponomariov's way to the throne, the leading lights of the Russian national squad – Alexander Morozevich, Evgeny Bareev and Peter Svidler – were overwhelmed, while in the final Vasily Ivanchuk was literally crushed. This speaks volumes. However, even prior to the Championship, objectively speaking, young Ruslan was not exactly short of chess experience....

Pauses on the way

Here is one more advantage of chess over all other sporting disciplines. The world enthuses over veteran gymnasts aged thirty, footballers aged thirty-five, hockey players aged forty, or fifty-year-old equestrians and yachtsmen. In chess, half a century of participation in major contests is not at all exceptional. There is even a world chess crown for players over sixty! And in the course of such a long chess journey, players have taken time off. They still do so, and most probably will in future, even if the benefits from this are not great.

When the reigning champion Mikhail Botvinnik had what you could call an extra rook in one of his world title match games against David Bronstein in 1951, but failed to convert this advantage into a win, the overall verdict was unanimous. He was off form, they said, he was out of training; he had taken three years off chess for the purpose of defending his doctoral dissertation; even a king of chess couldn't afford such a break.

Unfortunately the massed chorus of experts and critics had clean forgotten about some far longer absences from the chess scene. We are not talking about the grave illnesses by which the brilliant careers of Carlos Torre, Aron Nimzowitsch and Enrique Mecking were interrupted for a long period – in effect for good. Subsequently these players could only observe the chess scene without taking part in the battle. Our present theme is *voluntary* seclusion. What was the record-breaking instance of it? Wilhelm Steinitz 'put in a claim' to this distinction even before officially ascending the chess throne. From 1873 until 1894 – a span of 21 years! – he only took part in two tournaments.

This was something that forcefully struck the entire chess world. What was much less noticed at roughly the same time was the absence from chess of the young Englishman Amos Burn. After taking up the game at the age of 16, he had quickly joined the circle of the strongest British players – only to disappear again for a decade and a half! There is not even any evidence of isolated appearances at the chessboard in a café or club. His return was all the more resounding. He finished equal first with the already famous Joseph Blackburne in the London tournament of 1886, won at Nottingham in the same year, and shared first and second prizes with Isidor Gunsberg at London 1887. The highest point in Burn's career was first place, with an individual victory over Steinitz, at Cologne 1898; but even immediately after his prolonged break, his play was of no mean quality.

Nonetheless Burn never rose above the status of England's number two player, whereas it is the stars above all – whether in chess, art or politics – that the world has grown accustomed to watch closely. Hence the 'sabbatical' periods of the World Champion Emanuel Lasker – and there were more than enough of them – were far more attentively discussed. His return match with Steinitz was scarcely over when he settled in Manchester and travelled to Heidelberg university to prepare his dissertation for a doctorate in philosophy and mathematics. Incidentally he succeeded in both these fields. Mathematicians are familiar with 'Lasker's module' and 'Lasker's ring', while his books *The Struggle* and *Philosophy of the Interminable* were diligently studied by Albert Einstein himself. The latter book became a forerunner of modern games theory and, in broad terms, of cybernetics as a whole.

These activities alone make Lasker's 'defections' from practical chess understandable, but on top of this he was a dramatist, he wrote books for children and brilliantly edited *Lasker's Chess Magazine*, to which he was also the chief contributor. Yet after his first absence which lasted nearly three years, he came back without any preparation to win first prize in superb style in the London tournament of 1899, scoring 23½ points out of a possible 28. Geza Maroczy, Harry Pillsbury and David Janowski finished 4½ points behind; the size of the winner's lead was itself a record at the time. And Lasker took the first brilliancy prize into the bargain! (The following notes are by B.Weinstein.)

Steinitz – Lasker

15...♘xg2!!
Nearly all annotators have given this move at least two exclamation marks, and we will go along with the majority.
16 ♔xg2 ♗xh3+ 17 ♔f2
It's 'easy to see' (now!) that taking the bishop allows mate: 17 ♔xh2 ♕h5+ 18 ♔g2 ♕g4+ 19 ♔h1 (or 19 ♔f2 ♕g3 mate) 19...♕h3+ 20 ♔g1 ♕g3+ 21 ♔h1, and now the manoeuvre ♖e8-e4-g4 is decisive.
17...f6
Capturing the rook was playable, but Lasker's move is more attractive and stronger.
18 ♖g1 g5
This pawn has to be captured, as otherwise a defence against g5-g4 is hard to find.
19 ♗xg5 fxg5 20 ♖xg5 ♕e6 21 ♕d3 ♗f4 22 ♖h1
The rook on g5 has nowhere to escape to. On 22 ♖h5, Black has 22...♕g4 23 ♘h4 ♖xe2+, while 22 ♖g7 is answered by 22 ♗f5, and 22 ♖g1 by the obvious 22...♗e3+.
22...♗xg5 23 ♘xg5 ♕f6+ 24 ♗f3 ♗f5 25 ♘xh7 ♕g6 26 ♕b5 c6
For one moment White was threatening mate (27 ♗xb7+ etc.).
27 ♕a5 ♖e7 28 ♖h5 ♗g4 29 ♖g5 ♕c2+ 30 ♔g3 ♗xf3 0-1

There followed another magnificent performance in Lasker's first tournament of the dawning twentieth century – in Paris in the summer of 1900. In the company of such leading world players as Pillsbury, Chigorin, Schlechter, Janowski, Marshall and Maroczy, he lost one game, drew one and scored fourteen (!) wins. After that he departed from the scene once again, for rather more than two years. Note that this was when he was at the height of his powers, at the best time of life for playing chess! Then from May 1904 until the beginning of 1907, there was another interval. Lasker's final pause on his journey lasted a full nine years, from the first Moscow international tournament in 1925 until the Zurich tournament in the summer of 1934. There, in the very first round, he played a positional queen sacrifice – at the age of sixty-six!

Euwe – Lasker

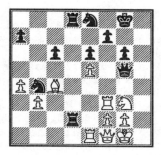

34...♘c2!! 35 ♘e4 ♕xe5!! 36 ♘f6+ ♕xf6 37 ♖xf6 ♘xf6 38 ♖c1 ♘e4 39 ♗e2 ♘d4 40 ♗f3 ♘xf2 41 ♕c4 ♘d3 42 ♖f1 ♘e5 43 ♕b4 ♘exf3+ 44 gxf3 ♘e2+ 45 ♔h2 ♘f4+ 46 ♔h1 ♖2d4 47 ♕e7 ♔g7 48 ♕c7 ♖8d5 49 ♖e1 ♖g5 50 ♕xc6 ♖d8 0-1

I need hardly say that the two gaps in Osip Bernstein's chess career, which come to nearly a quarter of a century when added together, were overshadowed by the periods of 'leave' taken by the great Champion and ex-Champion of the world. The Franco-Russian Grandmaster's aggregate time of absence – from 1920 to 1930 and from 1933

to 1946 – has a fair claim to record status, but I have already mentioned the subjective way we respond to these things.

If we are talking about a 'one-off' interval, then without any doubt the palm must be handed to Bobby Fischer. He conquered the crown on 1 September 1972 by scoring +7 -3 =11 in his match with Boris Spassky at Reykjavik (and we should not forget that the first two days in the schedule brought Spassky two points, one of them without any play). After that, exactly twenty years and one day were to pass before the eleventh World Champion sat down at the chessboard again for a public contest (a few games with a computer, which was still taking its first steps in chess, do not count). In the three years after Reykjavik, the young Anatoly Karpov had emerged as Fischer's opponent for a match at the highest level, but Fischer effectively declined to play him by imposing a large number of more or less unacceptable conditions. It was only on 2 September 1992 that he began his so-called return match (who was returning? the challenger?) with his old friend and rival Spassky. What was at stake, of course, was not the Championship title (which had long since passed into other hands) but the 5½ million dollars put up by the Yugoslav millionaire Jezdimir Vasiljević (soon afterwards Interpol was on his trail). Fischer began the match on the island of Sveti Stefan with a victory which to all intents and purposes was the most impressive in the whole of the lengthy contest of 30 rounds.

Fischer – Spassky

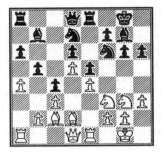

19 b4!? ♘h7?

A strategic mistake by an opponent thrown off balance. Black simply had to capture *en passant*. After 19...cxb3 20 ♗xb3 he would have had quite good counterplay against the queenside weaknesses. Now Fischer impeccably carries out his plan.

20 ♗e3 h5 21 ♕d2 ♖f8 22 ♖a3! ♘df6 23 ♖ea1 ♕d7 24 ♖1a2 ♖fc8 25 ♕c1 ♗f8 26 ♕a1 ♕e8 27 ♘f1!

Proclaiming his intention, which is to bring this knight back to its starting square b1; to open the a-file; and then, after exchanging all the major pieces, to play ♘b1-a3, attacking and winning the pawn on b5.

27...♗e7 28 ♘1d2 ♔g7 29 ♘b1

29...♘xe4!

The best practical chance – in the spirit of the young Spassky.

30 ♗xe4 f5 31 ♗c2 ♗xd5 32 axb5 axb5 33 ♖a7 ♔f6 34 ♘bd2 ♖xa7 35 ♖xa7 ♖a8

36 g4!

Recalling his best years! White transfers the play to the kingside where the black chieftain is anything but safe – even though, on the surface, there seems to be no basis for an attack.

36...hxg4 37 hxg4 ♖xa7

A more tenacious line might have been 37...f4, to avoid activating the white queen.

38 ♕xa7 f4 39 ♗xf4 exf4 40 ♘h4! ♗f7 41 ♕d4+ ♔e6 42 ♘f5!

White's threats are now irresistible.

42...♗f8 43 ♕xf4 ♔d7 44 ♘d4 ♕e1+ 45 ♔g2 ♗d5+ 46 ♗e4 ♗xe4+ 47 ♘xe4 ♗e7 48 ♘xb5 ♘f8 49 ♘bxd6 ♘e6 50 ♕e5 1-0

However, this match game, one of 10 wins alongside 5 losses and 15 draws, stands apart from all the rest. These days, the pace of change in the seemingly timeless game of chess has become too swift. Opening preparation, the intensity of the training that goes into every game – these and many other components of the struggle have progressed too far. At the end of the day, Fischer (like Spassky too, for that matter) was no more than a shadow of his great former self. In our time, then, a price has to be paid for taking 'time off' from chess 'service'.

Furthermore Fischer has a reckoning to face. Winning the match and receiving five-eighths of the stake money, he virtually forfeited the right to return to his homeland. (In America he can expect a ten-year prison sentence, fines to the tune of a quarter of a million, plus a tax on the prize money.) He took another period of leave – which up to the present moment has lasted for more than a decade. And it will probably never end.

A title for all ages

For many a long year, the title of chess Grandmaster did and did not exist. As early as 18 February 1838, through one of its readers, the London newspaper *Bell's Life* proposed awarding this title to William Lewis whom we have all now completely forgotten. Later, the five finalists of the St Petersburg tournament in 1914 received the title from Nicholas II, Tsar of All the Russias. However, even after the foundation of FIDE, it took exactly a quarter of a century before the International Grandmaster title was adopted officially. Why indeed should the top players have been interested in the opinion of what was essentially an amateur organization, albeit an international one? Up to that time, those who had won at least one notable tournament were respectfully referred to as 'great masters'. (That great hustler Ostap Bender assumed that a Grandmaster was just an 'older master'.) If the organizers of a tournament restricted the entry to such winners, the press would refer to the contest – for instance Ostende 1907 or St Petersburg 1914 – not as a Grandmaster tournament but as a 'tournament of champions'. At any rate, public opinion among chessplayers at that time was very powerful, and there was no discussion of who should be called a Grandmaster and who should not.

In this field, as in that of ballet, the Soviet Union proved to be the world leader. The Grandmaster title was officially instituted in our country way back in 1927, and less than two years later it was awarded to the 42-year-old Boris Verlinsky, the winner of the national championship in 1929. Prior to that he had won the championships of Ukraine and Moscow. In the first Moscow international tournament in 1925 his overall result had been relatively modest, but he had inflicted a sensational defeat on the 'invincible' World Champion Capablanca as well as 'incidentally' beating such leading lights as Rubinstein, Sämisch, Spielmann and Levenfish.

The land of near-victorious socialism had another record performance to its name: in 1931, the highest chess title was abolished (!). After four more years it was resurrected, and Mikhail Botvinnik became the 'second first' Grandmaster of the USSR. Incidentally, in the entire world of serious chess, Hungary was to be the only other country to recognize National Grandmasters.

On its revival after the Second World War, FIDE took over the system of competition for the chess crown and also introduced, among other things, the title of International Grandmaster. At the beginning of 1950, twenty-seven chessplayers were appointed Grandmasters on what you might call an honorary basis. The oldest of them was the German Jakob (Jacques) Mieses, who was soon to complete his 85th year! (Long afterwards the title was awarded to the 85-year-old George Koltanowski, again *honoris causa* – that is, on the basis of his earlier achievements including a simultaneous blindfold display which broke the currrent record. The Peruvian Esteban Canal, who enriched chess opening theory with two variations that bear his name, was also to become a Grandmaster, at 81.) The Hungarian Geza Maroczy was five years younger than Mieses; in all, eleven of the 'great firsts' had been born in the nineteenth century.

David Bronstein had most probably learnt the art of chess from the books of his titled colleagues; among this first batch of Grandmasters he looked 'indecently' young at 26. The world's number two player at that time, Vasily Smyslov, was three years older. Subsequently, however, the title was awarded to ever younger competitors.

The future World Champion Mikhail Tal was 21 when he achieved the Grandmaster title.

His successors on the chess throne, Boris Spassky, Anatoly Karpov, Garry Kasparov and Vladimir Kramnik, were around the age of 18.

The age at which another king of chess, Bobby Fischer, became a Grandmaster was long regarded as the benchmark; he was 15 years, 6 months and 1 day old. It seemed impossible to improve on this record until Judit, the youngest of the Polgar sisters, attained the *men's* Grandmaster title when more than a month younger – 15 years, 4 months, 28 days. At that moment the pundits were unanimous: the ceiling had been reached! But time passed, and the 2001 Girls' World Champion, the Indian Humpy Koneru, achieved her third norm for the (men's) title at 15 years, 1 month and 17 days – three months faster than Judit. So far this is the most rapid intrusion by a girl into the male Grandmaster family. But what about the highest official women's title? In this category, the diminutive Ukrainian schoolgirl Katerina Lahno comes (or rather, flies!) before all others. At 12, she became both the European Girls' under-14 Champion and a Woman Grandmaster. To be exact, she was aged twelve years six and a half months!

Earlier, Polgar's compatriot Peter Leko had raised himself into the Grandmaster camp at 14 years, 4 months, 22 days. The French boy Étienne Bacrot took two months and 22 days less than that to reach the coveted goal, but shortly afterwards Ruslan Ponomariov from Ukraine became the world's youngest 'great master' at the age of 14 years and 17 days.

Was that as far as things could go? Nothing of the sort! Ruslan was surpassed by three days (!) by the Baku player Teimour Radjabov, for whom incidentally Garry Kasparov (also a native of that city) predicted an excellent chess future. After that, the Chinese Bu Xiangzhi 'took over the baton' 62 days earlier in life – at 13 years, 10 months and 13 days. True, he had been losing a large number of games against Russian masters, and for our famous Grandmasters he was just easy prey – but that was back in 1999. Within a year, he had victories to his credit such as, for instance, the following one against a highly experienced opponent who was several times Champion of the USA:

**Larry Christiansen –
Bu Xiangzhi**
Reykjavik 2000

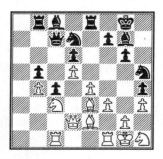

21...♘e5 22 f4 ♘d3! 23 ♘xb5 (23 ♗xd3 cxd3 24 ♕xd3 ♕c4) **23...♕d7 24 ♖xc4 ♗a6! 25 ♘xd6 ♕xd6 26 ♖c6 ♕xb4 27 ♖xa6 ♖xe4 28 ♗xd3 ♖xe3 29 ♕xb4 ♖xb4**
The mutual slaughter is at an end. For the moment White has an extra pawn, but Black's pieces are active enough to start hunting down the white king.
30 ♖d1 ♖d4! 31 ♘f2 ♘xf4 32 ♗c2 ♖xd1+ 33 ♘xd1 ♖e2 34 ♗b3 ♗d4+ 35 ♔f1 ♖xg2 36 ♔e1 ♘d3+ 37 ♔f1 ♖g1+ 38 ♔e2 ♘c1+ 0-1

But Grandmasters keep on getting younger! In January 2002 Ruslan Ponomariov from the Ukrainian town of Kramatorsk arrived in Moscow for the final of the FIDE World Championship. He was accompanied by his official second, his 12-year-old fellow-countryman Sergei Karjakin. Everyone's first reaction to this pair was to smile – but Ponomariov became Champion, while within half a year Karjakin gained his third and final Grandmaster norm at the age of 12 years 7 months exactly. He had outdone the Chinese Bu by one year, three months and thirteen days!

Who's next, my young friends?

Old and little

These words don't characterize Grandmasters in general (heaven forbid), they are just a Belorussian catch-phrase. One of the fortunate things about chess is that unlike almost all other types of sport it allows its warriors to do battle until their hair goes grey or vanishes altogether. At the age of 63 years 17 days, Vasily Smyslov was still in the hunt to regain his chess crown. By the following evening he had lost the Candidates Final match to Garry Kasparov, but remained number 3 in the official world ranking list. Sammy Reshevsky won the US Championship for the first time in 1936, and for the last time thirty-three years later (recalling Ilya Muromets in the Russian folk tale). There will be more about this in the chapter 'Occupation: Champion'.

Examples of chess longevity abound. The Englishman John Keeble, for instance, was champion of Norfolk and Norwich Chess Club in 1884 and ... in 1933, that is nearly half a century later. Among those who played, or have been playing, for over 50 years in major tournaments, we may name the Yugoslav Svetozar Gligorić, the Argentinian Miguel Najdorf, the Englishmen Harry Golombek, Joseph Blackburne and Henry Bird, the Hungarian Geza Maroczy and the Germans Wolfgang Unzicker and Wolfgang Uhlmann. 'Gligo' has even been granted the right to play in the Yugoslav Championship for the rest of his life without qualifying, and every year in that event he manages to do a fair amount of damage to his 'chess grandchildren'. Golombek became a Grandmaster at 74 – for his earlier successes, of course. Another of his achievements, though not a record one, was to have conducted the chess column in the venerable *Times* newspaper from 1945 until 1985. Blackburne played in both the second international tournament in world chess history – London 1862 – and the 'Tournament of Champions', St Petersburg 1914.

The Swede Erik Lundin stepped into the ranks of the Grandmasters just before completing his eighth decade. The traditional Hastings tournament of 1931/32 was the Englishman Edward Jackson's first serious international event; in chess terms the newcomer's age was a round figure: 64 years! Admittedly he lost all his games against the top

four players in the tournament, but he managed fifth place out of ten nontheless. Grandmaster Milan Vidmar the elder, whose life embraced big-time chess in parallel with big-time science, won the Basle tournament in 1952, defeating ex-World Champion Max Euwe in their individual game; the victor was 67 at the time, having started his international chess career half a century earlier! However, the currently unsurpassed record belongs to Viktor Korchnoi. Within a month of celebrating his seventieth birthday he finished first in the tournament at Biel 2001, where some of the Grandmasters taking part might have been his great-grandchildren! Here is his game against a distinguished 'grandson':

Gelfand – Korchnoi
Slav Defence [D44]

1 d4 d5 2 c4 c6 3 ♘c3 ♘f6 4 ♘f3 dxc4 5 a4 ♗f5 6 e3 e6 7 ♗xc4 ♗b4 8 0-0 ♘bd7 9 ♕e2 ♗g4 10 e4 ♘b6 11 ♗b3 ♗xf3 12 ♕xf3 ♕xd4 13 ♖d1 ♕e5 14 ♗f4 ♕h5 15 ♕d3

In return for the pawn White has two fine bishops, control of the d-file and the initiative. Almost any player in the world would attend to the black king by playing 15...0-0 here, but Korchnoi goes his own way.

15...♘bd7 (?!!) 16 e5 ♘xe5 (?!!) 17 ♕d4 ♗xc3 18 bxc3 ♘g6 19 ♗d6

Horror of horrors!

19...♕a5!? 20 ♗c5 b6 21 ♗b4 ♕e5

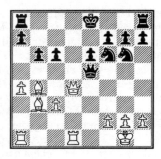

It now turns out that White has no mate and is left two pawns down. He resigned on the 51st move **(0-1)**.

One year on, all-powerful Time received a further slap in the face. The 40th anniversary of the Candidates Tournament in Curaçao arrived, and the authorities of the island decided to remind the chess world, indeed the *whole* world, of this fact. They organized a tournament to which they invited players who had faced each other in the four cycles of that earlier distinguished event. Of those eight players, four were still alive and two of them came: Grandmaster Pal Benko as a guest and commentator, and Viktor Korchnoi as a participant! The contingent of 'Curaçao old-stagers' was completed by Yuri Averbakh. In 1962 he had been coach to the Soviet Grandmasters; in 2002 he acted as Chief Arbiter.

Of course, the format of the tournament itself was altered with the lapse of time: thirty-eight Grandmasters and masters, from eleven different countries, took part in a nine-round Swiss. The main contenders for first place were the

Dutchman Jan Timman (until recently one of the strongest players in the world), the reigning European Champion Bartlomiej Macieja from Poland, the Israeli Grandmaster Yona Kosashvili (who 'for good measure' is married to one of the three famous Polgar sisters), and Korchnoi. The top finishers with 7 points were the 'chess grandfather and grandson', Viktor and Yona, but the Sonneborn-Berger score gave preference – and first prize! – to the veteran, who (I should add) had played 'youthful chess' as always.

Baldur Hönliger's level of play certainly falls a long way short of the world-class performances of Korchnoi. However ... in 1986, in the *Bundesliga* of what was then West Germany, there was no shortage of either masters playing on home ground or Grandmasters in the 'foreign legion' invited from outside (the mere names of Mikhail Tal and Boris Spassky speak volumes). This did not stop Hönliger from playing top board for the Wuppertal club at the age of eighty-one!

Naming the the youngest player to take up our game of the intellect is a less realistic task. On the domestic level, Capablanca and Kramnik were doing battle with their fathers and uncles at the age of four. In London, the five-year-old Lucinda Kate Gibson was beating her father and elder brothers (while incidentally solving grammar school maths problems). At the age of 7-8, Reshevsky was giving simultaneous displays in Paris, London, Berlin and Vienna....

At Lucerne in 1982, the twelve-year-old Kim Tjongtjinjoe became the youngest participant in a World Chess Olympiad up to that date. The Surinam squad placed him on board three. This was probably an even 'stiffer' test than that faced by Daniel Yanofsky at the Buenos Aires Olympiad in 1939, when the fourteen-year-old played on second board – sometimes even top board – for Canada, which was no weak team.

The record held by the Surinam player lasted until the Olympiad at Bled, Slovenia, in 2002. That town had already been associated with chess records; it was there in 1931, on the shore of that magnificent lake, that Alexander Alekhine finished a tournament 5½ points clear of his rivals.

It is true that Roela Pasku, playing on second board for the Albanian women's team and looking like a perfect child, was actually 'getting on in years': she was a full 12 years 10 months old. But the Singapore girl Jeslin Tay Li-Jin, aged 11 years 4 months and 10 days, was, as they say, in a class of her own!

At this point there is even something to be said for closing our search. The new time-control introduced by FIDE – an hour and a half for the game, with 30 seconds added per move (an arrangement made possible by 'Fischer clocks') – is inexorably shifting chess in the direction of youth, and it is almost a safe bet that in the next Olympiads there will be participants barely above pre-school age.

The youngest Olympiad *team* was the men's team fielded by Azerbaijan, again at Bled in 1902. It was headed by Grandmaster Teimour Radjabov, who at the official opening of the tournament was 15 years, 7 months and 13 days old. The average age of the 'core' Azeri team – that is, Grandmasters Shakhriyar Mamedyarov, Vugar Gashimov and Gadir Guseinov in addition to Radjabov – was 16 years, 5 months, 15 days! As to the squad as a whole, its age was 'spoilt' by the 'ageing' reserves, International Masters Rasul Ibrahimov (21 years) and Javad Maharramzade (26), who pushed the average up to all of eighteen and a half! At the same time the Azeris were as high as 20th in the list of ratings, above 121 other teams.

These youngsters, by the way, had a good deal of success – an assertion which could be made purely on the basis of, for example, their win against the Ukrainian team, headed by Ruslan Ponomariov (FIDE World Champion) and Vasily Ivanchuk, one of the world's strongest Grandmasters! The quality of play also commanded respect.

Radjabov (Azerbaijan) –
Braga (Italy)
Queen's Gambit [D10]

1 d4 d5 2 c4 c6 3 ♘c3 ♘f6 4 e3 a6 5 ♘f3 b5 6 b3 ♗g4 7 ♗e2 e6 8 0-0 ♘bd7 9 h3 ♗h5 10 ♗b2 ♕b8 11 ♘e5 ♗xe2 12 ♕xe2 ♘xe5 13 dxe5 ♘d7 14 cxd5 cxd5 15 ♖fd1 ♗e7
Serious players would hardly consider variations like 15...♘xe5 16 ♘xd5 exd5 17 ♖xd5.

16 ♕g4 g6 17 ♘e2 ♘xe5 18 ♕f4 f6 19 e4 g5

19...dxe4 20 ♕xe4 0-0 would be completely reckless due to 21 f4.

20 ♕e3 dxe4 21 ♕xe4 ♔f7 22 ♖ac1 ♖a7 23 f4 gxf4 24 ♘xf4 ♗d6

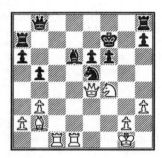

Black's aim is to start exchanging major pieces next move. White has nothing against this; he simply switches his attack to a different object.

25 ♘h5 ♖c7 26 ♖xc7+ ♕xc7 27 ♕f4 ♗e7 28 ♘xf6

Now the king is naked: if 28...♗xf6, then 29 ♖f1.

28...♕c2 29 ♘d7+ ♔e8 30 ♖c1! ♘f3+ 31 ♔xf3 ♕xb2 32 ♖d1 ♖g8 33 ♕c6 ♖g5 34 ♘c5+

Now 34...♔f7 35 ♕xe6+ ♔e8 36 ♖d8+ leads to mate.

1-0

The 11-year old Elina Danielian from Erevan officially achieved a Woman International Master norm at Moscow 1991, inflicting defeat on both the tournament winners, Elena Fatalibekova and Tatiana Chekhova. Maia Chiburdanidze was two years older when she gained her first international title (in much more difficult conditions), but she became a star of the first magnitude!

The St Petersburg player A.Grachev had a much harder time of it. He had been striving all his life to gain the 'silver medal' of the master title. It was not until the age of 83 that he took the coveted prize, in the 1992 international tournament of veterans of the Great Fatherland War. The contest, in the town of Zhukovskoe, was dedicated to the 50th anniversary of the battle for Moscow. It comprised exactly 50 players from 8 countries including England, Denmark – and Germany. Their average age was very slightly above the 70-year mark. The winner was the 75-year-old International Master Semyon Zhukhovitsky, while the freshly promoted Master of Sport found his way into the Guinness Book of Records.

Given such a substantial 'age spread', we can only regard it as natural that 'young and old' should be constantly facing each other in mortal combat. The record age gap for a World Championship contest was seen in 1896/97, at the return match in Moscow – where the ex-World Champion Wilhelm Steinitz was almost 61, while the Champion Emanuel Lasker was one month over 28. Similarly in the Botvinnik-Tal matches, Mikhail the elder was more than twice the age of Mikhail the younger, but the disparity in absolute terms (25 years) was less than in the case of Steinitz and Lasker (32 years).

For Candidates Matches, the record is and perhaps always will be the final at Vilnius in 1984. There the 63-year-old ex-World Champion Vasily Smyslov faced the future Chess King Garry Kasparov, who was exactly one-third his age! Vasily had become a Grandmaster when Garry's parents had only just been born!

This match, incidentally, proved to be a record in another respect too: all 13 games opened with the Queen's Gambit (as long as you count the Slav Defence, which occurred in just one of them, as a variety of that opening).

Smyslov was also involved in another match that established an absolute record at Grandmaster level. In 1996, in the little French town of Albert, the 75-year-old 'senior' played the 13-year-old junior Étienne Bacrot. Here again success was on the side of youth – with a score of 5:1!

Bacrot – Smyslov
Nimzo-Indian Defence [E35]

1 d4 ♘f6 2 c4 e6 3 ♘c3 ♗b4 4 ♕c2 d5 5 cxd5 exd5 6 ♗g5 h6 7 ♗h4 g5 8 ♗g3 ♘e4 9 e3 h5
More popular choices are 9...♗e6 and 9...c6, fortifying Black's position in the centre.

10 f3
An interesting moment. Étienne takes a considered decision that is out of keeping with his years; he chooses a purely positional continuation. In Seirawan - Al Hadrani, Novi Sad 1990, White had offered a piece sacrifice with 10 ♗d3!? h4 11 ♗e5. Black could have accepted the gift with 11...♗xc3+ 12 bxc3 f6 13 ♗xe4 dxe4 14 ♕xe4 fxe5, but shied away from such sharp play – unwisely, it seems. After 11...f6?! 12 ♗xe4 dxe4 (12...♗xc3+ 13 ♕xc3!) 13 d5!

♔f7?! (13...♕xd5 was worth considering) 14 ♕xe4 ♕e7 15 ♕c4! Seirawan emerged with a sound extra pawn.

10...♗xc3+ 11 bxc3 ♘xg3 12 hxg3 ♘d7 13 ♔f2 ♘f6 14 ♖b1 b6 15 c4 c6 16 cxd5 cxd5 17 ♗b5+ ♔f8 18 ♘e2 ♔g7 19 ♖b3 ♗e6
It would be dangerous to weaken the queenside with 19...a6, but now White seizes the c-file.

20 ♗a6 ♕d6 21 ♖c3 ♖ae8 22 ♕c1 (taking aim at the g5-pawn) 22...♗d7 23 e4 dxe4 24 ♕xg5+ ♔f8 25 ♖e3

25...exf3?
25...♗c6, maintaining the tension in the centre, might have been better.

26 ♖xe8+ ♔xe8 27 gxf3 ♖g8 28 ♕e5+
Going into a favourable ending; sooner or later Black's weak pawn on h5 will fall.

28...♕xe5 29 dxe5 ♘d5 30 ♗c4
White isn't in a hurry to pick up the pawn. After 30 ♖xh5 ♘b4 31 ♗c4 b5 32 ♗b3 a5 Black would obtain counter-chances.

30...♗e6 31 ♘d4 ♖h8 32 ♘xe6 fxe6 33 ♗xd5 exd5 34 f4!
White's pawn duo is irresistible. There is no point in going after material gains; after 34 ♖d1 ♔e7

35 ♖xd5 ♔e6 36 ♖b5 ♖c8, Black would have an active position.

34...♔f7

Nor can Black save himself with 34...♔d7 35 f5 ♖e8 36 e6+ ♔d6 37 ♖xh5 ♔e5 38 g4 ♔f4 39 f6 ♖xe6 40 f7 ♖f6 41 ♖f5+.

35 f5 d4 36 ♖c1 ♔g7 37 ♖c7+ ♔h6 38 ♖f7 ♔g5 39 e6 h4 40 e7 1-0

With all this in mind, the 'mere' 52 years difference between Ruslan Ponomariov and Viktor Korchnoi, who played each other in a match at Donetsk in 2001, would not merit a mention in this book, were it not for one additional circumstance: in the eighth and last game of the match, 'experience' succeeded in winning and levelling the score. In his two analogous duels with 'youth' in 2002, Viktor didn't manage to rescue himself, hence his opponents will remain unnamed....

Incidentally, veteran champions have not only battled with youth face to face and given simultaneous displays to budding kings of chess (see the chapter 'All onto one'); they have also devoted long years to preparing those who subsequently constituted the glory of the game. The first 'teacher-pupil' relationships to become famous were those involving the brilliant Hungarian (originally Austro-Hungarian) Grandmaster Geza Maroczy. The World Champion Max Euwe, the first Women's World Champion Vera Menchik and Grandmaster Isaac Kashdan all considered Maroczy their mentor.

The record in this field belongs nonetheless to the patriarch of Soviet chess, Mikhail Botvinnik. His school was attended, in different years, by the 12th, 13th and 14th Chess Kings – Anatoly Karpov, Garry Kasparov and Vladimir Kramnik – to say nothing of dozens more first-class Grandmasters. Interestingly, Mark Dvoretsky too studied at this school or rather academy; he went on to become a trainer himself, and coached Grandmasters Artur Yusupov, Sergei Dolmatov and others.

Presidents have a long life

We aren't talking about heads of state, of course. *They* not only get replaced, they can be overthrown or even killed. Running a chess club is different. We can take it as proven that this job imbues the club president with the same inexhaustible energy that a grateful audience in a packed-out concert hall imparts to a conductor.

Two men may be regarded as record-holders in this department. First there was the Englishman John Watkinson. On his 20th birthday (in 1853) he took over the chess club that had been founded in the town of Huddersfield. He remained its president for 70 years (!), right up until 19 December 1923 – when, ten months after crossing the ninety-year threshold, he departed this life.

In that same year of 1923, in the holy city of Jerusalem, in what was then the League of Nations mandate territory of Palestine, a chess club named after Rubinstein was founded. Three years later, Lev Osipovich Mogilyover – who, alas, had never met the great Akiba – was elected president. He had been born in Bialystok and emigrated to Palestine from Odessa – where anyone and everyone had held power during the Russian Civil War, and the chief instrument of government had been the bullet. He very quickly acquired Arabic, German, French and English to add to the languages he already knew: Russian, Ukrainian, Yiddish, Hebrew and Latin. He became a well-known chess problemist.

The club, however, was always the main thing in Mogilyover's life, and the experience he accumulated enabled him to organize nothing less than the the the 16th International Chess Olympiad in Tel-Aviv in 1964. The Soviet authorities sent their team to the hated Israel with heavy heart and gritted teeth. (Twelve years on, when the Olympiad was held in Haifa, the USSR sacrificed the gold medals they would have been certain to win, and in their absence the Americans were victorious.) After being its president for 70 years, Mogilyover left the club at the age of ninety-two when his earthly existence came to an end....

But there was one astonishingly versatile man, Alexander Kazantsev, who composed studies over an even longer period. He was also President of the Composition Committee of the USSR Chess Federation. Even more important, he was a brilliant engineer and inventor, a world-class author of fantasy fiction, and a philosopher. He published his first chess composition in 1926, and his last in 1996! Admittedly he could not, generally speaking, count as a particularly 'prolific' composer. He only produced 120 studies in the course of 70 years, and 12 of them were the result of collaboration. He

was one of the first to receive the International Master title, and was content to go no further.

Longevity, however, is not confined to chess organizers. The strong player Jean Ladi Karev lived in the 18th, 19th and 20th centuries; he was born in 1797 and died in November 1901. It has not been possible to find examples of his play; no games of his are in print.

Much the same can be said about the biography of the Englishwoman Jane Carew. The question as to how far she was seriously involved with chess is even more open.

Russia's oldest chessplayer appears to have been Mikhail Mikhailovich Segel, with whom I had the honour to be closely acquainted; I even played a few games against him, and once published the following lines on the subject of my opponent:

"In the mid-1950s the championships of Kazan and Tartaria were held concurrently if Rashid Nezhmetdinov was taking part. The latter was among the strongest masters in the country, and he would collect an almost unbroken string of 'ones' on the tournament chart. Why 'almost'? Basically, this was the 'fault' of Mikhail Segel. To me he appeared lanky, gaunt and broad of frame. He would push his glasses up onto his forehead, clasp his head between his big palms, and build up a position that was utterly impossible to breach. 'I don't like to have a 30-per-cent chance of winning if my opponent has a 20-per-cent chance. I'm happy with 1 per cent as long as my opponent has 0 per cent,' he once said to me, and I stress that we were not talking in private.

"At the time I didn't understand him. Nor did I understand what he said one evening when I had some success at the chessboard. I was in good form and facing an opponent old enough to be my father. With a series of sacrifices I demolished his position in about 25 moves. Suddenly I heard these words of reproach, which *were* spoken in confidence:

"'Yakov old fellow, you shouldn't be so cruel to your opponent.'

"'How *am* I supposed to win, then?' I inquired, not very cleverly.

"Mikhail Mikhailovich made no reply. He just looked over his spectacles at me. Today I would give anything not to have received that look, on that evening in the distant past....

"His reproach stemmed from a particular delicacy of character which the old Russian intelligentsia measured with neither titles nor ranks nor grades. I am convinced that in this respect he is the current Champion of Russia! And perhaps not only of the Russian chess world."

Furthermore Mikhail Mikhailovich became the first-ever Champion of the Republic of Tatarstan, way back in 1920. (At the same time he was playing as a defender in the Kazan football team and had a hand in introducing the sport of shooting into the Republic.) In 1923, as one of the best chess-players of the Volga region, he took part in the 'Cities Tournament' which was held simultaneously with the USSR Championship in Petrograd. I should add that the schedule was arranged according to all the rules of economy: three rounds and an adjournment session in two days. In his group Segel settled down, as they say, in the middle of the table, winning a game against S.Slonim who was well known in the country at the time.

Segel's manner of conducting the following game is most typical of him.

Segel – Efremov
Kazan Championship 1931
Queen's Pawn Opening [A46]

1 d4 ♘f6 2 ♘f3 e6 3 e3 d5 4 ♗d3 c5 5 c3 ♘bd7 6 ♘bd2 ♗d6 7 0-0 ♕c7 8 ♕e2 0-0 9 e4 dxe4 10 ♘xe4 ♘xe4 11 ♕xe4 g6 12 ♕h4 ♕d8 13 ♗g5 ♕c7

Marking time like this cannot go unpunished.

14 ♘d2 (setting out for f6) 14...b6 15 ♖fe1 ♗b7 16 ♗e4! ♖fe8 17 ♗xb7 ♕xb7 18 ♘e4 ♗f8 19 dxc5 ♗xc5 20 ♖ad1 1-0

At the age of 100 Mikhail Mikhailovich enjoyed playing blitz and skittles games, with or without clocks, and took a lively interest in everything that was going on in the chess world. One year later, he was no more.

The post of President of FIDE has existed for three quarters of a century now. It would have been downright impossible for one person to hold office for so long, if only because of the international composition of this body. All the same, the first FIDE President, the Dutchman Alexander Rueb, remained in office for 25 years and then held the title of Honorary President for another ten. One of the main reasons for appointing him was that, among the 'founding fathers' of the organization, he was the only one representing a small country that wasn't at loggerheads with the others. None of Rueb's five successors held the post for a longer period. The Filipino Florencio Campomanes might be thought to rival him, but only through the accumulation of various separate posts. As well being President of his own national chess federation for a fair stretch of time, Campomanes was President of the FIDE Asiatic Zone for 4 years, FIDE Vice-President representing Asia for 8 years, and FIDE President for 13 years. He has been an Honorary President since 1995, after plunging the international federation into a full-scale crisis! Furthermore 'Campo' was the only President to draw a salary from FIDE funds – on no mean scale, either – and it was only during his presidency that a special resolution of a FIDE Congress stipulated the class of automobile and hotel suite which were to be put at his disposal on arrival in any country. 'On the other hand,' his campaign to create Grandmasters in every corner of the globe led to an unprecedented devaluation of this and other international titles.

FIDE Presidents have played the game themselves – in their different ways, ranging from World Championship standard (Max Euwe), through Grandmaster standard (Fridrik Olafsson), to this:

Caro-Kann Defence [B15]

1 e4 c6 2 d4 d5 3 ᒍc3 ᒍf6 4 e5 ᒍfd7 5 e6 fxe6 6 ᒍd3 ᒍf6 7 ᒍf3 g6 8 h4 c5 9 dxc5 ᒍc6 10 ♕e2 ᒍg7 11 ᒍd2 ♕c7 12 0-0-0 e5 13 ᒍg5 ᒍe6 14 ᒍb5 ♕b8 15 h5 gxh5

16 ᒍfd4! ᒍg4 17 f3 e4 18 fxg4 ᒍxd4 19 ᒍxd4 exd3 20 ᖴxd3 ᒍe4 21 ᒍf5 ♕e5 22 ᒍxg7+ ♕xg7 23 ᖴxd5 ᒍxg5 24 ♕b5+ ♔f7 25 ᖴf1+ ♔g6 26 ♕d3+ ♔h6 27 ᖴh1 1-0

In this game from the first round of the Leipzig Olympiad in 1960, the black pieces were handled by... **Florencio Campomanes**, a national master from the Philippines. The one fact which might count as a 'mitigating circumstance' was that, as fate would have it, his opponent was **Mikhail Tal**. But even getting on for thirty years later, at the World Championship match in Seville when Campomanes was already the all-powerful FIDE President, he scored zero points from four half-hour games in the press centre, against me – after which he visibly lost interest....

A council of judges

Venerable old age is by no means always a quantity with a minus sign in front of it. Since prehistoric times, primitive tribes have heeded their elders. The latter might have been past hunting sabre-tooth tigers and mammoths themselves, but with their experience of life they knew the best way the hunt should be organized.

To this day in most countries of the world, there is an age limit – a *lower* limit, that is – on the appointment of judges. This is only natural; youthful impetuosity is unsuited to ruling on the destiny of human beings. In chess, one small compartment of human existence, the same principles apply. At any tournament where brilliancy prizes are offered, the jury is made up of people possessing both the specific qualifications and the wisdom imparted by life itself.

The record age for a panel of chess judges was established at the Alekhine Memorial Tournament, Moscow 1992. The panel consisted of Mikhail Botvinnik, ex-World Champion; Andrei (or Andor) Lilienthal, the Hungarian, then Soviet, then again Hungarian Grandmaster; and the Polish-Argentinian Grandmaster Miguel Najdorf. Their combined age was 244 years! All of them in their time had played against the third World Champion. And the game they judged to be best was one in which a strategically paradoxical decision, as Botvinnik put it, took the place of sacrificial beauty or dashing attacks.

Karpov – Kamsky

"Over the last five moves Black could not have been more active. Deserting his king, he has thown himself into an attack on the queenside, but unexpectedly his initiative has come to a total standstill. That formidable-seeming pair, the bishop on b2 and knight on c2, require defending and are merely hampering the action of Black's own rooks. Having dealt with his opponent's aggression (even if only temporarily), White starts to develop his own offensive." (Karpov)

26 ♔h1

A customary unhurried manoeuvre by the ex-World Champion. A square is provided for the bishop's retreat, after which the white king's rook comes to life.

26...♕e7 27 ♗g1 ♘d7

Obviously glad that it doesn't need to guard the a4-square (to stop its opposite number from jumping there, and then to c5), the black knight hastens to relocate, clearing the path of the b-pawn at the same time. Nonetheless it ought to have waited! There was some sense in starting to pursue the white queen at once, with 27...♕b4. If then 28 ♕f4 (28 ♕h6 ♕f8), Black has 28...♘a3!?, giving his pieces access to the important square c1. After the move played, it's too late for this plan.

28 ♖f3 ♕b4 29 ♕h6 ♕f8 30 ♕g5 ♕g7 (practically forced) **31 ♕d2 b6 32 ♖df1 a5 33 h4 ♘b4 34 a3**

Of course not 34 ♕xb2?? ♖c2 35 ♕a1 (or 35 ♕a3) 35...♖xa2, trapping the queen.

34...♖c2 35 ♕f4 ♘c6 36 ♗h3 ♘d8 37 ♗e3 b5 38 ♖3f2!

"Having made his kingside position much stronger, White

changes tactics; after rook exchanges, Black will perish in the place where he recently dominated. In a few moves' time the white queen will be mistress of the c-file." (Karpov)

38...b4 39 axb4 axb4 40 ℤxc2 ℤxc2 41 ℤf2 ℤxf2 42 ♕xf2 ♗a3 43 ♕c2

Needless to say, with virtually an extra piece, White wins easily.

43...♘xe5

White's virtual extra piece is transformed into a real one, and although some tactical precision is still required, the outcome of the fight is a foregone conclusion.

44 dxe5 ♕xe5 45 ♕c8 ♕e4+ (45...♕xe3 allows mate in three) **46 ♗g2 ♕xb1+ 47 ♔h2 ♗b2 48 ♕xd8+ ♔g7 49 f6+ ♗xf6 50 ♗h6+ ♔xh6 51 ♕xf6 ♕c2 52 g5+ ♔h5 53 ♔g3**

It was still possible to let the win slip with 53 ♔h3? ♕f5+ 54 ♕xf5 gxf5 55 ♗f3+ ♔g6.

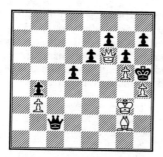

53...♕c7+ 54 ♔h3 1-0

It would not have come amiss if Herman Helms had been present too – though only a time machine could have made this possible. One of the founders of the US Chess Federation, Helms was awarded the title of International Arbiter in 1954

– when he was already 84! It was then that he ceased editing the chess section in the *Brooklyn Daily Eagle*, a job he had done for 61 years. As for the *American Chess Bulletin* which he founded himself, Helms edited and published it for a rather shorter period: 59 years only! (The Grandmaster and record-breaker George Koltanowski, whom we have mentioned before, signed the chess column of the *San Francisco Chronicle* for a 'mere' 52 years!) An additional record achievement in Helms's 93-year life was to have issued daily chess bulletins for the first time in history, at the Cambridge Springs international tournament of 1904.

Caissa's favourites and pariahs

"There's an Island of Misfortune in the ocean," sings the hero (or anti-hero?) of a highly popular Soviet comedy film. He is right; in the chess world there *is* such a place, and virtually every participant in the universal chess process has been permitted to reside there, even if only temporarily. Which of us has never blundered a piece away or missed a mate in a couple of moves? Whose flag has never fallen in a winning position? Who has not toiled to build up an advantage, only to see it wafted away like cigarette smoke in the time scramble?

In principle, though, this is normal. The pure chess struggle involves not only the player's talent, skill and knowledge, but also his nervous system, the speed at which his brain functions, his complexes, and dozens of other factors whether known or assumed. For that reason we are only going to talk about patent absurdities which can be viewed as cases of ill luck with full justification.

On the chessboard, the first thing this means is a 'finger-slip': you accidentally touch a piece, which then has to move in a way that is not just useless but harmful. To enumerate the record holders in this department is practically impossible – the quantity of candidates is too great. Here are three cases all the same.

At the Berlin tournament of 1897, the general consensus was that Mikhail Chigorin was likely to win first prize. (Tarrasch, at any rate, twice voiced this opinion in the *Berlin Daily* newspaper.) For one thing, it was not long since he had turned in a brilliant performance in Budapest. Secondly, many of the strongest masters of the day – Lasker, Steinitz, Tarrasch, Pillsbury, Maroczy – were absent from this event. The prediction might possibly have come true. However....

In a game against **Johannes Metger**, a perfectly ordinary opponent, **Chigorin** achieved what was close to a winning position on the Black side of a King's Gambit.

After the normal and obvious 27...♕e7, Black would both keep his extra pawn and wrest the initiative from his opponent, but for some incomprehensible reason the rook on h4 found its way into Chigorin's hand. Since 27...♖f4 was unplayable on account of 28 ♕xf4, there followed **27...♖xh2+ 28 ♔xh2 ♖h8+ 29 ♔g3 f5**, and then **30 ♖xg6+** whereupon Black resigned. This put paid to all dreams not only of first place but of any high placing at all. The only thing left for Chigorin to do was overhaul his competitive routine, which he did – with such evident success that he ended the tournament with four losses in a row!

Fate dealt an even harsher blow to **Viktor Korchnoi** in his game with Black against **Vladimir Bagirov** in the 1960 USSR Championship. The contest took place in Leningrad which was then Viktor's home city, in the Palace of Culture commemorating the First Five-year Plan. The hall was packed to overflowing and there were hundreds more fans in the freezing cold outside; it was under their eyes that the incident occurred.

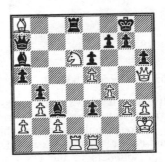

It's clear that after 27...♗xe1 28 ♖xe1 ♖xa8 29 ♕f3 e2 Black would reach a superior ending and have winning chances. That was what Korchnoi intended to play, but he mechanically reached out for his light-squared bishop which is aiming at empty space, instead of his dark-squared one. His immediate capitulation was all the more tragic since it meant losing the lead in one of the strongest Soviet Championships, with the finish just a couple of steps away.

Eventually, however, everything turned out happily for Viktor. In the final round he even had some luck, which just goes to show that no one on the Island of Misfortune has a *permanent* residence permit.

What happened on 23 July 1927, in a game between the Argentinian **Palau** and the Yugoslav **Kalaber** in the first 'Tournament of Nations' in London, can only be called a tragicomedy. After the opening moves of a Bogo-Indian Defence, 1 d4 ♘f6 2 c4 e6 3 ♘f3 ♝b4+ 4 ♝d2, it seems that Black momentarily forgot which way round the king and queen go at the start of the game; he played 4...♚e7??, then in answer to 5 ♝xb4+ he calmly continued with 5...♚xb4!!?. The indescribable astonishment on his opponent's face and the spectators' hearty laughter compelled the Yugoslav master to look at the board and ... resign on the spot.

However, chess history, with its wealth of events and nuances, contains a unique case in which the inadvertent touching of a piece resulted in instant victory, and in an utterly hopeless position too. This surely belongs in the record books.

It occurred in one of the subsidiary tournaments at the traditional Hastings congress of 1990/91. A ten-year-old boy called Nikolai, the son of Soviet Germans who had been repatriated to Germany, was playing an elderly bespectacled lady, and set up mating threats against her king. Short-sighted as she was, she leaned so far over the table that she touched her own king with her nose (!) and knocked it off the board. The boy took this as a sign of resignation and stopped the clock, whereupon the controller immediately scored the game as a loss to him amid stern words of reproach.

In purely human terms, two players could probably claim to be record-holders in the sphere of bad luck. In the nineteenth century, there was the inventor of the counter-gambit 1 d4 d5 2 c4 e5, Adolf Albin; and in the twentieth – Julio Bolbochan.

The originally Romanian, later Hungarian (or Austro-Hungarian?) maestro took part in a fair number of international contests – over 25. He won at Vienna 1891 and 1892, and finished second in the New York tournaments of 1893 and 1894 (behind Lasker and Steinitz respectively). Albin was invited to such super-tournaments as Hastings 1895 and Nuremberg 1896 – where, to be sure, he failed to make the running. But it was only in the first memorial tournament to the great Ignatz Kolisch, one of the world's strongest chessplayers of 1860s, that he had serious cause to lament his fate. The double-round tournament with nine participants took place in Vienna in 1890. Albin, needless to say, fared poorly – he scored a mere 5 points (including one by default) and finished eighth. But even this wouldn't have been so bad if he had not been the only player to come away without a prize at the end of the tournament. The point is that although Joseph Holzwarth finished below him, scoring only one win and two draws from 11 games, he (Holzwarth) was not done out of a reward – a consolation prize! It came from a tender-hearted patron who suddenly took pity on this contestant who had withdrawn from the tournament after falling ill!

The younger of the Bolbochan brothers, Julio, became a Grandmaster at 57, which is 'indecently' late by our present-day standards. By that time he had practically retired from big-time chess and switched to coaching, but a quarter of a century earlier he had been a most prominent figure. Playing as high as board 2 in the the 1950 Olympiad, he made the top score for that board; later, in the four-round USSR-Argentina match of 1954, he held his own against none other than Keres; he twice won FIDE Zonal Tournaments, and took part in the 1962 Interzonal. He was also supposed to have played in two other Interzonal Tournaments, but that is where his record-breaking bad luck comes in.

In 1952 in the little Swedish town of Saltsjöbaden, Bolbochan only managed to play his opening game with Geller before falling so seriously ill that he had to abandon the battlefield. Oh well, these things happen; such is life. FIDE nominated him as a candidate for the next Interzonal, together with Grandmasters Kotov (USSR) and Pirc (Yugoslavia). He therefore assumed that he didn't need to play in the Zonal Tournament of 1954 at Buenos Aires in his own homeland. In the following year Bolbochan arrived on time at Göteborg, where precisely three places in the Interzonal had been reserved. However, the FIDE Congress, which was in session in the same place, suddenly decided not to allow the nominees into the tournament but to limit the number of participants to twenty-one. In terms of kilometres, then, the Argentinian had circled the entire globe for the purpose of playing one solitary game in two Interzonals!

In Olympiads, Caissa played more tricks on the Yugoslav Grandmaster Milan Matulović than on anyone else. His personal character, quite frankly, was none too estimable, but his play, over a relatively brief stretch of time, was simply superb, and he rightfully took his place in the 'Rest of the World' team which confronted the USSR in the 'Match of the Century'.

Matulović started playing for his country in 1964, and at the Tel-Aviv Olympiad he achieved the best result among the second reserves: +10 -1 =2. These 11 points out of 13 earned him a prize. He was to take part another three Olympiads. On all three occasions he scored the greatest number of points for his board – but no more prizes came his way!

At Lugano in 1968 he won 8 games, drew five and lost two. International Master Kogan made the same score of 10½, but he had only played 13 games! The Soviet Grandmaster Geller and the future Grandmaster Keene (England) also fared better than Matulović – on percentage, which is what takes precedence at Olympiads – so that the Yugoslav didn't even figure among a trio of fourth-board prizewinners.

Two years later at Siegen, Matulović performed well on third board with +10 -1 =6, that is 13 out of 17. The Englishman Hartston was half a point behind – but he had played a games less, so that once again the percentages were unkind to Matulović.

Finally, in the Jubilee 20th Olympiad at Skopje in 1972, in the role of first reserve, Matulović went through all his 18 games without loss, winning exactly half of them! His 13½ points enabled Yugoslavia to finish in the prize list, but brought nothing to him personally: the rising star Anatoly Karpov scored half a point less, but this was from 15 games only.

In my view, a firm place among these 'victims of fate' goes to one of the most outstanding players of the modern era – Leonid Stein. He became a master only at the age of 24, but within another 5 years he had attained that most difficult of goals: the gold medal in the national championship. Soon afterwards he twice repeated this superlative result. (He thus became the third player – after Botvinnik and Keres, and before Tal, Korchnoi, Karpov and Beliavsky – to win three USSR Championships.) He emerged as winner in one of the strongest tournaments of our time: Moscow 1967, dedicated to the 50th anniversary of the Great October

Socialist Revolution. Apart from Fischer and Korchnoi, practically all the world's strongest Grandmasters were present at this event. Stein also took part in the famous 'Match of the Century', but never once figured among the Candidates for the World Championship – through no fault of his own.

In the 1962 Interzonal he finished sixth, which would have qualified him for the Candidates Tournament – but for an insurmountable barrier in the shape of the FIDE ruling which only permitted a limited number of Candidates from any one country (read: 'from the USSR').

Two years later the situation repeated itself with just the difference that Stein was fifth – but the rule was still in force.

By the time of the next Interzonal, in 1967, FIDE had recognized the absurdity of its former ruling, so that this time the battle was fought out purely on the chessboard. Alas, out of inertia or whatever, Stein only obtained a share of 6th-8th places. An extra match-tournament was held as a play-off for the sole remaining place in the Candidates. It ended with the scores all level, whereupon the conventional Sonneborn-Berger tie-break system was applied to the original Interzonal result. Needless to say, the 'verdict' went against the man whom World Champion Karpov acknowledged as a stupendous talent.

Add to this the fact that, as a twenty-year-old candidate master, Stein had won a semi-final of the RSFSR Championship but didn't go forward to the final because the Soviet Army couldn't do without his services as a lance-corporal. And add the fact that four years later he was excluded from the Ukrainian Championship final because during the semi-final, which he won, he had been partial to spending the nights playing cards – which was frowned on by Soviet ideology. Should we perhaps conclude that Stein, who departed this life at 39, held the world record for ill luck?

Or was that record beaten by a chessplayer who was going to play in the US Open Championship in 1975 in the town of Lincoln, and whose story was told shortly afterwards in the American journal *Chess Life and Review*?

This player might possibly have won the tournament, but he was twice mugged on his way to the venue. Bearing up under the blows of fate, he drank away his troubles and then lobbed a brick through the plate glass of a shop window – for which he was arrested by the police. He was faced with a psychiatric examination and punishment for the damage he had caused. He telephoned the tournament director to appeal for help. On learning who the detainee was, the magistrate simply drawled, "Oh, a chess-player," and at once cancelled the psychiatric examination. The punishment was *not* cancelled, however, and the luckless fighter against fate and shop windows remained behind bars for precisely the twenty days during which the championship was held.

Peter Nielsen's performance in the Danish Championship of 1995 also stands out. The sole Grand-master on the list of competitors, he didn't succeed in winning a single game!

All connoisseurs and lovers of our ancient game were even more astonished by Viswanathan Anand's result in the category-21 tourn-ament at Dortmund in 2001. Anand was the reigning FIDE World Champion and occupied third place in the world ranking list – yet he finished last! In the double-round contest he lost nearly half his games and didn't win a single one. True, there were only six contestants, but that still doesn't explain Anand's resounding failure. He was just on the Island of Misfortune....

Chess is a game for individuals, but we may still try to identify a kind of 'group failure' that can count as a record. In January 1949 in a New York tournament, the last three lines on the score chart were filled by Isaac Kashdan, Arnold Denker and Herman Steiner – the US Champions of 1946, 1947 and 1948!

But what about the *luckiest* chessplayer? The balanced structure of our world – plus and minus, hot and cold, attraction and repulsion – definitely suggests that there must be such a person. As you will appreciate, candidates for this 'title' are legion – ranging from any tournament victor who had 'winner's luck' (in chess this expression is not unwarranted), to someone like Max Euwe, against whom Alexander Alekhine lost a World Championship match with rather less than a sober head (putting it mildly). But perhaps it is worth recalling the following story from over a century ago; will this not settle the question as to who was the luckiest of the lucky?

It happened in 1889 in Wroclaw, which in those days bore the German name of Breslau. The annual congress of the German Chess Federation was in progress there. The master tournament was for players who held that honourable title, while the 'main' tournament was for those who were seeking it. Among the latter were the three characters in our tale: Lipke, later to become a well-known master; Feyerfeil, a most gifted chessplayer whose name means nothing to anyone today; and the student philosoper from Berlin, Emanuel Lasker. To use the German expression which is more eloquent than 'poor student', Lasker was a *Hungerstudent*. He was studying philosophy and mathematics, striving to penetrate the essence of the world order, the imperfection of which was affecting him directly in the area of his stomach. What was chess to him at that time? A model of thought, as it is for present-day cybernetics? Or an intellectual recreation? Whatever the answer, one thing is definite: chess was far from being an activity to which he was prepared to devote his whole life. It is, however, an established fact that a year earlier Lasker had won a tournament held in the Berlin *Kaiserhof* café, and received a prize of a few marks – which for a brief period enabled the future World Chess Champion to cast his eyes on the menu. First tournament, first success. Lasker decided to try his hand at chess once more. But what if he was unsuccessful this time?

One of his biographers maintains that Lasker had repeatedly told his brother Berthold of his intention to quit chess at once if he should fail to gain the master title at his first attempt.

So here he was, in the Breslau 'main' tournament. It was overshadowed by the master tournament in which the 27-year-old doctor of medicine Siegbert Tarrasch, himself a master of less than two years' standing, was trouncing the star players of Europe. Feyerfeil beat Lasker – a storm in a teacup. Lasker suffered one other defeat against a complete outsider. At the end of the tournament he had conceded two points. Feyerfeil finished with the same score – he had drawn two games and lost to Lipke. On tie-break, first prize and the master title were awarded to Lasker.

But the whole point is that Feyerfeil ought *not* to have lost to Lipke. And the reason has nothing to do with chess ability, nothing to do with (say) an unsound combination. It was a sheer accident – they forgot to place a pawn on the board after the adjournment!

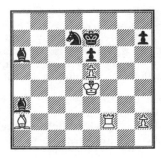

On resuming the game, Feyerfeil with White played ♖f2-h2. As the reader will have guessed, this move was only made possible because the white h-pawn had been left off through someone's carelessness. Thus a rook's pawn which, by an irony of fate, had remained unmoved all game, fulfilled its historic role. If it had stayed in place, White might well have secured a draw, and the course of chess history might have been radically altered. And Feyerfeil? His name was not to appear in any more tournament tables....

No, it is not at all a *fact* that if Lasker had come second in the Breslau tournament he would have focused all his powerful intellect on mathematics (game theory and all), on philosophy, and on drama – while expunging chess from his life. At the end of the day, a seed fallen on the ground will even push its way up through concrete. And yet – who knows, who knows?

Profession: champion

First place, the top step on the winners' podium – this is what literally everyone aims for. It is no accident that a special commission at the end of the twentieth century demonstrated that our game of the intellect is a sport, and that chess ought therefore to be accepted into the great Olympic family. And of course, a victory is especially heartwarming if the victor starts to be called a champion just after it.

One earnest and convincing bid for Champion status was made by the English player Michael Adams in the 1982-83 season, when he became the simultaneous holder of his country's Under-11, Under-13, Under-15 and Under-18 titles, as well as being adult champion and blitz champion of the County of Cornwall. However, ten years passed, and though Adams duly became one of the world's strongest Grandmasters, his laurel wreaths are not at the moment increasing.

And yet many people have contrived to win championships several times over. Within a specific country, especially one where mass interest in chess is in its early stages of development, the game has tended to be dominated by a very narrow group of players, one of whom gains the highest national honours more often than the rest. Among those who have been national champion 5, 6, 7, 9 or 10 times, I may name Gösta Stoltz of Sweden, Fridrik Olafsson of Iceland (masters and Grandmasters with this surname, an extremely common one in their country, have won the Icelandic Championship 13 times between them), the Bulgarian master Alexandar Tsvetkov (who had taken part in the Chigorin Memorial tournament in Moscow shortly after the Second World War and finished last by a wide margin, registering only four draws in fifteen games), the Romanians Victor Ciocaltea and Florin Gheorghiu, the Englishman Jonathan Penrose (in the period 1958-69 he only twice relinquished the British Championship), the Italian master Stefano Tatai, the American Grandmasters Samuel Reshevsky and Robert Fischer, and the two Wolfgangs – Uhlmann of the German Democratic Republic and Unzicker of the Federal Republic of Germany. (The latter was the first post-war champion of both German states, which at that time could not even hope for reunification.)

Some of the champions have gone even further. Svetozar Gligorić won the Yugoslav Championship 11 times, but even prior to that he had been national amateur champion. In recognition of this and other achievements, the illustrious Grandmaster was accorded the right of participation in the championships of his very chess-minded country for the rest of his life, and at least until the age of 75 he was glad to make use of such an unusual privilege. In the years 1926-36 the Dane Erik Andersen only once conceded the palm of victory to another participant in his country's championship, which he won 12 times in all. His 'neighbours' Karle Ojanen and Max Euwe 'reigned' over Finnish and Dutch chess for many a long year. Eight of Euwe's 13 championship titles were gained when he already held the rank of ex-World Champion.

Nonetheless the Dane Ingrid Larsen and the New Zealander Ortvin Sarapu remain the absolute record holders in this field, with 17 and 16 gold medals respectively in their national championships! Statements that the latter also won the Australian Championship crop up here and there in chess literature, but they are unconfirmed. The Estonian New Zealander or New Zealand Estonian amassed his collection of titles over the course of 30 years, but only became an International Master after the first half of these triumphs; and in his infrequent top-ranking

tournaments, such as the 1967 Sousse Interzonal and the World Olympiads, he basically played the role of a 'chopping block'. There is an old Russian folk fable about the 'top dog' in the village, which inevitably comes to mind here.

We should take all this into account when assessing Sarapu's chess 'reign', which in terms of duration was lengthy but far from a record. The epoch of Paul and Hans Johner in Switzerland – that well-ordered country which was not, however, too 'chess-minded' in those years – is more significant. The brothers shared victory in the country's championship for the first time in 1908, and for the third time 24 years later.

In addition the elder brother won two championships on his own and the younger won nine, the last of which was in 1950 when he was 61 years old – that is, 42 years after his first success! Yet though this is a record figure, I cannot help highlighting Grandmaster Robert Hübner's achievement in Germany, a country which *is* very much geared to chess. In 1999, when already past the age of 50, he won the country's championship which had first fallen to him 32 years earlier as a young man of nineteen! Needless to say, in the little town of Altenkirchen near Cologne he was competing with many opponents young enough to be his children or grandchildren. After drawing three games with world-class Grandmasters – Artur Yusupov and others – he scored six wins thanks to his deep positional understanding and outstanding technique. Here is one example of how he exploited his advantage:

Hübner – K.Müller

**52 ♘d4 ♕c7+ 53 ♔e4 f5+
54 ♔d3 ♕e7 55 ♘e6+ ♔f6 56 ♘c5
g5 57 ♘xb7 g4 58 ♘d6 ♕e6
59 ♕d4+ ♔g6 60 ♘c4 g3 61 ♕f4
♕d5+ 62 ♔e3 ♕g2 63 ♔d4 ♕g1+
64 ♘e3 ♕a1+ 65 ♔d3 ♕b1+ 66
♔c4 ♔f6 67 ♘d5+ ♔e6 68 ♕h6+
♔d7 69 ♕g7+ ♔e6 70 ♕e7 mate**

The Soviet Grandmaster Efim Geller's achievement calls for very special acclaim. Twenty-four years after his first victory in the championship of the world's strongest chess power, he repeated this feat at the age of 55. Veteran as he was, he displayed youthful energy in games such as the following.

Geller – Anikaev
USSR Championship, Minsk 1979
(notes by Geller)

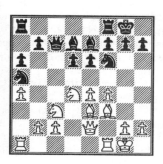

13 g4

The plan with 13 ♖ad1 ♘c4 14 ♗c1 was more solid and perhaps stronger, but I was in an aggressive mood that evening.

13...♖fc8?

Black wants to bring his rook into play, and counts on repelling the kingside attack without its aid. However, he is not only losing time but irreparably weakening f7. In this situation 13...♖ac8 would also be slow, and would be no improvement on account of 14 g5 ♘e8 15 f5 ♘c4 16 fxe6 fxe6 17 ♗g4 ♘xe3 18 ♕xe3 with a very strong initiative.

The sharpness of the position demands immediate action on Black's part, and this purpose would be served by 13...♘c4. During the game I considered the reply 14 g5 ♘e8 15 ♘f5! ♗d8 (if 15...exf5, then 16 ♘d5 ♕d8 17 ♕xc4) 16 ♗d4 exf5 17 ♖ae1 or even 17 ♔h1, with a powerful attacking position for the sacrificed piece.

14 g5 ♘e8 15 f5 ♘c4 16 ♗h5

A perfectly adequate alternative was 16 fxe6 fxe6 (or 16...♗xe6 17 ♘xe6 fxe6 18 ♗g4) 17 ♗g4, and Black is unable to defend e6 properly – since after 17...♘xe3 18 ♕xe3 ♕c4 the simple 19 ♕f2 is decisive. But the move played is highly effective too, as it forces a drastic weakening of Black's king position. White had, in fact, calculated everything almost to the end.

16...g6 17 fxg6 fxg6 18 ♕f2 ♘e5 19 ♘f3

If Black's sole defender – the knight on e5 – is exchanged off, his position will collapse. He therefore contrives to bring up his reserves.

19...♘g7 20 ♘xe5 ♖f8 21 ♘f7 ♘xh5?

Allowing White to finish the game by force in a striking manner. Instead 21...gxh5 was more tenacious, though after 22 ♗d4 it would still be virtually impossible to stem White's attack; if 22...♗xg5, then 23 ♕g3.

22 ♘d5!

White needs to prevent his opponent from blocking the long black diagonal with e6-e5.

22...exd5 23 ♘h6+ ♔g7

Alternatively 23...♔h8 24 ♗d4+ ♘g7 25 ♗xg7+ ♔xg7 26 ♕d4+ ♗f6 27 ♖xf6 ♕c5 28 ♖f7 mate.

24 ♕f7+!

This is much quicker and more rational than 24 ♗d4+ ♗f6 25 gxf6+ ♔xh6 26 ♕h4 g5 27 ♗e3 ♖g8 28 f7 etc.

24...♖xf7 25 ♖xf7+ ♔h8 26 ♗d4+ ♗f6 27 ♖xf6

Now if 27...♘xf6 then 28 ♗xf6 mate.

1-0

The game was rewarded with a special prize.

If we make no division between men's and women's chess, then the record laurels should rightfully be handed to the Englishwoman Edith Price. She won the Ladies' Championship of her island in 1922, 1923, 1924, 1928 and 1948, at the ages of 50, 51, 52, 56 and 76 respectively! All the same it is essential to note that this happened partly before and partly after the era of the first Women's World Champion, Vera Menchik-Stevenson.

In the USSR, where first place in a championship was harder to achieve than anywhere else in the world, the national record was held by two Mikhails, Botvinnik and Tal, who won six times each. It is true that Botvinnik also triumphed in the tournament for the title of 'Absolute Champion of the USSR', but that contest was clearly artificial and remained unique in the chess history of the country and the world.

There are also some record instances of a player collecting championship titles from different countries. First in line was the Englishman Henry Ernest Atkins. To begin with he made a 'clean score', 15 out of 15, in the tournament at Amsterdam in 1899, thereby becoming the first foreign Champion of the Netherlands. After that he 'got to grips' with his own compatriots, winning the British Championship nine times between 1900 and 1925. The phenomenon of 'champion foreigners' did not become widespread, however, until roughly half a century later. After winning the US Championship five times and reaching the Interzonal Tournament by a roundabout route, Grandmaster Walter Browne went on to win the Championship of Australia. After immense difficulties which took up seven years of his life, the USSR Champion Boris Gulko extricated himself from the clutches of the Soviet authorities and went to the USA where he won the Championship twice. His wife Anna Akhsharumova gained the same combination of titles – this may rightly be considered a record for a family. After two victories each in USSR Championships, Boris Spassky and Anatoly Karpov both won the West German Open Championship twice, and Spassky came first in the French Championship also. Leonid Stein won the East German Championship before becoming three-times Champion of the USSR.

Some chessplayers were positively compelled by destiny to collect different titles like this. Thus, the Austrian Grandmaster Erich Gottlieb Eliskases, a highly prominent figure in the 1930s (he won three matches against Rudolf Spielmann and one long one, consisting of 20 games, against Efim Bogoljubow) was of course champion of his own country, and also (in his spare time, so to speak) won the Open Championship of Hungary – a tournament dedicated to Geza Maroczy's fifty years of chess activity and comprising a very impressive list of entries. After Austria was swallowed up by Hitler, Eliskases twice had occasion, whether he liked it or not, to be champion of 'Greater' Germany. After the 1939 Olympiad, not wishing to return to the fascist paradise, he remained in Argentina, but unfortunately the championship of a fourth country eluded him; unlike the Polish Champion Miguel

Najdorf, who won the Argentine event several times, Eliskases only managed second or third place.

Viktor Korchnoi too won national championships in three countries – in the USSR (four times), and then, after leaving his native land for good, in the Netherlands and Switzerland.

They were all outdone, however, by Grandmaster Leonid Shamkovich, that 'chess workman' as he called himself. To start with, he twice came first in the Championship of the RSFSR, the largest of the Soviet Republics which has become present-day Russia. Then after emigrating to Israel he acquired the title of Champion there too. Later moving to the USA, he finished first in two American Championships and also took part in the Open Championship of Canada – where he gained one further title to add to his sporting trophies. Set beside such a service record, Grandmaster Roman Dzhindzhikhashvili's exploits pale somewhat – *he* won the championships of Soviet Georgia, Israel and the USA 'only'.

But should not Cecil John Seddon Purdy be considered the outright record holder in this area? In the first place, he won the Australian Championship four times. (Another two wins in the contest went to his son, John Spencer Purdy; another four had gone to the latter's maternal grandfather, Spencer Krekkentorp.) Cecil's play in these events was enterprising, fresh and exuberant; the following game, against another player who several times won the championship, is only one example.

Koshnitsky – Purdy
Sydney 1945
Catalan System [E01]

1 c4 e6 2 ♘c3 ♘f6 3 g3 d5 4 d4 c5 5 cxd5 ♘xd5 6 ♗g2 ♘xc3 7 bxc3 cxd4 8 cxd4 ♗b4+ 9 ♗d2 ♕xd4 10 ♖c1 0-0 11 ♘f3 ♗xd2+ 12 ♘xd2 ♘c6 13 0-0 ♖d8 14 ♘b3 ♕b6 15 ♕c2 ♗d7 16 ♘c5 ♘d4 17 ♘xd7 ♖xd7 18 ♕c4 ♕b2 19 ♖fe1 ♖ad8 20 e3 b5 21 ♕f1 ♘c2 22 ♖ed1 ♖xd1 23 ♖xd1 ♖xd1 24 ♕xd1 g6 25 ♗e4 ♘a3 26 ♕d8+ ♔g7 27 h4 ♘c4 28 h5 ♕e5 29 ♗f3 a5 30 a4 ♘xe3 31 axb5 ♕a1+ 32 ♔h2 ♕b2 33 h6+ ♔xh6 34 ♕f8+ ♔g5 35 ♕e7+ f6 36 ♕c5+ ♘d5 37 ♗xd5 exd5 38 ♔h3 h5 39 f4+ ♔h6 40 ♕f8+ ½-½

Secondly, Purdy twice won the Championship of New Zealand. Thirdly, he became Champion of Australasia. Fourthly and fifthly, he won the Australian and Australasian correspondence championships. A sixth and final achievement was victory in the World Correspondence Chess Championship, the first ever to be held. Can over-the-board and postal titles be placed in the same basket? I wouldn't know, and I can only suggest that each reader resolves this question for himself.

In the matter of world chess crowns, the record belongs to Anatoly Karpov. He has three laurel wreaths to his name, as the 12th outright World Champion, FIDE World Champion and World Speed Chess Champion. As to his victory in the very first Speed Championship of Europe in 1988, his two gold medals in the USSR Championship, and the title of World Junior Champion as far back as 1969 – these, so to speak, are a supplement,

and an important and worthy one, to his chief honours. Emanuel Lasker could have had 6 different wreaths if they had been awarded in his day, while Mikhail Botvinnik really did receive 5 awards for his outstanding chess prowess. Garry Kasparov too received 5, as well as some others for speed chess. In short, my friends, it's up to you to choose between them.

Personally, though, I would single out Nona Gaprindashvili – and for reasons that have nothing to do with chivalry. The incomparable Nona – as they call her in Georgia – won the Women's World Championship five times, and was five times champion of the the strongest chess power, the USSR. As a member of the Soviet women's team she was 10 times an Olympic gold medallist. Furthermore Nona was the first holder of the title of Woman Grandmaster and the first woman to gain the corresponding men's title.

Quite a few chessplayers have won their first championship not in their own homeland but after moving to another country. This mainly applies to Grandmasters (or even just masters) who were once Soviet citizens: Gennady Sosonko became Champion of the Netherlands, Anatoly Vaisser of France, Vladimir Liberzon of Israel, and Igor Ivanov of Canada. But the record here, which is hard to surpass, must be accorded to the Swiss player who won the British Championship in 2001. This player was none other than ... the Englishman Joe Gallagher, who had relocated to a country where English is one language missing from the list of four official ones.

Such are the quirks concocted by life in general and chess life in particular!

In the sphere of team performances at national level, there is no one to rival the USSR team or their successors the Russian team. Making their first appearance in the international arena as late as 1952, they accumulated a record collection of Olympic gold medals, not to mention victories in European Championships, world telex chess championships, world Internet championships and numerous Women's Olympiads. One generation took over from another; even the national champion in an 'Olympic year' couldn't always be sure of a place in the team. In a word, Fischer was right when he once said to me, "One brilliant player can be be born anywhere, but as a team, *you* are invincible." Who knows if these words will still hold good in the future ...?

One other record of sorts beongs to the Grandmaster from Lvov, Alexander Beliavsky. A four-times USSR Champion, he has headed the Olympic teams of three different countries – the USSR at Buenos Aires in 1986, the independent Ukraine at Yerevan in 1996, and Slovenia in subsequent Olympiads. Naturally he always had a passport in his pocket from the respective state.

One final thought. Although child labour is severely restricted and sometimes prohibited outright by the legislatures of many civilized countries, the profession of 'champion' in chess is taken up literally by little boys and girls. Thus, Niaz Murshed won the Championship of Bangladesh in 1979 at the age of 12 years and 309 days. Luke McShane played in the much stronger British Championship in 1995 at an even younger age – he was 11, and World Under-10 Champion – but first place was then out of the question. José Raoul Capablanca, the brilliant *Wunderkind*, won his match against Juan Corzo at the age of 13, and from 1901 he was considered the strongest player in Cuba – although officially the title of Champion was not recognized there until a year later. Likewise at 13, Enrique Costa Mecking came first in the Championship of Brazil; he was later to be the only player to win two World Championship Interzonals. However, the Cuba of the early 20th century, Bangladesh, and even Brazil at the time in question, were somewhat out-of-the-way countries in chess terms, and the emerging young talents were clearly superior to their none-too-numerous compatriot rivals – or even head and shoulders above them. In its context, Robert James Fischer's achievement was much greater: at the age of 14 he defeated and surpassed all the strongest Grandmasters and masters of the USA, before gaining 7 further victories in the championship of what was one of the world's highest-ranking chess countries. One of the championships of the chess super-power, the USSR, was won by Svetlana Matveeva, now a Grandmaster, when she was just 15! The same feat was accomplished by the Spaniard Arturo Pomar in 1946 (Alekhine himself had worked with him a short time earlier) and the Norwegian Simen Agdestein in 1982. Maia Chiburdanidze won a very strong USSR Women's Championship at the age of 16, before putting on the world chess crown three years later (a female record!). However, it is Judit Polgar who can and must be considered the absolute record holder here. The youngest of the three legendary sisters, at the age of 15 she became Champion of Hungary – in the men's event! That 1991 Championship was a category 12 tournament and included nearly all the strongest Grandmasters of this very strong chessplaying country; they were attracted by the lucrative prize fund of a million forints.

Judit covered the distance without loss, registering 3 wins and 6 draws and finishing half a point ahead of such aces as Grandmasters Andras Adorjan and Gyula Sax. She immediately gained a double entry in the Guinness Book of Records – for becoming the youngest Grandmaster in the men's category at that time, and for being the first female player to win a men's championship. Here is the style in which she did it:

Tolnai – J.Polgar

20...♘c4! 21 ♘xe6 ♘xe5 22 ♕g3 ♘xe6 23 ♗f5 ♔b8 24 ♗xe6 bxc3 25 ♘xc3 d4 26 ♖hf1 ♗b4 27 ♘a4

♖he8 28 ♗f5 ♗c6 29 ♗b2 g6 30 ♗b1 ♗xa4 31 bxa4 ♗c3 32 ♗xc3 ♕xc3+ 33 ♕xc3 dxc3 34 ♖c1 ♖c8 35 ♖f4 ♖c5! 36 ♖b4+ ♔a7 37 ♖b3 ♖ec8 38 ♗e4 ♖8c7 39 ♖cb1 ♘c6 40 ♗xc6 ♖5xc6 41 ♖b4 ♖c4 42 a3 ♖xb4 43 axb4 ♖c4 44 h5 a5! 45 hxg6 hxg6 46 ♔a2 ♖xb4 47 ♖g1 c2 48 g5 ♔b6 0-1

This success enabled young Judit, officially still only a master, to head the women's world ranking list.

But even earlier – by a full 4 years! – in 1988 at Saloniki, she had become the youngest-ever gold medallist in a Chess Olympiad. The Hungarian women's team, consisting of the three Polgar sisters – Zsuzsa, Zsofia and Judit – and Ildiko Madl, finished in front of the previously invincible Soviet team with the reigning World Champion Maia Chiburdanidze at its head. As you can easily work out, Judit was then 11 years old; it will hardly be possible to break such a record. After all, to do so, it wouldn't be enough to play brilliantly yourself; you would also have to belong to a very strong team. Incidentally, a few days before this, Judit had been awarded the women's International Grandmaster title!

In the Men's Olympiad, practically no one apart from the Soviet or Russian players has had the chance to be a youthful champion, seeing that the Soviet team and its Russian successor have won every Olympiad in the past half century with just two exceptions (putting aside one occasion when they didn't take part, for the sordid political 'reasons' of the authorities). When the overall best result – 8½ out of 9 – in the 1992

Manila Olympiad was achieved by the 17-year-old Vladimir Kramnik for Russia, this seemed to raise the record hurdle to an unattainable height; we should note that in all of that half-century Kramnik was the first team member to be under 20, let alone by a margin of two and a half years.

Kramnik's record feat appeared to receive indirect confirmation when he became World Champion in the autumn of 2000. However, at almost exactly the same time the Russians were winning another Olympiad, at Istanbul – and one of their number, Alexander Grischuk, gave a magnificent performance. He too was 17 years of age, and indeed a few months younger than Kramnik had been at Saloniki!

Very well then – is the world chess throne destined for him too?

Negative distinction

"If you chop wood or write novels instead of playing chess, it is sometimes much more useful to humanity."

These words are by that well-known wit Professor Josef Krejcik, and there have been plenty of lovers of the ancient game who could very well have written them on their chess CV's. But which of these players was worst of all? Or – to paraphrase Eric Birmingham, the chess columnist of *L'Humanité* – which of them achieved the greatest negative distinction? On a local level this is practically impossible to establish, but international level is another matter. Here the Englishman George Hatfield Dingley Gossip, who lived for

alternate spells in the USA and Great Britain, can probably feel safe from competition.

He entered the third London international tournament in 1972, and came second to last with the score of +1 -6. (Naturally he beat the contestant who 'achieved' zero.) Next, he had a perfectly decent result – by his own standards! – in the New York tournament in the spring of 1889. (He finished 17th-18th out of 20 participants, collecting 13½ points out of a possible 38. The winners were Mikhail Chigorin and the Austro-Hungarian Max Weiss; they scored 15½ points more!) After that, Gossip persistently finished in last place in all the contests in which he took part: the 6th German Chess Federation congress, Breslau 1889; Manchester 1890; the 7th British Chess Association congress, London 1892; New York 1893.... His tally of points was always small: 4 out of 19, 3 out of 17, 2½ out of 13.... And yet against one group of opponents, all with identical or similar surnames, Gossip played with vastly more success than against anyone else! Thus, in New York 1889, he twice won crushingly against such an experienced and solid master as Henry Edward Bird, while conceding only one point out of four against J.W.Baird and D.G.Baird. In the summer of the same year, in Breslau, Gossip held his own against no less an opponent than Amos Burn. The latter had not only defeated Steinitz in his time; in the general estimation he was virtually England's strongest player. Twenty years later he would be invited to the Chigorin Memorial super-tournament in Moscow. In the Breslau tournament we are speaking of, he finished second only to Tarrasch himself.

Our hero G.H.D.Gossip didn't rest content with this. In Manchester he scored half a point against the third prize winner – that same Henry Bird, who incidentally devised a system in the 'Lopez' that is still seen today: 1 e4 e5 2 ♘f3 ♘c6 3 ♗b5 ♘d4. Bird also bequeathed to us the opening 1 f4 which bears his name, and was the first player in chess history to win a brilliancy prize.

Explaining Gossip's astonishing good fortune against Bird, the Bairds and Burn is scarcely possible; it is not within *my* powers, at any rate. As for constantly finishing at the foot of the table, it is perfectly possible that Mr Gossip possessed neither a herculean constitution nor even a normal level of health. And the schedule of those tournaments was punishing: 17 rounds in 12 days, 19 rounds in 13 days.... This was all the more significant since Gossip didn't conserve his energy: he would fight on in every game, literally until mate. Never mind if the opponent had two queens to his one, or a 'whole' extra rook or bishop!

Perhaps Chigorin was taking this stubbornness into account when he spent a mere 18 minutes on his game with Gossip in New York 1889, delivering mate on the 15th move:

Chigorin – Gossip
Scotch Gambit [C44]

1 e4 e5 2 ♘f3 ♘c6 3 c3 d5 4 ♕a4 f6 5 ♗b5 ♘ge7 6 exd5 ♕xd5 7 0-0

♗d7 8 d4 e4 9 ♘fd2 ♘g6?
The right move was 9...f5, fortifying the advanced post on e4 in good time.
10 ♗c4 ♕a5 11 ♕b3 f5?
Here this is a mistake; the least of the evils was 11...0-0-0.
12 ♗f7+ ♔e7?
Just how many wrong moves is it possible to play?
13 ♘c4 ♕a6 14 ♗g5+ ♔xf7 15 ♘d6 mate!

It was perhaps only Colonel C.Moreau who could to some extent rival Gossip for the title of 'anti-chessplayer'. Moreau was admitted at the last minute to the extremely strong Monte Carlo tournament of 1903, and not only finished in last place but lost all 26 of his games! He appears to have been yearning for a draw just as passionately as his compatriot General Bonaparte yearned for victory at Waterloo – he played the Exchange Variation against Schlechter's French Defence, for instance – but was routed by all the devices of both the old and the new schools.

After this, the colonel broke all records by the number of gifts he received! Sarcastic spectators brought him (or even posted him) hens' and quails' eggs, potatoes, tomatoes, apples, beads – in a word, anything shaped like a zero. Needless to say, each gift consisted of precisely 26 articles.

In Moreau's defence I must add that there are no reports of his participation in any other tournaments of any note at all, either before or after the Monte Carlo fiasco. This was quite unlike the frequent performances of

Gossip, who, as they say, lost no sleep over them.

We may note by the way that M.Didier, the Frenchman at the bottom of the table of the very first Monte Carlo tournament in 1901, succeeded in scoring just one quarter of a point from 13 games, but this quaint episode is explained in the chapter 'Sergeant-major's orders'.

From studying some old tournament charts you may unearth a similar 'achievement' by a genuinely strong player, the well-known theoretician and chess writer Curt von Bardeleben (never mind that the great Steinitz defeated him in what is possibly the most beautiful game in the whole of chess literature). In 1897 he was credited with half a point out of 19 in a tournament in his native city, Berlin. Don't believe your eyes, however; research has ascertained that this aristocrat (a most democratic one, by the way) withdrew from the contest after only playing a single game. The 18 zeroes, discrediting him for posterity, were entered against his name in accordance with primitive regulations of that time, which were soon to be discarded.

The absolute record for the number of lost games (games *actually* lost!) in one tournament was established for all time by the American Nicholas MacLeod. In the 1889 New York tournament that we have mentioned already (it was known officially as the Sixth American Chess Congress), this contestant finished bottom with 6½ points out of a possible 38, having lost 31 games (!). There can be no 'improving' on this 'achievement' if

only because such monster tournaments have not been held for more than a hundred years and are unlikely to be held in future.

In recent times, the record for failure may be claimed by two players. One is Kamran Shirazi, who scored half a point from 17 wholly genuine games in the 1984 US Championship. The other is Arnold Sheldon Denker. He was Champion of the USA in 1944 and 1946, and still capable of second place in the US Open Championship several years later. In 1981 FIDE corrected its own injustice and granted him the Grandmaster title at the age of 67. In 1971, however, he had ended up in last place in the master tournament at Wijk aan Zee, where he was the most experienced participant. He explained his failure by his long absence from competition. The following year Denker entered for the tournament again, announcing that he would be first this time. At the opening ceremony his letter to the organizers was read aloud, and at the drawing of lots the venerable American drew ... number one!

"See, I've kept my word!" Denker exclaimed – and again he was to finish last.

The most learned, the most eminent

Who *was* most learned or eminent? No arithmetically precise answer exists, because no one has established any absolute criteria for learning or eminence – and no one ever will. Who, for instance, was more influential within his own historical epoch – Alfonso X 'the Wise', King of Castille and Léon, on whose orders the first chess book in Europe was written? Or the master of all Europe and terror of all ruling houses in the Old World, the revolutionarly General Bonaparte who later stooped to taking the imperial title of Napoleon I? As it happens, he played chess quite often! As a rule he would win, although his grasp of the game was weak even for those philosophical times. As a tactician he was tolerably competent. There are two authentic encounters of his that history has preserved for us.

Napoleon I –
Madame de Rémusat
Paris, 20 March 1804
Napoleon's Opening (?) [A00]

1 ♘c3

Away from the chessboard, the warlord of genius would never have begun his battles with a cavalry attack.

1...e5 2 ♘f3 d6 3 e4 f5 4 h3 fxe4 5 ♘xe4 ♘c6 6 ♘fg5 d5 7 ♕h5+ g6 8 ♕f3 ♘h6 9 ♘f6+ ♔e7 10 ♘xd5+ ♔d6 11 ♘e4+ ♔xd5 12 ♗c4+ ♔xc4 13 ♕b3+ ♔d4 14 ♕d3 mate

The Emperor truly cut a dash, then – among sheep. But as soon as he faced a rather stronger opponent, the tables were turned with a vengeance:

Napoleon I –
Kempelen's Automaton
Schönbrunn 1809
Queen's Opening (?) [C24]

1 e4 e5 2 ♕f3 ♘c6 3 ♗c4 ♘f6 4 ♘e2 ♗c5 5 a3 d6 6 0-0 ♗g4 7 ♕d3 ♘h5 8 h3 ♗xe2 9 ♕xe2

♘f4 10 ♕e1 ♘d4 11 ♗b3 ♘xh3+ 12 ♔h2 (12 gxh3 ♘f3+) **12...♕h4 13 g3 ♘f3+ 14 ♔g2 ♘xe1+ 15 ♖xe1 ♕g4 16 d3 ♗xf2 17 ♖h1 ♕xg3+ 18 ♔f1 ♗d4 19 ♔e2 ♕g2+ 20 ♔d1 ♕xh1+ 21 ♔d2 ♕g2+ 22 ♔e1 ♘g1 23 ♘c3 ♗xc3+ 24 bxc3 ♕e2 mate**

But perhaps the hero of this chapter should be Pope John Paul II. At an advanced age, this holder of the supreme spiritual office continued playing chess by correspondence (albeit under a pseudonym), and the Milan newspaper *Corriere della Sera* reported that he had discussed some opening variations with Garry Kasparov when the World Champion was received at the Vatican in 1990. In Paris in 1999, at FIDE's 75th birthday celebrations, a personal representative of the Pope stated that his Holiness devoted two hours to chess every day. The Spanish King and the Emperor of the French possessed power, in the full sense of the word, over the lives of their subjects. The Pope, on the other hand, held sway over the minds and hearts of billions (!) of Catholics including Japanese and Chinese, Africans and Australians, and inhabitants of all countries in Europe and both American continents. We have no scale with which to measure the importance of these three historical figures. Yet in terms of personal attachment to our game, **Karol Wojtyla** – such was his worldly name before he took holy orders – far surpassed the others. In 1987 the English journal *The Problemist* even published a problem he had composed in his youth.

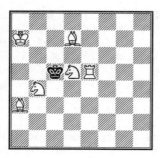

White mates in 2 moves

The first thing to note is that this is a miniature – a category of problems held in special esteem. Secondly it is a so-called 'aristocratic' problem – there are no pawns on the board. And thirdly, the solution is beautiful: **1 ♗b5!!**, and then 1...♚d6 2 ♘d3 mate; or 1...♚d4 2 ♘c6 mate; or 1...♚xb5 2 ♘b6 mate.

Most probably the young man of many talents was drawn to chess compositions under the influence of his own uncle, Marian Wrubel – one of Poland's leading problemists. There was only about a decade separating the two relatives – any age barrier between them would soon have disappeared, and the successes of the older one simply could not fail to exert a gentle influence on the younger. In a word, while chess did not become central to the life of God's future representative on earth, it occupied a favoured corner of his heart.

For this reason I think there is much symbolic significance in the fact that in 1992, the firm *Superpukar Polski* chose the John Paul II Museum of Art as a place to stage the match for the national championship, between Alexander Wojtkiewicz and Alexander Sznapik.

The Pope – who was, after all, probably the most eminent figure who ever played chess – is sure to have followed the course of the match, despite the fact that in the medieval statutes of the Order of the Knights Templars, chess was stated to be neither more nor less than the 'eighth deadly sin' after the seven biblical ones!

As for scientists, there have always been plenty of them in chess. On an amateur level there was Albert Einstein, the greatest mind of the 20th century; Dmitry Mendeleev, originator of the periodic table of elements; the Nobel Prize winners Frédéric Joliot-Curie and Pyotr Kapitsa; the mathematician Leonhard Euler; the father of cybernetics, Norbert Wiener – it would be impossible to list them all. Like for example the outstanding mathematician Andrei Markov the elder, they would sometimes prevail against players of world repute and win modest-sized tournaments at local level. But Vasily Omeliansky – the famous microbiologist, member of the Russian Imperial Academy of Sciences, corresponding member of the Turin Medical Academy, the Lombard Academy and the American Society of Bacteriologists – was once even invited into the professional forum. In 1905/06 he played in the Fourth All-Russian Tournament, in other words the championship of the country!

So perhaps the scientist who 'went furthest' in chess was Vasily Leonardovich Omeliansky. Or was he?...

On more than one occasion the British team included Sir Robert

Robinson, who became a Fellow of the Royal Society (the British academy of sciences) at the age of 34. A quarter of a century later he assumed the post of President of that body, and was honoured with the Nobel Prize for Chemistry. He was also asked to head the International Correspondence Chess Association, but his scientific workload was too great for him to take up the offer. To Grandmaster Erik Lundin, Sir Robert said, "I've played chess all my life, but these days I can only spare the time for postal play." This play was admittedly not lacking in talent!

Gannholm – Robinson
Correspondence match
Sweden v England, 1947-9
Queen's Pawn Opening [D05]

1 d4 ♘f6 2 ♘f3 e6 3 e3 c5 4 ♗d3 d5 5 b3 ♘c6 6 ♘e5 cxd4 7 ♘xc6 bxc6 8 exd4 c5 9 ♗b2 ♗d6 10 ♗b5+ ♗d7 11 ♗xd7+ ♕xd7 12 dxc5 ♗xc5 13 0-0 h5!

The signal for a fierce kingside attack.

14 ♘d2 ♖d8 15 ♕f3 ♖h6 16 ♖ad1 ♕c7 17 ♕e2 ♘g4 18 ♘f3 d4! 19 h3 ♖d5 20 c4 ♖f5 21 ♗xd4

21...♗xd4?
A sad lapse. By sacrificing the exchange and then his queen, Black could have pursued his plan to victory: 21...♖xf3! 22 hxg4 hxg4 23 ♗e5 (or 23 g3 ♕c6) 23...♖f5!! 24 ♗xc7 ♖fh5 with unavoidable mate.

22 ♖xd4 ♖xf3 (too late!) 23 hxg4 hxg4 24 g3 f5 25 ♖d3 ♕b7 26 ♖xf3 gxf3 27 ♕d3 ♔f7 28 ♖e1 f4 29 ♕e4 ♕xe4 30 ♖xe4 fxg3 31 fxg3 g5 32 a4 ♖h8 33 b4 ♖d8 34 ♔f2 ♖d3 35 b5 ♔f6 36 g4 e5 37 c5 ♔e6 38 ♖c4 ♔d7 39 c6+ ♔c7 40 ♖e4 ♔d6 41 a5 ♖d5 42 ♖c4 e4 43 c7 ♖d2+ 44 ♔e3, and Robinson had to acknowledge defeat in a game which by rights should have gone the other way (**1-0**).

Innumerable chess professionals have distinguished themselves additionally in the world of learning. Among those who attained professorial chairs and high academic honours, I may name the following. In *philology*: Larisa Volper, three times USSR Women's Champion and Candidate for the world chess crown; Alexandra van der Mije (Nicolau), six times Women's Champion of Romania and likewise a World Championship candidate; and Robert Hübner, who went as far as the Candidates Final. In *medicine*: the famous surgeon and Swiss Champion Oskar Naegeli. In *history*: the World Correspondence Champion Vladimir Zagorovsky. In *mathematics*: the ex-World Champion Max Euwe, and the English Grandmaster John Denis Martin Nunn – who was the youngest student in Great Britain for 400 years, winner of many major tournaments and silver medallist in the World Problem Solving Championship. In *technology*: Alexander Guliaev, a chess Grandmaster of Composition; and Milan Vidmar the elder, member of the Slovene Academy of Sciences, Rector of Ljubljana University and perhaps the most 'learned' of all chessplayers – who at Hastings 1925/26 scored an astonishing 8½ out of 9 to share victory with Alekhine. In *chemistry*: the chess composer Boris Sakharov, corresponding member of the USSR Academy of Sciences and recipient of the Lenin prize. But then again, many people of multiple talents have opted firmly for one activity; Paul Keres, with a higher degree in mathematical sciences, became a great chessplayer, while Roald Sagdeev, the Kazan Junior Chess Champion, became the USSR's youngest 'full' Academy member – aged 32 years!

For the sum of his achievements, however, the palm of supremacy here must handed to Mikhail Botvinnik, the Doctor of Science and Professor of Electrical Engineering who was successful in 5 World Championship contests and reigned over the chess kingdom for 13 years. It is not possible here to give a résumé of his scientific work; suffice it to say that he has enriched his scientific field with a new technical term, something given only to a few. Nor is there the slightest need to give examples of his chess art.

To round off this subject, I cannot help telling of one other man of learning whom the chess world has forgotten not just largely but totally. He was H.T.Buckle, the author of *History of Civilization in England* and a major background influence even on the distinguished British historian and thinker Thomas Carlyle (with whom Goethe conversed and Dickens was on friendly terms; his ideas can be seen in Tolstoy's *War and Peace*, Herzen's *My Life and Thoughts* and Marx's *Communist Manifesto*).

Buckle's book, translated into all European languages including Russian, covers a much broader field than its title suggests. Buckle elucidates the effect of climate, soil and food on the human character; he explains how Indian, Arab and Greek culture were shaped by the influence of natural conditions. He was much discussed and had an enthusiastic readership. He is even mentioned in *The Ballet*, a dramatic verse sketch by the Russian poet Nekrasov, where a general says, "Don't read that Buckle all the time!"

Now to the point. After winning the first international tournament in chess history – London, 1851 – and gaining universal recognition as the uncrowned king of chess (as we would put it today), Adolf Anderssen stayed on in the English capital, and, in true democratic spirit, played friendly games against practically all comers. It was then that this same Henry Thomas Buckle 'fell into his hands'. Or rather, who fell into whose hands?

Buckle – Anderssen
Giuoco Piano [C54]

1 e4 e5 2 ♘f3 ♘c6 3 ♗c4 ♗c5 4 c3 ♘f6 5 d4 exd4 6 cxd4 ♗b4+ 7 ♗d2

White rejects the sharper 7 ♘c3, no doubt out of respect for the creator of the 'Immortal' and 'Evergreen' games.

7...♗xd2+ 8 ♘xd2 d5 9 exd5 ♘xd5 10 ♕b3 ♘ce7 11 0-0 0-0 12 ♖fe1 ♘f4 13 ♖e4! ♘eg6 14 ♖ae1 ♕f6 15 ♘e5 ♕g5?

An unjustified attempt at counterplay instead of the obligatory 15...♘xe5; admittedly White would hold the initiative anyway.

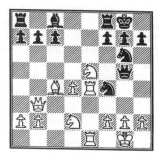

16 ♗xf7+ ♔h8 17 ♘xg6+ hxg6 18 ♕g3! (radically clarifying the situation in his own favour) **18...♕xg3 19 hxg3 ♖xf7 20 ♖xf4 ♖xf4 21 ♖e8+! ♔h7 22 gxf4 1-0**

Incidentally Buckle had even sent in his entry fee for that first-ever international tournament, but simply didn't arrive in time for the start....

In the same year Buckle defeated Löwenthal by 4½:3½ in a match. Earlier, in 1848, he had travelled to Paris to play Kieseritzky, and beaten him by the same score. And in London in 1847 he had overcome Bird in quite a lengthy contest by a two-point margin, with 9 points to 7. Now if you consider that Johann Jakob Löwenthal achieved the best result of any European in a match against Morphy, and finished ahead of both Steinitz and Anderssen in tournaments; if you recall that Lionel Adalbert Bagration Feliks Kieseritzky is famous not only as Anderssen's victim in the 'Immortal' friendly game, but also as a man who gave his name to a standard variation of the King's Gambit and as one of France's strongest chessplayers; if, finally, you take into account that Henry Edward Bird not only devised the opening that bears his name and won the first brilliancy prize in chess history, but also conceded a mere two points in a match against Steinitz; then the great historian's results are something you can judge for yourself.

Postscript: Straight after those battles of 1851, Buckle settled down to his life's main work. He completed it and sadly died shortly afterwards. He was only 41 – a distressingly early age, even by the standards of the mid-19th century.

Among artists, it is musicians who have been the most attracted to chess, while chessplayers conversely have turned to music more often than to anything else in the aesthetic domain. Two names that stand out here are François-André Danican Philidor, one of the fathers of modern chess and a creator of the of French comic opera genre; and Ferenc Erkel, a classical figure in Hungarian music and founder of the national opera, a composer (he gave Hungary its present national anthem), a conductor and a pianist – who at the same time was one of his country's strongest chessplayers of the mid-

19th century, and the organizer and leader of Hungary's first chess club.

In our own time the record for these two combined fields is held by the Soviet Grandmaster Mark Taimanov. His piano duo with his wife Lyubov Bruk is widely known as one of the 20 best in the whole history of music. Together with their son they also formed a piano trio – a particularly rare ensemble. However, when the pianist Taimanov is teamed with the vocalist Vasily Smyslov – who came through two stages of an extremely complex selection process for the Bolshoi theatre troupe – their 'number' is the most popular in any festive programme, as well as the most distinguished in terms of chess titles.

Nevertheless I consider that in Taimanov's life, music 'lost' to chess by a score of 49:51. For the Swedish pianist Michael Wiedenkeller, a similar 'balance of forces' came down on the side of music. Perhaps for that reason, he 'only' became an International Master who took part in numerous national and European tournaments.

The greatest stir, however, was caused not by these fully professional musical performances of chessplayers, but by a chess duel between two players who were formally amateurs. In the summer of 1937, posters were put up all over Moscow inviting chess enthusiasts to come to the Central House of Workers in the Arts, for a match between the distinguished composer Sergei Prokofiev and the great violinist David Oistrakh. They were both first-category players, whose standard was roughly that of a present-day FIDE Master. The match stake was not kept a secret, either: the loser was to give a solo concert for the winner and spectators. In the end it was Prokofiev who had to do this. Oistrakh, whose musical star had risen after he won first prize in a highly prestigious competition in Brussels under the patronage of the King of Belgium, played confidently to win the match, albeit by the smallest possible margin.

When the violinist's guest appearances coincided with events where Soviet chessplayers were participating – at the Leipzig Olympiad, or in South America – Oistrakh would take an active part in analysing adjourned games, and was delighted to be called an unofficial reserve in the Soviet squad.

Artists from the Middle Ages to the present day have very often turned to the theme of chess, utilizing the most varied chess motifs and 'accessories' on their canvases, but they have much more rarely lived 'parallel lives' in chess and art. We may of course recall Mecislovas Ostrauskas of Vilnius, who became a chess master in 1961; there were not many who acquired the title in the USSR at that time. However, the palm in this department belongs unquestionably to the Frenchman Marcel Duchamp, one of the founders of contemporary visual art – modernism, surrealism – and creator of the famous 'Fountain' urinal which was scandalously put on public display in 1917. Duchamp played in the first World Amateur Championship, held in Paris in 1924 on the occasion of the founding of FIDE. (He performed with middling success, winning a game against the Latvian master and well-known problemist Herman Mattison.) He also won the Paris Championship and was included four times in the French team at the 'Tournaments of Nations'. Here is the kind of play of which he was capable:

Duchamp – Feigin
The Hague Olympiad, 1928
(notes by Yuri Averbakh)

In this radically unbalanced position White has chances of a kingside attack, but Duchamp first sets about forestalling Black's counterplay on the queenside.
14 b4! ♕e7 15 ♖b1 ♘b6 16 0-0 ♘c7 17 a4 ♖b8 18 ♖fc1 ♗d7 19 a5 ♘c8 20 ♘a4
Black hasn't succeeded in thwarting his opponent's plan. White's positional advantage is plain to see.
20...♘b5 21 ♘c5 ♖a8 22 ♗xb5! cxb5 23 f4
The queenside is sealed, and White starts his attack on the enemy king. Black has no active possibilities in sight and is compelled to wait.
23...♗h6 24 g5 ♗g7 25 ♔g2 ♖d8 26 h4 ♗e8 27 h5 ♕a7 28 hxg6 hxg6 29 ♖h1 ♘e7 30 ♖h3 ♘f5

Somewhat facilitating his opponent's task; 30...♔f8 and 31...♘g8 would be more tenacious.
31 ♘xf5 exf5 32 ♖bh1 ♗d7 33 ♖h7 ♗c8 34 ♕e1

An entertaining position. Black is defenceless against ♕e1-h4 followed by ♖h7xg7+. He therefore resigned **(1-0)**.

Alas, the artist chessplayer was *also* capable of this:

Müller – Duchamp
The Hague Olympiad, 1928
English Opening [A28]

1 c4 e5 2 ♘f3 ♘c6 3 ♘c3 ♘f6 4 d4 exd4 5 ♘xd4 ♗b4 6 ♗g5 h6 7 ♗h4 ♘e4? 8 ♗xd8 ♘xc3 9 ♘xc6 ♘xd1+ 10 ♘xb4 **1-0**

On the subject of titled dignitaries who have taken an interest in chess, we have already mentioned Alfonso X and Napoleon I, to whom Charles V of Spain may be added. Then there was his Excellency Prince Dadian of Mingrelia, who incidentally liked to make up brilliant games, supposedly played by him – against opponents no one had heard of. And there was 'mere' Prince Eliashov, who won a handicap tournament in

117

Moscow in 1901 with the score of 8½ out of 11 ... etc. etc. etc. To regard these people seriously as chessplayers is either downright impossible or requires a very strained interpretation of the word. Yet Countess Chantal Chaude de Silans, who (it goes without saying) was born in the former residence of the Kings of France at Versailles, was another matter. She not only repeatedly won the women's championship of her country (aged 15 the first time!) and led the French team in the first Women's Olympiad; she also participated in men's championships, and in 1950 became the first female player in the world to be a member of a men's Olympic team. Moreover in the first post-war Women's World Championship – where one day she captivated her opponents and the spectators with her black-and-white chequered dress – it was Chaude de Silans who was anything but a walk-over for the Soviet contestants finishing in the first three places. With three rounds to go she moved to the head of the tournament table, playing splendidly – though regrettably not every day.

Chaude de Silans – Keller
Moscow 1949/50

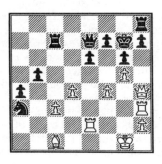

Sacrificing a second pawn, White crowns the final attack.
43 f5! gxf5 44 ♗f4 ♘c4
The bishop mustn't be allowed to check on e5.
45 ♕h6+ ♔g8 46 ♗xc7 ♕xc7 47 g6! fxg6 48 ♖xe6 ♕g7
Or 48...♔f7 49 ♖xg6.
49 ♖e8+ ♔f7 50 ♖e7+ 1-0

To all this I must add that the Countess and International Master managed the famous Paris chess club 'Caissa' for many years.

Her 'peer' by rank, the Belgian Count Alberic O'Kelly de Galway, 'collected' even more chess titles: International Grandmaster, Grandmaster of the International Correspondence Chess Association, and World Correspondence Champion – the third in chess history. In addition O'Kelly was an International Arbiter, and held the position of Chief Arbiter at the Petrosian-Spassky World Championship matches. His authority in human matters stood very high; in chess matters it was fully adequate. He took part in roughly a hundred (!) international tournaments and won about 25 of them, though admittedly the opposition in these contests was not of the strongest. The Count considered that his best game was the following one from his victorious World Correspondence Championship:

Balogh – O'Kelly
Correspondence game, 1959-61

In this game it's hard to say who is attacking....

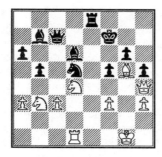

**36 ᗡxf5 ℤe2 37 ᗡbd4 ♗c5
38 ♔f1 ♛h2! 39 ᗡh6+ ♔g7
40 ᗡxe2 ♛h1+ 41 ᗡg1 ♗xg1
42 ♔e2 ♛g2+ 43 ♔e1 ♗h2
44 ℤxd5! ♗g3+ 45 ♔d1 ♛xf3+
46 ♔c1 ♗xd5 47 ♛d4+ ♔h7
48 ♗e3 ♗d6 49 ♛a7+ ♗b7
50 ♛b6 ♗f4! 0-1**

These successes stood as an unqualified record until an unforeseen situation arose involving the former World Championship Candidate Mark Taimanov and the seventh World Champion Vasily Smyslov. On the occasion of their jubilees (Taimanov's 70th birthday, Smyslov's 75th), the resurgent Russian gentry conferred on them the titles of count and prince respectively! This might call for no further comment, except that both Count Mark Evgenievich and Prince Vasily Vasilievich had already conquered all their resplendent honours in a different and, so to speak, democratic sense. Whether the law of heraldry (unlike the law of the land) works retroactively is nowhere explained.

In England, the post of Chancellor of the Exchequer has existed since medieval times. In plain language the title means 'Minister of the Chessboard'. In the subsequent centuries this post was held by dozens of gentlemen who, I regret to say, had no serious concern with chess. The point is that anywhere outside the United Kingdom, such an officer would simply be called Finance Minister! The English title arose because originally these people reckoned up their accounts on a chequered cloth.

George Alan Thomas's 'weak point' emerges in this connection. On the one hand Thomas played in over 80 national and international tournaments, sharing first prize at Hastings 1934/35 with Flohr and Euwe, ahead of Capablanca and Botvinnik. On the other hand, quite apart from chess championships, he won the English Badminton Championship several times, and in the 1920s he participated in the illustrious Wimbledon tennis tournaments. But as for his title ... in this respect Sir George rather 'fell short', being 'only' a baronet – a rank which comes somewhere in between the aristocracy and the minor gentry in the British 'rating list'. Still, he *was* the son of Lady Edith Margaret Thomas, the winner of the first-ever international women's tournament which was held concurrently with the legendary Hastings 1895 event. That was quite something!

Among high-ranking officers of state, it was probably the Yugoslav Bozidar Ivanović who had the most success at chess. He won his first gold medal in his country's championship while still only a master; later, as a Grandmaster, he repeated this feat twice. Afterwards he was appointed Minister of Sport and Tourism in Montenegro – the former Yugoslav republic which is now a sovereign state – and practically gave up chess for some years. However, in 1996, when the national championship was held in the capital Podgorica, the Minister felt a hankering for the past. He became champion once more, a quarter of a century after his first victory!

As regards parallel involvement in chess and some other form of sport, we may of course recall Paul Keres who at one time was Estonia's leading tennis player, and also his fellow Estonian Ruslan Mironov. The latter was Pärnu city champion, at chess ... and boxing. Viktor Kraiushkin won the chess and free-style wrestling champion-ships of Kazan University within the space of a month. Incidentally Bozidar Ivanović, whom we have just mentioned, won the table tennis championship of Montenegro more than once. Rashid Nezhmetdinov was the only chess International Master to be simultaneously a master of draughts (10x10 version). He won ten medals (five of them gold!) in Chess Championships of the RSFSR, and was a silver medallist in the Draughts Championship of this, the largest of the Soviet Republics.

Yet however strange it may seem, the favourite alternative occupation for chessplayers is football. Being a football fan is one thing. World Champion Tigran Petrosian was a truly 'fanatical' supporter of the Moscow 'Spartak' club. His colleague on the chess summit, Mikhail Tal, was no less keen, being partly a fan of the Riga club 'Daugava' and the Moscow 'Dynamo', but still more a fan of the beautiful game itself. The brilliant Grandmaster Ljubomir Ljubojević, however, went much further: nicknamed the 'Yugoslav Tal', he had first shown promise as a football star rather than a chess star; he played in the junior team of the famous Belgrade club 'Crvena zvezda'. His older colleague Svetozar Gligorić was already a chess master when he played for 'Partisan', the strongest team in Yugoslavia at the end of the 1940s. Later, having crossed the 60-year threshold (!), he regularly took the field for the 'Partisan' veterans' team and played in the traditional 'Chessplayers versus Journalists' matches. (World Champion Garry Kasparov played with passion in these same contests, as a striker; but *he* was 30-35 years younger.)

The outstanding Yugoslav footballers Milos Milutinović and Dragoslav Sekularec, key members of their national side, were not at all bad at chess either; they played at first-category standard. And Nikola Mijutković, a chess candidate master who was also centre forward for the 'Crvena zvezda', 'Sarajevo' and 'Sutesk' teams, once confessed: "I am quite sure that not a single goal I have scored has ever given me so much pleasure as the finish of my game with Grandmaster Dragoljub Velimirović in the 1966 Vrnjacka Banja tournament."

Mijutković – Velimirović

**32 ℤ1xe5! dxe5 33 ♕f6! ♗e6
34 h5 gxh5 35 ♕g5+ ♔h7
36 ♕xh5+ ♔g7 37 ♕g5+ ♔h7
38 dxe6 ♕d1 39 ♕h5+ ♔g7
40 ℤxf7+ 1-0**

All that now remains is to choose between the Romanian Bela Soos and the Norwegian Simen Agdestein. Soos, who received his international chess title when already a resident of West Germany, gained a place in his country's national football team; Agdestein played in the Norwegian football Premier League and and made his début in the international team on 10 May 1989 in a match against Italy – at the same time as being a chess Grandmaster. Which of them progressed further along the path of dual occupations? I personally have no view either way.

On the other hand it is perfectly obvious that the West German master Paul Tröger, who was national champion in 1957, could claim a kind of record in this area. He enjoyed particular respect within his country's football community because he worked as chief editor of the magazine *Fussballsport*.

Gentlemanly conduct

To ascertain the record performances in this field of mutual relations is especially difficult, because, apart from anything else, a 'gentleman' can be defined only very approximately. The English themselves, who gave the world both the word and the image of the gentleman, remain in some perplexity about it: "We invented football as a game for gentlemen, and it's played by hooligans. We invented rugby for hooligans, and it's played by gentlemen...."

The question as to what makes a gentleman arises in chess as elsewhere. How many times has a player forgotten to press the clock after making his move? And who nonchalantly studied the position while the hands of his opponent's clock were turning? The answer is not just anyone, but Vasily Smyslov, Anatoly Karpov and Alexander Khalifman – Chess Kings each in his own time, and eminently worthy people. We are not speaking of Mikhail Tal, who would immediately remind his opponent about the clock; by nature he was from another planet.

Of course, the conduct I have just mentioned is quite within the Laws of Chess, which don't require any gentlemanly gestures from the players. Accordingly, Cecil de Vere was not obliged to insist on continuing the game when Louis Paulsen overstepped the time limit against him in the Baden-Baden tournament of 1870. "My honour as a gentleman forbids me to score a point in this way," the English champion explained. However, his compatriot Joseph Blackburne regarded Paulsen as his rival, and protested to the tournament committee. The arbiters took a decision that was a far cry from the wisdom of Solomon: they made Paulsen and de Vere replay the game.

Another Englishman, Henry Bird, behaved in a similar manner in the 1882 Vienna tournament. His opponent, the Irishman James Mason, achieved a winning position and ... overstepped the time limit. Bird's response to this was to declare that *he* was resigning the game! Did he do so because he recalled another game against the same opponent six years earlier, which had earned him the first brilliancy prize in history? Hardly. It was just that Bird's notion of a rightful and worthy victory didn't include the purely competitive factor of the clock.

The arbiters, however, insisted on upholding the law – the *letter* of the law, not some abstract concept of justice.

This tradition of noble conduct was continued by **Milan Vidmar**, the Yugoslav Grandmaster and one of the highest authorities in the field of electrical engineering. In the summer of 1922 he was playing the World Champion **José Raoul Capablanca** in the London international tournament, and adjourned the game in a lost position.

When Vidmar wrote down his move and sealed the envelope, Capablanca asked him if he was really thinking of playing on. Unperturbed by this less than wholly tactful question, Vidmar said he would analyse the position first and then give an answer.

On the day for resumption, Vidmar returned. He had concluded that resistance was pointless, and aimed to resign the game to his opponent as soon as he arrived. The minutes passed, but Capablanca didn't appear. Suddenly Vidmar looked at the clock and saw that Capablanca's flag was going to fall in about ten seconds, so that he, Vidmar, would be formally awarded a win in a game he had intended to resign. He rushed to the table just when the controller was about to record Capablanca's forfeiture, and in the nick of time knocked his king over as a sign of surrender. The English press called this move of Vidmar's the most splendid that had ever been made in a chess game.

Can we call this a record? I don't know, because chess history contains a similar sort of episode which may, for good measure, be viewed as a record curiosity. In

122

1979 in the championship of Wyoming, two opponents, sitting at the board, spoke the words "I resign" in perfect unison. One of them did so because his position was hopeless, the other because of his pangs of conscience. Earlier in the game he had made a move and then immediately noticed it was a mistake. His opponent was absent from the board and there was no controller nearby, so he took the opportunity to move his piece back.

May the supreme judicial bodies of all chessplaying countries give their verdict on what constituted the highest degree of gentlemanliness!

Postscript: The English chess writer Ken Whyld, who unearthed this last story, doesn't give the names of the protagonists.

But most probably the Danish player Lars Hansen – a gentleman through and through – should be considered the record holder in this field. In the Erbanen Chess Club magazine he published and annotated the game he had lost to the young Bulgarian Evgenia Peicheva in the 1989 Copenhagen Open Championship (see the chapter 'Where is the king going?'). Voluntarily broadcasting the injury he suffered in a game against a young girl must have required some strength of character. Nor would he have reflected that this might get him into a book of chess records!

Gens una sumus

Probably no organization in the world has a worthier motto than that of FIDE: "We are one family." Were the Founding Fathers in the summer of 1924 influenced by Rudyard Kipling and his famous words about the same blood running in the veins of the wolves, the bear Baloo, the panther Bagheera and the boy Mowgli? Or were they just appositely expressing their feelings? Either way, the deed was done; and this motto, felicitously discovered, has accompanied most official communications from all chess Presidents ever since. Within this motley family, scandals have repeatedly erupted and shaken more than just the world of chess; but that is another story.

Apart from this *gens una*, however, chessplayers have their own families: fathers and mothers, wives, husbands and children, brothers and sisters, nephews and nieces, brothers-in-law and even mothers-in-law. Unfortunately, aside from blood relationships which last for ever (even when connections between the relatives are severed), family ties quite often disintegrate, so that deciding which family has the most to do with chess is not a simple matter. But here goes....

On an amateur level, there are cases where a father and as many as five children have played not only among themselves but in local competitions – successfully, too! Take the Nikologorsky family from Vladimir district in Russia. In September 2002, the magazine *Shakhmatnaia nedelia* ('Chess Weekly') had this to say about them:

"The father, Sergei Nikologorsky, is a poet and songwriter and edits his own journal. On the basis of the number of medals collected by his pupils during the past year, he is the best coach in Vladimir Province.

"Alexander Nikologorsky is a young poet and author of books of free verse; he is lightning champion and Junior Champion of Vladimir District.

"Matfey Nikologorsky won the Vladimir Province lightning championship at age 12 and is a silver medallist in standard chess.

"Russia's youngest first-grade player at age 6, Konstantin ('Kotik') Nikologorsky won the Under-8 Championship of Vladimir Province in all forms of chess, and was a bronze medallist in the Russian Championship for that age group.

"At age 8, Tania Nikologorskaia won the Girls' Under-10 Championship of Vladimir Province in all forms of chess – standard, speed and blitz.

"The Nikologorsky team finished second in the 1992 'White Rook' speed chess team championship of Russia.

"In the contests among Russia's best chess schools, the Nikologorsky family team (Alexander, Matfey, Kotik and Tania) also took the silver medals!"

At master and Grandmaster level, such a success *en masse* is of course almost impossible. Yet there is no lack of distinguished duos and trios. For instance we may name Purdy father and son, and the brothers Johner (who were mentioned in the chapter 'Profession: champion'); the Hungarian Grandmaster G.Forintos and his English son-in-law A.Kosten (at the 1991 Chess Festival in Catania, Sicily, they finished 2nd and 5th respectively); the Armenian Grandmaster A.Petrosian and his Hungarian son-in-law Peter Leko who is currently one of the best players in the world (furthermore the elder member of this pair is the coach of the younger); the Yugoslav sisters Alisa and Mirjana Marić, both Grandmasters; and the brothers Levon and Karen Grigorian who were Soviet Masters. However, as groups of siblings go, there is no one to rival the three Platov brothers (in the field of chess composition) or the three Polgar sisters. Of the latter, the eldest – Zsuzsa – has been Women's World Champion; the middle sister, Zsofia, was silver medallist in the (boys') World Under-14 Championship; and the youngest, Judit, has become the outright best female chessplayer of all times and all nations. Her participation in the top tournaments at the end of the 20th century no longer surprised anyone. Nor did her victories against the strongest opposition.

J.Polgar – Kasparov
Speed chess match, Russia v. Rest of World, Moscow 2002
Ruy Lopez [C67]

1 e4 e5 2 ♘f3 ♘c6 3 ♗b5 ♘f6 4 0-0 ♘xe4 5 d4 ♘d6 6 ♗xc6 dxc6 7 dxe5 ♘f5 8 ♕xd8+ ♔xd8 9 ♘c3 h6 10 ♖d1+ ♔e8 11 h3 ♗e7 12 ♘e2 ♘h4 13 ♘xh4 ♗xh4 14 ♗e3 ♗f5 15 ♘d4 ♗h7 16 g4 ♗e7 17 ♔g2 h5 18 ♘f5

After this it becomes clear that Black has a very difficult position.

18...♗f8
Black can't win a pawn by 18...hxg4 19 hxg4 ♗xf5 20 gxf5 ♖h5, in view of 21 ♖h1!, when 21...♖xf5? fails to 22 ♖h8+ ♗f8 23 ♗c5.

19 ♔f3
In the opinion of Grandmaster N.Rashkovsky, Kasparov was continuing to look for winning chances even when he could no longer see a draw.

19...♗g6 20 ♖d2 hxg4+ 21 hxg4 ♖h3+ 22 ♔g2 ♖h7 23 ♔g3 f6?! (merely bringing the dénouement closer) **24 ♗f4 ♗xf5 25 gxf5 fxe5 26 ♖e1!**
Already Black's position is indefensible.

26...♗d6 27 ♗xe5 ♔d7 28 c4 c5 29 ♗xd6 cxd6 30 ♖e6 ♖ah8 31 ♖exd6+ ♔c8 32 ♖2d5 ♖h3+ 33 ♔g2 ♖h2+ 34 ♔f3 ♖2h3+ 35 ♔e4 b6 36 ♖c6+ ♔b8 37 ♖d7 ♖h2 38 ♔e3 ♖f8 39 ♖cc7 ♖xf5 40 ♖b7+ ♔c8 41 ♖dc7+ ♔d8 42 ♖xg7 ♔c8, and Black resigned without waiting for the reply **(1-0)**.

There is nothing unnatural about chessplaying married couples either – with their common interests, the same circle of contacts, and, for the chessplaying bride, the possibility of obtaining a reliable, faithful and devoted coach as well as a husband.

One of the first such cases was the union between Valentina and Georgi Borisenko which lasted half a century. Surviving the severest elimination process, they took part in the USSR Championships 32 times (!) between them – and these were the most gruelling and strongest tournaments in the world. In her 24 championship finals Valentina gained 5 gold, 2 silver and 4 bronze medals – the outright best result among Soviet women chessplayers. Together with three compatriots she played in the first Women's World Championship of the post-war era (that is, after the death of Vera Menchik) – but alone of the three, she never became Chess Queen.

Georgi made his name first and foremost as a major chess theoretician, contributing abundant new material to at least half a dozen of the most topical and essential openings. A Grandmaster of the International Correspondence Chess Federation, he was both USSR Champion and World Championship runner-up in the field of postal chess.

In our own day we saw what looked like a very powerful union between Joël Lautier (the leader of French chess (his country's team won the 2002 European Championship), and Grandmaster Almira Skripchenko-Lautier who had been awarded the highest civil distinction in Moldova for her chess achievements. Incidentally her mother Naira Agabebian is also a Grandmaster who has several times won the Moldovan Women's Championship, while her father Fedor Skripchenko is an international chess arbiter. At the 2002 Bled Olympiad, Skripchenko-Lautier was already the leader of the French women's team; sadly, though, her union with Joël broke up.

Alexei Shirov, a pupil of the great Mikhail Tal and, after him, Latvia's best player, has done even more in the way of creating strong matrimonial chess alliances. Departing from his homeland and participating in the most prestigious contemporary tournaments, he first married Marta Zelinska, Poland's strongest female player and a bronze medallist at the Bled Olympiad. In chess their 'family rating' was very high, but playing a game is not the same as living your life.... Shirov's present wife is Viktoria Cmilyte; she is a Grandmaster and Lithuanian Champion, but being only 19 she has yet to attain a high Elo rating.

Grandmasters Susan and Bogdan Lalić were awarded the highest chess title at the same FIDE congress (Susan, née Walker, was previously married to Keith Arkell.) And yet one day it fell to their lot to be divorced – albeit only in chess terms. It happened in a Swiss tournament on the British island of Jersey. By the luck of the draw they were paired against each other in the last round. They were both in the running for first place, and both wished to take it – and not simply to gain the prize of 1500 pounds sterling for the family. Bowing to the wishes of the Grandmaster couple, the arbiters' committee contravened the regulations by 'divorcing' them. Alas, the family budget seriously suffered. Bogdan failed to win his final game and received only £450 for sharing 2nd-3rd places, while Susan lost and had to make do with a modest prize for the highest-placed female competitor. On the other hand, their honour and good name – things which are worth a lot! – were preserved.

If we turn to cases where both parents and children play chess, then the widest fame belongs rightly to the Hund family – father, mother and two daughters – from Darmstadt in Germany. The head of the family, Gerhard, became a national master, while the female trio went even further. The mother, Juliana, became an International Correspondence Master, first in the women's and then in the men's category, and won two postal championships of what was then West Germany. The younger daughter Isabel won the national Girls' and Women's Championships, both within a year. The elder daughter Barbara became the first German player to gain the International Woman Grandmaster title; she won FIDE Zonal Tournaments and performed creditably in World Championship Interzonals.

Another family just as active in the chess world is that of Vladimir Makarov, a Russian master from the Orenburg region. He met his bride-to-be Zoia at local chess contests in the Far East of the country, where he was an 18-year-old soldier doing national service. At present, the couple have six children! They are champions of Orenburg province on both an individual and a family team basis. The father of the family has played several times in Russian Championship finals. The mother works as a coach while looking after the family; she has frequently played for the corespondence team of the Russian Federation, and possesses a silver medal from the USSR Championship. Their eldest son Vladimir has also earned the right to play in the Russian Championship, while their daughter Olga has won the regional championship in her age group. Their other four children too have obtained creditable gradings.

However, the Wood clan in England could have competed with these families on equal terms. The 'patriarch', Baruch or Barry, played in several national championships, and in 1945 he won the British Correspondence Championship. His daughter Peggy was one of the strongest female players in the country. His son Christopher was a member of the national student team and played for it in Students' Olympiads. Admittedly the other two sons rather let the side down: Frank and Philip didn't rise above mediocre grades. On the other hand Peggy's husband, Peter Clarke, was considered England's number two player in the 1960s, though that was a time when the country didn't have a single Grandmaster of its own.

But one other family achieved much more. It contained the surnames of Poliak, Rubtsova and Fatalibekova. The father, Abram Borisovich Poliak, became a chess

master back in the days when only two or three players in the USSR would obtain the title in a year– if that. The mother, Olga Nikolaevna Rubtsova held the Women's World Championship title from 1956-58 and was three times USSR Women's Champion and twice Moscow Champion. Their daughter Elena (Fatalibekova by marriage) finished first or in the prize list in several USSR Women's Championships. She won the Moscow Championship three times, came first in the Tbilisi Interzonal of 1976, and reached the semi-final in the World Championship Candidates matches. True, her brothers and sisters, four in number, never went very far as chessplayers.

On one occasion in the national championship, the mother and daughter played each other. This was a unique case. Everyone expected a draw between relatives, but there was no hint of that.

Elena Rubtsova –
Olga Rubtsova
USSR Women's Championship,
Kishinev 1965

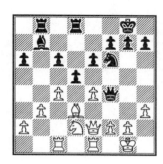

White's placid conduct of the opening is not at all a sign of peaceful intentions.

17 cxd5 cxd5 18 e5 ♘d7
19 ♘f1!?

On 19 ♘f3, Black plays 19...d4
with good counterplay.

19...♘f8 20 ♖c7 ♖dc8

Allowing a 'small combination'
in Capablanca style.

21 ♖xb7 ♖xb7 22 ♗xa6 ♖bc7
23 ♗xc8 ♖xc8 24 ♕d3 ♖c1

Probably facilitating White's task
of exploiting the extra pawn;
24...♘d7 was preferable.

25 ♖xc1 ♕xc1 26 a4 ♕a1
27 ♕b5 d4 (Black has no time for
27...♕xe5) 28 ♔h2 d3 29 ♕xd3
♕xe5+ 30 ♔g1 h6 31 ♕d8 ♕c3
32 ♕b6 1-0

Part Three: Tournaments, Matches, Events

In contention for the crown

It began upwards of 100 years ago, and has always been the quintessence of world chess life. Its vicissitudes have been followed by vastly more people than there are chessplayers in the world. Nor is this surprising; very many people have tacitly equated the World Chess Championship with the highest manifestation of intelligence to be found, if not among humanity at large, then at least among all competitors in sport.

The list of record holders in this department was opened by the first World Champion, Wilhelm Steinitz. He ascended the chess throne on 29 March 1886, forty-five days before his half-century jubilee. He stepped down at the age of 58 years and 10 days. Since then the chess world has never known a 'sovereign' of more advanced years.

The youngest Chess King was Garry Kasparov, at the age of 22 years 210 days. In January 2002, however, the FIDE version of the Championship was sensationally won by the Ukrainian Grandmaster Ruslan Ponomariov; he won the last game of the final match at the 'indecently' early age of 18 years 104 days. And although the format of that contest is plainly geared to youth, we can hardly expect an improvement on this record in the foreseeable future.

Emanuel Lasker reigned over the chess kingdom for the longest: 26 years, 11 months and 2 days. Alexander Alekhine kept the Championship title for more than 16 years, Garry Kasparov for nearly 15.

Mikhail Tal's 'reign' turned out to be the shortest: one year and five days.

It was Max Euwe who held the title of ex-World Champion for the longest time – 44 years!

The throne was gained (yes, *gained* – not just defended!) three times by Botvinnik and twice by Alekhine; at the present time (mid-2004), Kasparov retains chances of doing likewise. After Karpov lost the title he never managed to regain it, but by taking advantage of the schism in the chess world in the 1990s he twice became FIDE World Champion.

Two Chess Kings – Mikhail Botvinnik and Garry Kasparov, who incidentally were teacher and pupil – competed at the highest level the greatest number of times: they played 8 matches each (if the 1948 World Championship Match Tournament counts the same as one of these duels). Emanuel Lasker and Anatoly Karpov each have 7 matches to their name, although the 12th king considers himself the absolute record-holder in this sphere; after all, he was successful in another three matches for the FIDE world title, against Jan Timman, Gata Kamsky and Viswanathan Anand.

But even if these three matches are disregarded, Karpov remains the record-holder for the sheer number of games played in duels for the crown; he played 194 of them (!), chiefly thanks to two matches of unrestricted duration. Garry Kasparov is in second place here; he has currently played one game less (!). And if Kasparov and Vladimir Kramnik had not declined to play the final game of their London match in 2000, Garry Kimovich's tally would have precisely equalled that of Anatoly Evgenievich.

The longest title match (1984/85) dragged on for more than five months (to be precise, 159 days!) between these same two rivals. Then ... "the FIDE authorities broke off the match – an absolute absurdity, unequalled (thank heaven) in the whole history of chess" (Botvinnik). I may add that the then President of the International Chess Federation, the Filipino Florencio Campomanes, did this at the prompting and veiled behest of the Soviet chess and non-chess functionaries, who didn't

want the occupant of the throne to change.

Compared with this, the previous lengthiest match, between Anatoly Karpov and Viktor Korchnoi in the Philippines in 1978, seems almost of fleeting duration: it lasted a 'mere' 93 days (!) before Karpov won the 32nd game to retain his title. Interestingly, almost three quarters of a century earlier, Capablanca and Alekhine had managed to play 34 games in 75 days.

But then, these monster events in chess have probably shared the fate of the dinosaurs. In our own era wth its quickened pace, matches of unlimited length are not to be expected in the foreseeable future. Still, who knows? After all, by rights, everyone should have been put on their guard as early as 1861 by the match between Louis Paulsen and Ignatz Kolisch which began after a small tournament in Bristol. The match conditions stipulated that the winner would be the first to win 9 games, with draws not to count. The first 17 games gave no cause for worry: Paulsen won 6 of them, with one loss and 10 draws. But at that point Kolisch fought back, and after the 31st game, with the score at +7 -6 =18 in Paulsen's favour, it was decided to call this marathon a draw; it had been going on for nearly three months.

The shortest matches for the crown were played by Emanuel Lasker – against David Janowski in 1909 and Karl Schlechter in 1910. They lasted for 10 games each (though in the latter case a 30-game match was originally planned). The battle with Janowski was over in just 22 days, which again is a record of sorts. Another Lasker-Janowski match (in 1910) incorporated only one game more, since the World Champion very quickly achieved the requisite 8 wins.

It was this last match, incidentally, that saw the record disparity in scores – 9½:1½. In their first match Lasker had won by 8:2.

An absolute overall record which cannot be broken was established twice (!) by Bobby Fischer when he beat both Mark Taimanov and Bent Larsen by 6:0. However, these were 'nothing more than' the quarter-final and semi-final matches in the 1971 Candidates series, so we are justified in mentioning them only in passing. Generally speaking, 'clean scores' are no rarity in chess history, but we will come to them in the chapter 'Unbroken runs'.

The best set of results for a whole series of title matches was achieved by Garry Kasparov with 5 wins, one drawn result and one loss, as well as one match which, as we know, was broken off. Lasker too won 5 matches, drew one and lost one. But here again, a kind of record belongs to Bobby Fischer: having won his only match, he abandoned the throne undefeated. Alexander Alekhine did the same, with the difference that he was still World Champion when he departed this life.

The longest rivalry between two players at the highest level was that between the two 'K's': Anatoly Karpov and Garry Kasparov played 5 matches between 1984 and 1990. Mikhail Botvinnik and Vasily Smyslov faced each other three times: in 1954, 1957 and 1958. Wilhelm Steinitz played Emanuel Lasker and Mikhail Chigorin twice each. Lasker and David Janowski played each other twice. Alexander Alekhine played two matches each against Efim Bogoljubow and Max Euwe; Botvinnik played two against Mikhail Tal, Tigran Petrosian two against Boris Spassky and Anatoly Karpov two against Viktor Korchnoi.

Five of these contests had the status of 'return matches', but only three were 'successful' ones: Alekhine regained his title against Euwe, as did Botvinnik against Smyslov and Tal. Steinitz and Karpov failed to restore their monarchies.

Interestingly, among challengers whose first attempt failed, it was only Spassky who achieved the goal after all and became the tenth Chess King in history.

It was Lasker who defended his title with the shortest interval between matches – twice in 1910, and once 57 days earlier, at the end of 1909. The longest gap between title matches also occurrred within his reign: 10 years, 3 months and 8 days (from 1910 to 1921). Of course, the First World War and its devastating consequences must be taken into account here. In the period of the Second World War, competition for the Championship was halted by 10 years, 2 months and 26 days. This alone would be enough to put a stop to wars once and for all, but who in any time or place has listened to the voice of reason?

It was Botvinnik who won the largest number of games – 46 – from all the matches in which he played. Lasker won one game less. Steinitz and Alekhine each saw their opponents capitulate 43 times.

Steinitz also holds a record for sequences of losses in World Championship matches. In 1894 he lost five games in a row against his successor on the throne, Emanuel Lasker. In his unsuccessful return match two years later, he started off with four defeats. But a curious point is that even in the match which first gained him the title, Steinitz began with a win and then succumbed in the next four games. The public was already betting on Johannes Zukertort, but in the end....

On this point, the first World Champion had some 'close competitors'. Lasker finished his match with David Janowski in 1910 by celebrating five victories running; against Frank Marshall in 1907 he had won his last four games. Three games in a row were also lost by Mikhail Chigorin (against Steinitz of course), Max Euwe (against Alekhine in their return match), Mikhail Botvinnik (in his first match with Smyslov in 1954), Vasily Smyslov (in the 1958 return match with Botvinnik – at the very start!), Mikhail Tal (in 1961, in

Botvinnik's other return match) and Garry Kasparov (against Karpov, in history's final return match in 1986).

Chess 'anti-records', if I may put it that way, were attained by Marshall (against Lasker in 1907), Janowski (in 1910, also against Lasker) and ... Kasparov (in 2000 against Kramnik), through failure to win a single game!

As for draws, Anatoly Karpov's record of 135 was more recently surpassed by Garry Kasparov's 143, and if he comes out of retirement *he* will still be attempting to recover his crown. Now a piece of mysticism: in each of his matches with opponents other than Karpov (that is, Nigel Short, Viswanathan Anand and Vladimir Kramnik), the 13th World Champion drew 13 games, although the number of wins varied.

What about the longest *series* of draws? Boris Spassky and Bobby Fischer concluded peace seven times running at Reykjavik in 1972, as did Kasparov and Kramnik in their London 2000 match. Kasparov and Anand drew eight times in a row in New York in 1995. But it goes without saying that the sequence of 17 consecutive draws (from the 10th to the 26th game inclusive) in the unlimited record-breaking match between Karpov and Kasparov that we have mentioned already, is a record with nothing to rival it. The young challenger, who had suffered 4 defeats before this sequence began, was already being dubbed 'the long-playing loser' by wits among Karpov's supporters.

We may conclude this theme by recalling one match of absolute record status. It was fought out between the strongest chessplayers of its era, but unfortunately it was before anyone had thought up the idea of competing for the World Championship. It was Wilhelm Steinitz versus Adolf Anderssen, London 1866. Almost all the games were either King's Gambits (Steinitz) or Evans Gambits (Anderssen). Each contestant registered a string of 4 victories, and in the end the future World Champion came out on top with the score of 8:6.

And there wasn't a single draw!

In official title matches, the lowest number of draws occurred at Havana in 1889 between Steinitz and Chigorin. For some details of the longest-ever World Championship game, see the chapter 'The shortest and the longest'. Mikhail Botvinnik made only 9 moves in the 21st and final game of the match in Moscow in 1963, thereby handing the Championship title to Tigran Petrosian.

The quickest win – in 19 moves – was scored by Steinitz against Zukertort in the final game of the 'opening' match in this endless succession of confrontations. There is nothing surprising in the fact that this game is omitted from numerous monographs on Wilhelm Steinitz; his opponent made just too many mistakes. What *is* surprising is its omission from some of the modern electronic databases.

Steinitz – Zukertort
New Orleans, 29 March 1886
Vienna Game [C25]

1 e4 e5 2 ♘c3 ♘c6 3 f4 exf4 4 d4!?

Steinitz isn't afraid of the check on h4; according to his theory the king can look after itself. Reasonably enough, Zukertort postpones the crucial events by one move.

4...d5 5 exd5 ♕h4+ 6 ♔e2 ♕e7+ 7 ♔f2 ♕h4+ 8 g3 fxg3+ 9 ♔g2

Much later, in the Berlin tournament of 1897, Chigorin tried 9 hxg3 against Winawer. After 9...♕xd4+ (9...♕xh1 10 ♗g2 ♕h2 11 dxc6 looks very much like suicide for Black) 10 ♗e3 ♕xd1 11 ♖xd1 he acquired a huge lead in development for the pawn.

9...♘xd4 10 hxg3

Steinitz himself considered the position after 10 ♕e1+ ♗e7 11 hxg3 to be very complicated and unclear.

10...♕g4 11 ♕e1+ ♗e7 12 ♗d3

Here too Steinitz gave an alternative: 12 ♖h4 ♘xc2 13 ♕e5 ♕g6 14 ♖b1 ♕f6 15 ♗b5+ ♔d8, after which he judged White's initiative to be worth more than the sacrificed material.

12...♘f5?!

A dubious move, cutting off the queen's retreat. Steinitz thought 12...♔d8 was relatively best, though after 13 ♘e4 White has a serious initiative.

13 ♘f3 ♗d7 14 ♗f4 f6

There is no other way to stop 15 ♘e5, trapping the queen.

15 ♘e4

White's threats are growing with the speed of an avalanche. One of them is 16 ♘f2 ♕g6 17 g4, when the pin will cost Black a piece. In parrying this, Black commits an oversight which loses by force.

15...♘gh6?

Here Steinitz examined 15...0-0-0 16 ♘f2 ♕g6 17 g4 h5 18 ♗xf5 ♗xf5 19 ♘h4, and also 15...h5 16 ♘h4 ♗c8 (preparing a retreat for the queen) 17 d6!. In either case White wins. It seems there is already no salvation for Black.

16 ♗xh6 ♘xh6 17 ♖xh6 gxh6

Better an end without torment than torments without end. Steinitz gives two other lines, neither of which alters the result: 17...♗c8 18 ♖h4 ♕d7 19 d6 cxd6 20 ♗b5 ♕xb5 21 ♘xd6+, and 17...♔d8 18 ♘f2 ♕a4 19 ♖h4.

18 ♘xf6+ ♔f7 19 ♘xg4 1-0

As for the symbolic game in which not even one half-move was made – that too is discussed under 'The shortest and the longest'.

Standing out from the rest

This is about tournaments – but not about those tens of thousands of competitions which have been going on every day at various levels of chess for the past century and a half. We are speaking of those with some feature that sets them apart from all similar ones.

Record age

Here we need to start a long way back. At the end of the summer of 1946 – the first peaceful summer since the Second World War, that conflict so terrible in its consequences and the number of its victims – the Staunton Chess Club in the totally devastated Dutch town of Groningen attained its seventy-fifth birthday. In honour of the occasion it assembled virtually all the strongest players on the planet to take part in the first major post-war international tournament.

In 1995, the 125th anniversary of the club's foundation was celebrated. According to an ancient Greek philosophical maxim, you cannot enter the same river twice – the water will be different. In disregard of this, the members of that original star contingent were invited back to Groningen. There were seven of the twenty left, and they all accepted. The sum of their ages was little short of five and a half centuries – 547 years! Their elder statesman was the irrepressible Miguel Najdorf. He was already past 86, but he still enjoyed playing blitz chess (after finishing a serious game), and on winning he would declare, "You're a bit old to be playing me." It's interesting that half a century earlier, when talking about Groningen '46, Grandmaster Kotov had stressed this same hobby of the 'impetuous Najdorf': "Any time when there was no play, the ringing laughter that went with his bouts of lightning chess could be heard from the hotel vestibule."

But then in serious play too, the 'grand old man' retained the *élan* which had enabled him to beat the first prize winner – Mikhail Botvinnik – in that far-off tournament. With logical play he reached the following position:

Najdorf – Denker
Groningen 1996

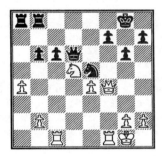

On **23 ♖xc6!** Black resigned at once.

Out of consideration for the participants' age, the organizers created a record by holding the shortest of all tournaments on the Swiss System – it lasted for just three rounds! The ex-World Champion Vasily Smyslov scored 2½ points. The youngest players, the Swiss M.Christoffel and the Canadian D.Yanofsky (who were only 71 and had also been the youngest in the earlier tournament) scored half a point each.

Incidentally the Swiss International Master had similarly finished last at Groningen '46, where he received a 'consolation' prize. The Canadian had been awarded the third brilliancy prize on doubtful grounds, for his sensational win against Botvinnik.

Record distance

We have just spoken of the shortest tournament. The longest one dates from far-off times. In 1889 in New York, 20 players faced each other for a double-round contest in which, for good measure, any drawn games from the second cycle were to be replayed. As a result, a total of 430 games took place between 25 March and 18 May: 380 in the 'basic' tournament and 46 'supplementary' ones. (N.Grekov's monograph *M.I.Chigorin* gives the erroneous figure of 423.) In addition, the players who shared first and second places spent 9 days on a match for first prize! Of necessity, then, the individual record holders among all these hard workers at the chessboard were the tournament winners: the Russian Mikhail Chigorin, and the Austrian of Hungarian origin Max Weiss (or Miksa, to use a version of his forename that sometimes occurs in chess literature). The latter had handed in 47 signed scoresheets to the organizers, including 5 for replayed games and 4 for his play-off match with Chigorin. Mikhail Ivanovich had had one replay fewer, but ... on the day after the close of the tournament, that is day 65, he went on to give an 8-board simultaneous blindfold display at the Manhattan club. One of his opponents, who sat down to play without batting an eyelid, was D.W.Baird, a contestant in the tournament that had just ended! He had finished last but one in that event, and had no success in the 'simul' either; presumably Chigorin (who made the score of +5 =2 -1) took particular care in his game with this opponent.

With such a stupendous chess ordeal in mind (Chigorin's opening game against E.Delmar, for instance, had lasted 135 moves!), it can be downright embarrassing to hear the complaints of some of today's Grandmasters about how tired they are after 9 rounds – including rest days! Especially since the play of these record-breaking New York contestants remained perfectly creditable right up to the finish.

Weiss – Chigorin
Play-off, 1st game
(notes by Chigorin)

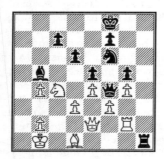

34 ♔c2! d5! 35 ♘a3!
After 35 exd5 ♘xd5 White can't take the pawn on e5 with either the queen or the knight, while Black is threatening ♗b5xc4 and ♘d5-e3+.
35...♗c6 36 b5 ♗b7 37 ♖f2
Essential. On 37 ♕d2, Black plays 37...dxe4 38 dxe4 ♘xe4 39 fxe4 ♗xe4+.
37...♖g1 38 ♕d2 ♕g3 39 ♖h2 dxe4 40 dxe4

40...♖xd1! 41 ♖h8+
If 41 ♔xd1, then 41...♕xf3+ 42 ♔c1 ♕f1+ 43 ♕d1 ♕xd1+ 44 ♔xd1 ♗xe4, and picking up the g4-pawn for good measure, Black obtains a won position.
41...♔g7 42 ♕xg5+ ♔xh8 43 ♕xf6+ ♔g8 44 ♔xd1 ♕f2! 45 ♘c2 ♕f1+ 46 ♔d2 ♕xb5 47 b4 ♗a6 48 ♕d8+ ♔h7 49 ♕xc7 ♕d3+ 50 ♔c1 ♕xf3 51 ♕xe5 ♕xg4 52 ♕f5+ ♕xf5 53 exf5 ♔g7 54 ♔d2 ♔f6 55 ♘d4 ♔e5 56 ♔c3 f6 ½-½

Or take this example, played a few games earlier in round 36 (!):

Chigorin – Bird
(notes by Steinitz)

34 ♖xg7+!!
A magnificent combination!
34...♔xg7 35 ♖b7+ ♔g6 36 ♕f7+ ♔f5 37 ♖b5+ ♔e4

38 f3+ ♔e3

After 38...♔d3 there would be no immediate mate, but Black still wouldn't be able to save the game.

39 ♕b3+ ♔e2

If 39...♔d2, then 40 ♗f4+ ♔e1 (or 40...♔e2 41 ♕b2+ followed by ♕b2-d2+ etc.) 41 ♕b1+ ♔e2 42 ♕f1 mate.

40 ♕b2+ ♔d3

There would be a curious finish after 40...♔d1 41 ♕b1+, when 41...♔d2 or 41...♔e2 leads to the same mate as in the actual game, while 41...♖c1 is answered by 42 ♕d3+ ♔e1 43 ♗g3 mate.

41 ♕b1+ ♔e2 42 ♖b2+

All superbly played. White refrains from winning the queen and forces an elegant mate.

42...♔e3 43 ♕e1+ ♔d4 44 ♕d2+ ♔c4 45 ♖b4 mate

The Vienna tournament of 1898 was almost as long. It was a double-round event with 19 participants, and included nearly all the strongest players in the world. The struggle (including an extra 4-game match to decide first prize) went on for exactly two months, or, to be absolutely precise, 61 days! And one striking fact is that after the space of just twenty-four hours, during which they travelled from the Austro-Hungarian imperial capital to Cologne, a magnificent seven headed by the nearly sixty-year-old Steinitz went into battle again, in the 11th German Chess Federation congress.

Of these seven, the venerable ex-World Champion performed with fair success, as did Mikhail Chigorin, Carl Schlechter and Jackson Whipps Showalter who was many times Champion of the USA. David Janowski, who had been making his mark brilliantly and occupying ever higher places in tournaments, failed to endure the stress and strain; this was the first warning bell to sound for him, though it went unheard. Emanuel Schiffers, a devotee of the sharp combinative style and Russia's number two player in those years, played generally up to his strength. But it was one of the best English masters, already a 'great master' in the unofficial terminology of the time, who won the most resounding victory of his career. He not only took first place with a one-point lead over his nearest competitors; he also played his best game, and against such a formidable opponent too.

Burn – Steinitz

Black has obviously been comprehensively outplayed on all parts of the board, but the position is of the closed type, there aren't that many pieces left, and, most importantly, the bishops are on opposite colours. Is there some hope of salvation, then?

35 f5!!

This may be set beside Lasker's similar move in his classic game with Capablanca, St Petersburg 1914.

35...♖dd8 36 ♖h4 ♗f8 37 f4 ♖d6 38 ♔c3!

This places Black in *zugzwang*.

38...b5 39 axb6+ ♖dxb6 40 ♖xb6 ♖xb6 41 ♖h1 ♗e7 42 b3 ♖d6 43 ♖a1 ♖b6 44 ♔d3 ♔b8 45 ♔e2 ♖d6 46 ♔f3 ♔c8 47 ♔g4 ♔d8 48 ♔h5 ♔e8 49 ♔g6 ♔f8 50 ♖a5 ♖b6 51 ♗c4 ♗d6 52 ♖a1 ♗e7 53 ♔h7! ♗d6 54 ♖d1 ♖c6 55 ♖d5 h5 56 ♔g6 a5 57 ♔xh5 ♖b6 58 e5 fxe5 59 fxe5 ♗e7 60 ♖d7 ♖b8 61 ♖a7 ♖d8 62 ♖xa5 ♖d2 63 ♖a8+ ♖d8 64 ♖a7 ♖d1 65 f6 gxf6 66 exf6 ♗d8 67 g4 ♖g1 68 g5 ♖g3 69 ♔g6 ♔e8 70 ♗b5+ ♔f8 71 ♖f7+ ♔g8 72 ♗c4 1-0

Seeing that Cologne was a 15-round contest, each of the seven players I mentioned had played 51 games in 80 days! "Yes, men in our time were not like today's breed. *You* are not the heroes!" Indeed such an insatiable appetite for the game has every reason to be considered a record.

The most complicated tournament in chess history was undoubtedly the one held in the health resort of Ostende in 1906. The organizers invited 36 contestants. With the exception of World Champion Lasker and Dr Tarrasch, perhaps all the strongest players were there. The experts in the press tipped Geza Maroczy for first place. In the event he performed excellently, although he allowed the Austrian Carl Schlechter, a pretender to the chess crown, to finish above him. It was the best result of Schlechter's life. Both these players and 7 other prizewinners played 32 games each – thanks to the imagination of the organizers which knew no bounds.

To begin with, they divided all the players into 4 groups of roughly equal strength. In the first cycle of the contest, group A played against group B according to what was later known as the Scheveningen system (see the chapter 'Where history is made'), while group C played against group D. After this, three players from each 'team' were eliminated; among them, naturally enough, was the the well-known chess patron Peter Saburov. The son of a senator who was also a chess enthusiast, Saburov chaired the management of the St Petersburg Chess Association and would later organize the famous Chigorin Memorial in 1909; but he had little personal success as a player. At Ostende he was the only one to lose all 9 of his games.

In the second cycle, group A, now reduced to six players, played group C, again on the Scheveningen System; and group B played group D. Again the participants with the worst results were eliminated, this time two from each group. Mikhail Chigorin was among them; his time was already running out, in chess as in life.

138

In the third cycle the quartet from group A played against group D, and group B played group C. This time no one dropped out, and in the fourth cycle the members of each group played amongst themselves. Finally, the fifth cycle consisted of the "winners' group". It was originally meant to consist of 6 players, the same as the number of prizes being offered. In the course of the tournament, however, some individual donations had been made to the fund, so that on the eve of the last lap the number of finalists, and consequently prizewinners, was increased to nine.

Dissatisfaction with this concocted system arose in all quarters, both in the world press and among the participants, inasmuch as it radically increased the role of chance. 'On the other hand', we have here another record-breaking tournament (according to one possible criterion) which we may add to the rest.

What was the largest of all single-round tournaments? Let us disregard various multi-stage competitions and indeed the 'Swisses' that have firmly taken over the world. Instead let us point to the the third Ostende Chess Congress, held in 1907. However, we are not speaking of the so-called 'Tournament of Champions' (which will be mentioned later under 'Summit meetings') but of the second-string 'master tournament'. Within a few years, an entire galaxy of competitors from this event would be setting the tone in world chess: Nimzowitsch, Rubinstein, Spielmann, Bernstein.... At Ostende

these young players squeezed the 'old-stagers' out of the top group, and in this they were undoubtedly helped by the sheer length of the tournament: 28 rounds. It would have been even longer if Paul Johner, later to be six times Champion of Switzerland, had not withdrawn after six games. As it happened, none of the five leaders had played him.

Jakob Mieses for example, who had already lived a 'full' 42 years, went to the top of the table after three quarters of the lengthy distance with the brilliant score of 16½ out of 21, but afterwards tired so much that from his last seven games he only scored 2½, even losing to three tail-enders.

However, to make up for his 'failure' – he shared 3rd and 4th prizes with Nimzowitsch, half a point behind the joint winners – Mieses elegantly earned the brilliancy prize on the 36th (!) day of play, five rounds from the end.

Perlis – Mieses
20 June 1907

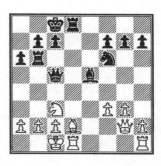

Playing his favourite Scandinavian Defence, Black has seized the initiative, and the storm clouds

are gathering over the white king.
21 ♗e1
Not 21 ♘a4 ♗xb2+! 22 ♘xb2
♕a3, or 21 f4 ♕b4!. However, the
move White plays promises him no
relief either.
21...♕e3+! 22 ♗d2
In answer to 22 ♔b1 Black
had prepared the spectacular
22...♖xb2+! 23 ♔xb2 ♖xd1, and
White can resign. In that case,
though, the 'prizewinning' queen
sacrifice would not have occurred.
**22...♗xc3!! 23 ♗xe3 ♗xb2+
24 ♔b1 ♗d4+ 25 ♔c1 ♗xe3+
26 ♖d2 ♗xd2+ 27 ♕xd2** (the
queen would be lost anyway)
27...♖b1+ 28 ♔xb1 ♖xd2 0-1

After this, no one had reason to
be surprised at the Carlsbad
tournament of 1911, where 'only'
26 mainly first-class players were
competing, let alone at Baden-
Baden 1925 or the first Moscow
international tournament, comprising 21 players each – just as no
one was surprised at the earlier, and
famous, Hastings 1895 (22 players)
or the later Carlsbad 1929 (the same
number). Vera Menchik's last place
in the latter event is wholly
explicable: the Women's World
Champion simply didn't have the
strength to last such a distance.

In more modern times, an event
that stands out is the grandiose 1953
Candidates Tournament for the
right to play a match with the World
Champion. Almost the whole of
the chess élite met to settle its
differences in the course of 58 days
in Switzerland. In the 30 (!) rounds
of the double-round contest, the 15
Grandmasters played 210 games

which to everyone's delight
included such a brilliancy as
Averbakh-Kotov, examined in the
chapter 'No one ever saw further'.

Strictly speaking, no one had
originally intended to organize such
a 'monster' tournament; the plan
was to restrict the entry to 10
players, but 9 of these came from
the USSR. This meant that the
Candidates Tournament would be
virtually a Soviet internal affair; it
was practically 100% certain that
one of the Soviet Grandmasters
would take first place and hence
that there would be a 'Soviet' match
for the crown. FIDE therefore went
back on its initial decision and
incorporated ex-World Champion
Euwe into the tournament (doing
him a highly dubious service),
together with the American
Reshevsky, the Yugoslav Gligorić,
the Hungarian Szabo and the Swede
Stahlberg. The ratio of Soviet to
non-Soviet players changed from
9:1 to 9:6, the tournament acquired
an 'international character' and the
entire chess world had a unique
spectacle to watch.

Two other Candidates Tournaments (or more exactly Match
Tournaments), in Yugoslavia (1959)
and Curaçao (1962), were almost as
long, comprising 28 rounds each –
but only 112 and 105 games
respectively were played by the 8
players in the 4 cycles. Mikhail Tal,
who won the first of these two
tournaments, was a 'non-starter' in
the fourth cycle of the second,
owing to ill health.

By way of a curiosity, another
peculiar record of endurance –

concentrated endurance, so to speak – was demanded from the players in a tournament entitled 'The 24 Hours of Le Lionnais' (Switzerland) in the summer of 1991. That's right – in the course of a full twenty-four hours, each contestant spent 1000 minutes at the chessboard playing 100 blitz games. As you can easily work out, there was hardly more than a four-minute break between rounds; that was all the time these chess marathon runners had for catching some sleep and something to eat, and attending to other needs.

In terms of points scored, the player with most powers of endurance proved to be the Yugoslav A.Komljanović, at that time an International Master. He finished with 93 out of 100! The Soviet Grandmaster V.Gavrikov scored one point less and came half a point ahead of the Yugoslav Grandmaster V.Kovacević. No ambulances were called to the tournament hall; in the language of official communications, 'there were no casualties.'

If the criterion is length of time irrespective of the number of games, then of course it is postal players who have been involved in the longest tournaments. This was especially true after Soviet players stepped into the international correspondence arena. "Chessplayers in a postal tournament have to wait three months for every reply from their opponents" – the poetic exaggeration here is only slight. In fact the secret but obligatory censorship extended the games

immeasurably. "We're lucky to play 10 or 12 moves a year against foreign opponents," Ludmila Belavenets recalled. Indeed the Women's World Championship which she won lasted nearly 7 years, from 1 December 1984 until the end of April 1991. But the 26th European Championship went on for even longer – a full 7 years. A curious fact is that the Lithuanian Vladas Gefenas started the tournament as an adolescent and finished it in full adulthood as a husband and father.

Record pacifism

This record was established in June 1999 by ten Grandmasters whose names are known to the entire chess world: the Russians Vasily Smyslov, Mark Taimanov, Vitaly Tseshkovsky and Yuri Balashov, the Dane Bent Larsen, the Czech Vlastimil Hort, the Hungarian Lajos Portisch, the Yugoslavs Svetozar Gligorić and Borislav Ivkov, and finally Boris Spassky of France. They assembled in Moscow for the tournament in memory of ex-World Champion Tigran Petrosian, who would have reached the age of 70 during the event. Without a vast number of wins – including wins against each other – these players would simply never have scaled the heights as they did, but here in the Cosmos Hotel, star wars were sadly lacking. In some games no particular struggle arose, in others the player with the advantage failed to conduct it to its logical conclusion. Here is an example.

Portisch – Hort
Grünfeld Defence [D93]

**1 d4 ♘f6 2 ♘f3 g6 3 c4 ♗g7
4 ♘c3 d5 5 ♗f4 0-0 6 ♖c1 c6 7 e3
♛a5 8 ♛d2 ♗e6 9 b3 ♘bd7
10 ♗d3 ♗f5 11 ♗xf5 gxf5 12 0-0**

With the idea of 13 ♘d5.

12...dxc4

12...♛a6!?.

13 bxc4 ♖fd8

At this point Hort only had 35 minutes left....

14 ♛c2 e6 15 ♖b1

The opening has turned out in White's favour; he has a spatial advantage, the better pawn structure, and control of the centre.

15...♛a6 16 ♘d2 ♘f8 17 c5

Portisch seizes some more space; at the same time he is counting on a sly trap.

17...♘g6

28...♖b8 29 ♛b3 ♘c3 30 ♔h1!

Planning ♖f1-c1.

**30...♗f6 31 ♘b6 ♖d8 32 ♖c1
♘d5 33 ♘c4 ♖a7 34 ♖c2 ♗g7
35 ♖d2 h6 36 ♖d1 f4 37 ♘d6 fxe3
38 fxe3 f5 39 ♖f1 ♖f8 40 ♖f3 ♖aa8
41 ♘c4 ♖a7 42 e4**

With time trouble over, Portisch starts the decisive action!

**42...fxe4 43 ♖xf8+ ♗xf8 44 ♛g3
e3!?**

With time running short, Hort overlooks the danger. A better move was 17...♘d5.

18 ♗c7 ♖d7 19 ♖b4! (the black queen is trapped!) **19...♘d5 20 ♖a4
♛xa4 21 ♘xa4 ♖xc7 22 ♘c3 ♘ge7
23 ♘c4 b5 24 ♘xd5 ♘xd5 25 ♘d6
a5 26 h3**

Exploiting White's material advantage is not simple, but technique is Portisch's forte!

26...♔h8 27 a4 b4 28 ♘c4

This time it is Hort who sets a trap.

45 ♛e5+ (45 ♘xe3 is simpler)
45...♗g7 46 ♛b8+ ♔h7 47 ♘xe3

Capturing the rook turns out to be bad – after 47 ♛xa7 e2 there is no stopping the pawn. The position now becomes sharp.

47...♖f7 48 ♘c4

A possibility was 48 ♛e8 ♖f4, with an unclear outcome.

48...♗xd4 49 ♛e8 ♖f1+ ½-½

After 49...♖f1+ 50 ♔h2 ♗g1+ 51 ♔g3 ♗f2+ 52 ♔f3 ♗xc5+ the winning chances would rather be on Black's side.

As it turned out, the first round saw Tseshkovsky, twice Champion of the USSR, prevail with Black against Gligorić, eleven times (!) Champion of Yugoslavia. In round two, the nine-times champion of Hungary with White beat the seventeen-times (!) Champion of Denmark. In round four Ivkov, the first-ever World Junior Champion, playing Black, took Gligorić's 'revenge' on Tseshkovsky. And all the other 42 games were drawn! The two tournament winners were separated by only one point from the two tail-enders, while 60% of the competitors had identical scores. In a word, not a tournament but purely a record factory; the records produced were admittedly not the kind that chess enthusiasts most desire.

An almost equally 'non-belligerent' event had occurred nearly three decades earlier. In the spring of 1970, Leiden Chess Club organized a match-tournament to celebrate the 75th anniversary of its foundation. Four illustrious Grandmasters – World Champion Boris Spassky, ex-Champion Mikhail Botvinnk (this was his last appearance at the board), Bent Larsen and Jan Hein Donner – delivered one decisive game for every two rounds! Spassky and Donner drew 10 games out of 12, Botvinnik 9 and Larsen 7. They fought, they exerted themselves – but the 'peaceful will' of Caissa proved stronger.

Individual outbreaks of pacifism in a chessplayer arise inexplicably and spontaneously. Thus for example in 1992 the eminent Grandmaster Lev Psakhis, twice USSR Champion and later Champion of Israel, an enterprising and aggressive player, drew all eleven of his games in a tournament in Greece. Among his opponents were Vladimir Kramnik, Joël Lautier, Michael Adams, Ivan Sokolov and Vladimir Akopian. A record? Probably not, I am afraid. In the French Championship a year earlier, the master Mershad Sharif, who had not been noted for anything special until then, drew all 15 games without trouble! The event included ex-World Champion Boris Spassky and Grandmasters Bachar Kouatly and Olivier Renet, as well as Marc Santo Roman who had achieved a Grandmaster norm. You might object that it wasn't an international tournament, but it was nonetheless in category 8 according to FIDE's classification.

It's interesting that such great peace-lovers as Richard Teichmann (on the boundary of the 19th and 20th centuries) and Petar Trifunović (at the end of the 1940s) never had any similar 'achievements' to their name.

Among chessplayers known to me personally, Mikhail Segel, the 1924 champion of the Volga region, more than once produced results that were close to being records. I have spoken of him already in Part 2 of this book; he set up the record for longevity among Russian chessplayers. Mikhail Mikhailovich celebrated his hundred-year jubilee, naturally enough, with a feast, two glasses of vodka, and, curiously, a small lightning tournament. In general, up to the age of 90, Segel had neglected 'new-fangled' blitz chess, preferring the friendly games without clocks which were the accepted thing in the days of his youth.

As to his pacifism ... as far back as the beginning of the 1950s, in the championships of Kazan and Tartaria, Segel's score line on the tournament chart would have an exceptionally uniform appearance: one win and all the rest draws, no matter how many players were participating. Even Rashid Nezhmetdinov, five times Russian Champion, failed to overcome him; the International Master's brilliant combinative conceptions would founder on the 'Maginot Line' of reinforced concrete which the future 'grand old man' of Russian chess ingeniously constructed and still more ingeniously defended. But then, the Romanian Florin Gheorghiu played in just the same manner in the 1981 Moscow 'tournament of stars', as did Lubomir Kavalek at Wijk aan Zee 1982 (interestingly, Mikhail Tal made the same score with five wins and four losses) and the Swede Ulf Andersson at Mar del Plata three weeks later....

Draws have never been very highly regarded by lovers of chess, and at the first Moscow international tournament, in 1925, there was even an extra prize (constituting a record in itself) for the prizewinner with the fewest drawn games. It was shared between the tournament victor Efim Bogoljubow, Grandmaster Frank Marshall who finished fourth, and Peter Romanovsky who shared 7th-8th prizes. Each of them had concluded peace in five games out of twenty – insofar as peace is the right word for encounters such as this:

Bogoljubow – Marshall
Queen's Gambit [D38]

1 ♘f3 ♘f6 2 c4 e6 3 d4 d5 4 ♗g5 h6 5 ♗xf6 ♕xf6 6 ♘c3 ♗b4 7 ♕b3 c5 8 cxd5 exd5 9 a3 ♗xc3+ 10 ♕xc3 0-0 11 ♕xc5 ♗g4 12 e3 ♗xf3 13 gxf3 ♕xf3 14 ♖g1 ♘d7 15 ♕d6 ♘f6 16 ♕g3 ♕xg3 17 hxg3 ♖ac8 18 ♗d3 ♖c6 19 ♔d2 ♖fc8 20 f3 h5 21 ♗f5 ♖8c7 22 ♖ac1 g6 23 ♖xc6 ♖xc6 24 ♗d3 ♘h7 25 ♖f1 ♘g5 26 b4 ♖f6 27 f4 ♘e4+ 28 ♗xe4 dxe4 29 ♖c1 ♖a6 30 ♖c3 f6 31 ♔c2 g5 32 b5 ♖a5 33 fxg5 ♖xb5 34 gxf6 ♔f7 35 ♖b3 ♖g5 36 ♖xb7+ ♔xf6 37 ♖xa7 ♖xg3 38 ♔d2 ♖g2+ 39 ♔e1 ♖a2 40 ♖a5 ♔g6 41 ♖e5 h4 42 ♔f1 h3 43 ♔g1 h2+ 44 ♔h1 ♖xa3 45 ♖xe4 ♖a2 46 ♖g4+ ♔f5 47 ♖g2 ♖a3 48 ♖g3 ♖a2 49 ♖g2 ♖a3 50 ♖e2 ♔e4 51 ♔xh2 ♖a8 52 ♔g2 ♖f8 53 ♖e1 ♔d3 ½-½

However, at times the thought involuntarily crosses your mind that some contests which break records by their peaceful tendencies are in full accordance with the will of Caissa. After all, in a friendly match between the Dutchman Jeroen Piket and the Frenchman Joël Lautier, both still young but already distinguished Grandmasters, nearly every game saw sacrifices on both sides – yet all eight of them ended in draws!

Lautier – Piket
Monte Carlo 1996

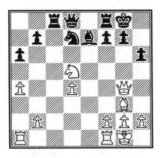

20...♘f6?? 21 ♘xe7+??

The elementary 21 ♕xc8 wins the exchange.

21...♕xe7 22 ♕f3 ♕d7 23 ♗e5 ♘d5 24 ♖ac1 f6 25 ♗g3 ♖xc1 26 ♖xc1 ♖d8 27 ♕b3 ♕f7 28 h3 g5 29 ♖c5 ♔g7 30 h4 ♖d7 31 ♕f3 ♕e6 32 ♔h2 ♘e7 33 ♕e3 ♕g4 34 f3 ♘f5 35 fxg4

Why not 35 ♕xg5+, with quite good chances in the rook endgame?

35...♘xe3 36 ♔h3 ♖xd4 37 hxg5 hxg5 38 ♖xg5+ ♔f7 39 ♖c5 ♖xa4 40 ♖c7+ ♔g6 41 ♖xb7 ♘xg4 42 b3 ♖e4 43 ♖a7 ♘e3 44 ♖xa6 ♖b4 45 ♖a3 ♘c2 46 ♖a2 ♘e3 47 ♖b2 ♘c4 48 ♖c2 ♘a5 ½-½

And while we are on the subject of matches, a final word. I have already mentioned history's longest string of draws in the first encounter between Anatoly Karpov and Garry Kasparov, and also the 'mere' eight draws at the start of Kasparov's World Championship match with Anand (New York, 1995). More than a century earlier, however, the rising Austrian star Carl Schlechter, aged 19, drew all ten games of a match against his very experienced compatriot Georg Marco. And yet the games were extremely hard

fought! A game between the same players in the 1905 Ostende tournament lasted 13 moves only – and Marco won!

Record bloodshed

As far as matches are concerned, this record was established nearly a century and a half ago and will probably stand for ever! In 1866 on a rainy June evening in London, Wilhelm Steinitz, still young and a 'rising star of chess', began his dispute with Anderssen, the winner of two international tournaments – the first two in history. It was Anderssen, in fact, who used the phrase I have just quoted to describe his opponent. I would mention in passing (this has nothing to do with our topic) that the winner could expect the modest prize of 100 pounds sterling, and the loser 20 (!). The prize fund and the players' accommodation expenses had been guaranteed jointly by three London chess clubs.

It's true that in those days defence was viewed with disdain and players were incapable of serious defensive strategy, so that rivers of chess blood flowed. Even so, fourteen games between players of roughly equal strength, and not one peaceful result – this was extreme! The final score was 8:6 to the future World Champion. Both he and his unofficial champion opponent gained their wins more or less in the style of the following game – the 8th, played when the score stood at 4:3. Incidentally Steinitz played the King's Gambit every time he had the chance, while Anderssen offered the Evans Gambit in six games out of seven.

Steinitz – Anderssen

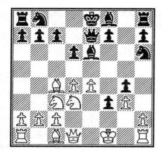

11 d5?!

The prelude to a rash piece sacrifice which Anderssen accurately refutes. In his next game with White, Steinitz played the quiet 11 &b3 and obtained an excellent position after 11...&g7 12 &e3 &xb3 13 axb3 c6 14 ♕d2 ♘g8 15 e5! d5 16 &g5 ♕e6 17 ♘a4.

11...&c8 12 e5

This and the following move show how far Steinitz still was, at that time, from the ideas of the Classical School. The piece sacrifice he undertakes here is unsound. After some complications Anderssen succeeds in wresting the initiative from him with an astute manoeuvre.

Instead 12 &f4, followed by ♕d1-♕d2 and ♖a1-e1, was stronger. On 12...f6, White could also consider 13 &b5+.

12...dxe5 13 ♘xe5 ♕xe5 14 &f4 ♕g7 15 ♘b5 &d6!

Against 15...♘a6 White would continue his attack with 16 &xc7. However, Anderssen isn't concerned to keep his material plus – he has a rook sacrifice in mind. After 16 &xd6 cxd6 17 ♘c7+ &d8 18 ♘xa8 ♕xb2, Black would seize the initiative.

Steinitz in turn prefers to play for attack at any cost. Without exaggeration, in this match he was more of an Anderssen than Anderssen!

16 ♕e1+ &d8 17 &xd6 cxd6 18 ♕b4 ♘f5 19 &d3

Of course 19 ♘xd6? would be met by 19...♕f8 20 ♘xb7+ &xb7 21 ♕xb7 ♘e3+.

19...♘a6 20 ♕a3 ♘c5

21 &xf5 ♕h6!

An unexpected 'quiet' move, after which the white king comes under a devastating attack. Black threatens both 22...♕h3+ followed by ♖h8-e8+, and 22...♕d2.

22 &d3

The simplest answer to 22 ♕c3 is 22...♖e8 (after 22...♕h3+ 23 &f2 ♕g2+ 24 &e3 ♖e8+ 25 &f4, or 24...♕e2+ 25 &f4, Black has no checks while White is threatening 26 ♕f6+) 23 h4 &xf5, with an extra piece and an attack.

22...♖e8 23 h4 ♕d2 24 ♖g1 ♖e2! 0-1

In justice it must be said that in the 19th and early 20th centuries, matches without draws were not uncommon. But either it was a case of Steinitz, Lasker or Capablanca winning 5:0 against opponents known to be weaker; or it was this

146

same result between La Bourdonnais and Saint-Amant, in a couple of their endless succession of duels; or else we are generally speaking of games at odds, as between La Bourdonnais and the Hungarian Josef Szen. Hence such encounters from the 'early dawn' of modern chess may be disregarded.

In more recent times, ex-World Champion Max Euwe and Paul Keres gave each other exceptionally little quarter. They could not of course improve on the record of Steinitz and Anderssen, if only because their own match in Amsterdam, from December 1939 to January 1940, consisted similarly of 14 games and no more. By rights, however, they could hope to repeat the 'feat' of their great prececessors. Alas, a draw in the very first game put paid to the theoretical possibility of one-hundred-per-cent 'bloodshed', and then another draw followed. What happened next, however, was the longest series of decisive games in modern chess! The players resigned to each other in ten games running, and since in six cases this was done by Euwe, the match organizing committee refused to finance his next prospective duel for the world crown against the reigning champion Alexander Alekhine.

Still, Euwe did win one of the last two games of the match.

Bobby Fischer's 'clean scores' in Candidates matches are mentioned in the Chapter 'Unbroken runs'. If we put matches aside, the record for 'blood-thirstiness' belongs to the 1862 tournament in London, which is often referred to as the second international tournament in chess history. The official table doesn't contain a single drawn result, and there were 14 participants. However, for one thing, they were too varied in calibre; of nine players who received personal invitations, only two accepted – Anderssen and Louis Paulsen. The others entered for the tournament on their own initiative. Secondly and most importantly, the 'normal' total of 91 games was increased by 20 extra ones – since drawn games were replayed. The tournament winner Anderssen had to do this three times, including once against the second prize winner Paulsen; incidentally by the normal system of scoring, they would have changed places in the tournament table. Steinitz, whose glorious chess career began with this contest, was even forced to sit down for two replays against the Englishman Green, who ended up sharing last place in the official reckoning. Furthermore, at that time, there was never any hint of so-called Grandmaster draws, so that the games replayed included hand-to-hand battles such as this:

MacDonnell – Steinitz
Evans Gambit [C51]

1 e4 e5 2 ♘f3 ♘c6 3 ♗c4 ♗c5
4 b4 ♗xb4 5 c3 ♗c5 6 d4 exd4
7 0-0 d6 8 cxd4 ♗b6 9 ♘c3 ♗g4
10 ♕a4 ♗d7 11 ♕b3 ♘a5
12 ♗xf7+ ♔f8 13 ♕d5 ♘f6
14 ♕g5 ♔xf7 15 e5 ♘e8 16 ♕f4+
♔g8 17 ♘g5 ♕e7 18 e6 ♗c8
19 ♘d5 ♕f8 20 ♕f7+ ♕xf7
21 exf7+ ♔f8

147

22 ♖e1 ♗d7 23 fxe8=♕+ ♖xe8 24 ♗b2 ♖xe1+ 25 ♖xe1 h6 26 ♖e7 hxg5 27 ♖xd7 ♖h4 28 ♘xc7 ♖e4 29 ♗c3 ♘c6 30 d5 ♘e5 31 ♘e6+ ♔e8 32 ♖xg7 ♖e2 33 h3 ♖xf2 34 ♗d4 ♗xd4 35 ♘xd4 ♖xa2 36 ♖xb7 g4 37 ♘f5 gxh3 38 ♘xd6+ ♔f8 39 ♖b8+ ♔e7 40 ♘f5+ ♔d7 41 gxh3 ♘f3+ ½-½

This unfortunate practice devised by our chess ancestors is discussed in more detail under 'Sergeant-major's orders'. Now for the authentic record-breaking tournament without draws. It did not originally figure in the sporting calendar for 1961, but the trouble was that when the RSFSR Championship finished, only one player had emerged as a qualifier for the USSR Championship final. Those who shared 2nd to 6th places were assigned to a supplementary contest for the two remaining vacancies. All five were International or National Masters, well known throughout the country; two were shortly to become Grandmasters. Problems with financing and organizing such unscheduled events did not arise in Soviet times, and in Dubna, the town of physicists near Moscow, four of these players assembled in

the autumn (one had declined). The contestants in the double-round tournament had no time for draws; nothing but victory inspired them! Furthermore, the future Grandmasters Anatoly Lein and Vladimir Antoshin ended up playing an extra match between themselves. The first player to win a game was to win the match, and as it turned out, there was no 'limbering up' with draws – the very first game was decisive.

Lein – Antoshin
(notes by M.Yudovich jr.)

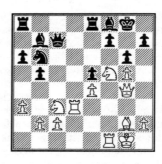

White has some difficult problems to solve. If his attacked knight withdraws to g3 or h4, the initiative passes to Black. Also 22 ♘h6+ ♗xh6 23 gxh6 ♖ad8 promises nothing good. Lein therefore takes a decision that is risky but fully justified from the psychological viewpoint: to attack his opponent without shrinking from sacrifices, rather than concede the initiative just when Black was hoping to seize it.
22 ♖h3 gxf5 23 ♕h5 f6 24 ♖xf5
White only has one pawn for the sacrificed piece, but his major pieces have taken up menacing positions opposite the black king.

Antoshin has to switch over to defence against his opponent's desperate attack. In such an important game this demands a great effort.

24...fxg5

Up to here Black has played accurately, but now he misses his chance to repulse the attack while keeping a material plus.

The right move was 24...♗c8, after which 25 ♕xe8 ♗xf5 26 ♕h5 ♗g6 would be unsatisfactory for White, while 25 gxf6 would be met by 25...♗xf5 26 ♖g3+ ♔h8 27 f7 ♗c5+ 28 ♔h1 ♖f8. Now White's attack increases and, as often happens, one error leads to another – but the second one is much more serious.

25 ♕xg5+ ♗g7

If 25...♔h8, then 26 ♕f6+ ♗g7 27 ♕g6 h6 28 ♖f7.

26 ♕h5 h6

On 26...♗f8 White could return with 27 ♕g5+; then after 27...♗g7 28 ♕h5, Black would have to play h7-h6 anyway, or consent to a draw by repetition.

27 ♕g6 ♕c6

The only defence against the threat of 28 ♖xh6. But now White manages to restore the material balance almost entirely.

28 ♕f7+ ♔h7

On 28...♔h8, White plays 29 ♖g5 ♕c5+ (or 29...♖g8 30 ♖g6) 30 ♔h1 ♕f8 31 ♕xb7, regaining the piece while keeping a strong attack as well as an extra pawn.

29 ♖xh6+! ♕xh6 30 ♖h5 ♖ab8?

The decisive mistake. Instead 30...♕xh5 31 ♕xh5+ ♔g8 leads to a sharp position that isn't so simple to assess: for the queen and two pawns Black has obtained two rooks and a bishop. At any rate,

with his dangerous passed h-pawn and actively placed pieces, White's chances would be no worse.

31 ♕f5+! ♔h8 32 ♖xh6+ ♗xh6 33 ♕f6+ ♗g7 34 ♕xb6 ♗xe4 35 ♕f2 ♗xg2 36 ♕xg2

White emerges with a queen and pawn for two rooks, in other words approximate material equality. However, the queen supported by the knight is considerably stronger than the two rooks and bishop. In addition White has a passed h-pawn, and the black king is most awkwardly placed while its opposite number isn't threatened by anything.

All this enables us to assess the position as hopeless for Black.

36...e4

Otherwise the knight will take up a dominating position on e4. However, opening the long diagonal for his bishop brings Black no relief.

37 ♘xe4 ♖bd8 38 ♕g6 ♖e7 39 ♘g5 ♗d4+ 40 ♔g2 ♖f8

At this point the game was adjourned and White sealed his move. Although Black drags out his hopeless resistance for forty moves more, the outcome of the game is settled.

41 ♕h6+ ♔g8 42 ♕g6+ ♖g7 43 ♕e6+ ♔h8 44 ♕h3+ ♔g8 45 ♕b3+ ♔h8 46 h4 ♗f6 47 ♕b4 ♖c8 48 ♔h3 ♗xg5 49 hxg5 ♖c6 50 ♕f8+ ♖g8 51 ♕f5 ♖g7 52 ♕e5 ♔h7 53 ♔g4 ♖gg6 54 ♕e7+ ♔g8 55 ♔f5 ♖b6 56 ♔e5 ♖bc6 57 c3 ♖b6 58 ♔d5 ♖b8 59 b3 ♖f8 60 ♔e4 ♖c8 61 ♔f5 ♖gc6 62 ♔g4 ♖g6 63 ♔h5 ♖cc6 64 ♕e8+ ♔g7 65 ♕d7+ ♔g8 66 c4 bxc4 67 bxc4 ♖gd6 68 ♕e8+ ♔g7 69 c5 ♖e6 70 ♕d7+ ♔f8 71 ♔g4 a5 72 ♔f5 ♖g6 73 ♕d8+ ♔f7 74 ♕xa5 ♖a6

149

75 ♕c7+ ♔e8 76 ♕b8+ ♔d7
77 ♕b5+ ♔c7 78 a4 ♖gc6 79 ♔e5
♖g6 80 ♔d4 ♖a8 81 a5 ♖b8
82 ♕f1 ♖bg8 83 a6 ♖xg5 84 ♕f7+
♔c8 85 a7 ♖g4+ 86 ♔d5 ♖8g5+
87 ♔c6 ♖g6+ 88 ♔b5 1-0

In conclusion, here is a singular mixture of bloodshed and peace. In 1949 in New York, a match took place between one of the world's strongest Grandmasters, the American Reuben Fine, and the 'new Argentinian' Miguel Najdorf who was impetuously breaking into the chess élite. An unusual scenario unfolded. At the start the player on home ground won with both White and Black, whereupon the guest proceeded to do likewise. (The finish of one of these games is given in the chapter 'Peace, perfect peace') After that there were four draws in succession. None of them were short; all featured a desperate struggle with fluctuating chances. But the outcome was a happy end. Is this fate?

Record secrecy

The mid-1970s saw an upsurge of interest in chess in England. The country acquired its first Grandmaster, tournaments multiplied, books were published in large quantities. Nor was television left out. Even before the film *Where Karpov is King* was produced, 8 players were invited to an original type of tournament at the beginning of August 1977. They competed on the knockout system, and the games were to be televised. If a game was drawn, the time limit – 40 moves in 2 hours – was shortened for the replay.

The masters and Grandmasters supplied the organizers with commentaries on their play, but also signed a non-disclosure agreement so that for quite a long time the content and even the results of the games were kept secret. This kept up the viewers' interest in the BBC programmes devoted to the tournament. It was only three weeks after the struggle ended that they all found out who was winner: the World Champion Anatoly Karpov.

Prizes for back-markers

In theory it is possible to win a tournament in which you occupy last place! Or more precisely, in which you share it. For this, the only requirement is that all contestants without exception should score fifty per cent, only to rack their brains for a long time to come, wondering whether it was an achievement after all to share first place, or a disaster to share the last one.

Admittedly no such thing has occurred in any contests of note, and yet in tournaments with a small number of participants there have indeed been prizewinners who brought up the rear! This has happened more than once! For instance in Linares 2000, the joint winners, Garry Kasparov and Vladimir Kramnik, came a point and a half ahead of the third prize winners – and back-markers, since all the other four competitors had identical results and shared third to sixth places.

In the following year, the same Linares tournament ended even more amusingly. Again six Grandmasters, again a double-round event, again only two final scores – but this time Garry Kasparov came three points ahead of all his competitors, who thus finished second to sixth. When Alexei Shirov faced Judit Polgar in the last round, the sole woman in this company only needed to draw to secure second place in the table, in which case Shirov would finish bottom. However....

Shirov – J.Polgar
(notes by S.Shipov)

17...♗g5 18 ♗f2 f5!
Correct. We play in the sector where we are stronger.
19 ♔h1 ♛f6
You feel that Black's strategy is succeeding. Her position already looks a little better.
20 ♘b1
Logically played. The knight approaches the desired square c3.
20...♛h6
Classic chess! Judit plays on the black squares according to all the rules of chess art. Now the black bishop is ready to jump to f4 or e3.
21 ♘c3
Both sides have their assets. The white knight can continue its

journey by heading for b5. Another possibility is a2-a3 and b2-b4.
21...♖ce8
Objectively the position is equal. Subjectively, Black is better.
22 a3!
Both sides are playing logically. Let us see whose logic is the *more* logical.
22...e4
Judit plays to complicate the issue. In my view 22...♗e3 would be more logical and sounder; the exchange of dark-squared bishops is most important to Black. There could follow 23 b4 ♗xf2 24 ♖xf2 ♛e3 25 ♖ff1 ♘a6, with chances for both sides.
23 b4 e3 24 ♗e1
Not 24 bxc5 exf2 25 c6, on account of 25...♗f4 26 h3 ♛h4 and ♛h4-♛g3.
24...♘b7?!
An ugly square for the knight; 24...♘a6 looks more attractive.
25 ♘b5
White can't establish a pawn on the f4-square; if 25 g3, then 25...f4!.
25...f4
The wrapping-up job is completed. What next?
26 ♘c7
The knight continues its extraordinary journey. We are off to e6! With the black knight on a6, this would not have been possible.
26...♖e5
Why not 26...♖e7 ?
27 ♗c3
There would seem to be no objection to 27 ♘e6! ♖f6 28 ♗c3, when White wins the exchange and penetrates with his queen via a4 into the enemy's rear.
27...♖e7 28 ♘e6 ♖a8!
In this way Judit forestalls the white queen's sortie to a4.
29 ♛f5 ♗h4!

In the event of 29...♗f6 30 ♗xf6 ♕xf6 31 ♕xf6! ♘xf6 32 ♘xf4 axb4 33 axb4 ♖a2 34 ♖fe1, Black has no real counterplay on account of the badly placed knight on b7.

30 ♕g4

Not 30 ♗xg7 ♖xg7 31 ♘xg7 ♕xg7 32 ♕xf4 in view of 32...♗f2, and White can't dislodge the pair of units on e3 and f2. For the moment, of course, taking the f-pawn would be bad: 30 ♕xf4? ♖xe6, or 30 ♘xf4 ♖f8.

30...♗f6

On 30...♗g3 Black would have to reckon with 31 ♕h3 ♕xh3 32 gxh3, and after the bishop retreats the f-pawn falls.

31 ♗xf6 ♕xf6 32 ♘xf4 ♕b2

So the *black* queen reaches the enemy's rear.

33 ♕h4 ♖f7

Better 33...♘f6!?.

34 ♗d3 ♘f8?!

Too passive; Better 34...h6!, after which the black knight jumps to e5.

35 ♖fe1 ♕xa3

Or 35...axb4 36 axb4 ♖a2 37 ♖e2 ♖a1 38 ♕e1 ♖xd1 39 ♕xd1 ♕xb4 40 ♘e6.

36 ♘e6!

Black is hard pressed!

36...g6 37 ♘g5 ♖g7 38 ♕d4 ♕xb4 39 ♘e4 ♘c5 40 ♖b1 ♕a3 41 ♘f6+

The complications are in full swing. White has substantial winning chances. The centre is in his hands. The black knight on f8 is bad; placing it there was futile.

41...♔h8 42 ♖xe3 ♘xd3 43 ♘e8!

A small combination leading to the win of the exchange.

43...♖xe8 44 ♖xe8 ♔g8 45 ♖e3 ♘f2+ 46 ♔g1 ♕a4

The knight can't be saved anyway: 46...♕a2 47 ♖xb6!.

47 ♖e2 ♖c7

Perhaps Black should have opened up the white king with 47...♘h3+ 48 gxh3.

48 ♔xf2 ♖xc4 49 ♕xb6 ♖c5 50 ♕xd6 ♕d4+ 51 ♔g3 ♖xd5 52 ♕f4

The rest is uncomplicated technique.

52...♕c5 53 ♖c1! ♖g5+ 54 ♔h4 ♖h5+ 55 ♔g4! ♕d5 56 ♖d2

An immediate queen exchange would lead to loss of the h-pawn.

56...♕e6+ 57 ♔g3 a4 58 ♕c4 ♖a5 59 ♖e2 1-0

This event was unique and record-breaking in one other respect. For the first time in the history of international tournaments, the winner was the only contestant to finish with what chessplayers call a 'plus score', and a substantial one at that – 7½ out of 10. All, repeat *all* the others finished with a minus score, namely 4½, and thus in their way played the role of 'benefactors' for the thirteenth World Champion Kasparov.

In a word, some funny things do happen in this world!

Where history is made

As has long been known, the appearance of a new scientific term is an event, however small; it doesn't by any means happen every day. In chess, things are similar. Only one tournament has been permanently commemorated in two stock phrases – namely, Scheveningen 1923. In the first place, it gave its name to a special competition format. Ten Dutch masters fought against ten foreigners, putting aside internecine strife; everyone had a new opponent in each round, but only from the 'other camp'. This was the so-called 'Scheveningen System'. It was later employed repeatedly (suffice it to recall Ramsgate 1929, where the English players took on the rest; the Moscow-Prague match of 1946; and the testing which the young Soviet masters received from the Grandmasters at Sochi 1970), but the original 'Scheveningen' was the one on the largest scale.

Secondly, this tournament gave its name to the Scheveningen Variation of the Sicilian Defence which was later to become so popular. Strictly speaking, this opening set-up had been seen before – its first occurrence was probably in Chigorin-Paulsen, Berlin 1881 (!) – but such anomalies are quite usual. In any case, it *was* at Scheveningen that the 'Scheveningen' emerged as a fully-fledged system. Here, for example, is one of the encounters in which Black was just feeling his way towards the correct path.

Maroczy – Euwe
Scheveningen 1923
Sicilian Defence [B96]

1 e4 c5 2 ♘f3 ♘c6
In the modern Scheveningen this move is played much later if at all.
3 d4 cxd4 4 ♘xd4 ♘f6 5 ♘c3 d6 6 ♗e2 e6
This pawn-couple is the distinguishing feature of the variation.
7 0-0 ♗e7 8 ♔h1
Thirty years on, it became obligatory to play this move,

following Geller's example; but it appears that the Soviet Grandmaster had a predecessor.
8...0-0 9 f4 ♕c7 10 ♘b3 a6 11 a4 b6
A set-up that became fashionable half a century later, under the name of the 'hedgehog'.
12 ♗f3 ♗b7 13 ♗e3 ♘b4 14 ♕e2 d5 15 e5 ♘e4 (risky – *very* risky) **16 ♗xe4 dxe4 17 ♕f2 b5 18 axb5 axb5 19 ♘d4 ♗c6 20 ♕g3 ♖xa1 21 ♖xa1 ♖b8 22 f5 exf5 23 ♘xf5 ♗f8 24 ♗f4 ♖a8 25 ♖c1**

25...g6?
After this error, the game can't be saved. After 25...♕d7 there would still be everything to play for.
26 e6 ♕b7 27 e7 ♗g7 (or 27... ♗xe7 28 ♘xe7+ ♕xe7 29 ♗d6) **28 ♘xg7 ♔xg7 29 ♕h4 f6 30 ♕h6+ ♔g8 31 ♗d6 1-0**

* * *

When we speak of a game in which the opponent is invisible, this naturally refers to correspondence chess, irrespective of what means of communication (traditional or modern) the players are using. There have been innumerable postal contests both for individuals and for teams, but the most massive team encounter hitherto remains the

153

match between the English and Americans which carried on for almost 3 years between 1936 and 1938. There were 1000 participants on each side, and to state the final score under such circumstances seems to me absurd....

Sixty-odd years passed, and this record was due to be put completely in the shade. The FIDE President Kirsan Ilyumzhinov, whose soaring ambition in many undertakings can only be admired, announced that in the year 2000 he was going to hold an Internet match involving all five inhabited continents of the globe (anyone wintering in the Antarctic was left out), and that each team would consist of 100,000 people! Ostap Bender himself, who planned an interplenetary chess congress, would have been struck dumb. I am afraid the project has yet to be realized, perhaps just because of its grandiosity.

Summit meetings

By definition these should be matches for the World Championship and tournaments featuring the chief pretenders to the chess crown. But public opinion has not always agreed unreservedly with such formal definitions. Thus for example the Steinitz-Lasker duel of 1894, which brought about the very first change of rulers in the chess kingdom, took years to be acknowledged as a genuine meeting of the strongest. Until then Lasker had not enjoyed wide recognition, and his victory was considered fortuitous.

Many matches on the highest chess level were *not* indeed genuine summit meetings. In the days when a more or less objective selection process did not exist, the challenger was simply a player who sent the champion a challenge and whose gauntlet was picked up. This explains, for instance, the downright 'indecent' scores of Lasker's own victories against Marshall (+8 =7 without a single loss) and Janowski (+7 -1 =2 and +8 =3!), as well as Alekhine's against Bogoljubow.

At first sight it seems even more hopeless to try to work out which tournament holds the record for the quality and strength of its participants, even though such attempts have been undertaken more than once and are sure to continue. Of course, new mathematical formulae and computers are brought into play. But here is a candid admission by the author of one such attempt, A.Ivanov from the Ukrainian town of Donetsk. He is the author of the *Encyclopaedia of Chess Statistics (1851-1996)*.

The attainments of chess-players from different generations cannot be set beside each other and evaluated comparatively. Such problems are not peculiar to chess. Take the history of the queen of sciences, mathematics. Schoolchildren of today know more than the greatest mathematician of antiquity, Archimedes; while a student of mathematics and physics knows more than Newton.... If we were able to assess mathematicians by how far their knowledge exceeded that of their contemporaries, then we *could* say who was who.

It was with these aims that a virtual tournament was 'conducted' between the world's 36 leading chessplayers from a period of 30 years in the mid-19th century, whether or not they had faced each other in real life. Individual ELO scores in present-day format have been extrapolated and assigned to players of the past without even omitting a corrective to the constant inflation of the ratings.

Needless to say, the first-ever category 21 tournament, held in Las Palmas towards the end of 1996, has not been neglected by the statisticians. In this category, the average rating of the contestants has to be above the 2750 mark, even if only by one point. At that time only seven super-Grandmasters had a rating of 2700 or over, and the top six duly lined up for the contest: Kasparov, Karpov, Anand, Kramnik, Ivanchuk and Topalov.

Further tournaments in category 21, which at present is the highest possible for a six-player event, were held at Linares in 1998 and 2000. But perhaps objectively no less significance should be attached to the first chess congress of the 3rd millennium AD, held in the tiny Dutch town of Wijk aan Zee in January 2001. There, the nine (!) top names in the world ranking list went into battle. To be sure, they were 'diluted' by five other Grandmasters (who weren't exactly weak), so the category 'dropped' to 19, but what of it?

Other events that could very well stand comparison with this were Linares 1993, 1994 and 1999, as well as some older tournaments:

Vienna 1922, Nuremberg 1896, AVRO 1938, and of course St Petersburg 1895/96, where the participants were 'only' the world's four strongest players: the Champion Lasker, ex-Champion Steinitz, Pillsbury and Chigorin. Ostende 1907 and St Petersburg 1914 were also designated 'tournaments of champions'.

Thus the word 'champion' has somehow cropped up of its own accord in our assessment of these contests. Should not the participation of World Champions be taken as the criterion for the most significant events? At the end of the day it is they, the Chess Kings, who have dictated fashion to the entire chess world and sometimes opened up radically new paths of development for the ancient game.

Well, then – the first of the greatest gatherings of World Champions occurred in 1936 in the English town of Nottingham. There were five of them: the reigning Chess King, Euwe; three of his predecessors, Lasker, Capablanca and Alekhine; and the 25-year-old Botvinnik, post-graduate student and Young Communist League member (it was compulsory to mention this in the Soviet newspapers of the time), whose coronation was still a long way off. Sharing first place with Capablanca, Botvinnik was also awarded the brilliancy prize.

Botvinnik – Tartakower
Old Indian Defence [A46]

1 ♘f3 ♘f6 2 c4 d6 3 d4 ♘bd7
4 g3 e5 5 ♗g2 ♗e7 6 0-0 0-0 7 ♘c3

c6 8 e4 ♕c7 9 h3 ♖e8 10 ♗e3 ♘f8
11 ♖c1 h6?! 12 d5 ♗d7 13 ♘d2
g5?

"After this, in principle, the game can hardly be saved. By far the lesser evil was 13...♘g6 14 f4 exf4 15 gxf4 ♗f8." (Alekhine)

"I would therefore have preferred 14 b4." (Botvinnik)

14 f4 gxf4 15 gxf4 ♔g7

A relative improvement was 15...exf4 16 ♗xf4 ♘g6, giving up a pawn but obtaining at least *some* counterplay.

16 fxe5 dxe5 17 c5 cxd5 18 ♘xd5 ♕c6 19 ♘c4 ♘g6 20 ♘d6 ♗e6

Unfortunately 20...♖f8 is met by 21 ♘xe7 ♘xe7 22 ♗xh6+.

21 ♘xe7

"Instead of winning the exchange and a pawn with 21 ♘xe8+ ♖xe8 22 ♘xe7 followed by ♗e3xh6+ and ♖f1xf6, White prefers to make material sacrifices of his own in order to launch a mating attack. It's hard to say which of these two methods is stronger, as both guarantee victory – but the line Botvinnik chooses is definitely more elegant." (Alekhine)

"White can't resist the temptation to decide the game with an attack." (Botvinnik)

21...♘xe7

After 21...♖xe7 22 ♘f5+ ♗xf5 23 exf5 a piece is lost.

22 ♖xf6 ♔xf6 23 ♕h5 ♘g6 24 ♘f5! ♖g8 25 ♕xh6 ♗xa2 26 ♖d1 ♖ad8 27 ♕g5+

Strictly speaking, 27 ♖xd8 first was more accurate.

27...♔e6 28 ♖xd8 f6 29 ♖xg8 ♘f4 30 ♕g7 1-0

One other 'prize' became a chess record: Botvinnik was the first player to be rewarded with a state decoration (afterwards in the USSR this became usual).

The next event featuring five World Champions was Moscow 1971, where the portrait of a sixth hung above the stage; this was the Alexander Alekhine Memorial Tournament, honouring the Champion who had departed this life undefeated a quarter of a century earlier. Again two players shared victory. It was the first major success for the 20-year-old future Champion Anatoly Karpov. For the immensely talented Leonid Stein, it was sadly one of the last; within a year and a half he would be no more.

Finally, five Chess Kings once competed among themselves within the context of a team tournament! Of course this could only happen in our country, seeing that for more than half a century Bobby Fischer alone among foreign Grandmasters has been able to scale the chess Olympus. In the contest for the 1966 USSR Cup, teams representing various sporting bodies were headed by the reigning Champion Tigran Petrosian, his future conqueror Boris Spassky, and the ex-Champions Mikhail Botvinnik, Vasily Smyslov and Mikhail Tal. And yet none of them was destined to win the top-board super-tournament. That honour went to the leader of the Armed Forces team, Grandmaster Efim Geller, who incidentally had a better score against the Kings of Chess than anyone in the world!

But there was a paradox here – an uncommon episode which, if you like, can count as a record. Geller's best move of the tournament was not discovered against any of the World Champions or indeed in any of his own games, but on someone else's board. The following position arose in the match between the army team, of which Efim was captain, and 'Daugava' which was synonymous with the team of Latvia.

Eduard Gufeld – Janis Klovans

White sealed the obvious and natural move:
42 ♖d7+
He then set about analysing the position after Black's only reply:
42...♔f8
Many hours of work led to the conclusion that in view of the mate threats to his own king, White would have to force perpetual check. In the morning, however, a smiling Geller called at Gufeld's hotel room and without a word made a move on the chessboard:
43 ♗f4!!
It now beame clear that Black could resign! After 43...exf4 he would come out a rook down: 44 ♖d8+ ♔e7 45 ♖e8+ ♔d6 46 ♖d1+ ♖cd3 47 ♖xd3+ and 48 ♖d8+.
After 43...♗xg1 44 ♖f7+ ♔g8 45 ♖e7 the threat of mate on e8 is decisive, since Black's counterplay

involving a check on g3 is eliminated.
On resumption, Klovans reacted to White's 43rd move by sinking into thought for nearly an hour. He then played:
43...♖hd3
The concluding moves were:
44 ♖xd3 ♖xd3 45 ♖h1 ♔e7
(again, if Black takes the bishop on f4 he loses his rook) **46 ♖h8 1-0**

Chess history contains one other wholly unique case in which six (!) World Champions competed on the same stage at the same time, with a seventh also present. But they didn't all play against each other. Five of these Chess Kings were playing in the USSR team, while one was a member of the team representing all the Rest of the World, captained by Max Euwe who by then was at a ripe old age. The event – the 'Match of the Century', in Belgrade in the spring of 1970 – was itself absolutely unique, and not only in the world of chess. It happens that here, once again, the best game was played by the 'non-champion' Efim Geller in the first round against Svetozar Gligoric.

Geller – Gligorić
(notes by Geller)

23 ♘xe5!
Just in time! In giving up two minor pieces for a rook and pawn, White reckons that the rapid advance of his pawn-couple on the e and f-files will drive the black forces into bad positions.
23...♖xe5 24 ♗xe5 ♕xe5 25 f4 ♕e6
After 25...♕c3 26 ♕f2 the black queen would be trapped, for instance: 26...♘c6 27 e5 ♘e8 28 ♖e3 ♕b2 29 ♘xh6+ gxh6 30 ♗h7+.
26 e5 ♘e8

This gives White a chance to let the win slip by playing the tempting 27 ♘d6 ♘xd6 28 exd6 ♕f6 29 d7 ♘c6 30 ♖e8 ♘d4!.
Black could hardly be happy with 26...♘e4 27 ♖xe4! ♕xf5 28 ♖ee1 ♕e6 (if 28...♕h5 then 29 ♕d3 is unpleasant) 29 f5 with a very strong attack. The trouble is that his queenside pieces are merely looking on while his king's position is being demolished.
27 ♘h4!
The most energetic continuation. The weakness of h7 takes on a fatal significance for Black.
27...♘c6 28 ♕d3 g6 29 f5 gxf5 30 ♘xf5
Threatening mate in three moves with 31 ♘e7+ etc. Black's reply is

forced, as after 30...♗g7 31 ♘xg7 ♔xg7 (or 31...♖xg7 32 ♕h7+ ♔f8 33 ♕h8+) 32 ♕h7+ ♔f8 33 ♗f5! his queen has nowhere to go; 33...♕e7 allows 34 ♕h8 mate.
30...♕g6 31 ♕e2!
White could also win by 31 ♕d7, but he wants to deprive his opponent of any chances whatsoever.
31...♕g5
This leads to loss of the queen, but Black's position is already indefensible. Thus, in answer to 31...♕e6 32 ♕e4 ♕g6, there were two winning continuations that I examined during the game:
(a) 33 ♖e3 ♘d8 34 ♖d5 ♗xd5 35 cxd5 etc.
(b) 33 ♖d7! ♗c8 34 e6! ♗xd7 (or 34...♕xe6 35 ♘e7+) 35 exd7 ♘g7 (or 35...♘c7 36 ♘h4!) 36 ♘xg7 ♔xg7 37 ♕xg6+ fxg6 38 ♗e4.
32 h4 ♕f4
A queen trapped in the middle of the board is something you don't see all that often. The rest is simple.
33 g3 ♕xe5 34 ♕g4+ ♕g7 35 ♘xg7 ♘f6 36 ♕f4 ♗xg7 37 ♕c7 ♖b8
Three minor pieces are enough for a queen, but here White has an extra rook too.
38 ♖d6 ♘g4 39 ♖xc6 ♗d4+ 40 ♔f1 1-0

There has so far been one other occasion when six World Champions, in the presence of a seventh (Boris Spassky), played in one event. It was the third match between the team of a single country (in this case Russia) and another representing the entire rest of the world. It took place in the autumn of 2002 in the Great Kremlin Palace in Moscow. It is true that they were playing speed chess, and the Champions were of 'two sorts'. Three of them – Anatoly Karpov, Garry Kasparov and Vladimir Kramnik – belonged to the traditional, century-old line of Chess Kings, while another three – Alexander Khalifman, Viswanathan Anand and Ruslan Ponomariov – had won so-called FIDE World Championships on the knockout system. Given these 'attendant circumstances', can this Scheveningen-type contest be given a place in the record books? It should be borne in mind that the fast time limit gave rise to a quality of game such as the following.

Khalifman – Ponomariov

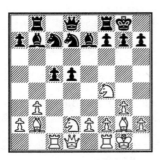

Amazingly, although White hasn't a single weakness, he comes out a pawn down within the space of just five moves.
16 e4 d4 17 ♘c4? (what about blockading with 17 ♘d3 and following with f2-f3 ?) **17...♗g5 18 ♖c2 ♗xf4 19 gxf4 ♕h4 20 ♕f3 ♘e6 21 ♕g3** (on 21 ♗c1, Black has 21...f5) **21...♕xf4**, and White was no longer able to save the game **(0-1)**.

Competitions with *four* World Champions taking part have been far more numerous – from the famous 1938 AVRO tournament to various Championships of the USSR, the 1981 'tournament of stars' in Moscow (another event with the same title, Montreal 1979, brought together three Champions only, although objectively its strength was no lower) and the 1983 contest in Niksic, Yugoslavia. They were always emphatically acclaimed with worldwide press coverage, but by purely formal criteria they cannot pretend to record status.

The Botvinnik Memorial in December 2001 promised to be an absolute record. All the participants without exception had occupied the chess throne one after another: the 12th World Champion Anatoly Karpov, the 13th, Garry Kasparov, and the 14th (by the ancient time-honoured sequence) Vladimir Kramnik. It had already been christened 'the tournament of the three K's', but ... Anatoly Evgenievich, the oldest of the three pupils of the patriarch (as chessplayers respectfully called Mikhail Moiseevich), evidently gave it due consideration and realistically weighed up his chances – which pointed clearly towards third prize, in other words last place. He therefore opted instead for the FIDE World Championship which was fixed for the same time, also in Moscow. The splendidly conceived record died before it was even born.

Finally the so-called 'Aeroflot Tournament', in Moscow again, broke the records not for the quantity of champions but of 'mere Grandmasters'. On 16 February 2004, one hundred and sixty-four of them, aged between 14 and 79 years, sat down to play among more than 600 participants in all. Of course, without a blatant and progressive devaluation of the highest chess title, this would have been physically impossible. All the same, a tournament containing approximately every sixth Grandmaster in the world was impressive. Moreover, by the strength of their play, very many of them fully lived up to their venerable chess rank.

Year after year, century after century

In chess, one of mankind's oldest 'pastimes', traditions are stronger than they have ever been in other sporting disciplines. And as chess traditions go, it is the English who stand out, in full accordance with their national mentality and their marked devotion to continuity.

Evidently for this reason, the most traditional of all the world's traditional tournaments remains the Christmas chess congress in the small town of Hastings, where a medieval battle – *not* a chess battle – decided the fate of England for many centuries to come. It was here, in 1895, that one of the greatest battles of the nineteenth century was fought – and this *does* mean a chess battle. The tradition of the Christmas tournaments dates from 1920, although in August 1919 the future World Champion José Raoul Capablanca scored 10½ points from 11 games at Hastings, mainly against English masters.

Only the Second World War interrupted these contests, and only between 1940 and 1944. Most Kings of Chess have taken part in them, as have most of the serious pretenders to the throne. The greatest number of victories went to the Yugoslav Svetozar Gligorić; he finished first on five occasions. To Salo Flohr, Hastings was home from home. He gained four outright victories without losing a single game, as well as one second place and one third – a peculiar record of winning consistency, with which nothing can compete except Vladimir Kramnik's results in the traditional Dortmund tournament: four victories in a row, again without loss, and a second place before and after this series.

At Hastings 1932/33, Flohr played one of his finest games.

Flohr – Sultan Khan
English Opening [A16]
(notes by Tarrasch)

1 c4 ♘f6 2 ♘c3 b6
Here 2...c5 is more correct. Mir Sultan Khan doesn't wish to put pressure on the centre or doesn't think it necessary.
3 d4 ♗b7 4 ♗g5 h6 5 ♗xf6 exf6 6 e4 ♗b4 7 ♕g4!
The more natural developing move 7 ♗d3 could be met by 7...f5, ridding Black of his doubled pawns.
7...g6?
A much better reply would be 7...0-0, especially as it threatens 8...♗xe4 9 ♕xe4 ♖e8. Now Black is left with a weak square which will give him a great deal of trouble later.
8 ♗d3 h5
This and the following moves look rather artificial, but they involve an idea which is

characteristic of the Indian master's original and inventive style.

9 ♕g3 h4 10 ♕g4 ♕e7 11 ♘e2 ♗xc3+ 12 ♘xc3!

In the event of 12 bxc3, Black would gain a clear advantage after 12...h3! 13 g3? f5. This was his intention in pushing the h-pawn. White should actually have played his queen to e3 on move 10.

12...f5 13 ♕e2 fxe4 14 ♗xe4 ♗xe4 15 ♕xe4 ♕xe4+ 16 ♘xe4 ♘c6

Skipping the middlegame, the play goes straight into an ending which, on the face of it, you might evaluate as equal.

17 0-0-0 0-0-0

18 ♘f6!

Revealing the astonishing justice of chess! The knight occupies the square weakened by Black's 7th move and thereby practically settles the result of the game. The e-file, the only open one, is now entirely at White's disposal.

18...g5 19 ♖he1

Threatening 20 d5 and 21 ♖e7. White answers 19...♖h6 with 20 ♘g4.

19...d6 20 h3 ♖df8

Black's choices are severely limited. Still, a better option was 20...♖h6 21 ♘g4 ♖g6 22 d5 ♘a5.

21 f4! gxf4 22 ♖e4 ♖h6 23 ♖xf4

♖g6 24 ♖d2 ♖h8 25 ♘d5 ♖g7 26 ♖e2 ♘d8

Black had the chance to double rooks on the g-file, so as to seek chances in the rook endgame after 26...♖hg8 27 ♘e7+ ♘xe7 28 ♖xe7 ♖xg2 29 ♖fxf7 ♖h2. Instead, however, White would reply 27 ♘e3, winning the h-pawn after 27...♖h7 28 ♘f5 ♖gh8 29 ♖ee4.

27 ♘e7+ ♔d7

The king is badly placed here, being immediately exposed to a rook check; 27...♔b8 was better.

28 ♘f5 ♖gh7 29 ♖e7+ ♔c8 30 d5

Now the black knight is condemned to the role of a bystander for a long period.

30...a5 31 ♘d4 ♖g7 32 ♘b5 ♖xg2 33 ♖xc7+ ♔b8 34 ♖e7 ♖g3 35 ♖f6!

Threatening a mating attack. The alternative 35 ♘xd6 ♖xh3 36 ♘xf7 ♖f8! 37 ♖d7 was weaker, even though White would remain a pawn up.

35...♖g6 36 ♖xd6 ♖hg8 37 ♖dd7

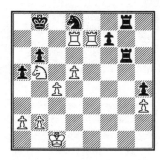

Flohr is going all out for mate but doesn't achieve this aim, since his opponent's counter-attack against the lonely white king is also taking on a menacing character.

37...a4!

161

Depriving the king of the b3-square, which might have supplied a path to shelter on a4. The threat now is 38...♖g1+ 39 ♔c2 ♖1g2+ 40 ♔c3 ♖8g3+, and if 41 ♔b4 then 41...♖xb2+; or if the king goes to the centre, Black exchanges one pair of rooks and eliminates the threats to his own king.

38 ♘c7 ♖g1+ 39 ♔c2 ♖1g2+ 40 ♔d1 ♖g1+ 41 ♖e1 ♔c8 42 ♖de7 ♘b7 43 ♘b5 f5 44 d6

This passed pawn will finally decide the game. The immediate threat is 45 ♘a7+ ♔b8 46 ♘c6+.

44...♘d8 45 ♖xg1 ♖xg1+ 46 ♔e2 ♖g2+ 47 ♔d3 ♖xb2 48 ♖c7+ ♔b8 49 d7

The game would seem to be over, but Sultan Khan still finds a way to make the win difficult for his opponent.

49...♘f7 50 ♖c8+ ♔b7

White now has various options: the simple 51 d8=♕ ♘xd8 52 ♖xd8, the elegant but bad 51 ♘d6+ ♘xd6 52 d8=♕ ♘xc8, or the line Flohr actually chooses, which wins but only with difficulty.

51 ♔c3 ♖xa2 52 ♖f8 ♘d8!

Astounding tenacity!

53 ♖xd8 ♔c6 54 ♘d4+ ♔d6 55 ♘xf5+ ♔c7 56 ♖h8 ♔xd7 57 ♖xh4 ♖f2 58 ♖h7+ ♔d8 59 ♘d4 a3 60 ♖a7 a2 61 h4 ♖h2 62 h5

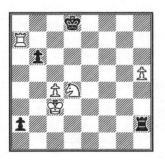

The struggle remains tense to the very end. Flohr evidently considered that the endgame after the exchange of pawns would be easily won; otherwise he would have protected the h-pawn with his knight.

62...♖xh5 63 ♖xa2 ♔c8 64 ♖a7 ♔b8 65 ♖f7 ♖h1! 66 ♘c6+ ♔c8 67 ♘b4 ♖c1+ 68 ♔b3

The right method was 68 ♔d4, followed by 69 ♔d5 and bringing the king to c6 to set up a mating attack.

68...♔b8 69 ♘d5 ♖d1 70 ♔a4 ♖b1 71 ♘b4 ♔c8 72 ♔b5 ♖b2

Black overlooked that White could break out of the pin by threatening mate. He should have played 72...♔b8 73 ♖f6 ♔a7, when 74 ♖xb6? fails to 74...♖xb4+ with a draw. White would have had to go in for further lengthy manoeuvres to reach the correct formation (♘d5 and ♔c6).

73 ♔c6 1-0

An interesting game in all its stages, testifying to the exceptional abilities of both players.

Although other traditional tournaments – Reggio Emilia, Sarajevo, Varna, Wijk aan Zee and others – have been going for 40-60 years, they fall a long way short of their older English counterpart. In the most recent decades, however, they have attracted much more attention; as a result of financial problems the composition of the Hastings tournaments is becoming less and less imposing.

The absolute record for a chess tradition, which scarecely anyone will surpass, belongs to the match between the universities of

Cambridge and Oxford, from whose walls so many outstanding scholars, Nobel Prize winners, writers and politicians have issued forth. Incidentally, the youngest student in Great Britain for 400 years was the 15-year-old John Denis Martin Nunn at Oxford; he is now a professor, a Grandmaster, and World Problem Solving Champion as a member of the English team. The first match between the universities took place on 28 March 1873. (There is only one Oxford-Cambridge contest with a longer tradition: the Boat Race between crews of eight on the Thames.) The teams consisted of seven men each, to whom in recent years a woman has been added. In the 101st match, by the way, the Cambridge team was rescued from a 'whitewash' by the solitary point scored by its female member.

This age-old duel has been interrupted only by the two world wars. In the 100th or jubilee match in the summer of 1982, the following game was judged to be best.

Cox – Nyman
Match Oxford v Cambridge, 1982
English Opening (what else?)
[A10]

1 c4 f5 2 g3 g6 3 ♗g2 ♗g7 4 ♘f3 d6 5 ♘c3 ♘f6 6 ♖b1 e5 7 d3 0-0 8 b4 ♘h5 9 ♕b3 ♔h8 10 0-0 f4 11 c5 ♘d7?

A dubious decision. The knight should be routed to the kingside via c6 and e7.

12 cxd6 cxd6 13 ♗a3 ♘df6 14 b5 h6 15 ♕b4!

Preparing a queen exchange that favours White, and tying the opponent's forces down.

15...♘e8 16 ♘d2 ♖f7 17 ♘c4 ♗f8 18 ♕a5! ♗e6 19 ♕xd8 ♖xd8 20 ♘a5 ♖dd7 21 b6 a6

22 ♗c6! ♖de7 23 ♘xb7 ♖xb7 24 ♗xe8 ♖g7 25 ♖fc1 ♘f6 26 ♗c6 ♖b8 27 gxf4!? exf4 28 ♘e4 ♘xe4 29 ♗xe4 d5 30 ♗xf8 ♖xf8 31 ♗f3 ♖b8 32 ♖c6 ♗g8 33 a4 a5 34 ♖d6 ♔h7 35 ♗xd5 ♗xd5 36 ♖xd5, and in a hopeless position Black overstepped the time limit on the 40th move (**1-0**).

In England there is a 'chess café' which has existed for a record length of time. Back in the past it was generally in this type of establishment that chess enthusiasts would meet. There was the *Café de la Régence* in the centre of Paris, frequented by Philidor and Légal, Rousseau and Diderot (who went on record as saying that "the best chess" was played there), Franklin, Robespierre and Napoleon. Morphy played in this café, and it was the scene of the match between the Frenchman Saint-Amant and the Englishman Staunton – as well as another between the Russian novelist Turgenev and the Pole Maczuski. There was the *Caffè Pastini* in central Rome, the

Krepsha café in the centre of Riga, the 'Partridge' café in central Vienna, the *Pechkina* coffee-house in central Moscow – etcetera etcetera. Some of these had a 'chess biography' lasting for years, in other cases it was decades; with *la Régence* it was nearly a century and a half. But there was also Simpsons-in-the-Strand in London. As early as 1839, a match between the strongest chessplayers of the time – the Frenchman La Bourdonnais and the Irishman MacDonnell – took place there. A year later, the first British tournament was won there by the historian Buckle. It was at Simpsons that Anderssen played his 'Immortal' game against Kieseritzky. Staunton, Morphy (whose entry in the visitors' book is preserved), Steinitz, Zukertort, Lasker ... who did *not* visit Simpsons?

Later on, there was a lengthy interval – and then a renaissance. Today the walls of the restaurant are adorned with contemporary portraits of many of the leading lights from a byone era, and daguerreotypes of past tournament battles. In 1993, the busy press centre for the World Championship match was located at Simpsons; Garry Kasparov and Nigel Short were playing in the neighbouring Savoy Theatre. From time to time I myself enjoy wearing a Simpsons chess necktie, sold exclusively in their chess souvenir shop.

However, the record for a chess gastronomic tradition belongs to a different tournament and a different country: Holland. It was there in 1938 that the large metallurgical firm of Hoogoveen began organizing its own chess contests – national ones at first, then international as from 1946. In that first year after the war, the hospitable country was not positively starving but did suffer from shortages of everything and was distinctly underfed. Yet how could the tournament's participants be sent away without the traditional banquet? Well, amid the festive surroundings, after the worthy speeches and the prizegiving, the diners at the banqueting table were served pea soup, the modest daily fare of Dutch farmers and townsfolk.

More than half a century has passed since then. There may be no pigeon's milk, in Holland or anywhere else in Europe; yet to commemorate that year of 1946, the concluding banquet at Beverwijk and Wijk aan Zee (the later venues of the tournament) has always begun with a bowl of pea soup.

A long, long memory

The spring of 1991 brought delight to a group of 100 little boys and girls from various corners of the USSR, India and Afghanistan. They were delighted with the blossoming mountain-slopes of the little health resort of Firiuz in Tajikistan; with the traditional hospitality of the hosts; and with tough and interesting struggles on the chessboard. The only surprising

164

thing about it was that this tournament was dedicated to the memory of Abu-Bakr Muhammad ben Yahya as-Suli, whose life had ended 1045 years earlier! Of all the memorials in chess history, this one reached back the furthest. The arbiter, Shorkhat Muratkuliev from Ashkhabad, has this to say about the man being commemorated:

> The most illustrious chess-player of the medieval period, in essence the World Champion, was considered to be the Turcoman Abu-Bakr as-Suli, the author of two significant Arabic manuscripts dealing with the game. In these works he collated all previous studies of *shatranj* and subjected them to a critical overhaul; he gave a voluminous analysis of standard opening positions *(tabiyat)* and chess problems *(mansubat)*.
>
> In European countries the name of as-Suli became known in the middle of the last century thanks to his extensive treatise 'on the Abbasids and their poetry', regarded by many historians as an original biography of the political and literary life of the Abbasid period. One copy of the manuscript, acquired in 1857 in Tebriz by Russian philologists, is now preserved in the Saltykov-Shchedrin State Library in St Petersburg. The treatise was published in 1935 in London, and after the war in Paris. It was later possible to unearth a good many other manuscripts by as-Suli. Collecting and classifying the numerous poetic productions of his time, he provided them with many-sided literary analyses.
>
> Scholars interested in as-Suli's life history usually refer to the 'Book of Song', the multi-volume work of the Arab philologist al-Isfahani, which observes that the chessplayer's grandfather, Sul-takin, was of Turcoman descent. As-Suli's ancestors lived in the territory of present-day Turkmenia – in the basin of the river Atrek. Today the state frontier between Turkmenia and Iran partly follows that river.
>
> As-Suli lived for many years in Baghdad. As to the time and place of his birth, nothing is known to this day. It is only from the manuscript mentioned above that we know that in 890-91 he worked for two or three nights in the capacity of a scribe for the well-known poet Ibn-Taifur in the town of Basra. Notwithstanding his youth, the impression is that as-Suli possessed comprehensive scholarly and literary equipment. Of Ibn-Taifur, he writes: "He did not justify my expectations, and I therefore had to part with him."

As we see, as-Suli would express his opinion without regard for authority. From early years he began collecting the works of medieval poets, compiling a bibliography and writing commentaries. From remarks by his contemporaries, it appears that his personal library was held to be one of the most richly endowed in Baghdad. In the art of calligraphy, he had no equals. Nevertheless he has become known in the west largely thanks to chess.

A passionate lover of chess at that time was the caliph al-Muktafi, who reigned from 902-908. He kept the chessplayer al-Mawardi in his palace and followed his games with great interest. Then the caliph was informed by his retinue that a player of uncommon strength named as-Suli was living in Baghdad. One day in 905 a contest between the two best chessplayers began. The caliph didn't doubt for a minute that his favourite would triumph. Yet the latter lost game after game. After his impressive victory as-Suli began to be treated with particular respect in Baghdad. A well-known poet of the time, Ibn-Mutazz, had a high regard for his mind and abilities and took him under his wing. As-Suli was a sociable man who paid no special heed to religious dogmas. Yet despite all the attention accorded to chessplayers in the palace, the spiritual authorities viewed this game as barbarous, as an invention of the powers of darkness. The fabrication of images as chess pieces was forbidden by Islam outright. It was only natural that as-Suli, who had linked his fate to chess, could not arouse sympathy among the devotees of the cult.

In 940, al-Muttaqi came to the throne. He was a ferocious ruler concerned only with himself and his power, and this led to unrest in the caliphate.

The courtiers who had long concealed their enmity towards as-Suli decided to take the opportunity to kill him. As-Suli fled from Baghdad to Basra, where he spent the last years of his life, forgotten by everyone, destitute, ailing and in constant fear for his life. He died in 946.

Over a thousand years have passed, but in the memory of the nations of central Asia and the Near East, as-Suli lives on as a man of letters, historian, poet and chessplayer. His works of scholarship are of great interest for the study of the medieval period, while researchers even today are struck by the comprehensiveness of his bibliographical writings.

In chess history too, as-Suli is accorded a prominent place. During his lifetime he had no equals; he defeated all who tried their strength with him. His contemporaries gave him the honorary title of *ash-Shatranji* (in Arabic, 'the great chessplayer').

As-Suli was the first player of the Middle Ages who attempted to discover and formulate the fundamental principles of the game. He was even credited with inventing chess, and became a truly legendary figure. In the East to this day, some chess moves are termed 'as-Suli moves'.

I may add that in a twelfth-century manuscript from the library of the Turkish Sultan Abdul-Hamid there is a diagram with the accompanying caption: "This ancient position is so difficult that there is no one in the world who would be able to solve it, except those I have taught to do so. I doubt whether anyone did this before me." A note in the manuscript adds, "This was said by as-Suli."

Black moves first, and White wins – that is the task. Don't forget that this was *shatranj*, in which the queen was a very weak piece; it only moved one square at a time along the diagonal.

I don't think there is any need here for me to report the investigations of Grandmaster Yuri Averbakh, who solved the problem. (The Englishmen Hooper and Whyld also applied themselves to it in the mid-1980s, but went down the wrong track.) But if the works of an encyclopedist from the early Middle Ages are still attracting attention more than 1000 years later, it just goes to show....

One further point is that Firiuz held its *second* as-Suli Memorial in August of the same year (1991), bringing together around 100 young men and women including the junior champions of India, the country where chess was born, and neighbouring Afghanistan.

In a word, Abu-Bakr Muhammad ben Yahya as-Suli has been fortunate in the way posterity has remembered him. So have many great chessplayers of the modern age.

In Cuba, José Raoul Capablanca y Graupera was commemorated 'only' after twenty years, but since that time his memorials have been held almost annually. Emanuel Lasker's memorial took place after 21 years. Wilhelm Steinitz's birth in Prague was celebrated 120 years after it occurred, that is 56 years after his death. Howard Staunton, England's strongest chessplayer in his day, was granted a memorial tournament after 77 years (!), and that was basically inspired by the centenary of the 1851 London event which he organized – the first international tournament in chess history. Ah yes, it seems that the ancient Romans were right: 'O tempora, o mores!'

Now for a case of long memory on what you might call an everyday, mundane level. In 1989 the American newspaper *Pittsburgh Press* printed the story of how a certain Robert Peer was stopped on the road for speeding. Exceptionally, the policeman didn't fine the offender but let him off with a warning. The delighted Peer was on the point of driving on, when he heard the policeman say:

"Do you know why I didn't fine you?"

"No."

"Well, thirty-five years ago we were at school together. We played each other in the school chess championship, and you threw your queen away in a won position."

God bless chess!

Sergeant-major's orders

Chessplayers have now and again had to submit to conditions wholly dictated by tournament committees and their leaders, who have sometimes applied the philosophy of a certain sergeant-major. The latter explained to a recruit what military subordination was all about: "I'm in command – you're a fool. When *you're* in command, *I'm* a fool." The world's strongest players have repeatedly found themselves in the position of recruits like that.

Perhaps the most harmless of such scenarios arose from a clause in the official regulations for the Cambridge Springs tournament of 1904. "On Sundays *[no rounds were played on that day]* the participants shall devote themselves to analysis of the Rice Gambit." It isn't hard to guess the reason. The tournament was financed almost single-handedly by Isaac Rice of New York. The trouble arose from a line of the King's Gambit beginning 1 e4 e5 2 f4 exf4 3 ♘f3 g5 4 h4 g4. After 5 ♘e5 ♘f6, as proposed and analysed by Kieseritzky, the American professor and sponsor had tried to introduce the line 6 ♗c4 d5 7 exd5 ♗d6 7 0-0 into practice. This gambit had been played exclusively in a match between Chigorin and Lasker in the previous year. Later, two tournaments would be devoted to it: a Russian one (St Petersburg 1905), and an international one (Munich 1911). Actually, at Cambridge Springs, half a dozen of the 'analysts under examination' might just have 'gone

through the motions'. Pretending to analyse and doing it properly are two very different things, but practically indistinguishable to an outsider.

Or take the big tournament organized in 1873 on the occasion of the international exhibition in Vienna. It was an all-play-all, but the participants didn't all play the same number of games. How could this be? It was very simple. Each player played a three-game match against every other player. If you won the match, you received a single point on the tournament chart. If the result was 1½-1½, the players scored half a point each.

But of course you could win the match just by winning the first two games. Thus it was that Wilhelm Steinitz gained his final score of 10 out of 11 by playing 25 games, while Joseph Blackburne, who shared 1st-2nd places with him, had had to sit down at the chessboard 30 times. And although Blackburne had crushed the future World Champion by 2½:½ in their individual encounter, it was Steinitz who finally took first prize by winning two games in a row in the play-off match.

There is no need to comment on the fact that under such conditions you didn't have White and Black an equal number of times.

This tournament under 'sergeant-major's orders' bequeathed to us the following game among the total of 1666 played.

Steinitz – Blackburne
Irregular [A00]

1 a3 (?!) g6 2 d4 ♗g7 3 e4 c5
4 dxc5 ♕c7 5 ♗d3 ♕xc5?! 6 ♘e2
♘c6 7 ♗e3 ♕a5+ 8 ♘bc3 d6 9 0-0
♗d7 10 b4 ♕d8 11 ♖b1 b6 12 ♘d5
♘f6 13 ♘xf6+!
Fixing the black king in the centre.
13...♗xf6 14 ♗h6 ♘e5? 15 h3
Parrying the threat of 15...♘g4.
15...♖g8 16 f4 ♘c6 17 ♕d2 ♕c7
18 c4 ♘d8 19 ♖fc1
A hint that castling long is unsafe for Black.
19...♘e6 20 ♘c3 ♕b7 21 ♘d5
♗h8 (or 21...♗g7 22 f5!) 22 ♔h1
♖c8 23 ♕f2 ♗c6 24 ♕h4 ♘d4
25 ♗g5 ♗xd5 26 cxd5 ♔d7
Black loses one of his pawns anyway; if 26...h5, then 27 ♗xe7!?.
27 ♗xe7 ♖xc1+ 28 ♖xc1 ♖c8
29 ♖d1 ♖c3 (has Black seized the initiative, then?) 30 ♗f6! ♕c8
31 ♕g4+ ♘f5 32 ♗b5+ ♔c7
33 ♗xc3 h5 34 ♕f3 ♘h4 35 ♗xh8
♕xh8 (or 35...♘xf3 36 ♖c1+)
36 ♖c1+ ♔b7 37 ♕c3 ♕d8
38 ♕c6+ ♔b8 39 ♗a6, and at last Black resigned (1-0).

Who holds the record for regulations in 'sergeant-major style'? The organizers of a whole range of contests in the late nineteenth and early twentieth century competed for that distinction. The Lord knows their names. They were united by what you might call a form of robbery which their regulations sanctioned.

Thus for instance a present-day mathematics graduate would be nonplussed if he studied the table of the third major tournament in chess history, which was held in Paris in 1867 concurrently with a notable event in the Europe of the time – the trade and industry exhibition. The scoreline of the winner – the successful banker and fine chessplayer Ignatz Kolisch – was adorned with twenty proud 'ones' interspersed with two 'halves' and two 'zeroes', yet his total was given as ... twenty points. An arithmetical error? But then the second prize winner Szymon Winawer, who as it happens only entered the tournament by chance, also had a drawn game disregarded in his total; while with Steinitz, who took third prize, no less than three draws were left out of account! But our mathematician's fright would be unfounded; by order of some sergeant-major figure, draws were equated with losses (!), so that the two-game matches between the players could very well have a 0:0 result, and in theory all 13 participants might have had nothing but 'ducks' on the final tournament chart.

Just imagine – 156 games played, and not a single point scored!

Our mathematician might also have been flabbergasted on reading that the great Philidor won his match against the renowned Phillip Stamma with the score of 8:2 after registering eight wins, one draw and one loss. But this time the sergeant-majors had nothing to do with it. It was simply that the young François-André Danican had given his opponent record odds: in the first place he took Black in all the games, and secondly draws were counted as wins for Stamma!

And then of course, such whimsicality of a more or less harmless sort may be seen in the rules for the 1867 tournament at Dundee, where the future World Champion Wilhelm Steinitz was playing in addition to the local contestants. The arrangements for the games in each round were made by mutual agreement between the players. The organizers reckoned that this free-and-easy schedule was the most suited to the Scots with their traditional love of liberty!

The fundamental laws of chess have been subjected to attacks at practically all times. For example the right of the first move, giving White the initiative and a certain advantage, might seem impossible to abolish; if you gave this right to the other side, nothing at bottom would be changed. And yet in 1893 the New York chess association attempted to level the players' chances completely, by holding a tournament in which a draw counted as a win! For Black, of course.

But let us return to our topic and pursue it further. It is in the general nature of things that players should always be divided into favourites and outsiders, sometimes before a tournament starts but more often while it is going on. One player may simply surpass the bulk of the field in strength; another may be in bad form; someone else, on the contrary, may be caught up and propelled forward by the wind of success, and everyone will say he has the luck of a first prize winner. The favourites, of course, will plan to collect points at the expense of the under-achievers. As a rule they succeed – but what about the record in this department?

Well, in terms of the gulf between leaders and back-markers, there is nothing to set beside the Paris tournament of 1900. A player at the bottom of the table will almost always escape loss in a small number of games, perhaps a minimal number; but in this event, the top 11 players dropped only half a point from their 66 games against the 6 tail-enders – a record which will scarcely ever be repeated! True, the attainment of this record was facillitated by one circumstance which has now disappeared from the chess scene for good: following the weird fashion of the time, the first drawn game between any two opponents was replayed, whereupon only the result of the second game would be entered on the score chart. In this way the 'strongest' robbed the 'weaklings' without compunction: the back-markers were to forfeit eight half-points which they originally earned in the sweat of their brow. The terrible Geza Maroczy was especially successful in the 'replays'. Without 'robbing' the also-rans Brody and Rosen, he would never have managed third prize behind Emanuel Lasker and Pillsbury.

Brody – Maroczy
Ruy Lopez [C65]

1 e4 e5 2 ♘f3 ♘c6 3 ♗b5 ♘f6 4 d4 ♘xe4 5 dxe5 ♗e7 6 ♕d5 ♘c5 7 ♗e3 ♘e6 8 0-0 0-0 9 ♘c3 f6 10 ♖ad1 ♔h8 11 ♘e4 ♘xe5 12 ♘xe5 fxe5 13 ♕xe5 d6 14 ♕c3

c6 15 ♗e2 d5 16 ♘c5 ♘f4 17 ♗f3
♗d6 18 ♘d3 ♘xd3 19 ♖xd3 ♕c7
20 h4

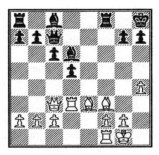

20...♖xf3 21 gxf3 ♗f5 22 ♖d2
♕f7 23 ♖e1 ♗h3 24 ♗g5 ♕g6
25 f4 ♗xf4 26 ♖d3 ♗f5 27 ♖f3
♗d6 28 ♔f1 ♗e4 29 ♖h3 h6 30 f3
♗f5 31 ♖h1 hxg5 32 hxg5+ ♔g8
0-1

In this same Paris tournament, following the 'sergeant-major's rules', the future German Grandmaster Carl Schlechter was deprived of the third prize he fully deserved. He had scored the same number of points as Marco and Mieses but had drawn more games, so the organizing committee divided the prize sum into two parts only.

The penchant of the 'sergeant-majors' for rulings of this kind reached its apogee in the fourth London tournament in the summer of 1883. There were 14 participants in the double-round contest, but rather than play the 'normal' total of 182 games, they had to battle it out a full 256 times! Not just the first draw, but the first *two* were replayed! Small wonder that the tournament dragged on for three days short of two months. Among

the players were George Henry Mackenzie – a captain of the northern army in the American Civil War, and three times winner of American Chess Congresses – and the Austrian Berthold Engels, winner of the first congress of the German Chess Federation. In order to register two half-points each, these two were compelled to sit down opposite each other six times! Their tournament colleagues were no less afflicted. The record-breaker (or champion?) for ill luck – and not only in that long summer of chess – was poor Samuel Rosenthal. He had been involved in the Polish rebellion of 1863, and after its defeat he was forced to abandon his homeland and flee to France in fear of the noose or forced labour in Siberia. In this tournament, he replayed 20 draws (!), so that in place of a normal batch of 13 games he had to play 33! In essence, then, his 8th prize – the last one – is perhaps equal in value to a much higher and more weighty distinction.

The organizers of the first so-called 'health-resort tournaments' in Monte Carlo went even further. (Gatherings of famous chessplayers were widely reported in the press, and this reminded everyone of the existence of such refined places of relaxation and cure as Ostende, Cambridge Springs, San Sebastian, Pistyan and, later, Carlsbad, Baden-Baden, San Remo, Bled, Kemeri, Palma de Mallorca and Linares.) By that time, the system of replaying draws had brought down countless shafts of criticism on its head. Notably, its former fervent advocate Mikhail Chigorin had ceased to

171

support it. The main point of the criticism, more or less, was that the original drawn result was deleted outright and thus of course forgotten. Well, the tournament tables of Monte Carlo 1901 and 1902 contained a merry scattering of (wait for it) quarter points! That's right – a draw brought the opponents a quarter of a point each, and after the replay the victor received three quarters in all, while the loser remained where he was. A second draw added another quarter-point to each player's total. The upshot was that in 1901, apart from the 13 regulation games, the tournament winner David Janowski played two supplementary ones; the second and third prize winners, Carl Schlechter and Mikhail Chigorin, played four each (if draws had not been replayed, they would have finished level); Frank Marshall played six, and the unfortunate Simon Alapin a full eight, so that in essence he was playing a second tournament.

In 1902 there were many more participants – 20 in total – and with the fairly large basic workload, the Englishman John Mortimer was the only one to avoid any 'tie-breaks'. (His chess life in general had not been uneventful; in the London tournament a decade earlier he had defeated the swiftly rising Emanuel Lasker in most dashing style with an Evans Gambit, but in Monte Carlo Mortimer was not the player he had been, winning just one game amidst 18 losses.) Schlechter by contrast, and Richard Teichmann who was almost playing blindfold owing to an eye complaint, each sat down at the board 26 times in the

course of the 38 days. This was sheer madness, but what did the sergeant-major organizers care about that?

The well-known chess historian N.Grekov commented:

Objections to this system had been raised before, and now a further argument was added; the Monte Carlo tournament illustrated it blatantly. It concerned the unjust way the prizes were allocated on the basis of the points system in use. Even the first two prizes were affected: as a result of the peculiar way of scoring draws, Maroczy was awarded first prize and Pillsbury second. If draws had been scored conventionally – if, that is, they had not been replayed but had gained half a point in the first place – then the scores of the top two prizewinners would have been level.

The system incurred resolute condemnation from all sides and was never to be used again.

We may also add that there was a record price for the quarter-point separating the winners: 2000 francs, in those days a very tidy sum in a currency on the gold standard.

By rights, that remarkable Hungarian Grandmaster Geza Maroczy should have thanked the 'goodwill of the sergeant-majors' for a similar stroke of fortune. One of his 'regular customers' was none other than Jacques Mieses, a man of dashing chess style and thoroughly decorous character. It was at Monte Carlo 1902 that Mieses obtained the draw against Maroczy which he had so longed for; but in the replay, of course, he stood no chance....

What didn't they think up, those would-be reformers of chess competitions, just to be that bit out of the ordinary – just so as to avoid resemblance to other, perfectly conventional, tournaments! In 1911, for instance, games played at the London City Chess Club were subject to the ruling that your clock time was never to exceed that of your opponent by more than five minutes. It was under this strange regulation (to put it mildly) that a masterpiece was created – the famous game between Edward Lasker and Thomas (quoted in the chapter 'Where is the king going?'). In that same year, a match took place in Munich between the oustanding Austrian Grandmaster Rudolf Spielmann, known as the last of the chess Romantics, and the strong Russian master Simon Alapin who had just won two minor Munich tournaments. In this match each player had the right, during his own thinking time, to analyse the position on a separate board! In our day this sort of thing would be called 'advanced chess'; in fact, we now see exhibition contests in which Grandmasters are aided by computers with their enormous memory of two and a half million games and comprehensive collections of known chess openings. But at that time, a century ago ... in a word, it was just another order from the sergeant major!

We must give Spielmann his due: he never once made use of the facility he had been offered, and nonetheless won convincingly with the score of +5 -1 =3. His 'fellow Grandmaster' (or 'older master') Ostap Bender was indeed right: if the fair-haired player plays well and the dark-haired one plays badly, no lessons will alter their relative strengths – allthough Alapin, generally speaking, was not playing at all badly.

But what do you say to this? After winning a match, can you end up as the loser? The question sounds absurd, but this is precisely what happened to Salo Flohr in London in 1932. At that time he was an aspirant to the chess Olympus. He prevailed in a duel with the most enigmatic player of all time and all nations – Mir Sultan Khan, the illiterate maestro (how does that phrase sound?). And yet Flohr was declared to have lost. Why? Because this, according to the will of the organizers, was a 'tandem' match. Flohr's 'workmate', the Dutch master Salo Landau (was the coincidence of names the reason why were they were paired together?) lost his match against the English master Victor Berger who was teamed with Sultan Khan – and the margin between the lesser players was greater than that between their superiors.

And what price the following record curiosity from the year 1912? Forty-five contestants of the most varied standards of play gathered in Richmond (England). Among them was the famous Frank Marshall. God alone knows what wind had blown him there. The American Grandmaster naturally won all 44 of his games – and finished third! What made this absurdity possible was merely a ruling that a win against a lower-rated opponent scored one point as usual, whereas for beating a higher-rated player you could be rewarded with two, three or even four points!

It remains to be added that this entire 'contest' was played to a fast schedule of two or sometimes three games a day. But who isn't used to 'rapid chess' tournaments in *our* time?

To some extent the sequence of these curious contests is being carried on by the ultra-modern 'FIDE World Championships'. Never mind that 100 chessplayers from all over the world suddenly find themselves fighting for the crown, not in Zonal and Interzonal Tournaments and Candidates matches, but all at once in the same playing hall! No one can take this seriously, even taking into account the weird devaluation of the Grandmaster title that occurred at the end of the 20th century. By definition there are not and cannot be so many super-class players in the universe; but that is not even the point. Following the logic of the sergeant-majors, the regulations of this one competition incorporate three varieties of chess: classical, rapid (25 minutes per player per game) and blitz (or five-minute chess in plain language). Of course, the board and pieces remain the same, and the knight always moves in an 'L-shape'; yet under such conditions, Lasker or Alekhine or Botvinnik (all of whom were averse to blitz chess) would no more have seen the world title than their own

ears. Just think how many times distinguished Grandmasters have been knocked out of FIDE World Championships without losing any classical games, or even any rapid ones either! It is quite enough to recall the fate of Vladimir Kramnik, the 14th Chess King, at Las Vegas in 1999. Incidentally my chess teacher, the respected Soviet coach and International Master Rashid Nezhmetdinov, who wasn't bad at blitz himself, more than once exhorted us: "Only idiots analyse five-minute games. Just have fun with them, that's all."

The harm done by this concocted system is understood by all chessplayers – and yet all dream of getting into that intimate circle of 100. Why? Because even if you drop straight out of the contest by losing two classical games at the start, you still receive a sum equal to the first prize in no mean international tournament. And life in this world cannot be lived without money, any more than without women. The sergeant-majors of chess, then, will probably exist for ever, like the game of the wise itself.

Unless perhaps, sometime, they get so much cleverer that they make it to the rank of lieutenant.

Phantoms of the chess world

Dictionaries define *phantom* as a phenomenon of fantasy, a spectre, an apparition – or as a model of the human body or part of it. And although this last meaning only applies in medicine, all the definitions, oddly enough, have a connection with the game on the chequered board. But which phantom may be viewed as the record-holder in terms of the resonance it created? Was it that famous chess automaton constructed by the brilliant engineer Wolfgang von Kempelen, which impressed everyone by its chess talents in more than half a century of guest appearances at Vienna and Bratislava, Paris and London, Berlin, Leipzig and St Petersburg? Asking the question is easier than answering it. Still, let us try....

At the end of 1929, a highly popular Leningrad newspaper published an announcement which seemed to come straight out of the world of medieval chivalry. A certain 'X' issued a simultaneous challenge to the city's 10 strongest chessplayers to play him in a match. Those players were headed by Alexander Ilyin-Zhenevsky, Mikhail Botvinnik and Yakov Rokhlin, all of them masters (at that time there was no higher title). The rest were first-category players (of whom there were 50 or 60 in the whole of the Soviet Union), and included such powerful talents as for example the future Grandmaster Viacheslav Ragozin. In a word, the challenge caused a considerable stir. It was immediately reprinted in the national papers *Izvestiia* and *Komsomolskaia Pravda*, as well as a number of Moscow and provincial publications. I do not know, and no one now will ever discover, whether the match was mentioned by the Comintern radio station – the chief one in the country. Two years earlier, it had sent the world's first

chess broadcasts out onto the airwaves (another record!) in the shape of reports from the First Spartakiad of the Peoples of the USSR by the Moscow master (and expert on pawn endgames) Nikolai Grigoriev. If it *was* mentioned on the radio, that impudent gesture from Leningrad will have been noticed by the entire nation. For propaganda purposes, the authorities had brought telecommunications to out-of-the-way villages much earlier than domestic electricity, and loudspeakers hung from lamp-posts wherever you went.

The conditions of the challenge sounded eccentric. 'X' was to take White in all the games, and the players' moves were to be handed to the newspaper's editorial office by 7 p.m. Then 'X' would reply to them within three hours! If 'X' lost three games, he would disclose his name.

The élite could not refuse the challenge; their high chess reputation was at stake. But no one doubted that in the next few weeks the mask would be stripped from 'X' and he would be ignominiously compelled to reveal himself.

That was until 'X', having started off with a draw against the well-known composer and strong player Leonid Kubbel, began extracting resignations from opponent after opponent. He mated two of them outright on the 33rd move! Those remaining grew nervous; they began to suspect that 'X' was one of the very experienced masters from the old Tsarist Russia – Ilya

175

Rabinovich perhaps, or Grigory Levenfish.... Suspicions also fell on the Leningrad Champion Ilyin-Zhenevsky; people said that he had beaten himself to avert suspicion, but then they remembered that after the game in question he had gone to Berlin for two weeks on official business, while moves continued to be made daily. The secretary of the Leningrad Chess Section, Yakov Rokhlin, a legendary figure in his own way, categorically 'pointed the finger' at the master Peter Romanovsky, a close rival of Alekhine in the earliest Soviet tournaments. On the other hand another master, Abram Model, was 'acquitted' simply because in the general opinion he was talented but prone to nerves; in such a gruelling match he would have lost eight games out of ten.

Meanwhile the contest continued, and the élite fell down like flies in late autumn. Botvinnik, who was to become USSR Champion within a year, 'escaped' with a draw by a miracle. A half point was also salvaged by Yakov Rokhlin from a game that was no joking matter:

Slav Defence [D25]
(notes by Rokhlin)

1 d4 d5 2 c4 c6 3 ♘f3 ♘f6 4 ♘c3 e6 5 ♗g5 ♘bd7 6 e3 ♕a5 7 ♗xf6 ♘xf6 8 ♗d3 ♗b4 9 ♕c2 dxc4
The tempting 9...c5 occurred to me in my analysis, but I figured that my invisible opponent was likely to possess encyclopaedic knowledge of opening theory. I therefore needed to nudge him into an uninvestigated and sharper line.
10 ♗xc4 b5 11 ♗d3 ♘d5 12 0-0

♗xc3 13 ♖fc1
It was also worth considering 13 e4.
13...♗xb2 14 ♕xc6+ ♔e7 15 ♕xa8 ♗xa1 16 ♘e5
This is stronger than 16 ♖xc8 ♖xc8 17 ♕xc8 ♕c7 etc., or 16 ♖xa1 ♖d8 17 ♘e5 ♗d7 18 ♕b7 ♕c7 with a dynamic equilibrium of forces.
16...♔f6!
My opponent later told me that he hadn't been expecting this manoeuvre, but though paradoxical, it is Black's best way out of the dangerous situation. Removing his king, he retains counter-chances based on penetrating with his queen to the enemy's back rank.
17 ♖xc8
White wouldn't obtain any winning chances with 17 ♖xa1, for instance: 17...♕c3! 18 ♖d1 a6! 19 ♕a7 ♕c7 20 ♕xc7 ♘xc7 21 ♖c1 ♘a8 etc.
17...♖xc8 18 ♕xc8 ♕e1+ 19 ♗f1 ♘xe3!

20 fxe3
A forced reply. If 20 ♕d8+, then 20...♔f5 21 fxe3 ♕xe3+ 22 ♔h1 ♕c1! (the careless 22...♕e1 would be met by 23 ♕g5+, giving Black some trouble) 23 ♔g1 ♕e3+ with a draw. After the move played, there are still some prospects of a fight.

20...♕xe3+ 21 ♔h1 ♕xd4!
22 ♘c6! ♕d1 23 ♕d8+ ♕xd8
24 ♘xd8 a6! 25 ♘c6!
At first sight both queenside pawns look doomed – White does, after all, have an extra piece. However:
25...♗e5!
It was only now that White perceived Black's far-sighted plan. After 26 ♘b4 ♗d6! 27 ♘xa6 b4, White would basically be playing without his trapped knight. The black king could come across and compel the bishop to keep protecting it.
26 ♔g1 ♗d6 27 ♔f2 e5 28 ♔e3 ♔e6 29 g4 h5!
The endgame with a piece less demands maxium accuracy from Black, and is instructive in itself.
30 h3 hxg4 31 hxg4 g6 32 ♘d8+ ♔e7 33 ♘b7 f5! 34 gxf5 gxf5 35 ♗h3 ♔e6! 36 ♗xf5+ ♔xf5 37 ♘xd6+ ♔e6 38 ♘e4 ♔d5 39 ♔d3 ♔c6! 40 ♔c3 ♔d5 41 ♔d3 ♔c6 42 ♔c3 ♔d5 43 ♘d2 ♔c5 44 ♘b3+ ♔c6 45 ♔b4
In this position the game was agreed drawn (½-½). The following line is a possibility: 45 ♔b4 ♔b6! 46 ♘a5 e4 47 ♘b3 e3 48 ♔c3 a5 49 ♔d3 a4 50 ♘c1 ♔c5 51 ♔xe3 ♔b4 52 ♔d3 ♔a3 53 ♔c2 b4, and the draw is obvious.

The final score of the match was 8½:1½, the news spread all round the country, and chessplayers were plunged into deep dejection. Were such things possible? Who was 'X'? Where did he come from?

But 'X' had no thought of abandoning his incognito. After all, he hadn't lost a single game! The newspaper editors maintained their proud silence and wouldn't give in to any persuasion. Then the journal *Shakhmatny listok* began its own investigations, entrusting them to Abram Model. The latter published an account of his researches in one of the issues for 1930. He considered all the chess celebrities, thoroughly analysed the probablity that they might have been in 'X's' shoes – then stated the conclusion that he himself was 'X'!

To quote a work by Vladimir Zak (the Leningrad master and eminent Soviet coach) and Y.Dlugolensky: "On going through the list of all possible candidates, the participants in the match had rejected such a sharp combinative player as Model – why was this? After all, most of the games positively bore the stamp of his 'authorship'."

The 'blame' here lay with Model himself. Having already attained the master title in pre-revolutionary times, he had also gained the reputation of a player extremely prone to moods. One day he would play brilliantly against a strong opponent, the next day he would lose in absurd fashion to a weak one.

Throughout the chess biography of Abram Yakovlevich Model (1895-1976), it is conspicuous how the high points and setbacks stand side by side. Thus, after finishing last (with 1½ out of 9!) in the 1926 Leningrad Championship, he shared 3rd and 4th places in the USSR Championship the following year, winning twelve games and drawing two. In 1929 Model shared 2nd and 3rd places in the championship of the city, but in the next national championship he only came eleventh. This list could be continued, but it is much more interesting so listen to the opinion of people closely acquainted with him.

Alexander Alekhine called Model an extremely talented chessplayer and predicted a great future for him, but made the proviso: "if he adopts the right attitude".

The 'right attitude' did not materialize. At some point Model decided that his 'chief' love should be music and mathematics, not chess. Mathematics, indeed, became the chief love of his life.

After hearing Model's recital of a Beethoven sonata, the famous pianist Flier categorically declared that Model should give up mathematics and chess and devote himself entirely to concert perform-ances. But this was just at the time when Abram Yakovlevich decided that he shouldn't sacrifice chess for the sake of music.

Let me add that if an anthology of verse devoted to chess and chessplayers should ever appear, a good half of it will be taken up by humorous poems and witty epigrams by Model.

Such was the man well known to Leningraders as 'chessmaster X'. He was, so to speak, a phantom made flesh, and no doubt the creator of the record mystification in the chess world.

In a way there was something reminiscent of this in the first chess game ever to be played by telex. The Yugoslav Grandmaster Borislav Ivkov was facing 1000 readers of a Rotterdam newspaper who decided on each move by a simple majority vote. Playing White, the readers gave hardly any thought to the opening and were clearly trying to copy Bobby Fischer's play from one of his World Championship match games in Reykjavik. To a query from Yugoslavia as to whether there was a World Champion among the readers, the Dutch players answered, "No, but we're in touch with him by telepathy."

Whether this joke took effect or whether there was some other reason, Ivkov suddenly offered a draw in the better position on the 31st move. The reply from Rotterdam was, "Fischer urges us to accept your offer." That might have been the end of the matter, but later the truth about the contest was disclosed by one of its organizers, the Dutch master and journalist Hans Böhm. It turned out that no thousand readers had had anything to do with it. The topic of 'chess as a source of creative inspiration' had been debated by Rotterdam's creative élite – actors, artists, musicians, writers and academics – at a gathering in the city's greatest concert hall. They had assigned the role of the mythical army of readers to Grandmaster Jan Hein Donner, and he it was who had been battling single-handed with his Yugoslav colleague. The fact that this misled, or positively cheated, several tens of thousands of Yugoslav chess fans, didn't bother anyone....

And then the following episode may very well be called a minor record in terms of mystification. In the spring of 1948 the World Championship Match Tournament was finishing in Moscow. On Victory Day with its exceptionally keen celebrations, Mikhail Botvinnik – the tournament leader, and leader of Soviet chess – was playing ex-World Champion Max Euwe. With two rounds still to go, the drawn result raised Botvinnik to the chess throne which had been vacant for two years. As you can easily guess, there was no great fight in this game. After White's 14th move the hall erupted with prolonged applause, and the arbiters even halted play on the other board.

There were film crews working in the Hall of Columns at Union House and in the surrounding streets that evening, but alas, they didn't manage to film that final move. Cinecameras in those days made a fair amount of noise, which as we know is not conducive to chess, so they couldn't be kept running for any length of time; but no one could foresee just when the game was going to end. The new Chess King refused point-blank to re-enact that moment for the sake of posterity; even as a young man, Botvinnik was no angel by nature. The producer, however, found a way out of what looked like a hopeless situation. He noticed that the game's demonstration board operator – young Yakov Estrin, later to be Botvinnik's friend and also World Correspondence Champion – was wearing a similar-coloured jacket. And so ... in the official newsreel which was compulsory at the start of all cinema programmes, Soviet citizens numbering around 150 million watched as the 'hand of Botvinnik', in a highly dramatic gesture, moved a pawn from b2 to b4 in a curve that distantly recalled the flight of a howitzer shell. Since this clip lasted for no more than two seconds on the screen, even the fierce Soviet film censors of the day failed to notice the hoax. Perhaps that was because they had never watched a *genuine* pawn move on the chessboard....

A game to be counted among the chess phantoms is the one supposedly played between Napoleon Bonaparte and General Bertrand on the island of St Helena in 1820. An Englishman, a certain Captain Kennedy, reported it in his memoirs which date from 1862, and it became widely known through numerous publications. The very serious English researcher Harold Murray, in his classic work *A History of Chess*, was the first to pronounce it a fabrication. A similar case is the famous encounter between the French masters F.Lazard and A.Gibaud: 1 d4 ♘f6 2 ♘d2 e5 3 dxe5 ♘g4 4 h3?? ♘e3, whereupon White resigned. Gibaud maintained that this was a figment of someone's imagination, although these players did once face each other in a game that was awarded a brilliancy prize. It was played in the championship of *La Régence*, the famous Paris 'chess café', in 1909.

Lazard – Gibaud

1 e4 e5 2 d4 exd4 3 ♘f3 ♘c6 4 ♗c4 ♗c5 5 c3 ♘f6 6 cxd4 ♗b4+ 7 ♘c3 ♘xe4 8 0-0 ♗xc3 9 d5 ♗f6

179

10 Re1 De7 11 Rxe4 d6 12 g4!? h6 13 h4 ♔f8 14 h5 g5 15 Dd4 c6 16 ♕f3! Dxd5 17 ♗d2! Dc7 18 Rae1! d5 19 ♗b4+ ♔g7 20 Re7! dxc4

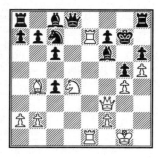

21 Dxc6 ♕d3 (if 21...bxc6, then 22 ♕xf6+! ♔xf6 23 ♗c3+ and mate next move) **22 Rxf7+ ♔xf7 23 Re7+ ♔g8 24 ♕xf6 Rh7 25 Re8+ Dxe8 26 ♕f8 mate**

On 4 September 1927, the following game, supposedly between Botvinnik and Rokhlin, appeared in *Pravda*, the chief Communist organ of the USSR. (For another ten years or so, everything published in that newspaper would be taken as authoritative and absolutely true; it never printed any corrections!) The notes are by Ilyin-Zhenevsky.

11 Da3 ♗a6 12 ♗b5!

Threatening to win the queen with Da3-c4.

12...♗xb5 13 axb5

This of course is stronger than taking with the knight, as it seals up Black's queenside pieces for good.

13...0-0 14 0-0 ♕b6 15 ♕a4!

Best! By sacrificing his knight White obtains a comfortable attacking position for his pieces.

15...bxa3 16 Rxa3 g6

Black is at a loss what to do. Instead of this move, 16...Dc6 was relatively best, though White would still have a won position after 17 bxc6.

17 Dg5 h6 18 De4 ♔h7 19 Rh3

Now that this rook has been brought to the h-file, White's attack decides the game quickly.

19...h5 20 g4 h4 21 ♗g5 ♔g7 22 Rxh4 Rh8 23 ♗f6+ ♗xf6 24 exf6+ ♔g8 25 Rxh8+ ♔xh8 26 g5 *[26 ♕b3 wins]* **26...Dc6 27 Dxc5!**

1-0

This was taken at face value for many long decades to come. It was only in 1980 – more than half a century later! – that ex-World Champion Botvinnik published the following lines:

"From White's 11th move, a 'fantasy game' began. At the end of it, instead of resigning, Black could play 27...♘cb4 28 ♕b3 ♕xd6 29 ♕h3+ ♔g8 30 ♘xd7 ♕f4, after which he would be guaranteed a draw by perpetual check. *[Better still, 30...♘f4 31 ♕g4 ♘bd3 or 31 ♕h6 ♘h5, winning for Black.]*

"The point is that Ilyin-Zhenevsky, who edited the chess section in *Pravda* at that time, had heard of a convincing win by me against 'Rokhlin himself' (my opponent was one of the most experienced players in Leningrad), and telephoned his friend Yakov to ask him for the game score. At first Rokhlin refused point-blank, maintaining that the game wasn't at all interesting, but Ilyin-Zhenevsky kept insisting. Then Rokhlin decided to play a trick on his friend and dictated the 'score' of the game which, in actual fact, proceeded as follows *[from the penultimate diagram].*"

Botvinnik – Rokhlin
Six-player match tournament,
Leningrad 1927
(notes by Botvinnik)

11 ♗g5
With this move, not an obvious one, White forces Black to give up a pawn. Now 11...♗xg5 is bad on account of 12 ♕xd5, as is 11...♗b7 in view of 12 ♗c4; while 11...♘b6 is answered by 12 ♗xd8 ♔xd8 13 ♘g5.

11...b3+ 12 ♗d2 ♘b4 13 ♕xb3
Now White has both a positional and a material plus.

13...0-0 14 ♘a3 ♗a6
Meeting the threat of 15 ♘c4, which Black would now answer by taking the knight.

15 ♗b5!
Again threatening 16 ♘c4, which this time would win the queen.

15...♗xb5 16 axb5
Now Black's queenside is bottled up.

16...♕b6 17 0-0 a5
In this way Black fortifies his knight's position on b4, but what about the other poor knight on b8?

18 ♖ac1 ♕a7
It's essential to defend the c5-pawn.

19 ♕c4 ♗b6

20 ♗g5
The bishop occupies the same square again, this time with decisive threats.

20...♕b7 21 ♖fd1
White prevents 21...♕d5.

21...♖e8 22 ♗e7
The situation is already grave for Black. The threat is 23 ♘g5.

22...h6 23 ♘h4
Now there is no defence against 24 ♘f5. The concluding moves were:

23...♘8c6 24 bxc6 ♘xc6 25 ♕e4
Preventing 25...♘d4.

25...♕a6 26 ♘f5 ♘d4 27 ♖xd4
White has to eliminate this knight in order to conquer the g7-square.

27...cxd4 28 ♘xh6+
Black resigned here, as he is mated after either 28...gxh6 29 ♗f6 or 28...♔h8 29 ♘xf7+ ♔g8 30 ♘g5.

1-0

One game of the match between Alexander Alekhine and Stepan Levitsky (St Petersburg, 1913) did not actually take place in the form in which Alekhine presented it in his own games anthology. When writing that book he was seeking a match with Capablanca for the world chess crown, and endeavouring to display himself to all the world – and potential sponsors – as a great master of combinative chess. Hence he decided to 'correct and refine' that far-off match of his youth against one of Russia's strongest players of the past. He shortened one of his seven wins by nearly half, replacing a fairly interesting but protracted endgame with an uncomplicated combination – which did not occur in actual play!

I should add that the fourth World Champion participated in one other game that never happened – or rather, he was *made* into a participant. In September 1959 in *Chess Review,* a certain Georgy Bogunovich, from the American town of Pittsburgh, published his recollections of a game between the young Alekhine and the well-known Russian master Vladimir Nenarokov, played in Moscow in 1907. Never mind that Nenarokov's initial is given incorrectly. Never mind that in the 'eye-witness' account of the game, the 15-year-old Alekhine – an aristocrat to the marrow of his bones – was smoking *makhorka* shag, the 'devil's weed' smoked by workers and peasants. Let us pretend we believe this; even so, the published score of Alekhine-Nenarokov is still extremely difficult to accept – given that it is

identical with Tolush-Aronson from the 1957 USSR Championship in Moscow. The question that will never be answered is whether Mr Bogunovich, the recipient of the fee for the article, borrowed the moves he had 'seen with is own eyes' from the Soviet tournament bulletin or copied them out of the *British Chess Magazine.*

Exactly 40 years on, this fiction was introduced into the pages of the journal *64* by my old friend Anatoly Matsukevich, but it didn't live for long. It was shot down by the precise marksmanship of the journalist Alexander Ponomariov from Kemerovo, who dug up the full story.

The contest that took place in August 1936 in Munich must also be counted among the phantoms. That was the year when the Nazi régime, victorious in Germany, was trying to improve its abysmal international reputation by means of sport. True, at the Olympic Games in Berlin, a furious Hitler had departed from the stand when the black American Jesse Owens won four gold medals by trouncing the blond German supermen. But chess could not be left out of account, and Germany hosted the next in the series of 'Tournaments of Nations', even suspending its zoological hatred of 'non-Aryans' – that is, Jews. However, some Grandmasters and masters (the Austrian Rudolf Spielmann, the Peruvian Esteban Canal and others) demonstratively stayed away from fascist Germany. The USA team – which had won the previous three 'Tournaments of Nations' –

declined to participate, as did the British, the Belgians and some others, although 21 teams did line up to do battle. They were mainly from states diplomatically close to Germany or small countries that were terrified of their rapidly rearming neighbour.

It was decided to make up for quantity with quality, and the size of the teams was increased from 4 boards to 8 with two reserves. First place went to Hungary with 110½ points out of 160, followed by Poland (108), Germany (106½) and Czechoslovakia (104). On top board, the Estonian Paul Keres scored 15 out of 20, the Yugoslav Vasja Pirc 12 out of 17, and the Swede Gideon Stahlberg half a point less; the Austrian Erich Eliskases and the Latvian Vladimirs Petrovs each scored 13½ out of 20.

Immediately afterwards, public opinion compelled the FIDE President, the Dutchman Alexander Rueb, to revise his earlier decision, with the result that the Munich tournament disappeared forever from the list of World Chess Olympiads. The following 'Tournament of Nations' was held in Stockholm slightly less than a year later. There the Americans reasserted the chess hegemony that they exercised at the time.

I will now say something about a star tournament which fared better in some ways and worse in others. It was not reported and not written about. It was held in the summer of 1953 in the health resort of Gagra on the shores of the Black Sea, with splendid conditions for the contestants; yet at the same time, in a sense, it was non-existent. Although it involved all the best Soviet chessplayers except for World Champion Botvinnik and his recent challenger David Bronstein, the games didn't become available to the chess world until nearly half a century later! The explanation is that the project for a match between the USSR and the USA was taking shape, and this tournament was organized as preparation for the team – in secret! And the Soviet authorities knew how to keep a secret safe, even in sport! This is why the book on Smyslov in the famous Soviet series in black covers (entitled 'Outstanding Chessplayers of the World') makes no mention of this tournament that he won, while the Petrosian volume says nothing about his creditable second place (he was only 22 at the time) and the Kotov and Geller volumes are equally uninformative. It will therefore be worth our while to look at both the tournament table and some fragments from the play.

Averbakh – Boleslavsky

White's advantage consists in the fact that Black's pawns are on the same colour squares as his bishop.

But so what? There isn't anywhere
to break through, and in addition
Black is threatening 46...♗e3.
46 g6+!
Yes there *is* somewhere! By
giving up a pawn in an ending and
straightening out his opponent's
pawn structure, White wins the
game! The pawn on f4 will be
safely defended by the king, and
Black won't be able to avoid
zugzwang.
**46...fxg6+ 47 ♔g5 ♗e3 48 ♗b2
♗c5 49 ♗f6 ♗b4** (or 49...♗e3
50 ♗e7 ♗c5 51 ♔f6) **50 ♗d4 ♗c5
51 ♗xc5 bxc5 52 ♔f6 ♔h6 53 ♔e6
g5 54 fxg5+ ♔xg5 55 ♔xd6 f4
56 ♔xc5 f3 57 d6 f2 58 d7 f1=♕
59 d8=♕+ ♔g4 60 ♕d4+ ♔g3 61
♔b5 ♕b1+ 62 ♔xa5 ♕e1+ 63 ♔b5
♕b1+ 64 ♔a6 ♕b8 65 a5 ♕b4 66
♕d5 ♕b3 67 ♕d6+ ♔h3 68 ♕d7+
♔h2 69 c5 ♕c4+ 70 ♕b5 ♕g8 71
♔a7 ♕d5 72 ♕b6 ♕d7+ 73 ♔a8
♔h3 74 c6 ♕d5 75 ♔a7 1-0**

Taimanov – Tolush

37 f5! gxf5 38 g6! f4+ (if
38...hxg6 then 39 h6) **39 ♔xf4 fxg6
40 ♘xe6 gxh5 41 ♕xh5+ ♔e7
42 ♕xh7+ ♔d6 43 ♘d4 ♕f8+
44 ♘f5+ ♔c6 45 ♕e7 ♕b8+
46 ♕e5 ♕d8 47 ♘d4+ ♔b7
48 ♔e3 ♔a8 49 ♔d2 ♕g8 50 ♔c1
♕g2 51 ♕e8+ ♔b7 52 ♕c6+ ♔b8
53 ♘b5 ♕g5+ 54 ♔b1 ♕g1+
55 ♔a2 ♕f2+ 56 ♔a3 ♕g1
57 ♕c7+ 1-0**

		Gagra 1953 Training Tournament									
		1	2	3	4	5	6	7	8	9	10	Total
1	Smyslov	*	0	½	½	1	1	1	1	½	1	6½
2	Petrosian	1	*	0	½	1	½	1	½	½	1	6
3	Boleslavsky	½	1	*	0	1	½	½	½	½	1	5½
4	Averbakh	½	½	1	*	½	½	0	½	1	0	4½
5	Geller	0	0	0	½	*	½	1	1	1	½	4½
6	Kotov	0	½	½	½	½	*	½	0	1	1	4½
7	Taimanov	0	0	½	1	0	½	*	½	1	1	4½
8	Keres	0	½	½	½	0	1	½	*	0	1	4
9	Tolush	½	½	½	0	0	0	0	1	*	1	3½
10	Ragozin	0	0	0	1	½	0	0	0	0	*	1½

Geller – Petrosian
French Defence [C15]

1 e4 e6 2 d4 d5 3 ♘c3 ♗b4 4 ♗d3 c5 5 exd5 ♕xd5 6 ♗d2 ♗xc3 7 ♘c6 10 ♘f3 ♘f6 11 ♘g3 0-0 12 ♘f3 ♗g4 13 0-0-0 ♗xf3 14 gxf3 ♕xa2 15 ♖hg1 g6 16 ♕h4 ♕e6 17 f4 ♘d7 18 fxe5 ♘cxe5 19 ♗b5 ♘f3 20 ♕f4 ♘xg1 21 ♖e1 ♕a2 22 ♗c4

22...♘e2+!! 23 ♖xe2 ♕a1+ 24 ♔d2 ♘b6 25 ♗xf7+ ♖xf7 26 ♕d4 ♖d7 0-1

Ragozin – Boleslavsky

21...♖xf2 22 ♖xf2 ♘xf2 23 ♔xf2 ♕e5 24 ♗c1?
The decisive mistake. White could maintain the balance with 24 b4! (to bring his queen into play)

24...♕xg5! 25 bxc5 ♕e3+ 26 ♔f1 ♕f4+ 27 ♔g1.

24...♕f6+ 25 ♔g1 ♘d3! 26 h3 ♖e1+! 27 ♔h2 (27 ♖xe1 ♕f2+ 28 ♔h2 ♘xe1 leads to mate) 27...♖xd1 28 ♕a4 ♖e1 29 ♗d2 ♘c5 30 ♕b4 ♖e8 31 ♗g5 ♕xg5 32 ♕xb6 ♘e4 33 ♘xe4 ♖xe4 34 ♘f3 ♕e7 0-1

Taimanov – Smyslov

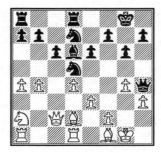

19...e5! 20 ♗g2 exd4 21 exd4 ♘f8 22 b5 ♘e6! 23 bxc6 bxc6 24 ♕xc6 ♖ac8 25 ♕a6
On 25 ♕xd5, Black wins with 25...♗h2+ 26 ♔xh2 ♖xd5 27 ♗xd5 ♕xf2+ 28 ♔h1 ♖c2.

25...♘df4 26 ♕f1 ♘xd4 27 ♗xf4 ♗xf4 28 ♘b4 ♕g5 (switching to the b8-h2 diagonal) 29 a5 ♗b8 30 ♕a6 ♕e5 31 ♔f1 ♘b3! 32 ♘d5 ♘d2+ 33 ♖xd2 ♕xa1+ 34 ♔e2 ♕e5+ 35 ♔d1 ♕a1+ 36 ♔e2 ♖e8+ 37 ♘e3 ♖c1 38 ♗d5 ♖e1+ 39 ♔f3 ♕e5 40 ♘f1 ♕f4+ 41 ♔g2 ♖xf1 42 ♖e2 ♖xe2 43 ♕xe2 ♖c1 44 ♕e8+ ♔g7 45 ♗xf7 ♕h2+ 0-1

An entire mini-chapter, so to speak, could be devoted to figures in tournament tables that don't correspond to any games played, and games which are not recorded in the tournament tables. Under the first of these headings, there are the 2:2 scores registered at the 1939 Buenos Aires Olympiad in the matches Palestine-Germany, Poland-Germany, France-Germany and also France-Czechoslovakia, Poland-Czechoslovakia and Palestine-Argentina. This had to do with the world war that had just broken out; a number of teams refused to play against the initiators of the fighting or their satellites and allies. Incidentally it may have been these imaginary matches that enabled the German team to take first place, a mere half point ahead of the excellent Polish team.

The converse of this arose in the 1967 Interzonal Tournament in the Tunisian town of Sousse. The American Grandmaster Bobby Fischer started brilliantly and was leading with 8½ points after 10 rounds ... and then dropped out, for an absurd reason of his own making. As a result, such a brilliant victory as the following was excluded from the tournament table. In one sense it exists, and in another it doesn't!

Fischer – Stein
Ruy Lopez [C92]
(notes by R.G.Wade)

1 e4 e5 2 ♘f3 ♘c6 3 ♗b5 a6 4 ♗a4 ♘f6 5 0-0 ♗e7 6 ♖e1 b5 7 ♗b3 d6 8 c3 0-0 9 h3 ♗b7

One of the more unusual of the many possibilities for Black from the well-thumbed position after White's 9th move, viz.: 9...♘a5, 9...h6, 9...♘b8, 9...♘d7, 9...♗e6, 9...a5 and 9...♕d7, all adopted at some time by Grandmasters.

10 d4 ♘a5 11 ♗c2 ♘c4 12 b3

With his pawn centre Fischer prefers not to exchange pieces – as happened in Kuijpers-Lutikov at Beverwijk 1967 and Yeropov-Lutikov, USSR Spartakiad 1967 – by 12 ♘bd2 ♘xd2 13 ♗xd2 followed by the centre break 13...d5.

12...♘b6 13 ♘d2 ♘bd7

As Stein lost this game, a lot of criticism is sure to be directed at the involved manoeuvrings of this knight.

14 b4 exd4

By departing from the Steinitzian concept of strongpointing the pawn at e5, Stein nullifies the idea behind his 13th move, which is to keep the white e-pawn on e4, blocking the diagonal of the white bishop at c2 and thus reducing White's attacking chances.

What changes Stein's mind? It must be the realization that with play in the centre blocked or stifled, the scenes of action switch to the wings. Fischer's 14 b4 has staked a claim on the queen's wing but perhaps it is also a weakening move. On the king's wing the prospect of Fischer's knight going from d2-f1-g3-f5 or via f1-h2-g4 may cause anxiety. Stein, who rarely shirks a rough-and-tumble phase, plunges....

15 cxd4 a5 16 bxa5 c5

Setting up a passed pawn on the queen's wing and one that can expect support.

This forces Fischer to explore the kingside possibilities.

17 e5 dxe5

After 17...♘d5 18 exd6 ♗xd6 19 ♘e4 ♗e7? 20 dxc5 ♘xc5 21 ♘xc5 ♗xc5 22 ♗xh7+ ♔xh7 23 ♕c2+, White regains the piece with advantage in pawns.

18 dxe5 ♘d5 19 ♘e4 ♘b4

An alternative plan of defence is 19...c4, to follow up with ♘d7-c5.

20 ♗b1 ♖xa5 21 ♕e2 ♘b6

The black queenside is compact and has its long-term menace. But now the storm gathers on the other wing. Stein was already extremely short of time.

22 ♘fg5

The threat is 23 ♘xh7.

22...♗xe4

After 22...♗xg5 23 ♘xg5 h6 24 ♘e4, the Black kingside remains dangerously weak with the pair of white bishops bearing down on it.

23 ♕xe4 g6 24 ♕h4 h5 25 ♕g3!

As 25...♕d4 is met by 26 ♘xf7!, e.g. 26...♖xf7 27 ♕xg6+ ♖g7 28 ♕xb6 or here 27...♔f8 28 ♗h6+ ♔e8 29 ♗e3 ♕xa1 30 e6.

25...♘c4 26 ♘f3

Threat 27 e6.

26...♔g7 27 ♕f4 ♖h8 28 e6! f5

29 ♗xf5!! ♕f8!

Regretfully the bishop is left alone, for if 29...gxf6, 30 ♕g3+ and then:

(a) 30...♔h7 31 ♘g5+ ♗xg5 32 ♗xg5 followed by 33 ♖ad1 threatening 34 ♖d7.

(b) 30...♔f8 31 ♕g6 ♕e8 32 ♗h6+ ♖xh6 33 ♕xh6+ ♔g8 34 ♘g5 followed in time by ♖a1-d1 and this rook entering the attack.

With this move, Stein at least weakens the attack by exchanging queens.

30 ♗e4

"I am surprised that Fischer did not examine an interesting line by which he can keep the queens on the board: 30 ♘h4!!, with these variations:

(a) 30...gxf5 31 ♕g3+ and mates.

(b) 30...♗xh4 31 ♕xh4, and either capture on f5 loses:

(b1) 31...gxf5 32 ♕g5+ ♔h7 33 e7! winning.

(b2) 31...♕xf5 32 ♕e7+ ♔g8 33 ♕d8+ ♔g7 (33...♕f8 34 e7!) 34 ♕c7+ ♔g8 35 e7!.

(c) 30...g5 31 ♕g3 ♕f6 32 ♘g6! ♕xa1 33 ♘xe7 ♕f6 34 ♗xg5 winning.

(d) 30...♘d6 31 ♗b2+ ♔g8 (if 31...♗f6, 32 e7 wins) 32 ♘xg6 ♕xf5 33 ♘xe7+ winning.

(e) 30...♗d6 31 ♕g5 ♕f6 32 ♘xg6! ♕xg5 33 ♗xg5 ♖e8 34 e7! ♖a7 35 ♖ad1 ♘xa2 36 ♖e6! winning." (J.E.Littlewood)

30...♕xf4 31 ♗xf4 ♖e8

Queried by Stein after the game. In its place he suggested immediately 31...♖a6 and the Soviet players, seconds and journalists thought a draw then reasonable. Larsen, working independently, however, found then 32 a3!! for if 32...♖xa3 33 ♖xa3 ♘xa3 34 ♗e5+ ♗f6 35 ♗d6 and the advanced e-pawn together with the two bishops maintains a winning position.

After 31...♖a6 32 a3 ♘xa3, then 33 ♘e5 threatening 34 ♘xg6 keeps up the pressure, or 32...♘c6 33 ♖ad1.

32 ♖ad1 ♖a6 33 ♖d7 ♖xe6 34 ♘g5 ♖f6 35 ♗f3! ♖xf4 36 ♘e6+ ♔f6 37 ♘xf4

Threatening 38 ♖e6+ followed by 39 ♗e4.

37...♘e5 38 ♖b7 ♗d6 39 ♔f1 ♘c2 40 ♖e4 ♘d4

Fischer is the exchange ahead and endeavours not to surrender the tactical initiative.

41 ♖b6 ♖d8 42 ♘d5+ ♔f5 43 ♘e3+ ♔e6 44 ♗e2 ♔d7

Or 44...b4 45 ♘c4 with pins *(and needles)*.

45 ♗xb5+ ♘xb5 46 ♖xb5 ♔c6 47 a4 ♗c7 48 ♔e2 g5 49 g3 ♖a8 50 ♖b2 ♖f8 51 f4 gxf4 52 gxf4 ♘f7 53 ♖e6+ ♘d6

Otherwise 54 ♖f6.

54 f5 ♖a8 55 ♖d2 ♖xa4 56 f6 1-0

Another chess spectre may be added to the foregoing. The book of the 4th All-Russian Tournament (in plain language, the national championship), held in St Petersburg in 1905, gives a game Rubinstein-Maliutin in which White resigned after throwing away a bishop, but in the tournament table it is put down as a draw. A mistake by the author and compiler? Nothing ot the sort. There had simply been some events that the broad chess public didn't know about.

The game had been adjourned with a clear advantage to Rubinstein. On resumption, there was a fair amount of noise in the hall. The spectators were behaving in a very relaxed manner, and so

were the contestants who were not playing, especially the one who was to gain the silver medal in this championship: the eminent theoretician and first professional psychologist in chess, Beniamin Blumenfeld, then twenty years old. Akiba more than once turned to the controllers and asked them to quieten things down; he said he couldn't play in such conditions, and was supported by his opponent – but in vain. As a result, with his nerves all on edge, Rubinstein first ran his position downhill for move after move, then made that 'blunder' which cost him a piece. After the end of the game he presented an appeal to the tournament committee, as the controlling team was called in those days. The council of arbiters consulted among themselves, then took a decision far removed from Solomon's wisdom: the game was to be replayed from the adjourned position.

By then, however, Rubinstein had been told the correct winning method by third parties, and didn't want to take advantage of this gift from the arbiters; so he offered Maliutin a draw, which was accepted. Thus another phantom arose, in a manner that has no analogies.

At any rate, the phantoms I have just mentioned were the product of external circumstances and efforts to cope with them. They didn't conceal any malicious intention towards the chessplaying community. There is, however, another type of chess mirage – of a much darker hue and a frankly unpleasant odour – which has more than once seen the light of day.

The following, for instance, was published in the 7th issue of the weekly *64* for 1969:

Copying a pattern

In a western magazine our attention was caught by a game between **Vrillestad** and **Friese**:

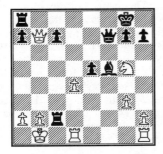

18...罝c1+! 19 含xc1 豐c4+ 20 含d2 豐d3+ 21 含e1 豐e3+ 22 含f1 罝f8! 23 含g2 豐e2+ 24 含g1 息e6, and it was all over (0-1).

This finish deserved to be published, and yet some inexplicable 'sixth sense' kept us from reproducing it – and with good reason. Soon afterwards in a different periodical we saw the familiar diagram, but the names under it were completely different. *Messrs Vrillestad and Friese had taken their cue from a game Spielmann - Van der Bosch (1935), and followed it without a single deviation!*

Well, I note the delicacy of my journalist colleagues who left it at that and didn't draw any inferences from the 'coincidence' that was perfectly obvious. Let us now

consider a much more glaring and more recent chess phantasmagoria containing 'malice aforethought'. In 1993-4, FIDE registered some interesting and, you could say, high-class games from two minor all-play-all international tournaments that had taken place in Moscow in the spring of 1992. Take a look at them, and you will scarcely have cause to lament any drop in the level of skill among so-called middle-ranking players in recent times.

Ruy Lopez [C78]

1 e4 e5 2 公f3 公c6 3 息b5 a6 4 息a4 公f6 5 0-0 b5 6 息b3 息b7 7 罝e1 息c5 8 c3 d6 9 d4 息b6 10 息g5 h6 11 息h4 g5 12 息g3 0-0 13 豐d3 公h5 14 公bd2 豐f6 15 息d5 罝ae8 16 a4 公xg3 17 hxg3 exd4 18 axb5 axb5 19 息xc6 息xc6 20 公xd4 息d7 21 公2f3 b4 22 公f5 息xf5 23 exf5 bxc3 24 bxc3 罝xe1+ 25 罝xe1 含g7 26 公h2 h5 27 g4 h4 28 公f3 罝a8 29 豐d2

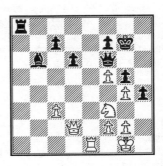

29...罝a4! 30 公h2 罝c4 31 罝c1 息a5 32 豐e3 d5 33 豐e8 息xc3 34 豐d7 息e5 35 罝d1 息xh2+ 36 含xh2 c6 37 罝e1 罝xg4 38 g3 hxg3+ 39 fxg3 罝b4 40 含g2 罝b2+ 41 含h3 罝b4 0-1

English Opening [A36]

1 c4 c5 2 ♘c3 ♘c6 3 g3 g6
4 ♗g2 ♗g7 5 e4 d6 6 ♘ge2 e6 7 d3
♘ge7 8 ♗e3 ♘d4 9 ♕d2 ♖b8
10 ♖c1?! h5 11 h3 a6 12 f4 f5
13 ♘d1 ♘xe2 14 ♔xe2 ♘c6
15 ♘f2 ♘d4+ 16 ♔f1 0-0 17 ♔g1
h4! 18 g4 e5 19 ♗xd4 cxd4 20 exf5
gxf5 21 ♗d5+ ♔h7 22 gxf5

22...♗h6 23 ♕e2 ♗xf5 24 ♖f1
♗xf4 25 ♕h5+ ♔g7 26 ♘e4 ♗g6
27 ♕g4 ♕e7 28 ♔g2 ♔h6 29 ♖f2
♗f5 30 ♕e2 ♗e3 31 ♖f3 ♕g7+
32 ♔f1 ♗g6 33 ♘f2 ♗h5 34 ♘g4+
♗xg4 35 hxg4 ♕xg4 36 ♗f7 ♔g7
37 ♖xe3 ♖xf7+ 38 ♔e1 ♕xe2+
39 ♖xe2 ♖h8 40 ♖g2+ ♔f8, and
emerging from time trouble, Black
converted his advantage into a win
on the 54th move (0-1).

English Opening [A22]
(notes by the winner)

1 c4 ♘f6 2 ♘c3 e5 3 g3 d5
4 cxd5 ♘xd5 5 ♗g2 ♘b6
Beginning the fight against the
'Dragon Variation' of the Sicilian
Defence (with colours reversed and
a move less), I proceeded from the
conviction that a shortage of one
tempo was not enough to turn this
congenial line of play into a bad
one. Sure enough, this game – just

like any other played recently –
leads us to a clear conclusion: in
this variation Black need not fear
that he will fail to equalize.
6 ♘f3 ♘c6 7 0-0 ♗e7 8 d3 0-0
9 ♗e3 f5
The idea of this advance is to
induce White to start a struggle for
the c5-square earlier than he would
like. The usual continuation 9...f6
would have given the opponent
more possibilities to choose from.
10 ♘a4 f4 11 ♗c5 ♗g4 12 ♖c1
♗d6
This manoeuvre forms a vital link
in Black's strategic plan. Otherwise
White could continue 13 ♗xe7
♕xe7 14 ♘c5, with some
unpleasant pressure against the
pawn on b7.
13 ♖e1
As a result of this move White
will sooner or later lose control of
the d4-square, where a black knight
will take up a very strong post.
13...♕e7 14 ♘d2 ♔h8!
Aiming to play ♘b6xa4 – which
at the present moment would be
premature in view of the simple
15 ♕xa4, and if 15...♗xc5 then
16 ♕c4+ etc.
15 ♘e4
Playing to win a pawn by
15 ♗xd6 cxd6 16 ♘xb6 axb6
17 ♗xc6 bxc6 18 ♖xc6 ♖xa2
19 ♖xb6 would be unsatisfactory on
account of 19...d5!, when Black
threatens 20...fxg3 followed by
21...♕c5 (or 20...♕c5 at once).
15...♗xc5
After this exchange, the threat to
the b7-pawn counts for less than
Black's pressure in the centre.
16 ♘axc5 ♘d4
With the strong threat of 17...f3!.
However, White finds the only
adequate reply.

17 ♘b3!

Now none of the variations guarantees Black a decisive plus, for example:

(a) 17...f3 18 ♘xd4 fxg2 19 ♘f3.

(b) 17...♘xe2+ 18 ♖xe2 f3? 19 ♖e1.

(c) 17...♗xe2 18 ♖xe2 f3? 19 ♘xd4.

(d) 17...♘xb3 18 ♕xb3 f3 19 exf3 ♗xf3 20 ♗xf3 ♖xf3 21 ♖e3 with equal chances.

17...c6

Black selects a quiet positional continuation. However, since ♖a8-d8 is essential in any event to protect d4, it should have been played at once. Then if 18 ♘xd4 exd4 19 ♕d2, Black has 19...♘d5 20 ♕a5 b6 21 ♕xa7 ♕b4 with fully adequate compensation for the pawn. After the move played, White achieves an equal position.

18 ♘xd4 exd4 19 ♕d2 ♘d5 20 ♖c4 ♕e5 21 b4

Threatening to win a pawn by 22 ♕b2; White has obtained some counterplay.

21...♖ad8 22 ♕b2 ♘b6 23 ♖c5 ♖d5

Now the threat is 24...♘a4!.

24 ♕a3 ♘d7

With this move Black defends the rook on f8 among other things; this will later prove highly important.

25 ♖xd5?

Having played some attacking moves White lets his optimism get the better of him, and ends up spoiling his position beyond repair. The modest 25 ♖cc1 was better (whereas 25 ♖a5 a6 26 ♘c5 would be refuted by 26...f3! as in the game).

25...cxd5

After this move, the forced evacuation of the white knight finally enables Black to carry out

his latent threat of f4-f3 to great effect.

26 ♘c5

26...f3 27 h3

The attack would have been particularly interesting if White had found the best defence at this point: 27 ♘xd7 ♗xd7 28 ♗f1! (but not 28 b5 in view of 28...♔g8!, and the b5-pawn falls). There could follow: 28...h5 29 ♕c1 (to forestall 29...h4, which would threaten 30...hxg3 31 hxg3 ♕xg3+!) 29...♖e8 30 e3 h4, with the strong threat of ♖e8-e6-h6.

Instead of this, White chooses a tempting move that allows a quicker and more convincing dénouement.

27...fxg2! 28 hxg4 ♘f6!

If now 29 ♘xb7, Black wins at once with 29...♘xg4.

29 b5

White parries the threat of 29...♘xg4 (which would now lose to 30 ♘d7), but cannot save the game.

29...♕e7!

The white knight is fixed to the spot. Now 30 ♕c1 is useless on account of the new pin 30...♖c8, while 30 ♕xa7 is met by 30...♘xg4.

30 ♕b4

This rescues the king (30...♘xg4 31 ♕xd4), but leaves the knight to its inescapable doom.

30...♘d7 31 ♕xd4
31 ♘a6 is also hopeless in view
of 31...♕f6!.
31...♘xc5
Technically simpler than
31...♕xc5 32 ♕xc5 ♘xc5 33 ♖c1,
followed by 34 ♔xg2.
32 ♕xd5
Or 32 ♔xg2 b6 33 ♕xd5 ♖d8
34 ♕f3 ♘xd3.
32...♖d8 33 ♕f3 ♖xd3
But not 33...♘xd3 on account of
34 ♖d1 ♘e5 35 ♖xd8+, with 36
♕xb7 to follow.
**34 exd3 ♕xe1+ 35 ♔xg2 ♕e7
36 d4 ♘e4 37 ♕e3 ♕e8 38 f3 ♘f6
39 ♕e5**
There are some games in which
the right moment to resign is
genuinely hard to decide. Since
White didn't do that earlier, there is
nothing left for him now but to play
on to the end.
**39...♔g8 40 g5 ♕xe5 41 dxe5
♘d5 42 f4 ♘c3 43 ♔f3 ♘xa2 44 f5
♘c3 45 b6 a5 46 ♔e3 ♘d5+
47 ♔d4 ♘xb6 48 e6 a4 49 f6 gxf6**
If instead 49...h6?, Black would
lose to 50 e7 ♔f7 51 fxg7.
50 gxf6 a3 0-1

The notes to this game were by ...
Alexander Alekhine. Mysticism? A
ghost story? How could the first
Russian World Champion, whose
life ended in 1946, annotate an
ordinary encounter between the
master Vladimir Kozlov and Andrei
Makarov, played in an ordinary
tournament nearly half a century
later? And why *would* a Chess King
do such a thing? It's true that
shortly before his death he devoted
some attention to the games of
undistinguished Portuguese players
so as to pay for his cigarettes, but as
for this...

In actual fact there was no
miraculous phenomenon. Alekhine
was annotating one of his *own*
games with Black in the 1939
'Tournament of Nations' in Buenos
Aires. His opponent was the future
International Master Czerniak, the
leader of the team from Palestine
(present-day Israel). The element of
fantasy consists in the fact that
the players in the Moscow
tournament were repeating the
World Champion's game move-for-
move. Similarly, in the first of the
three games I quoted, Normunds
Miezis and Andrei Makarov
'copied' an encounter between the
strong Grandmasters Dolmatov and
Beliavsky from Moscow 1990;
while in the second, Sergei Yuferov
and Andrei Makarov were
'thinking' in the same way as
International Master Ujtelky and
Grandmaster Bondarevsky in the
Chigorin Memorial, Sochi 1964.
Makarov, later to be President of the
Russian Chess Federation, enacted
some more of these phantom games
too; with their help he gained the
International Master title (!), after
only sitting down to play 5 or 6 real
games in the course of two
'qualifying' tournaments!

But what are these 'identical'
games from individual tournaments, when set beside a book
published as far back as 1822, by
Commendatore (this testified to his
noble origin) Ciccolini di Macerata
– the founder of the 'Chess
Academy' in the Roman *Caffè
Pastini*. Entitled *Endeavour*, the
book is made up exclusively of
fictitious games by the author! A
whole book! That means more than
just the isolated 'creations' of the

illustrious Prince Dadian of Mingrelia who published them from time to time in the pages of the periodical press.

Phantom chess also has another side, which emerged only in our own era of Elo ratings. As worthy claimants to the role of record-holder in this department, I would name the Georgian Grandmaster Zurab Azmaiparashvili, who in a four-player match-tournament in Yugoslavia scored +14 =4 -0 (sixteen out of eighteen!) and at once added 70 points (!) to his rating; the Turkmenian master Babakuly Annakov, who supposedly played 212 games in the course of half a year (183 days) or one year, thereby growing in stature by 205 points (!) in the ranking list; six players from Myanmar, who came from complete obscurity to break into the list of the world's top 100 players at one jump; the Romanian Alexandru Krisan, who pulled off something similar; and so on....

In short, there are no end of phantoms, including record-breaking ones, in chess as in life – although some of these chess apparitions are received with pleasure and a smile.

Thus for example on a free day during the 1966 World Championship match, Spassky and Petrosian unexpectedly did battle again, and their games appeared in the chess press! There was just one small 'but'. The opponents were not sitting at a single board, but at 20 at once; naturally they were playing 20 games. But not all the Spasskys on that occasion were called Boris,

and not all the Petrosians were Tigrans. It was just that these namesakes of the great masters had gathered at Moscow University Chess Club, and on their own amateur level were 'adding' to the creative interest of the match for the crown.

Furthermore I saw with my own eyes the score chart of a double-round tournament from the early 1950s, in which Botvinnik, Smyslov, Bronstein and Fine played each other with hardly any draws. There is no mystery here; it all really did take place. Only the players were not the chess titans known to all the world, but members of the chess club at the Moscow Palace of Pioneers and Schoolchildren.

Then again, the magazine *Deutsche Schachblätter* told of an encounter between such great names as Philidor, Anderssen, Morphy, Steinitz, Capablanca, Euwe, Botvinnik, Keres and Reshevsky; it took place in the post-war Berlin of 1948, when the city was still lying in ruins. But I am afraid these were not even name-sakes; some chess amateurs had assumed the illustrious names as pseudonyms, and conducted the tournament under that guise.

Finally, a whole 'family' of phantoms are closely linked to championship titles. For instance, Igor Kopylov (a master from Ufa), Sergei Glusevich and the St Petersburg player Vasily Malinin became champions of a non-existent country! The Soviet Union disappeared from the political map of the world, but its Correspondence Championship was still going on; furthermore the quarter-finals and semi-finals of the *next* two championships were already over. They didn't want this to go to waste, and the decision was made to see it all through to the end. And so they did. But ultimately the record here must be ascribed to Malinin. He was the last to receive the gold medal of Russia for a victory in the USSR Championship; this was as late as 2002 (!).

There was the same kind of absurdity, only on a larger scale, at the conclusion of the 10th World Team Championship – again for correspondence chess. While the letters were crossing mountains, seas and lands at a fast or leisurely pace, the USSR and the German Democratic Republic ceased to exist, as did Yugoslavia within its previous frontiers. Moreover the Soviet and Yugoslav teams contained players who were now citizens of different countries – for it wasn't only Muscovites who had played under the flag of the Soviet Union, or only Belgraders who had defended the Yugoslav colours. What was to be done? Should the championship be scrapped half way through? Of course not. The East Germans were simply labelled as such to distinguish them from the German Federal Republic, and the contest continued. Here again there was a touch of phantasmagoria in the proceedings. To clinch first place, the former Soviet team only needed half a point from the last game, which was being played by a former World Correspondence Champion, Professor Vladimir

Zagorovsky. A peace offer was duly sent from Voronezh to the Italian player Venturino. But it must not be forgotten that letters from the USSR to other countries and back took around 3 or 4 weeks, just as they would have done 300 years ago – so that Zagorovsky learnt of his opponent's acceptance literally a couple of days before his own death.

The 19-year-old Alexander Khalifman, later to be FIDE World Champion, once found himself in a phantom-like state, albeit only for twenty-four hours. In the Dutch town of Groningen he became European Junior Champion for a year that had not yet begun! It couldn't be helped – in the penultimate round on 31 December 1985, Alexander made sure of victory and in theory didn't need to sit down at the chessboard after seeing the New Year in. Throughout the annals of chess, no one else managed anything like that!

Defying the theory of probabilities

No, this branch of higher mathematics by no means excludes chance. It is known, for instance, that there are slightly more women in the world than men, but on stepping outside into the street, you could well find that the first 150 people you saw were all representatives of the stronger sex – a column of soldiers marching past. The probability formula *does* however define the possible frequency of such exceptions. Sometimes the probability of a coincidence is a fraction of one per cent, and by all the rules of worldly wisdom it can be ignored. And yet: "All theory, my friend, is grey; the golden tree of life is green." The poet after all comes closer to the truth than science.

Here are some coincidences which may very well claim record status.

Winners

The 1914 St Petersburg tournament was called a tournament of champions by Dr Siegbert Tarrasch – on the analogy of Ostende 1907 – and was truly a competition of the strongest. In the extremely fierce struggle the Chess King Lasker finished ahead of the young Capablanca, although he had been behind him at the end of the 'preliminary' stage. Third – a surprize to very many people indeed – was Alekhine, who had been admitted to the contest as winner of the All-Russian Master Tournament. Some stars of the first magnitude were left further down the list: Tarrasch and Rubinstein, Marshall, the aged Gunsberg....

Ten long years passed – under the shadow of the First World War and the upheavals and ravages it set in train. In New York in the spring of 1924, exactly 11 chessplayers assembled once again. By that time the crown had passed to Capablanca, and Alekhine had become the pretender; the 56-year-old Lasker was not even dreaming of returning to the chess throne. Richard Réti and Efim Bogoljubow were in their prime; the Soviet citizen living in Germany was to win the extremely strong Moscow tournament a year later, ahead of both Lasker and Capablanca.

In a word, the pack of chess giants might have been reshuffled – and yet the prizewinners lined up in precisely the same order as 10 years earlier: 1st Lasker, 2nd Capablanca, 3rd Alekhine. Nor is that all. The nearly fifty-year-old Frank Marshall finished just behind them; at St Petersburg he had been separated from the top three by Tarrasch, who was not present at New York. Of course everything could have turned out differently – after all, right up until the last minute it was doubtful whether the World Champion would participate, owing to a severe form of influenza. Caissa nonetheless arranged things just this way, and divine will is stronger than any mathematical theory.

Or take another case. In May 1972, shortly after the Soviet Team Championships in Moscow, another All-Union tournament was held: the unofficial USSR blitz championship. Some truly great masters of lightning play (and not only that, of course) flew in from various corners of the vast couontry: Mikhail Tal from Riga, Viktor Korchnoi from Leningrad, Leonid Stein from Kiev. On home ground, there were the Muscovites David Bronstein and Evgeny Vasiukov. But two others surpassed them all: the Leningrader Anatoly Karpov, still very young at the time (he had been a Grandmaster for only 3 years) and Vladimir Tukmakov from Odessa, who had joined the Grandmaster family just a couple of months previously. The contenders for the lead exchanged blows as follows.

195

Tukmakov – Karpov

21 Rcd1 g5 22 Bxg5 hxg5 23 Wxg5+ Bg7 24 e5! dxe5 25 Nh4 Ne7 26 Rxe5 Red8 27 Bd3 Rd5 28 Rxd5 Nfxd5 29 Nh5 Ng6 30 Nxg6 fxg6 31 Wxg6 Rc7 32 Re1 Re7 33 Nxg7 Rxg7 34 We8 mate

Karpov – Tukmakov

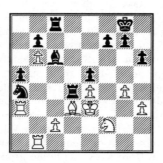

32 c3 Rd6 33 Bc2 Nc5 34 Rxa5 Nd7 35 Nd3 f6 36 Bb3+ Kf8 37 Ba2 Rd8 38 Bc4 Ke7 39 Rb4! Nf8 40 Nc5 Nd7 41 Nb3 Nf8 42 Ra7 Rd1 43 Nc5 Rb8 44 Bd5! Rxd5 45 exd5 Bxd5 46 Na6 Rc8 47 Nc7 Bxc6 48 Rc4 Nd7 49 Rxc6! bxc6 50 b7 Rb8 51 Na6 Kd8 52 Nxb8 Nxb8 53 Ke4 g6 54 Ra1, and Black lost at once after **54...Nd7? 55 Rd1**, although even the better **54...Kc7** would not have

saved him in view of the possible h3-h4-h5 **(1-0)**.

I remember full well the trepidation with which the two winners awaited the verdict of the arbiters who had set about calculating each player's Sonneborn-Berger score; the regulations had made no provision for a play-off match. When the results were announced at last, Tukmakov couldn't conceal his joy or Karpov his dejection.

Sixteen years passed, and in the Spanish town of Jijona the first European Championship of the newly popular rapid chess was held. One hundred and nine Grandmasters and masters played a 13-round Swiss. The undisputed favourite was Anatoly Karpov. To be sure, he had managed to add he prefix 'ex' to his World Championship title – but he still remained the chief rival to Garry Kasparov, and their matches for the crown continued to hold all chess enthusiasts in suspense. Others whose chances were rated highly were Grandmaster Viktor Gavrikov from Vilnius, who had become quite an expert at play with such an unusual time control; the Hungarians Istvan Csom and Andras Adorjan; Rafael Vaganian; and Oleg Romanishin. But at the end of the day, the player finishing equal with Karpov was once again Vladimir Tukmakov! He was already the veteran of all the participants. The best results of his chess career – 3 silver medals in USSR Championships – were behind him, although in 'Swisses' he was still performing with confidence. However that might be, he and Karpov had 10 points each! Once again the arbiters did their sums, this time using the Buchholz system – and 'revenge' was exacted: first place went to Karpov. This was largely due to their individual encounter.

Karpov – Tukmakov

16 ♔c3! 0-0 17 ♕e5! ♕f2
18 ♗d3 ♖ad8 19 ♖hf1 ♕h4
20 ♕e4 ♕h6 21 ♕e3 ♕h4 22 ♖f4
♕e7 23 ♘e5 ♕c5+

Instead 23...♘c7 would be dangerous in view of 24 ♗xh7+! ♔xh7 25 ♕h3+ ♔g8 26 ♖h4 ♕c5+ 27 ♔b3 ♕d5+ 28 ♔a3 ♕c5+ 29 b4.

24 ♕xc5 ♘xc5 25 ♗c4 ♘d7
If 25...f6, then 26 b4!.

26 ♘xf7! ♖xf7 27 ♗xe6 ♘f6
28 ♖af1 1-0

Opponents

Troubles caused by a 'jinx opponent' in chess are a secret to no one. For a whole variety of reasons, most of them psychological, a strong player X will perform catastrophically against player Y, when the latter is no stronger and

may even be weaker, perhaps *much* weaker. I experienced this myself at junior level, and in the ranks of the strongest players such examples abound. Suffice it to recall the two tournament games that the great Alekhine lost to the English master Yates, whose play in the main was a couple of classes lower. For a while, even after being World Champion, Tal had a 'five-all' score against Korchnoi. He had lost five games – and drawn the other five.

Korchnoi was reputed – rightly – to be an awkward opponent for Tigran Petrosian too. After losing his crown in 1969, the latter still kept on fighting to regain it, but in 4 cycles of Candidates matches the luck of the draw invariably brought him up against none other than Korchnoi. The ex-World Champion's second, Grandmaster Igor Zaitsev, testifies that in 1976, after coming through the Biel Interzonal and the subsequent play-off, Petrosian was reduced to tears of vexation on being told by telephone that he would have to play a match with Korchnoi next. I need hardly say that after winning their first match Petrosian lost all the others (including the scandalous one in Odessa). But one other thing is more important here: the probability of such a coincidence works out at 1 in 1029, that is less than 0.1 per cent. And yet it became 100% reality! There must surely have been a record grin on the face of the Fates!

Now a small digression. Reminiscing about Petrosian, Igor Zaitsev once observed:

In a purely external sense, his fortunes as a chessplayer were surprisingly like those of Capablanca. They both gained the World Championship title at approximately the same age: Capablanca was in his 33rd year, Petrosian was approaching 34. They both held the world chess crown for the space of precisely six years, and sad though it is to relate, they both ended their lives at about the same age too. There are also some other coincidences, in terms of their chess. Neither of them attached great significance to the opening; both were brilliant blitz players; they preferred static forms of advantage to dynamic ones, and finally the same extraordinary innate flair was common to both. The difference between their dates of birth is a little over forty years, and if we continue this magical sequence on the assumption that a chess phenomenon of such calibre appears once in a 40-year period, we arrive at the date of 1969 – in other words at Viswanathan Anand, whose manner of play is so reminiscent of both Petrosian and Capablanca! Surely this striking circumstance, which deserves special examination, prompts us to take a closer look at the gallery of champions – whereupon two other pairs immediately come to our notice: Botvinnik and Karpov, 1911 and 1951 (again pretty well exactly forty years between); Alekhine and Korchnoi, 1892 and 1932. Here

again, no doubt, there is a marked similarity of characters – and in some respects, definitely, a similarity of fortunes. Perhaps there really is something in this?

Two Grandmasters, Andrei Lilienthal and Igor Bondarevsky, displayed astonishingly similar results at a particular stage in their lives. They were born on the same day, 12 May, at a distance of 2 years. (As I write these lines, Lilienthal has completed his 90th year and is the oldest member of the world Grandmaster family.) They were more or less united by one aim. In March 1937, at the Moscow international tournament in which Reuben Fine was competing, they both scored 2½ points and shared the last two places (7th-8th), despite the disparity in strength which existed between them at the time. (Lilienthal was one of the world's strongest Grandmasters; Bondarevsky had only received the master title a month earlier.) Three years passed, and in the 1940 USSR Championship they finished level again – but on this occasion they scored 13½ out of 19 and shared the *first* two places, despite the fact that several other participants – Botvinnik, Keres, Smyslov, Boleslavsky, Petrovs – played objectively rather better.

In the subsequent match-tournament for the title of Absolute Champion of the USSR, Lilienthal and Bondarevsky once again finished close together, even though this time half a point separated them. But they and they alone had inflicted one defeat each on the winner, Mikhail Botvinnik.

Finally, at different times they acted as trainers and seconds to Vasily Smyslov during his duels with Botvinnik for the chess crown.

When chessplayers were rewarded with decorations and medals, Lilienthal and Bondarevsky both received the same one: the 'Mark of Honour'. Two figures of workers are depicted on it. It was the lowest in the official hierarchy of distinctions at that time, and among the populace it was rather sarcastically christened 'the Merry Children'.

And all this notwithstanding the fact that the characters of the two Grandmasters were utterly different – you might say diametrically opposed. Lilienthal was benevolence itself, amiability towards all and sundry; he had no enemies; the charming Andrei was even idolized by women whom he avoided. Bondarevsky was severity, going as far as cruelty; he displayed constant belligerence, and patent dislike – even hatred – of Jews, who numbered Lilienthal among their ranks.

Yet fate placed them on a parallel course, and nothing could be done about it.

Encounters

Chess games 'coinciding' from the first move to the last are mentioned in the chapter 'Phantoms of the chess world', and there are many more of them than we quoted there. But then again, there are plenty of analogies between games – whole or partial – that have nothing to do with downright fraud. What else can you expect? Smothered mates, bishop sacrifices on h7 and g7, interceptions of all possible kinds – these are the common property of the chess community, and every player makes the best use he can of what has been discovered and made permanently available.

There is no need to speak of the openings. How may times have we seen it? Two pairs of players in a top-level contest will divide their attention between their own game and the one on the neighbouring table! In an identical variation of one and the same opening, one player will employ a new continuation, which then gets copied on the next board ... in short, it's all a familiar scene.

Yet there was only one occasion in chess history when *three* games simultaneously took the same course. This was in round 14 of the 1955 Interzonal Tournament in Göteborg, when the draw placed all four Argentinian participants opposite Soviet Grandmasters in a novel kind of match (another of Caissa's record whims). In the games Geller-Panno, Keres-Najdorf and Spassky-Pilnik (the fourth Soviet Grandmaster had the white pieces too!), one and the same variation was played. Here is how the scenario was described by Efim Geller who played the leading role in it.

Geller – Panno
Sicilian Defence [B98]
(notes by Geller)

**1 e4 c5 2 ♘f3 d6 3 d4 cxd4
4 ♘xd4 ♘f6 5 ♘c3 a6 6 ♗g5 e6
7 f4 ♗e7**
In some games from the preceding rounds Black had failed to solve his defensive problems in this variation satisfactorily, and it was clear that the Argentinians had prepared something new for their unique three-board match against the USSR. All the same there was no particular reason for White to deviate.

8 ♕f3 h6 9 ♗h4 g5
This advance embodies the idea of the defence which the Argentine players had worked out. By exchanging the pawn on f4 they wanted to secure the e5-square permanently for a knight; in their view this could compensate for White's better development. However this whole manoeuvre is too slow, and for the price of two pieces White has the opportunity to start a direct attack on the king.

10 fxg5 ♘fd7

11 ♘xe6(!) fxe6 12 ♕h5+ ♔f8
Here something else occurred that was unexpected. The point is that at this moment Spassky and Keres were only just preparing to sacrifice the knight on e6, and so their opponents Pilnik and Najdorf were watching our game and having a lively discussion about something. Then Najdorf came up to me and said straight out, interrupting my thinking time: "You've got a lost game – we've analysed it all!"

By then I had already managed to find the continuation of the attack, so I answered with deeds rather than words.

13 ♗b5!
Indirectly aimed against Black's future knight outpost on e5, on which his whole system of of defence is grounded. The quiet 13 ♗e2 or 13 ♗d3 would allow him to reinforce that knight with the other one: 13...♘e5 14 0-0 ♔g7 15 ♗g3 ♘bc6. This won't work now, as White takes on c6 then on e5, and delivers mate!

It later emerged that this move had been briefly examined by the Argentinians in their home analysis, but they had found a 'defence' which reassured them. All the same, when I played this, Najdorf and Pilnik somehow became agitated and headed back to their own boards. Afterwards they took another look at our game and concluded that their preparation had a 'hole' in it.

13...♘e5 14 ♗g3!
This is the whole point! Black is no longer able to save the game. In their preparations the Argentine players had reckoned that after 14 0-0+ ♔g8! 15 ♗g3 hxg5! White's attack would founder. We now see what they left out of account: with the move-order in the game,

14...♔g8 fails to 15 ♗xe5 and 16 ♕g6+. If 14...♔g7, then if nothing else White has 15 ♗xe5+ dxe5 16 0-0 ♕g8 17 ♗e8 etc.

Najdorf and Pilnik, by the way, awaited events in our game, then when they realized that Black was in a bad way they varied from their home analysis by playing 13...♔g7. This merely enabled them to prolong their resistance.

Black's strongest defence was discovered a good deal later, after lengthy investigations that were published in virtually every chess magazine in the world. It consists of 13...♖h7!, envisaging the following main continuation: 14 0-0+ ♔g8 15 g6 ♖g7 16 ♖f7 ♗xh4 17 ♕xh6 ♖xf7 18 gxf7+ ♔xf7 19 ♕h7+ ♔e8, and White can either give perpetual check (20 ♕h5+ ♔f8 21 ♕h8+) or else continue the attack by 20 e5 or by 20 ♕h5+ ♔f8 21 ♖f1+ ♗f6 22 e5. It isn't my purpose to give an exhaustive analysis of this position; I will just say that in the end Black does appear to have a draw, which is why White more usually plays 11 ♗g3 from the diagram, avoiding such forced variations.

It's obvious moreover that after changing from the hunters into the prey, the Argentinians playing over-the-board couldn't find such a complex and unique continuation allowing Black to hold out on the edge of the precipice.

14...♗xg5 15 0-0+

An even simpler way to win was first 15 ♗xe5 dxe5, and then 16 0-0+.

15...♔e7 16 ♗xe5 ♕b6+

The outcome would not be altered by 16...♗e3+ 17 ♔h1 dxe5 18 ♕xe5 ♗d4 19 ♘d5+ ♕xd5 20 ♕c7+.

17 ♔h1 dxe5 18 ♕f7+ ♔d6 19 ♖ad1+ ♕d4

Or 19...♔c5 20 ♖d5+ exd5 21 ♕xd5+ ♔b4 22 ♕c4+ ♔a5 23 b4 (or 23 ♕a4) mate.

20 ♖xd4+ exd4 21 e5+ ♔c5

Or 21...♔xe5 22 ♕c7 mate.

22 ♕c7+ ♘c6 23 ♗xc6

Black resigned, in view of 23...bxc6 24 ♕a5+ ♔c4 25 b3 mate (1-0).

This episode was given a special name: the Argentine Tragedy.

Now for an astonishing case that was recounted 30 years ago by the English master and journalist Bernard Cafferty. In 1911, in the course of his European tour, the young Capablanca gave a simultaneous display in Birmingham, where one of his wins was the following game against a certain Mr Price.

Capablanca – Price
Queen's Pawn Opening [D00]

1 d4 d5 2 e3 e6 3 ♗d3 ♗d6 4 ♘d2 ♘d7 5 ♘gf3 f5 (the 'mimicry' ends) 6 b3 ♘h6 7 ♗b2 ♕f6 8 c4 c6 9 ♕c2 0-0 10 h3 g6?! 11 0-0-0 e5? 12 dxe5 ♘xe5 13 cxd5 cxd5 14 ♘c4! dxc4 15 ♗xc4+ ♘hf7 16 ♖xd6 ♕xd6 17 ♘xe5 ♗e6 18 ♖d1 ♕e7

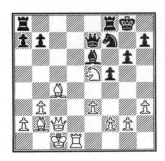

19 ♘xf7 ♗xf7 20 ♕c3 ♗xc4
21 bxc4 ♔f7 22 ♕g7+ ♔e8
23 ♕xe7+ ♔xe7 24 ♗a3+ ♔e8
25 ♗xf8 ♔xf8 26 ♖d7 ♖c8
27 ♖xb7 ♖xc4+ 28 ♔b2, and Black
refrained from continuing his
resistance in a rook endgame two
pawns down (1-0).

This occurred on 24 November.
In the following year, when Havana
was honouring its great son on his
return from Europe where he had
won the great tournament at San
Sebastian, **Capablanca** played a
blindfold game against a certain
Señor **Baca-Arus**. Up to the
position in the last diagram, this
game repeated Capablanca-Price,
that is, all 18 moves were played in
the same sequence! You might
suppose that the Cuban hidalgo
(to use the Spanish term) had
seen the English local newspaper
Birmingham Post and was
consciously acting out José Raoul's
script, but that belongs in the realm
of non-scientific fantasy.

This time, Capablanca concluded
the fight more spectacularly:
19 ♖d7! ♗xd7 20 ♘xd7 ♖fc8
21 ♕c3 ♖xc4 22 bxc4, and Black
resigned since he suffers big
material losses after 22...♘d6
23 ♕h8+ ♔f7 24 ♘e5+ (1-0).

However, the following perfectly
serious game would seem to hold
the record in the 'coincidence'
department.

Ruy Lopez [C82]

1 e4 e5 2 ♘f3 ♘c6 3 ♗b5 a6
4 ♗a4 ♘f6 5 0-0 ♘xe4 6 d4 b5
7 ♗b3 d5 8 dxe5 ♗e6 9 ♘bd2 ♘c5

10 c3 d4 11 ♗xe6 ♘xe6 12 cxd4
The present-day *Encyclopaedia
of Chess Openings* also recom-
mends 12 ♘b3 dxc3 13 ♕c2 ♕d5
14 ♕xc3 ♗b4 15 ♕e3 0-0. In the
game, White plays more naturally.
12...♘cxd4 13 ♘e4! ♗e7 14 ♗e3
♘f5 15 ♕c2 0-0
At the moment Black has no time
for 15...♘xe3 in view of the check
on c6.
16 ♖ad1 ♘xe3 17 fxe3 ♕c8
18 ♘d4 ♘xd4 19 exd4 ♕e6
20 ♘g3 f6?
White has retained the initiative
and straightened out his pawn
structure. At this point it was
imperative for Black to attack the
centre with 20...c5. Instead he does
so 'from the other side'.
21 ♘f5 fxe5

22 ♕b3! 1-0

This game was played in the
USSR in 1982, between Vitaly
Tseshkovsky and Artur Yusupov. A
few years later it was repeated,
move for move, by the no less
distinguished English players
Murray Chandler and John Nunn in
the 1985 Nimzowitsch Memorial.
That Nunn didn't know of the game
between his fellow Grandmasters
from the Soviet Union is obvious;

whether Chandler *did* know it, we cannot tell.

History can show some shorter games repeating themselves, if not daily or weekly or monthly or annually, then at any rate relatively often. Thus for example in the Moscow Junior Championship of 1937, the future World Champion **Vasily Smyslov** played the following miniature with White against **Yuri Poliakov**:

1 d4 d5 2 c4 ♘c6 3 ♘c3 ♘f6 4 ♘f3 ♗g4 5 cxd5 ♘xd5 6 e4 ♘xc3 7 bxc3 e5 8 d5 ♘b8

In the spirit of Chigorin's Defence, but Black should nonetheless have persisted with 8...♗xf3 9 ♕xf3 ♘a5.

9 ♕a4+ ♘d7 10 ♘xe5 ♕f6

11 ♗e2!! ♕xe5?

He had to resign himself to material losses with 11...c6 12 dxc6 ♕xe5.

12 ♗xg4 ♕xc3+ 13 ♗d2

Now 13...♕xa1+ 14 ♔e2 wins for White.

1-0

Precisely 50 years on, the very same thing occurred in an international tournament in Berlin, in a game between the Soviet Grandmaster Yuri Razuvaev and the Yugoslav Branimir Maksimović. Then a mere two months after that, the Swedish woman player Pia Cramling 'dispatched' Claude Landenbergue in essentially the same way. Who will be next?

The *very* short game **1 e4 c6 2 d4 d5 3 ♘c3 dxe4 4 ♘xe4 ♘d7 5 ♕e2 ♘gf6 6 ♘d6 mate** was discussed in the chapter 'The shortest and the longest'.

And finally, a truly extraordinary coincidence occurred in the realm of chess compositions – where having a predecesssor is a perfectly usual thing, but not to this extent.

The famous writer, poet and dramatist Alfred de Musset – whose romantic verses were on the lips of all cultured French people in the 1830s and whose *Confession of a Child of the Century* was praised by Pushkin, Leo Tolstoy and Gorky – had additional leanings towards the law, painting and medicine (!), and in parallel with all this he frequented the chess café *La Régence*. The games he played will hardly have been written down, and if they were, they have not been preserved. On the other hand, a problem he composed and proceeded to show at the café is widely known:

White mates in 3 moves

The solution goes: **1 ♖d7 ♘xd7 2 ♘c6 and 3 ♘f6 mate**.

Unfortunately, about three quarters of a century earlier, Lorenzo Domenico Ponziani – the inhabitant of the small city of Modena who invented the opening 1 e4 e5 2 ♘f3 ♘c6 3 c3 – had published an identical composition in his polemical tract *The Incomparable Game of Chess*. His book had not been re-issued anywhere outside Italy and has always been considered a rarity; moreover a plagiarism would have been virtually incompatible with Musset's personality.

It's a coincidence then – a record-breaking one. Although – God knows....

The prized apple of beauty

Remember what caused the downfall of ancient Troy? It was simply that an apple with the inscription 'for the most beautiful' turned up amidst the food on a banqueting table, and three goddesses who were famed as beauties fell into a deadly quarrel over it. When this unique 'beauty prize' was awarded to one of them by the Trojan Paris, the other two conspired together to destroy both the city and all the people in it. Which they did.

In chess, thank heaven, things have never gone that far. There have, however, been some serious arguments over the award of 'brilliancy prizes', known internationally as prizes for beauty – not of the players, but of the games they create.

Originating in 1876 at a fairly insignificant tournament in New York, this type of award has undergone a whole series of vicissitudes. There have been contests of the highest calibre where it was forgotten about. Then in another tournament they would make one sensible award and one senseless one. Sometimes they would alter the name of this prize which necessarily puts all the emphasis on questions of chess aesthetics.

However that may be, the 1929 Carlsbad tournament holds the record for the sheer quantity of brilliancy prizes. In rewarding those contestants who played imaginatively, it was as if the organizers were keen to help them out on the threshold of the world economic crisis. The composition of the tournament was, of course, impressive. All the strongest players were there, with the exception of World Champion Alekhine; and yet 14 brilliancy prizes (!) were too many. Quantity was not matched by quality, or if it was, there was a minus sign in front of it. The chief prizes went to games which the players themselves would have been embarrassed to count as achievements.

Fewer brilliancy prizes – 'only' twelve – had been awarded at Ostende 1905, but there the quality of the best games was immeasurably higher.

Janowski – Tarrasch
Queen's Pawn Opening [D02]

1 d4 d5 2 ♘f3 c5 3 c3 e6 4 ♗f4 ♕b6 5 ♕b3! ♘c6 6 e3 ♘f6 7 h3 ♗e7 8 ♘bd2 ♗d7 9 ♗e2 0-0

10 0-0 ♖fc8 11 ♘e5 ♗e8 12 ♗g3 ♘d7 13 ♘df3 ♘f8 14 ♖fd1 ♘a5 15 ♕c2 c4?!

"Up to here, true to his usual style, Tarrasch has maintained the tension without any positional concessions. He now begins a highly dubious attack on the queenside where White has no obvious weaknesses. The white d4-pawn is freed from pressure, while the black d5-pawn will soon (after e3-e4!) become weak." (Lasker)

16 ♘d2 f6 17 ♘ef3 ♗g6 18 ♕c1 h6 19 ♘h2 ♕d8 20 ♗f3! b5 21 e4 ♘c6 22 exd5 exd5 23 ♖e1 b4 24 ♘df1 bxc3? (24...a5, with ♖a8-a7 to follow if necessary, was better) **25 bxc3 ♕a5**

"Black still views the queenside as the main battlefield; 25...♕d7 was more cautious." (Tartakower)

26 ♘e3 ♗f7 27 ♕d2 ♗a3 28 ♖ab1 ♘d7 29 ♖b7!

"This deeply calculated penetration bears the stamp of genius. Observe how harmoniously and effectively the two bishops are co-operating." (Tartakower)

29...♘b6 30 ♘f5 ♕a6

"Nor would 30...♗f8 help, on account of 31 ♘g4 renewing the threat of a knight sacrifice on h6." (Chigorin)

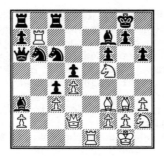

31 ♘xh6+! gxh6 32 ♖xf7! ♔xf7 33 ♕xh6 ♔g8

On 33...♗f8, Chigorin gave 34 ♗h5+ ♔g8 35 ♕xf6 and considered Black had no defence, but a much simpler method is 34 ♕h7+ ♔g7 35 ♗h5+ ♔f8 36 ♗d6+ ♘e7 37 ♗xe7 mate.

34 ♕g6+ ♔h8 35 ♕xf6+ ♔g8 36 ♕g6+ ♔h8 37 ♖e5! 1-0

"Truly a model of contemporary chess." (Tartakower, 1951)

It was the abundance of brilliancy prizes in one contest that enabled Akiba Rubinstein to set a record. In the Teplitz-Schönau tournament of 1922, he won only 6 games but collected 4 of the 7 prizes on offer. Since the conditions have now radically changed and no one, fortunately, offers so many prizes, Akiba's achievement is likely to stand unequalled for centuries.

Rubinstein – Mieses
Dutch Defence [A81]

1 d4 f5 2 g3 e6 3 ♗g2 ♘f6 4 ♘f3 d5 5 0-0 c6 6 c4 ♘bd7 7 ♕c2 ♘e4 8 ♘c3 ♗e7 9 b3 g5 10 ♘xe4 dxe4

After 10...fxe4 Black's last move would be completely unjustified.

11 ♘e5 ♘xe5 12 dxe5 g4 13 ♗e3 h5 14 ♖fd1 ♕c7 15 ♕c3 ♗d7 16 ♖d2 c5 17 ♖ad1 0-0-0 18 a3 ♗c6 19 ♖d6! b6

After 19...♗xd6 20 exd6 ♕d7 (or 20...♖xd6 21 ♕xh8+) 21 ♗xc5, Black's position would collapse even more quickly.

20 b4 cxb4 21 axb4 ♗xd6

White was already threatening 22 c5.

22 exd6 ♕d7 23 b5 ♗b7 24 ♕a3 ♔b8 25 ♖a1 ♕xd6

205

Black is mated after 25...♗c8 26 ♗xb6.

26 ♕xa7+ ♔c7 27 c5 bxc5 28 ♖c1

28 ♗xc5 was also adequate.

28...♖c8 29 b6+ ♔c6 30 ♗xc5 ♕d2 31 ♕a4+!

White has avoided the trap 31 ♗e3+ ♕xc1+ 32 ♗xc1 ♖a8, so Black resigns **(1-0)**.

At the 1923 Carlsbad tournament, Aron Nimzowitsch 'only' won 3 of the 8 prizes offered (they were divided into three first, three second and two third prizes).

Efim Geller attained another record of sorts. In the Budapest tournament of 1952 he gained the first brilliancy prize by beating Erno Gereben in a game that is widely known. On top of that, he received 'half a brilliancy prize' for the following happy miniature.

Geller – Golombek
Nimzo-Indian Defence [E41]

1 d4 ♘f6 2 c4 e6 3 ♘c3 ♗b4 4 e3 c5 5 a3 cxd4 6 axb4 dxc3 7 ♘f3 cxb2 (better 7...d5) **8 ♗xb2 d5 9 c5 b6 10 ♗b5+ ♗d7 11 ♗xd7+ ♘fxd7 12 ♕c2**

Natural, but ... it lets the advantage slip. After 12 ♕a4! bxc5 13 bxc5 ♕c8 14 0-0 Black would hardly be able to solve all the problems facing him.

12...♘c6! 13 ♗xg7 ♘xb4 14 ♕b1 ♖g8 15 c6!

What can Black do now? On 15...♘c5, White has 16 ♕xh7 ♖xg7 17 ♕xg7 ♘c2+ 18 ♔e2 ♘xa1 19 ♖xa1 and the black king is very uncomfortable. However...

15...♘xc6 16 ♕xh7

16...♘f6!!

Giving up a whole rook rather than the exchange, Black brings his queen out and gives it space to operate. Both kings will now be in the firing line.

17 ♗xf6 ♕xf6 18 ♕xg8+ ♔d7! (18...♔e7 would lose to 19 ♕g5) **19 ♘e5+**

A final winning attempt.

19...♘xe5 20 ♕xa8 ♘f3+ 21 gxf3 ♕xa1+ 22 ♔e2 ♕a2+ ½-½

The draw was agreed in view of 22...♕a2+ 23 ♔f1 ♕b1+ 24 ♔g2 ♕g6+.

"The judges took the unusual step of awarding a brilliancy prize to both players in consideration of the manner in which each side caps the other's combinations." (Golombek)

Second player wins

How many four-game matches there have ever been, no one knows. It may be that one in every five or six of them ended in a 2:2 draw. Or perhaps one in three, for with players of roughly equal class it isn't easy to tip the scales in your own favour within such a short distance.

It more rarely happens that the drawn match contains no drawn games. And there was probably only one case where all the games were won by Black! At any rate I have never personally seen any other match like it, or come across one in chess literature. It happened in 1991. The Soviet Union was still more or less in existence but provided very modest funding for sport in general and chess in particular. And then, with money from sponsors, two tournaments were held – one in Tbilisi followed by one in Moscow – in honour of the 5th Women's World Champion and the 7th Chess King, for both of whom it was a jubilee year. Neither tournament was lacking in lively play. Nona Gaprindashvili began with an energetic attack against one of the eventual winners, but ended up sharing last place; it was the first time she had ever finished at the bottom of the table. What awaited Vasily Smyslov, on the other hand, was a miniature copy of the most famous of all Candidates Tournaments – Switzerland, 1953 – in which he had gained a resounding victory and with it the right to play his first match against World Champion Mikhail Botvinnik.

It must be said, however, without disrespect to him, that the player celebrating his 70th year did not attract the most attention during those days. The Moscow chess fans were more or less used to Vasily Vasilievich, they had met him a hundred times before; in a word, he was 'one of them'. With one other contestant it was different. It was his seventh visit to the Soviet Union, but the first after a very long interval. This was a jubilee year for

him too, incidentally; Sammy Reshevsky was 80 years old, and could very well be counted among the chess record-holders. After all, at seven years of age and too small to be seen from behind the chess table, he had been giving simultaneous displays to adults.

I was therefore very keen to have a talk with the former child prodigy who was over from America.

"Grandmaster, there are some people who play good chess for a short time, and there are some who play a moderate game for a long time. *You've* been playing well for three quarters of a century! What's your secret?"

"It's all very simple indeed. I've always lived a life of moderation and kept to a routine. Even now I'm healthy and I've got a clear head. Apart from that, everything's in God's hands."

"When you gave simultaneous displays in Warsaw, Paris and London as a seven-year-old boy, did you have an inkling of where your chess career would lead?"

"No. I was just trying to beat each individual opponent in any display. I didn't even know about the World Championship title or that I was going to make a bid for it. I didn't know who *was* Champion then, either."

"What prevented you from gaining the title in the match-tournament of 1948 or a little later?"

"I know why I didn't succeed in winning then. But years have gone by, I'm here as your guest and right now I'd rather not talk about it. It's not worth raking over the past after nearly half a century."

(An interesting question is whether Reshevsky knew about Botvinnik's report to Andrei Zhdanov while he, Botvinnik, was leading that same match-tournament. Zhdanov was the secretary of the Communist Party Central Committee, in other words the number two functionary in the mighty and fearsome USSR. Botvinnik persuaded the supreme ideological authority that "in the struggle for the chess crown the capitalist Sammy will be unable to overcome three socialist heroes together....")

"And what is your chess life like at the moment?"

"My relations with the American national federation are complicated. They won't admit me to the US Championships because of my low rating. At the moment the players in America with high ratings are those who constantly play in open tournaments. I carry out my religious observances to the letter, and I can't play in 'opens' as they play on the sabbath. But I'm sure I wouldn't do too badly in the championship."

(Now a small digression. During the title match in Lyon, the US Chess Federation President, Grandmaster Max Dlugy – at that time the youngest president in the world – told me that they understood the awkwardness of this situation but couldn't do anything about it. The number of participants in the championship is fixed; if they included Reshevsky it would automatically mean excluding one of the young players, and the laws in that country, including chess regulations, are binding on everyone. But he also told me of something the lawyers had established after six months of painstaking investigations at the Federation's behest: there was nothing illegal about imposing an increase of one dollar – the price of a bus ticket! – on the entry fee paid by every competitor in every 'open', so as to set up an assistance fund for veterans....)

In the final round, the 80-year-old Reshevsky succeeded in defeating the 70-year-old Smyslov. It was the latter's only loss, after which Efim Geller, another participant from Zurich 1953 (alas, it had only been possible to reunite three of them) shared victory with the 'young veteran' Evgeny Vasiukov. Well, there you are – even Napoleon, invincible for many a year, had his Old Guard and his Young Guard. And on the day after the tournament ended, a match between Reshevsky and Smyslov began. It initiated something that was absolutely new in chess and had yet to be given its organizational form: a Veterans' World Cup.

In this match, only White moved first, as laid down by the rules – and only White lost.

Reshevsky – Smyslov
Game 1
Nimzo-Indian Defence [E38]

1 d4 ♘f6 2 c4 e6 3 ♘c3 ♗b4
4 ♕c2 c5 5 dxc5 ♘a6 6 a3 ♗xc3+
7 ♕xc3 ♘xc5 8 b4 ♘ce4 9 ♕d4 d5
10 cxd5 ♕xd5 11 ♕xd5 exd5
12 ♗b2 ♔e7 13 ♘f3 ♗d7 14 e3
♖hc8 15 ♗d3 a6 16 ♘d4 ♘d6
17 ♔e2 ♘c4 18 ♗c1 ♘e4 19 f3
♘c3+ 20 ♔f2

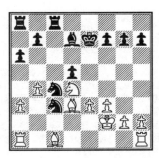

20...♘e5 21 ♗d2?? ♘xd3+ 0-1

In a position where Black was slightly more active, White evidently picked up the wrong bishop and thereby opened up Black's run of wins. The Grandmasters each had 30 minutes' thinking time for the game, but for some reason they were conducting this first encounter at blitz chess speed.

Smyslov – Reshevsky
Game 2
Ruy Lopez [C92]

1 e4 e5 2 ♘f3 ♘c6 3 ♗b5 a6
4 ♗a4 ♘f6 5 0-0 ♗e7 6 ♖e1 b5
7 ♗b3 d6 8 c3 0-0 9 h3 ♗b7 10 d4

♖e8 11 ♘bd2 ♗f8 12 a3 g6 13 ♗c2
♘b8 14 b4 ♘bd7 15 ♗b2 ♖c8
White has played the opening rather passively and Black seizes the initiative.

16 ♕b1 c5 17 bxc5 dxc5 18 dxe5
♘xe5 19 ♘xe5 ♕xd2 20 ♘f3 ♕f4
21 ♗c1 ♕b8
The weakness of his queenside and lack of prospects for his bishops make White's position difficult. His attempt to 'untangle' costs a pawn.

22 a4 ♗c6 23 axb5 axb5 24 c4
bxc4 25 ♗b2 ♗g7 26 ♕a2 ♘xe4
27 ♗xg7 ♔xg7 28 ♖ab1 ♕a8
29 ♕xc4 ♗d5! 30 ♕a4 ♘c3
31 ♕xa8 ♖xa8 32 ♖xe8 ♖xe8
33 ♖e1 ♖xe1+ 34 ♘xe1 ♔f6 35 f3
♔e5 36 ♔f2 ♔d4 37 g3 c4 38 ♘g2
♗c6 39 ♘f4 ♗a4 40 ♗xa4 ♘xa4
41 ♔e2 ♔c3 42 ♔e3 ♔b2 43 ♔d4
c3 44 ♘d3+ ♔b1 45 ♘b4 ♔b2
46 g4 ♔b3 47 ♘d3 c2 48 g5 ♘b6
49 ♘c1+ ♔b2 50 ♘d3+ ♔b1
51 ♔c5 ♘a4+

After the unavoidable 52...♘b2 White can't contrive to give up his knight for the c-pawn. He therefore resigned.
0-1

Reshevsky – Smyslov
Game 3
English Opening [A22]

1 c4 ♘f6 2 ♘c3 e5 3 ♘f3 ♘c6 4 g3 ♗b4 5 ♗g2 0-0 6 0-0 e4 7 ♘g5 ♗xc3

A favourite strategic device of the ex-World Champion: he calmly concedes the advantage of the two bishops to give his opponent doubled pawns.

8 bxc3 ♖e8 9 d3 exd3 10 exd3 d6 11 h3 h6 12 ♘f3 ♘e5 13 ♘h4 ♖b8 14 ♖e1 ♗d7 15 f4 ♘g6 16 ♖xe8+ ♕xe8 17 ♘f3 c5! 18 g4 ♗c6 19 ♕f1 ♖d8 20 ♗d2 ♕d7 21 ♖e1 ♖e8 22 d4 ♖xe1 23 ♕xe1 ♕e7 24 ♕xe7 ♘xe7

By bringing about exchanges Black extinguishes his opponent's aggressive designs, and now sets about exploiting the pawn weaknesses.

25 d5 ♗a4 26 ♘e1 b5 27 g5 ♘d7 28 gxh6 gxh6 29 f5 ♔g7 30 ♗f4 ♘xf5 31 ♗e4 ♔f6 32 ♗xf5 ♔xf5 33 ♗xd6 bxc4 34 ♗e7 ♔e4 35 ♔f2 ♔xd5 36 ♔e3 ♔e6 37 ♗d8 ♘b6 38 ♘f3 ♘d5+ 39 ♔d2 ♔f5 40 h4 ♔e4 41 ♘h2 f5 42 ♗a5 ♗d7 43 ♘f1 f4 44 ♔e2 ♗g4+ 45 ♔d2 ♔f3 46 ♔e1 ♔g2 47 ♘d2 f3 48 ♘e4 ♗f5 49 ♘f2 ♘e3

Black threatens 50...♘c2+, not only removing the blockade from f2 but taking his pawn through to queen. White resigns – for the third time in the match!

0-1

Smyslov – Reshevsky
Game 4
Sicilian Defence [B58]

1 e4 c5 2 ♘f3 ♘c6 3 d4 cxd4 4 ♘xd4 ♘f6 5 ♘c3 d6 6 ♗e2 e6 7 0-0 ♗e7 8 ♗e3 0-0 9 ♕e1 ♗d7 10 ♖d1 a6 11 ♔h1 ♕c7 12 f4 ♘xd4 13 ♗xd4 ♗c6 14 ♗d3 ♘d7 15 ♕g3 e5 16 ♗e3 ♔h8 17 ♕h3 ♘c5 18 ♗xc5 dxc5

Both sides have played the opening without any particular refinements, and White has obtained quite a tangible plus. His last move is evidently prompted by a wish to simplify; Smyslov took into account that a draw would be enough to win the match.

19 fxe5?! ♕xe5 20 ♖f5 ♕e6 21 ♘d5 g6 22 ♖ff1?

White used up nearly a quarter of his allotted thinking time on this move which hands the initiative to Black. After 22 ♘xe7 ♕xe7 (or 22...gxf5 23 exf5 ♕f6 24 ♘xc6 bxc6 25 c3 with sufficient compensation for the exchange) 23 ♖f4 there would still be everything to play for. Now Black acquires the two bishops and the better pawn structure. He realizes his advantage in a highly techincal manner with a small dose of ingenuity.

22...♕xh3 23 gxh3 ♗d6 24 c4 ♗e5 25 b3 b5 26 h4 h5 27 ♔g2 b4 28 ♗c2 ♖a7 29 ♘f4 ♔g7 30 ♔f3 a5 31 ♔g1 ♔h6 32 ♖g5 ♗d4 33 ♘e2 f6 34 ♖g2 ♗e5 35 ♘f4 g5 36 ♘e6 g4+ 37 ♔e3 ♖e8 38 ♘xc5 f5 39 ♖f2 ♖f7 40 ♘d3 ♗b8 41 e5 ♗a7+ 42 c5 ♗e4 43 ♔f4 ♗b8 44 ♖e1 ♖d8 45 ♔e3 ♗a7 46 ♖d2 ♖d5 47 ♖ed1 ♗xd3 48 ♖xd3 ♖xe5+ 49 ♔d2 ♗xc5 50 ♔c1 f4 51 ♖d5 ♖xd5 52 ♖xd5 ♗e3+ 53 ♔d1 f3 54 ♗d3 ♗f4 55 ♖xa5 ♗xh2 56 ♖a6+ ♔g7 57 ♖g6+ ♔f8 58 ♗c4 ♖d7+ 59 ♔c2 g3 60 ♖f6+

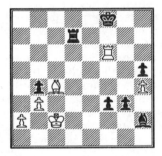

60...♔g7 0-1

In this objectively hopeless position White overstepped the time limit. The record was established – 4:0 in Black's favour!

Vertical distances

We play chess across horizontal distances on the earth's surface. What was the record distance between two correspondence chess opponents, using either traditional or modern means of communic-ation? This is quite impossible to establish.

On the other hand, the record-breaking game played across a *vertical* distance is known with complete precision. Since Yuri Gagarin's flight, mankind has started gradually making the cosmos 'habitable', and on 9 June 1970 the first and so far only consultation game was played between cosmonauts and 'earthlings'. The former were Adrian Nikolaev, the commander of *Soyuz 9* in its orbit round the earth, and the engineer Vitaly Sevastianov. Their opponents were General Nikolai Kamanin, who was head of the Soviet Cosmonaut Centre, and the cosmonaut Viktor Gorbatko. The game wasn't all that long, but took six hours to play; the radio communication only functioned while the spacecraft was above the territory of what was then the USSR.

Of course, none of the four participants in this game was a chess professional, but they all loved chess, and for Kamanin, who was renowned in his time as a polar aviator, the game was actually more than just a pastime. At a certain stage in Sevastianov's life it became a serious matter for him too; seven years later he was to be elected Chairman of the USSR Chess Federation, President of FIDE Zone 4 and a member of the Central Committee of that international organization.

Space – Earth
Queen's Gambit Accepted [D20]

1 d4 d5 2 c4 dxc4 3 e3 e5 4 ♗xc4 exd4 5 exd4 ♘c6 6 ♗e3 ♗d6 7 ♘c3 ♘f6 8 ♘f3 0-0 9 0-0 ♗g4

10 h3 ♗f5 11 ♘h4 ♕d7 12 ♕f3 ♘e7 13 g4 ♗g6 14 ♖ae1 ♔h8?! 15 ♗g5 ♘eg8 16 ♘g2 ♖ae8 17 ♗e3 ♗b4

18 a3 ♗xc3 19 bxc3 ♗e4 20 ♕g3 c6 21 f3 ♗d5 22 ♗d3 b5 23 ♕h4 g6 24 ♘f4 ♗c4 25 ♗xc4 bxc4 26 ♗d2 ♖xe1 27 ♖xe1 ♘d5 28 g5!? ♕d6 29 ♘xd5 cxd5 30 ♗f4 ♕d8 31 ♗e5+ f6 32 gxf6 ♘xf6 33 ♗xf6+ ♖xf6 34 ♖e8+ ♕xe8 35 ♕xf6+ ♔g8 ½-½

All the participants in this game were granted honorary membership of the Central Chess Club of the USSR. However, Kamanin, the initiator and organizer of the 'cosmic duel' – which, needless to say, had taken place on the space crew's official rest day – received quite a stiff reprimand from the Communist Party Central Committee, that organ which held undivided sway in the vast country. For what? There is no answer. The logic of Communist officialdom was impenetrable.

However that might be, when Vitaly Sevastianov returned from the flight, he declared that "people setting off on a distant voyage to the stars will take with them their favourite book, their favourite song – and a chess set."

No subsequent games were to take place between space and earth. Who could contradict the strict instructions of the true rulers in the land of the Soviets? Yet chess inside spacecraft has remained, thanks to a special chessboard that floats between the cosmonauts. It was invented about 10 years ago by the engineer M.Klevtsov, a graduate in biological sciences, who was accorded a patent for it. An ordinary chess set is unsuitable in space. A chance jolt or even heavy breathing can send the weightless pieces off into corners of the spacecraft from which you can't fetch them back. There is the same trouble with magnetism. A travelling set where the pieces plug into the board is better, but they are still very easy to lose. Clearly the pieces have to move across the board without detaching themselves from it. Klevtsov's solution was novel and uncomplicated, although the final design of his set had undergone several stages of modification. There is little point here in detailing the technical features with which each chess piece is equipped. The main thing is something else. A system of vertical and horizontal grooves along the lines between the squares enables the pieces to be moved as if on rails and stopped in the middle of the desired square. A captured piece leaves the battlefield and takes its place on the sidewalk.

The following game was played in space – but only in the cinema. In the famous film *2001: A Space Odyssey* by the American director Stanley Kubrick, an astronaut confronts the computer 'HAL' and is beaten by it.

212

Astronaut – Computer
Ruy Lopez [C77]

1 e4 e5 2 ♘f3 ♘c6 3 ♗b5 a6
4 ♗a4 ♘f6 5 ♕e2 b5 6 ♗b3 ♗e7
7 c3 0-0 8 0-0 d5 9 exd5 ♘xd5
10 ♘xe5 ♘f4 11 ♕e4 ♘xe5
12 ♕xa8 ♕d3 13 ♗d1 ♗h3
14 ♕xa6 ♗xg2 15 ♖e1

15...♕f3 0-1

For a long time it was supposed that Kubrick had thought up this game himself (in his youth he had made a living out of playing chess for money stakes), but eventually someone found out that it copies an encounter between Rösch and Schlage from a Hamburg tournament in 1910.

On earth, the tournament at the highest altitude was one which took place in the summer of 1982 during the first Soviet expedition to climb the world's highest mountain – Everest. Here too it was necessary to invent a special chess set, for the travelling set they took with them was no good: at the height of 7000 metres, where the base camp was pitched, the pieces were instantly swept off the board by the ferocious wind. It was then that one of the best mountaineers, Vladimir Balyberdin, fabricated a chess set of his own design. He marked out squares on a piece of plywood and drove a staple into each of them. He cut flat pieces out of plastic and fitted them with little wire hooks which attached themselves to the staples. The wind ceased to be terrible. But how were they to play without clocks? Balyberdin took two identical little bottles, poured sand into each, measured the time and adjusted the quantity; there would be four minutes per player per game. Eight people took part in the tournament, from Professor Anatoly Ovchinnikov to the cook Vladimir Voskoboynikov.

Then again, there was what you might call the other extreme. Day and night in the autumn of 1940, the British capital resisted the raids of the Nazi air force which showered it with thousands of high-explosive and incendiary bombs. Not daring to invade across the Channel, Hitler was trying to subdue England from the air. But the country held out, and the indomitable English national character showed itself in quite an impressive chess tournament. It was held under ground, in the city's largest bomb shelter. First, play took place in two preliminary groups, then the winners of these – the Women's World Champion Vera Menchik-Stevenson, and E.G.Sergeant, one of the strongest English masters of the time – met in the final. Menchik won, and thus finished first in the only underground tournament in chess history. Sadly, less than four years on, she was to perish in the rubble of a house destroyed by a German V2 rocket.

213

The march of progress

As an inspired model of life, chess has not been impervious to general laws of development during a span of more than a thousand years. What is remarkable, though, is that since time immemorial, while evolving in response to the very course of social progress, the game has resisted outright all revolutionary (and patently record-breaking) attempts to re-shape it.

Little stone figures fabricated some thousands of years ago in the land of ancient Greece are preserved in the St Petersburg Hermitage, but no one so far knows by what rules they were moved about, or what their role was. However, since the time when *shatranj* emerged – around the 7th century AD – the transformations of our game can be traced in every direction they took. The bishop and even the pawn gained in speed of movement; the queen was converted from a very weak piece into the strongest of all; castling arose; stalemate acquired a different significance. In brief, *shatranj* in Europe became chess, and sailed to America (historians surmise that it even travelled in Columbus's caravels). The 'game of a hundred cares' – as it was called at the courts of the Persian shahs and Turkish sultans – gradually conquered the world, and was to prove extremely resistant to most 'assaults' against its essence.

The reforms proceeded – or tried to proceed – in two fundamentally different directions.

One of them had to with accommodating chess to the changing rhythm of life itself; it became impossible to wait for an hour or two for your opponent's next move. It appears that the record for protracted thought was established in 1851, when shortly after the the end of the London international tournament (the first in history), some of its participants played a number of matches amongst themselves. In one of them, Elijah Williams faced Howard Staunton, who before the start of the tournament had been considered the world's best player – only to be crushed by Andersson and then, through inertia, to lose to Williams in the play-off for third place. The match that followed the tournament was unofficial although it did have a prize fund. It also set up a record by reason of its regulations: Staunton had to win 7 games for victory, Williams only 4. Yet with the score standing at +6 -2 =3, Staunton could take no more; he resigned the match when one step away from winning. This was understandable; games had lasted for 20 hours each (!), and Williams would quite often sit for nearly 3 hours over a single move!

Hence timing devices were introduced. Sand-glasses were used at first, and if you overstepped the time limit you didn't lose the game but incurred a penalty – something which Grandmaster Eduard Gufeld, that irrepressible fantasist, tried to re-introduce into modern chess. This rule was first applied in 1853, in the match between Harrwitz and Löwenthal in London. Eight years later, clause 2 of the conditions (or regulations) for the Paulsen-Kolisch match stated that if a player exceeded the time limit, a win for him would count as a draw, a draw would count as a loss, and a loss as a double loss. Clause 3.1 provided for an increase in the penalty: "If one player fully complies with the rules concerning the time limit and his opponent consumes twice the allotted time, then a win for the latter shall count as a loss, a draw as a double loss, and a loss as a triple loss."

Afterwards mechanical clocks arrived. This invention of the engineer Wilson from Manchester enjoyed undivided dominance in chess for over a century. Today it is coming to be replaced by the Fischer clock, mitigating the effects of time trouble which can otherwise be catastrophic. All these reforms are a natural development of the game.

On the other hand, some attempts were made to reverse the whole trend. Thus when Siegbert Tarrasch accepted a challenge from Karl August Walbrodt, his compatriot who had rapidly made a name for himself, he insisted on playing the match without clocks! And this was in August 1894! After winning by +7 -0 =1, Tarrasch wrote as follows in *300 Games of Chess*:

The thinking time for the moves was regulated in a novel manner. Clause 9 of the match rules stated: "The games will be played without clocks. If, however, the committee finds that the expenditure of time is excessive, it may demand that from a particular moment the game shall continue at the rate of 12 moves per hour with accumulation of unused time. Overstepping the time limit will not incur loss of the game but will give the committee the right to demand that the offending player shall make the remaining moves up until the 12th, 24th or 36th (etc.) within five minutes. Only if this time is exceeded will the game be counted as lost."

This 'novelty' – which was borrowed from Anderssen and Morphy, La Bourdonnais and MacDonnell, and the practice of the good old days in general – did not have the slightest adverse effect. The games took as much time as normal serious games do, i.e. 3-7 hours. Only one of them, the last, took 11 hours, and this was mainly due to Walbrodt who put a particular effort into this game and occasionally thought for a very long time. At any rate, neither player was under pressure from that frequent threat of losing on time which had affected both me and my opponent in an extremely harmful manner on several occasions in my match with Chigorin. I played with greater concentration than ever before or since; oblivious of all my surroundings, I devoted myself exclusively to the game. The result – I have to state this, to be true to my task as a biographer – was a degree of correctness in the play that has never been attained in any other series of games to my knowledge.

One further (and final!) attempt to do without clocks, again on Tarrasch's initiative, was undertaken at the Nuremberg tournament in 1906. It resulted in a fiasco which Rudolf Spielmann, a participant in the master tournament, described in his booklet *On Chess and Chessplayers*.

To avoid any abuse of unrestricted thinking time, an expedient from the Paris tournament of 1867 (!) was repeated. The players were required to play 15 moves per hour. After that, a five-minute period of grace was allowed, and then a fine of one German mark per minute was imposed. After the very first round, the sum of the fines ran to several hundred marks; very soon it reached thousands! Naturally, no one could pay such amounts. The organizers went back on their decision, the time restrictions were removed – and the tournament had to be prolonged! The game Schlechter-Marshall, for instance, which Spielmann considered to be without any content, ended in a draw on move 28 after the players had been sitting at the board for 8 hours!

It is worth observing incidentally that after clocks made their appearance and various time controls were introduced (for many decades the basic one was 40 moves in 2½ hours), players would still sometimes pore over a move for 60 or 80 minutes or even longer. At Bucharest in 1954, my teacher Rashid Nezhmetdinov thought for an hour and a half over a move in his game against the New Zealander Robert Wade.

Nezhmetdinov – Wade
French Defence [C11]
(notes by Nezhmetdinov)

1 e4 e6 2 d4 d5 3 ♘c3 ♘f6 4 e5 ♘fd7 5 f4 c5 6 dxc5 ♘c6 7 ♘f3 ♗xc5 8 ♗d3 f6 9 exf6 ♘xf6! 10 ♕e2 0-0 11 ♗d2 e5?! 12 fxe5 ♗g4?!

With his last two moves Black has unleashed immense tactical complications. I needed to take a long think, particularly since these moves had been played at lightning speed and I realized I might fall victim to some 'home analysis'. First of all I had to work out a large number of variations connected with accepting the piece sacrifice.

It should be observed that when calculating variations – especially in complex, intricate, double-edged positions – sang-froid and clarity of thought are essential; it is very important not to be enticed into pursuing "the will-o'-the-wisp of a mating attack", as Grandmaster Aron Nimzowitsch aptly put it in his day.

Here, for instance, a tempting line is 13 exf6 ♖e8 14 f7+ ♔xf7 15 ♘g5+ ♔g8! 16 ♗xh7+ ♔h8 17 ♘f7+ ♔xh7 18 ♘xd8, but this fails to 18...♖axd8 19 ♔d1 ♖xe2 20 ♘xe2 ♘d4 21 ♖e1 ♖e8 22 c3 ♗xe2+ 23 ♔c1 ♘c6 etc.

I thought for 90 minutes over my move here!

The first 15-20 minutes were spent thinking about acceptance of the piece sacrifice and establishing that the variations were unacceptable. I then immersed myself in the position anew. A move that immediately comes to mind is 13 0-0-0. But after 13...♘d4, how is White to carry on regrouping effectively? Another 35-40 minutes were spent on finding suitable defensive moves ('quiet' moves are always harder to find than forced sequences). Then I returned once again to the lines following 13 exf6, and re-checked them. After that, the regrouping that occurred in the game was gradually refined and given its final form.
  13 0-0-0 ♘d4 14 ♕e1 ♘h5
  On 14...♗xf3 15 gxf3 ♘xf3, White has 16 ♕g3! ♘h5 (or 16...♘xd2 17 exf6 and wins) 17 ♕g4 ♕h4 (17...♘xd2 18 ♕xh5) 18 ♕xh4 ♘xh4 19 ♘xd5 with a won position.
  15 ♗e2!
  This difficult move cost me a great deal of time.
  15...♖xf3
  From here on I had foreseen everything, and therefore played fast, while Wade was thinking for longer and longer. I was thinking during his time too, as I had little

more than 5 minutes for my last 20 moves before the time control.
  16 gxf3 ♘xf3
  If 16...♗xf3, then 17 ♗xf3 ♘xf3 18 ♕e2 ♘xd2 19 ♕xh5!.
  17 ♗xf3 ♗xf3 18 ♖f1 ♗xd1 19 ♕xd1!

This is the position I had evaluated in my own favour while analysing the variations after the 12th move. After all the exchanges, Black proves to be behind in development. The pawn on d5 is difficult to save.
  19...g6
  If 19...♕h4, then 20 ♕f3! ♖d8 (or 20...♖f8 21 ♕xd5+ ♔h8 22 ♖xf8+ ♗xf8 23 ♕f7, winning a piece) 21 ♕f7+ ♔h8 22 ♘xd5, when 22...♕xh2 fails to 23 e6.
  20 ♕f3
  Or 20 ♗h6!, which is even more accurate.
  20...♕d7 21 ♘xd5 ♖f8 22 ♘f6+ ♘xf6 23 exf6 ♗d4 24 ♕d3 ♖f7 25 c3 ♗e5 26 ♕e3 ♗xf6
  White's best reply to 26...♗xh2 is 27 ♕e4, preserving the important pawn on f6.
  27 ♕xa7 h5 28 ♖g1 ♔h7 29 ♕e3 ♗g7 30 ♕e4 ♕f5 31 ♕xf5
  Playing to simplify in time trouble.
  31...♖xf5 32 ♖g2 ♗h6 33 a4 g5 34 b4 g4 35 a5 ♖f3 36 ♔c2 ♗f8

217

37 b5 ♗c5 38 ♖e2 ♖f2 39 ♖xf2 ♗xf2 40 ♔d3 h4 41 ♔e2 1-0

Wolfgang Uhlmann once cogitated for 110 minutes over a move when playing Black against Mikhail Tal in the Alekhine Memorial Tournament, Moscow 1971. Interestingly, the German (then East German) Grandmaster also thought for an unconscionably long time in the opening.

Tal – Uhlmann
French Defence [C07]

1 e4 e6 2 d4 d5 3 ♘d2 c5 4 ♘gf3 ♘c6 5 ♗b5
"This way the game is least 'French' in character. In the 1971 USSR Championship, the following line (incidentally recommended by Alekhine in his day) was tried out in the game Tseitlin-Vaganian: 5...cxd4 6 ♘xd4 ♗d7 7 ♘xc6 ♗xc6 8 ♗xc6+ bxc6 9 c4 ♘f6? 10 ♕a4 ♕d7 11 e5, with advantage to White. An improvement (according to the annotators) is 9...d4 10 0-0 c5 11 f4, but that too gives a position that appealed to me in my preparations." (Tal)
5...dxe4
"Uhlmann is one of those players who aren't given to any cunning sophistication and as a rule play the opening quickly. The fact that he thought for over 30 minutes on move five showed that my psychological landmine had worked." (Tal)
6 ♘xe4 ♗d7 7 ♗g5!
Development above all! The open character of the position gives every tempo a special value.

7...♕a5+
White aimed to answer 7...♕b6 with 8 ♕e2 cxd4 9 0-0-0.
8 ♘c3 cxd4
Given the threat of d4-d5, this exchange is practically forced.
9 ♘xd4
"I very much wanted to sacrifice a piece here with 9 ♗xc6 ♗xc6 10 ♕xd4 ♗xf3 11 gxf3. However, in the first place, the variation 11...♕xg5 12 ♕a4+ b5! 13 ♘xb5 ♕e5+ 14 ♔f1 doesn't seem to give White anything substantial; and secondly Black can decline the sacrifice with no particular damage to himself, say by playing 11...♕b4. This last fact made me cut short any further investigations." (Tal)
9...♗b4
"During the game it seemed to me that my opponent's safest move was 9...♗e7. In reply I was planning 10 ♕d2 ♘f6 (of course not 10...♗xg5 11 ♕xg5 ♘xd4 12 ♗xd7+) 11 0-0-0, which was sure to lead to sharp play." (Tal)
10 0-0 ♗xc3 11 bxc3 ♕xc3!?
"The whole idea (which is borrowed from other variations) of exchanging the dark-squared bishop is probably ineffective; just too many files and diagonals are opened! Taking the pawn on c3 positively compels White to go for an immediate attack. The German Grandmaster must have missed something when examining White's tempting reply 12 ♘f5. After the game, 11...a6 was suggested; there could follow 12 ♗xc6 ♗xc6 13 ♘xc6 ♕xg5 14 ♕d6 ♘e7 15 ♖fd1! ♘xc6 16 ♕d7+ ♔f8 17 ♕xb7, with advantage to White." (Tal)

12 ♘f5!

12...exf5

"Obviously, opening another file like this should hand victory to White. But it's even more obvious that Black would lose if he declined the sacrifice." (Tal)

It was at this point that Black established what appears to be a world record for the length of time spent on thinking about a single move: 1 hour 50 minutes!

13 ♖e1+

This is too good to reject, but then White could also consider an immediate 13 ♕d6.

13...♗e6 14 ♕d6 a6

"There is nothing better. White's chief threat is not so much to play 15 ♖ad1 as to bring his bishop onto the opened diagonal a3-f8 (again by analogy with some other variations). Black hasn't the power to prevent this. However, against 14...♘f6 White *would* play 15 ♖ad1, as 15 ♗d2 ♘e4 isn't so clear." (Tal)

15 ♗d2

Better than 15 ♗a4 b5 16 ♗d2 ♕c4 17 ♗b3 ♖d8! 18 ♕c7 ♖d7.

15...♕xc2 16 ♗b4

"A false trail would be 16 ♖ac1 ♕xc1 17 ♖xc1 axb5 18 ♖xc6 ♖d8!." (Tal)

16...axb5 17 ♕f8+ ♔d7 18 ♖ed1+!

"Accuracy to the end, as they say. Instead 18 ♖ad1+ ♔c7 19 ♕xa8 ♘f6 20 ♗d6+ ♔b6 21 ♕xh8 ♘e4 would give Black some counterplay." (Tal)

18...♔c7 19 ♕xa8

"Now 19...♘f6 20 ♕xh8 ♘e4 would simply be met by 21 ♗e1, so the German Grandmaster stopped his clock. He had a minute and a half left." (Tal)

1-0

However, the absolute record in a modern chess game probably belongs to the Brazilian International Master Francisco Trois. In a game with Luis M.Santos at Vigo 1980 he took 2 hours 20 minutes to play 7 moves (!) and left no explanation of the reasons for this interminable cogitation.

For almost a whole century up until relatively recent times, games of chess were subject to an interruption prescribed by the rules: after 40 (or more rarely 45) moves, the game would be adjourned. One of the players would write down the so-called sealed move and seal it in an envelope. (The more academically minded players, above all Mikhail Botvinnik, even worked out a strategy for this moment in the game. They would make the sealed move themselves when it suited them and force their opponents to do so when that was preferable.) Then there would be analysis – endless, exhausting, exhilarating. It would go on through the night and morning, and sometimes for several nights more. Endgame theory was enriched by this; skills, even those of Grandmasters, were enhanced; energy was drained away; nerves were frayed.

On resumption, the time control also changed – from '40 moves in 2 hours' to '20 moves per hour'. And precisely here, a danger was concealed. How much time could you spend on the sealed move? If you were hasty, there might not even be any point in playing on. If you were slow, the ordeal of time trouble was in store for you.

In this mundane situation that had occurred hundreds of thousands of times, the record fell to **Georgi Borisenko**, International Master and later Correspondence Grandmaster. In 1956, in the USSR Championship in Leningrad, he reached the following uncomplicated position in his game with Black against Grandmaster **Yuri Averbakh**.

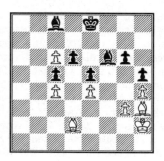

The Leningrad master, who was a noted theoretician, had to seal his move. Borisenko sank into thought. He could draw immediately with the elementary 41...♗xh3 42 ♔xh3 ♗d8 (after 42...♔d8 43 ♗a5+ ♔c8

44 c7, the black bishop has no way of getting at the white passed pawn; but even if it had, the resulting pawn endgame would still be a draw) 43 ♔g2 ♗b6 44 ♗g5, and there is nothing left to play with, or for. But the rhythmic ticking of the chess clock continued; the seconds flew by; the spectators and any players remaining on the scene began exchanging glances. Still Borisenko went on thinking. What about? It's hard to understand. Finally he wrote down his move and stopped the clock. He had thought for a full 56 minutes; there were only 4 minutes left to the next time control!

Needless to say, on resuming the game in conditions of prolonged time trouble, Black kept committing inaccuracies.

41...♗g4?! 42 ♗a5 ♗g7 43 ♗f1 ♗h6 44 ♘d3 ♗c1 45 ♔c2 ♗a3 46 ♗a4 ♗b4 47 ♗b6 ♔e7 48 ♗b5 ♗c8 (already the threat was 49 ♗a6 and c6-c7) **49 ♔g1 ♗e1 50 ♔g2 ♔e8 51 ♗c7 ♔e7 52 ♔h2 ♗f2 53 ♗a5 ♗e3 54 ♔g2 ♗c1 55 c7 ♗e3 56 ♔f3 ♗c1 57 ♔e2 ♗b2 58 ♗d2 ♗d4 59 ♗e1 ♗g4+ 60 ♔d3 ♗c8 61 ♔c2 d5**

Otherwise the white king will reach b8 by a forced march, but Black could already have resigned here.

62 cxd5 ♔d6 63 ♗a5 ♗f2 64 ♗e8 ♗xg3 65 ♗xg6 ♗xh4 66 ♗f7! ♗f2 67 ♗e6 ♗a6 68 c8=♕ ♗xc8 69 ♗xc8 h4 70 ♔d3 ♗g3 71 ♔c4 ♗f2 72 ♗h3 ♗g3 73 ♗d8 ♗f2 74 ♗g5, and Black resigned; not only is he a piece down, he is in *zugzwang* too.

1-0

Although it was played in the first half of the tournament, who knows? Perhaps this very game enabled Yuri Averbakh to share 1st-3rd places with Spassky and Taimanov, while causing Georgi Borisenko to finish third ... from the bottom.

Then of course, an utterly unique record of systematic lengthy thought was set up by Friedrich Sämisch, who has been mentioned more than once already in these pages. In the spring of 1969, quite a strong contingent of players, mainly Grandmasters, were invited to a tournament in the little seaside health resort of Büsum. Two Bulgarian Grandmasters were late for the drawing of lots; following the usual practice, they were assigned to the top and bottom lines on the tournament chart. Grandmaster Milko Bobotsov arrived literally at the last minute, but the national champion Nikola Padevsky failed to turn up at all and was replaced by the 73-year-old German Grandmaster – as Lev Polugaevsky later recalled:

> This 'grand old man' had graced the tournaments of the twenties, and he played some quite good chess at Büsum; in a number of games he was on the point of winning, but he finished all 15 of them in the same way: by exceeding the time limit! Sämisch did this wholly unperturbed, usually round about move 25 when there was plenty of time to use up on his move. But the interesting thing is that after the tournament he played in a lightning competition and took first place in the semi-final!

But then Sämisch had already 'distinguished himself' at a much earlier age. In one game in the Prague tournament of 1938, with a time limit of 2½ hours for 45 moves, he didn't even make it to move thirteen!

But let us return to the topic of reforming chess.

The second path of reform (leading to a dead end?) involved attempts to modify the game itself – for example by introducing new pieces. The first such proposals date from quite a long way back. Thus, as early as 1820-25, in the *Caffè Pastini* in Rome, the *Commendatore* di Macerata founded a chess club with the grandiose title 'Chess Academy', and it was there that he tried to insert 'bishop-knights' and 'bishop-rooks' into the play; that is, pieces that combined the moves of their 'forerunners'. By an irony of fate, when the *Commendatore* wheedled an artist friend into playing a 'reformed chess' match with him, he was resoundingly crushed.

The story continues. In the 1950s a certain Andreev-Kisel from Leningrad 'invented' the 'bear', which combined the moves of queen and knight. The name of the new piece was based on the Russian saying, "There's no animal stronger than a bear." Unfortunately there's nothing new under the sun. Back in 1890, exactly the same suggestion had been made by one Thomas Long and published in the *British Chess Magazine*. Dr Tarrasch promptly ridiculed it in the Berlin magazine *Deutsche Schachzeitung*, by proposing to give the queen the power of a *double* knight's move. Then White could score a win as follows: 1 d4 d5 2 ♕d1-c3-b5 mate! (♕xc7xe8.)

In our own day the recommendation has been made to increase the set of chessmen with a 'bomb' (referring to an atomic one); once in the course of the game it would obliterate everything within an area of 5x5 squares. Or we have been advised to insert 'princes', 'falcons' and 'dolphins' on the board while enlarging it to 100 squares. Out of artistic indloence, the genius Capablanca – who had not even had a chess set in his home – demanded in the late 1920s that the positions of bishops and knights should be swapped round in the starting position. This would nullify all the theoretical work on the openings, which, for all its modest dimensions at that time, was not the forte of the third World Champion. Across the span of the decades, he was echoed by another Chess King – Fischer. Gone were the days when the young Robert James's opening preparation dumbfounded his opponents and plunged them into gloom. A quarter of a century of absence from chess had duly left its mark. Catching up with the 'theoretical train' which had pulled off into the distance became unrealistic, so the ex-World Champion sought a different way out: by starting the game with the pieces arranged at random. *One Step Forward, Two Steps Back* is the title of a book by that chess lover V.I.Ulyanov or Lenin, and it is wholly pertinent as a judgement on Fischer's idea. Whereas 'Fischer clocks' immediately caught on,

'Fischerandom chess' has yet to establish itself in tournament practice, and is hardly ever likely to – even though semi-official Fischerandom world championships have already commenced....

The minds and hearts of all conceivable reformers have been particularly affected by social turmoil and cataclysms. It was not without astonishment that in *The Revolutionary Neurosis* (St Petersburg, 1906), a book by Dr Cabanes and L.Nass, I came across the chapter 'Chess and the Great French Revolution', which among many other things contains the following:

"Regarding chess, a very serious question has arisen as to whether it should be prohibited outright as an unfitting game for citizens.

"Can the French be permitted to play chess in future?"

This question was very seriously debated during several sessions of the assembly of 'good republicans'. A contemporary writes that " As was to be expected, it received a wholly negative answer." Afterwards, however, a further question emerged:

"Can this, the only game which truly cultivates the brain, not be democratized?

"By excluding from it the nomenclature and forms to which we have all sworn eternal hatred, is it not possible to preserve only the ingenious and exemplary combinations which are peculiar to chess alone, and which make it so attractive and irreplaceable?"

These are certainly not the words of just anyone; they were spoken by the famous chemist Guyton de Morveau, the very man whose service as an assistant prosecutor in the law courts at Dijon was combined in somewhat curious manner with his duties as a professor of chemistry and pharmacology.

"The whole world knows," the learned man continued, "that the game of chess is in essence an imitation of war. In this there is of course nothing inimical to republican ideas, since it is obvious that any free nation must always be ready to defend its liberty by force of arms. Even if the nation has no wish to take up arms for anything other than legitimate self-protection, it will not be so imprudent as to cease maintaining its armies and asssembling them periodically for exercises. Whatever the duration and scope of such exercises, their aim will not be achieved unless they take a military encampment as their model. From the start the camp has to be split into two detachments, each composed of forces with every class of weaponry; and these detachments must be placed under different banners, alternately figuring as attackers and defenders."

In Guyton's system chess should be, so to speak, a game of 'miniature war'. It was essential to consign the word *chess* to oblivion, since its derivation (from the Persian *shah*) had too uncongenial a ring. The chief actor in the game should be the banner, with moves identical to those of the former king. The piece which was "so absurdly called the queen" would be transformed into an adjutant, while the general would not be on the board but in the head of the player.

"The rooks or castles will become cannons, thus removing the former incongruity between their name and their mobility. The knights will be demoted to the status of cavalrymen; the officers will become dragoons. When the foot-soldier or pawn storms the enemy camp – that is, crosses the whole board – he will no longer change sex and become a lady, but will merely be raised to a higher rank."

Having thus performed a second regicide, albeit a peaceful one this time, Guyton is glad to have purged the game of those emblems and expressions that clashed with republican principles.

In conclusion he expresses the wish that the day may come "when the enslaved peoples will finally perceive that they, like pawns in chess, resemble strings on which the despots play their tunes, sparing or squandering them according to their whim."

In voicing his wishes the chemist Guyton was in some sense a prophet, probably without realizing it himself.

This passage is echoed in astonishing fashion by an appeal inspired by a different revolution:

Chess is an extremely interesting game of profound content, which is widely disseminated throughout the world. The distinguishing feature of this game is that it depends wholly – one hundred per cent – on the players alone, without any of the chance factors and causes that have a place in other games.

Chess arose in the period of monarchic rule, and this is reflected in its terminology. *Check* denotes the king, *mate* denotes death, and the whole purpose of the game is victory over the king in person.

I have no objection to preserving and developing the interesting game of chess, but in full accordance with the evolving socialist principle I have a proposal for a new method of playing it.... The essence of this new game can be briefly stated as follows. All the rules will be retained, but the result will be determined not by defeating the king but by liquidating all the adversary's pieces, as in draughts. In this new game the king will be renamed chairman and the queen will be his spouse.

It will be fitting to discuss and take decisions on this new variant of the game in connection with the preparations for the 50th anniversary of the Great October Revolution and in general with the triumph and development of socialism.

S.A.Belaiantsa, Tashkent
July 1967

In the interval between these cries from the heart, a certain A.Yurgelevich, keeping pace with the times, proposed at the end of the 1930s that chess *(shakhmaty)* should be renamed *shakhboy* to represent the 'battle' against the enemies of the socialist revolution; then in the 1950s he proposed *diashakhmaty*, dialectical chess. The rules of the latter are not worth reproducing here in view of their sheer absurdity. During the Lugano Olympiad, a chess set made at the beginning of the 1930s in Leningrad was displayed in the well-known collection of Halvour and Astrid Eger. The reds were agents of the world Communist movement, while the whites were Chamberlain, Krupp, Ford....

And finally, one truly amazing chess set saw the light of day and was comfortably accommodated in a suburb very close to Brussels, in the small living-room of Nikolai Golembiovsky, a subject of the Belgian crown whose origins were Cossack. The son of emigrants from the time of the First World War, he had never seen the expanses of their native land by the Don, and spoke Russian with great difficulty (his parents died before the Second World War, and his wife, naturally, was a local Belgian); yet in his heart he cherished pictures, rich in legends, of a past life in Russia. In a shed outside, there were saddles for horses (for about 30 years Monsieur Golembiovsky led a group of lovers of Cossack equestrian arts); and on a small, low table for newspapers, there was the chess set. In place of the black pieces there were red ones, and in place of the red knights there were two dogs, crouching and ready to spring; these were the 'curs of the GPU'. (Our grandfathers knew perfectly well that the GPU – the so-called State Political Administration, set up by the Bolsheviks – was the equivalent of the tsarist *Okhranka* or the later Gestapo, and the direct parent of the NKVD and KGB which live on in our memories.) The places of the kings were taken by the father-figure of the tsar on the white side, and by a sort of cross between Lenin and Trotsky on the red side. The bishops were respectively officers with shoulder-straps, and commissars with Mauser guns. In the early 1920s something similar was shaped in porcelain by Nina Danko, an artist from the former imperial porcelain factory near St Petersburg; the famous Venetian glassware artist Gianni Toso populated the chessboard with pieces in the style of the *Commedia dell'arte*; the American Doug Anderson manufactured a 'Clinton versus Dole' set; chess pieces out of *Star Wars* have appeared – etcetera, etcetera, etcetera. But you will agree that 'curs of the GPU' is extreme. And it can very well claim to be the record in terms of politicizing chess.

One against one

In the strict sense this is what chess is all about: confronting each other face to face, sometimes even without onlookers, to decide who is stronger and who can prevail in honourable single combat. Other aspects of the game – simultaneous displays, consultation matches, even team events – are not so much

corruptions as simply offshoots of the principal form of duel which sometimes acquires epic proportions and of course engenders its record-breakers.

As early as one and a half centuries ago, when international chess ties were essentially just starting to develop, there were witnesses to a grandiose personal encounter between two players. This was the contest between the Frenchman Lionel Adalbert Bagration Kieseritzky (true, they still called him a 'Russian', because he had been born inside the frontiers of the Russian Empire and only moved to Paris at the age when Jesus Christ went to Jerusalem) and the Englishman John William Schulten. They spent much of the year 1850 facing each other. The precise number of hours taken up by these 'sessions' is unknown; the thinking time was unrestricted. We may presume, however, that the players weren't seated at the board for excruciatingly long periods; a good many games were of a fleeting nature.

Kieseritzky – Schulten
Bishop's Opening [C23]

1 e4 e5 2 ♗c4 f5
Variations like 3 ♗xg8 ♖xg8 4 ♕h5+ g6 5 ♕xh7 ♖g7 don't frighten Black: 6 ♕h8 ♕g5, or 6 ♕h6 fxe4.
3 ♘f3 ♘c6 4 d3 ♘f6 5 ♘c3 fxe4 6 dxe4 ♗c5 7 0-0 d6 8 ♘g5 ♖f8 9 ♘xh7 ♖h8
White has won a pawn (9...♘xh7?? 10 ♕h5+) but used up a large amount of time to do so, while opening the h-file for his

opponent's counter-attack.

10 ♘g5 ♗g4 11 ♗f7+ ♔f8 12 ♘e6+ ♗xe6 13 ♗xe6 ♘d4 14 ♗h3 ♘h5 15 ♘e2?!

In that period of chess history, players were weak in defence. Today, any ordinary master would play 15 ♗e3.

15...♘f3+ 16 gxf3 ♕h4 17 ♗g4??

This loses, whereas the cool 17 ♗g2 would leave the issue open. On 17...♘f4 18 ♗xf4 exf4, White defends with 19 h3; while on 17...♔e7 he has 18 ♗e3, and if 18...♘g3 then 19 ♗g5+ ♕xg5 20 hxg3 ♕h6 21 ♖e1.

17...♘f6

White resigned, not before time either (**0-1**).

The contest ended with the overall score of 112:39 (+107 -34 =10) in Kieseritzky's favour. However, what we still don't know is whether they played all 151 games at one stretch or whether there was a whole series of shorter matches of 10, 20 or 30 games each. If the first supposition holds, then the record for a personal confrontation is established – once and for all, it would seem. (I must repeat the proviso that we are not counting off-hand games between friends and regular opponents in their thousands, who play each other in the evenings in all corners of the globe.) On the other hand if the second supposition is correct, we have reason to recall some other confrontations on a much higher level of both quality and sporting significance – in struggles for the chess crown, for example.

Thus, in the brief period from March 1954 to May 1958, Mikhail

Botvinnik and Vasily Smyslov played three World Championship matches comprising 69 games. On top of this, the famous Grandmasters faced each other about 50 times in individual and team tournaments. And yet today we can view this perfromance as a mere smile on the face of Caissa – because in the course the next great rivalry, that of Anatoly Karpov and Garry Kasparov, the world witnessed no less than 5 matches for the crown (between the autumn of 1984 and the end of 1990) comprising 144 games, as well as numerous encounters in tournaments of the highest calibre. There were 174 games in all, of which one was in a simultaneous display, 2 were blitz games and 4 were rapid chess. And as long as these two victors from many past title matches continue their careers, the figure has every reason to increase further. No one in the foreseeable future is likely to conduct a longer-running rivalry.

However that may be, the fact remains that Kieseritzky and Schulten packed everything into one year.

And then in some ways, two English bus drivers from Bristol went even further. They resolved to outdo the previous record-holders for uninterrupted play, a pair of Americans who had held out for 186 hours at the chessboard. Roger Long and Graham Croft settled down in a Bristol restaurant – this was in 1983 – and 'set to work' in the presence of a doctor and some spectators who were allowed into the room now and again.

On the fourth day, with the score standing at 45:37 in his favour, Long slipped down off his chair and fell asleep. He was woken up with a bucket of cold water, and the 'great chess session' continued. It ended after 200 hours (!) of non-stop play, when Croft was leading by 96:93.

Unbroken runs

At bottom, this is every chessplayer's dream: never to stop the clock and turn the king over as a sign of capitulation; never to speak those words which have an equally unpleasant ring in any language. Yet there is not a single maestro, even among the most brilliant, who has gone through his career without these 'minor tragedies'. Once Anatoly Karpov even compared losing a game to being knocked out by a punch to the head in the boxing ring. The difference is just that after the knockout the boxer can't fight again for at least three months, whereas a chessplayer more often than not has to return to the fray on the very next day.

In purely human terms, missing a win and making do with a draw is not so mortifying as losing from a drawn position – even though from the arithmetical standpoint you are simply dropping half a point in either case.

Which chessplayer went without defeat for the longest period? The well-known chess historian Ludwig Bachmann was the first to publish some interesting statistics. The list of record-holders began with Wilhelm Steinitz. From 4 August 1873 until 11 May 1882 – before he was even officially installed on the chess throne – he not only lasted without resigning a single game, he didn't draw a single one either! Nothing but wins, 25 in number!

This truly amazing sequence opened after 4 rounds of the Vienna tournament in 1873. In the chapter 'Sergeant-major's orders' we mentioned that the participants in that event played three-game matches against each other, with the match winner scoring one point. Steinitz didn't make a brilliant start. He won his first match with a 'clean' score, then had trouble against two undistinguished players who are totally forgotten today, beating each of them by 2:1. To Joseph Blackburne he lost 2½-½. Thereupon Steinitz accelerated to truly astronomic speed, winning every game against his seven remaining opponents including Henry Bird, Louis Paulsen and Adolf Anderssen! After that, in the play-off for first prize, Steinitz took convincing revenge on Blackburne, finishing the match after two games only. That made 16 wins in a row!

From then until the end of February 1876 – a full three years! – the future Chess King never sat down at the board, not counting guest appearances with friendly games and exhibitions of course. Finally he went into battle against that same Blackburne, who was then the most distinguished representative of the 'old', combinative school of play. By the rules of the match, victory went to the first player to score seven wins – and Steinitz incredibly pulled this off within the space of seven games, which you might have thought was a purely theoretical possibility!

It all began with this one:

Steinitz – Blackburne
London 1876
Ruy Lopez [C77]
(notes by Neishtadt)

1 e4 e5 2 ♘f3 ♘c6 3 ♗b5 a6 4 ♗a4 ♘f6 5 d3

The favourite continuation of Anderssen and Steinitz. White fortifies his centre so as to proceed with active kingide operations later.

5...d6 6 c3 ♗e7

Given that White has already played d2-d3 and would be losing a tempo if he advanced in the centre with d3-d4, it's worth considering the plan of fianchettoing the black king's bishop with 6...g6, ♗f8-g7 and 0-0, preparing a subsequent d6-d5.

7 h3

This is not, of course, played in order to prevent a pin against the knight on f3. White aims to continue with g2-g4, which in the first place will promote a kingside attack and secondly hinders Black's potential counter-stroke f7-f5.

7...0-0 8 ♕e2

The start of a plan which Steinitz implemented in various openings. White impedes d6-d5 for the time being, and, most importantly, bolsters his centre. If Black does carry out d6-d5, White is not going to exchange on that square.

8...♘e8

Is Blackburne's play correct? Now that Steinitz's plan has been employed in thousands of games, it's much easier to give advice. A modern master would probably play 8...b5 here, and answer 9 ♗c2 with

9...d5, seeing that 10 exd5 ♘xd5 11 ♘xe5 is strongly answered by 11...♘xe5 12 ♕xe5 ♗f6. If instead 9 ♗b3, then 9...♗e6.

9 g4

A committal decision.

9...b5 10 ♗c2 ♗b7

This bishop might be needed on the c8-h3 diagonal. Still, Blackburne's plan isn't as naive as it seems at first sight; he aims for ♕d8-d7 and ♘c6-d8-e6.

11 ♘bd2 ♕d7 12 ♘f1 ♘d8

If 12...g6, then 13 ♗h6 ♘g7 14 h4 is very strong.

13 ♘e3 ♘e6 14 ♘f5

14...g6

Before making this move it was worth withdrawing the bishop to d8 to preserve it from exchange – though this would lead to a passive position after (e.g.) 14...♗d8 15 ♗e3 g6 16 ♘h6+ and 17 0-0-0. The absence of the bishop weakens the dark squares. Blackburne's move demonstrates that at that time even famous masters only dimly appreciated the significance of positional factors which now (thanks to Steinitz!) are universally acknowledged.

15 ♘xe7+ ♕xe7

The white queen's knight reached f5 by an exhausting march – only to be exchanged off at once. But Black has paid a high price for this. The next stage will be the exploitation of the weak dark squares, but first Steinitz completes his development, and in so doing he commits an inaccuracy.

16 ♗e3

This move incurred no criticism, and yet 16 ♗h6 was much more promising. Then on 16...♘8g7 White has 17 ♖g1 – preventing the counter-blow 17...f5, which would be met by 18 gxf5 gxf5 19 ♗b3!.

16...♘8g7 17 0-0-0 c5

It was essential to take the opportunity to play 17...f5. Then after 18 gxf5 gxf5 19 ♗h6, Blackburne would obtain counterplay. If instead White refrained from opening the g-file, his attack would be much more difficult to play.

18 d4

The opening of lines enables the bishop on c2 to come into play. In addition this move is directed against the f7-f5 break.

18...exd4

At this point 18...f5 would be extremely risky. A more logical move was 18...cxd4, though White would have the better of it even then.

19 cxd4 c4?

A mistake characteristic of those times. Blackburne has visions of a queenside attack, but his assessment of the position is wrong. Today it would not take a very strong player to realize that Black shouldn't relieve his opponent of worries about the centre and leave him a free hand for an attack on the kingside (where White is clearly stronger!). But then Black's position was difficult already. The

answer to 19...d5 could be 20 e5!. Then if 20...c4 White has 21 h4, while 20...cxd4 21 ♘xd4 is also in his favour.

20 d5! ♘c7 21 ♕d2

The bishop is preparing to go to d4, and the queen to h6!

21...a5 22 ♗d4 f6 23 ♕h6 b4

Black's pawn storm is unsupported by his pieces and therefore promises nothing.

24 g5

The diagonal of the bishop on d4 needs to be opened.

24...f5

On 24...♘ge8, White would continue the attack with 25 h4, for example: 25...♕g7 26 ♕xg7+ ♘xg7 (or 26...♔xg7 27 h5 etc.) 27 gxf6 ♘h5 28 ♘g5 ♘xf6 29 h5!. Now if 29...♘xh5, then 30 ♖xh5 followed by ♖d1-g1, winning; or if 29...♔g7, then 30 hxg6 hxg6 31 ♖h7+ is decisive.

25 ♗f6 ♕f7 26 exf5

Steinitz opens up the g-file for the decisive assault.

26...gxf5

On 26...♘xf5, White wins with 27 ♗xf5 gxf5 28 g6!.

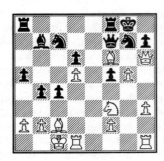

27 g6! ♕xg6

Forced, as 27...hxg6 loses at once to 28 ♘g5.

28 ♗xg7 ♕xh6+

Alas, 28...♕xg7 fails to 29 ♖hg1, which means that Black is left a piece down. Blackburne could very well have resigned here.

29 ♗xh6 ♖f6 30 ♖hg1+ ♖g6 31 ♗xf5 ♔f7 32 ♗xg6+ hxg6 33 ♘g5+ ♔g8 34 ♖ge1 1-0

Then came another interval – of 6½ years! Steinitz sent reports to the English magazine *Field* – where he conducted the chess column – from major tournaments in Paris, Wiesbaden and Berlin. He himself started playing again in the 1882 tournament that marked the jubilee of the Vienna Chess Association. The pleasant days of May brought him two initial victories, including one against the unfortunate Blackburne. But everything in this world comes to an end, and this victorious (hence undefeated) sequence ended too....

Of course, some other analogous cases may be recalled. Before Steinitz, the great Paul Morphy routed his opponents with a virtually 100% score at the first American Chess Congress in the autumn of 1857, but there was a huge gulf between his talent and theirs. Later in 1893, during his tour of America, Emanuel Lasker made an overall score of +10 -0 =1 from three of his four matches against local masters, but again the disparity in strength was obvious. It was in New York that Lasker accepted his opponents' resignation 13 times in a thirteen-round tournament, thereby setting up a record for the distance between the first and second prize winners – 4½ points. This was not surpassed until

38 years later (!), when Alexander Alekhine, at the height of his power and glory, finished 5½ points ahead of Bogoljubow at Bled in 1931; though that tournament was exactly twice as long as in Lasker's case. (Incidentally in the 1999 Linares super-tournament, which only lasted 14 rounds, Garry Kasparov won by a margin of 2½ points, but in the same place five years earlier Anatoly Karpov had done even better: the margin was the same, but the tournament only had 13 rounds. In a way this too is a record.) Add to this the fact that in his previous tournament, at San Remo at the beginning of 1930, the World Champion had conceded only two draws in 15 games; and that in the subsequent 'Tournament of Nations' in Hamburg he won all 9 of his encounters (though an interesting point is that he didn't play against the big names – Rubinstein, Maroczy or Flohr – or against the rising star Sultan Khan, but only against run-of-the-mill masters). If you consider too that in the Prague Olympiad, after Bled, Alekhine lost only one of his 18 games, and that this one was half way through the event; then the fourth World Champion turns out to have played a solid undefeated series of 55 games, 42 of which ended victoriously!

At various times, results close to 100% in major tournaments were registered by Mikhail Chigorin (16½ out of 17), Paul Keres (13½ out of 14) and Viktor Korchnoi (14½ out of 15; in the course of 5 contests in 1965 he won 27 out of 37 games without loss). At Buenos

Aires in 1970, Bobby Fischer 'only' scored 15 out of 17, but the second prize winner was 3½ points behind; the margin was the same at the Interzonal in the same year, though in that event the future 11th World Champion did lose one game. Soon afterwards he shook the chess world by winning 13 games in a row in his Candidates matches with Mark Taimanov, Bent Larsen and Tigran Petrosian; considering the 'not exactly weak' opposition, this had an aura of the fantastic about it.

Among the women, 100% results have not been all that rare. Vera Menchik towered above her rivals in World Championships, as did Nona Gaprindashvili and Nana Ioseliani at Olympiads.

But to return to the topic of sequences without defeat: in between his loss against the Soviet master Gunnar Uusi in a tournament in the little Estonian town of Viljandi in 1972 and his capitulation to Grandmaster Yuri Balashov in the Moscow match-tournament of three USSR teams in 1973, ex-World Champion Mikhail Tal was undefeated in 86 games from five major events. He finished first in the international tournament at Sukhumi. In the Skopje Olympiad he made the best result on his board, with a total of 14 out of 16. In the USSR Championship with Zonal status he came first, and if you disregard three quick draws at the finish, the half-distance mark was passed at the 'speed' of 10½ out of 12. He won the traditional international tournaments at Wijk aan Zee and Tallinn (in the latter case, ahead of Boris Spassky,

Paul Keres, David Bronstein, Lev Polugaevsky and Ulf Andersson...). The following illustrates the style of his victories.

Spassky – Tal
Tallinn 1973
(notes by Tal)

14...d4!
This combination leads by force to advantage for Black.
15 exd4 ♖xf3 16 ♗xf3 cxd4 17 0-0
Some interesting variations arise from 17 ♖c1. I was intending to continue with 17...♗xa6 (17...dxc3 18 bxc3 promises Black nothing) 18 ♗xc6 ♖d8, and Black should win. For instance after 19 ♕c2 dxc3 20 bxc3 ♕e5+ 21 ♗e4, Black has 21...♗d3 winning easily, although over the board I worked out a different variation that took my fancy: 21...♗xc3+ 22 ♕xc3 ♕xe4+ 23 ♕e3 ♕xg2 24 ♕xe6+ (the only move) 24...♔h8 25 ♕c6 ♕xc6 26 ♖xc6 ♗b7!, picking up a rook. The amusing thing is that if White tries to get a higher price for it with 27 ♖xh6+ gxh6, he is mated: 28 0-0 ♖g8 mate, or 28 ♖g1 ♗f3 followed by ♖d8-d1 mate.
17...dxc3 18 bxc3 ♗xc3 19 ♕d6 ♖xa6

Of course 19...♗xa1 would not do, on account of 20 ♕xc6.

20 ♗xc6

Against a move of the rook on a1, Black was intending 20...♘d4.

20...♗b4!

The culminating move of the combination. White loses his bishop on c6. Instead 20...♗e5 would be inadequate in view of 21 ♕e7.

21 ♕b8 ♖xc6 22 ♖ac1 ♗c5 23 ♖c2

Spassky endeavours to create pressure on this file, but it turns out that the Achilles' heel of his position is f2. Perhaps he should have looked for counter-chances by removing his rook from the c-file, say to d1.

23...♕a4 24 ♕b3

Not 24 ♖fc1, on account of 24...♗xf2+.

24...♕f4

Here I examined two moves – this one and 24...♕e4. I rejected the latter because after 25 ♖fc1 ♗b7 26 ♕xb7 ♗xf2+ 27 ♔f1! (but not 27 ♔h1? ♖xc2) 27...♕d3+ 28 ♔xf2 ♖xc2+ 29 ♖xc2 ♕xc2+, the queen ending with an extra pawn represents an extremely meagre gain for Black. Having decided on 24...♕f4, I planned to answer 25 ♕b5 with 25...♕d6; then on

26 ♖fc1 Black has 26...♗a6, when White can't play 27 ♕a5 in view of 27...♗xf2+.

25 ♕g3

Better 25 ♕f3, and if 25...♕xf3, then after 26 gxf3 e5 27 ♔h1! ♗b7 28 ♖b1 ♖b6 29 ♖xb6 ♗xf3+ 30 ♔g1 ♗xb6 31 a4 the ending remains unclear. Black would not have exchanged queens, however; he could preserve his advantage with 25...♕d6 or 25...♕c7.

25...♕f5 26 ♖fc1 ♗b7 27 ♕f3

White can't play 27 ♕b8+ ♔h7! (but not 27...♖c8 28 ♕xc8+ ♗xc8 29 ♖xc5, and it's White who wins) 28 ♕xb7, because again Black has 28...♗xf2+. However, 27 h3 was more tenacious.

27...♕g5 28 ♕b3

If 28 ♕g3, then once again 28...♗xf2+ is decisive: 29 ♕xf2 ♕c1+, or 29 ♔xf2 ♖xc2+ 30 ♖xc2 ♕f5+.

28...♖c7 29 g3

On 29 ♕xe6+, Black wins with 29...♖f7; while 29 ♕g3 is met by 29...♗xf2+ as before. The only move that doesn't lose at once is 29 ♕h3.

29...♗xf2+ 30 ♔xf2 ♕f6+

I played this move on the basis of what I had worked out earlier. There was a quicker method in 30...♕f5+ 31 ♔g1 ♕e4.

31 ♔e1 ♕e5+ 32 ♔f1

Neither 32 ♔d1 ♕d4+ 33 ♔e1 ♕g1+ nor 32 ♔f2 ♖f7+ 33 ♔g1 ♕d4+ is any good for White.

32...♗a6+ 33 ♔g1 ♕d4+ 34 ♔g2 ♕e4+ 35 ♔g1

If 35 ♔h3, then 35...♖xc2 followed by 36...♗f1+.

35...♗b7 36 h4 ♕h1+ 37 ♔f2 ♖f7+ 38 ♔e2 ♕e4+

White now resigned; after 38...♕e4+ 39 ♔e3 ♗a6+ 40 ♔d2 ♖d7+ he loses his queen. **0-1**

When his record-breaking sequence was halted, Tal's reaction was itself something for the record books: "Fine! Now I can start all over again!"

However, the chess community had to wait a quarter of a century before the young Vladimir Kramnik was launched on a bid to surpass this achievement at the start of 1999. He settled down to the task in earnest, and in a year and a half – playing in top-class tournaments and the FIDE World Championship, and even conducting an exhibition against the Swiss national team – he went through 89 games without defeat, though admittedly he won only 20 of them. I am not counting the odd twenty so-called semi-rapid, rapid and even faster games, or 'blindfold' ones; within this conglomeration of modern 'deviations' from the classical time control, Kramnik suffered two defeats. We can only regret that a loss in a 'normal' game at Dortmund 2000 prevented him from extending his record sequence right up to the World Championship match in London, where he didn't allow the 13th Champion Garry Kasparov to score a single win. (Such a result had not been seen since the days when Lasker was undefeated in his title matches with Frank Marshall in 1907 and David Janowski in 1910 – but failed to win a game against Capablanca in 1921.)

Today the target for an undefeated run should probably be reckoned as 100 games. Present-day Grandmasters play so much in a year. But who will shape up for the attempt, and when?

We may have to wait another quarter of a century before this is answered. Or then again ... should not the supreme prize have been awarded once and for all to a certain inhabitant of Morshansk, a little town in the sticks that God and time forgot about? He it was who sent an indignant letter to Moscow, where the return match between Lasker and Steinitz was taking place, way back in 1896. How could these gentlemen presume to play each other for the World Championship when he, N.Shumov, *had not lost a single game in ten years?* At the end of the letter, to be sure, the unbeaten chessplayer switched from anger to affability and consented to play the winner of the Moscow match; let them just send him the conditions, financial and otherwise, for the coming encounter.

He didn't wait long enough for a reply....

Part Four: Around the Chequered Board

All onto one

If the first great distinguishing feature of chess is the notation which enables everything achieved on the chessboard to be preserved down the centuries, the second is the possibility of simultaneous play between one (the strongest, of course) and many (the less skilled players, needless to say). This is something practically excluded from any other form of sport. I know from my own experience that thousands of recruits come to serious chess by way of these simultaneous exhibitions. I also know how pleasant it is for a small boy to shake hands as the simultaneous player congratulates him, and then afterwards to show the scoresheet proudly to his classmates, pointing to the signature of Smyslov himself below the result '½-½' – or that of Grandmaster Lilienthal, below the even more coveted result of '0:1'.

But then, it appears that this form of confrontation is not without interest for the strong chessplayers of this world either. "For a chess master, simultaneous displays have a very definite value. In terms of opening theory and technique, they constitute useful preparation for individual contests.... Even among weak players there are bound to be some who find the right thing at the right moment – a correct plan, a cunning defence, an unusual manoeuvre – and thereby lead the master to new ideas.... By their mistakes, they give him opportunities for practice in incisive exploitation." Alekhine once said this, and there is no reason to argue with him. At any rate, in the books I have written with Mikhail Tal, we reproduce a good many gems from the latter's extremely rich experience of giving 'simuls'.

I may add that the line-up of opponents is sometimes a little unusual. Garry Kasparov, for instance, once played against 32 members of the clergy; thank God the church has long since ceased to regard chess as something sinful. Mikhail Botvinnik, David Bronstein and other stars have more than once given displays in the parliaments of many countries. When Bronstein offered the choice of colours to his opponents at the British House of Commons, all twenty MP's with one accord turned the boards round to give themselves White. This was in the Cold War years, and the following day the English press commented on

"Parliament's rare unanimity in response to the Soviet proposal." Bobby Fischer and Anatoly Karpov (and I myself too, if you excuse the immodesty) have given displays in prisons, or more exactly in penal colonies. To play against the Russian ex-World Champion, some chess enthusiasts were even brought to Tver from other places of detention – an unprecedented case.

Conventional displays

All-time records in this department have been set up with uncommon ease. If the number of boards with chess amateurs seated at them increases by one, you can send your report to the *Guinness Book of Records*. Let us therefore start from the year 1911, when the Swiss master Hans Fahrni took on exactly 100 opponents, beating 55 of them, agreeing draws with 39 and losing to six. This result didn't greatly impress his contemporaries, though it did not go unnoticed. Then 11 years later in Cleveland, the new World Champion José Raoul Capablanca faced 103 players for 7 hours and conceded a grand total of one half point to them! Almost immediately afterwards, Frank Marshall raised the record level by giving a display on 155 boards in Montreal, but with a far more modest result: +126 -8 =21. Indeed, the score of nearly 100% achieved by the third World Champion in mass exhibitions exceeding 75 boards is thought to be unequalled to this day. Overall, Capablanca may be viewed as the record-holder for simultaneous play. Between his exhibition in Havana on 26 October 1901 (before his 13ᵗʰ birthday) and his final one in New York on 6 November 1941, he took on the chess enthusiasts 491 times. Playing 13,545 games, he won 11,912, drew 1,063 and lost 570 for a score of 91.13%. One of his opponents was a fourteen-year-old future World Champion.

Capablanca – Botvinnik
Leningrad 1925
Queen's Gambit [D51]
(notes by Botvinnik)

1 d4 d5 2 c4 e6 3 ♘c3 ♘f6 4 ♗g5 ♘bd7 5 e3 ♗b4
At that time this variation was only just coming into fashion. I chose it because I reckoned that in the simultaneous display Capablanca would have more trouble with a game where the fight was less familiar in character.
6 cxd5 exd5 7 ♕b3
Capablanca was fond of playing this move in queen's pawn openings, but he himself taught beginners to develop their minor pieces first. Accordingly 7 ♗d3 should have been preferred.
7...c5 8 dxc5
There was no reason at all to exchange off the central d4-pawn and lose control of the square c5.
8...♕a5 9 ♗xf6
A forced exchange (Black was threatening both 9...♘e4 and 9...♘xc5), after which Black has an easy game.
9...♘xf6 10 0-0-0
Seeing that he was playing against a boy, Capablanca decided to take a risk. But then, castling long is all the more risky in an open position with your kingside not yet mobilized. It was essential to clarify the situation with 10 a3.

10...0-0 11 ♘f3

Of course White couldn't take the centre pawn, as after 11 ♘xd5 ♘xd5 12 ♕xd5 ♗e6 Black would win easily.

11...♗e6 12 ♘d4 ♖ac8 13 c6

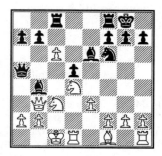

This natural effort to close the c-file leads unavoidably to an ending with an extra pawn for Black.

13...♗xc3!

White can't reply 14 bxc3, as after 14...♘e4 his position would be indefensible. This means he has to give up a pawn.

14 ♕xc3 ♕xa2 15 ♗d3 bxc6 16 ♔c2 c5

So that on 17 ♖a1, Black can win with 17...cxd4.

17 ♘xe6 ♕a4+

An essential refinement. After 17...fxe6 18 ♖a1, Black's operation to save his queen (with 18...d4) would inevitably mean forfeiting his advantage. Now the game reduces to the ending which I had evaluated when making my 13th move.

18 b3 ♕a2+ 19 ♕b2 ♕xb2+ 20 ♔xb2 fxe6 21 f3

Otherwise 21...♘g4 would follow.

21...♖c7 22 ♖a1 c4

Creating a passed pawn and stripping the white king's position.

23 bxc4 dxc4 24 ♗c2 ♖b8+ 25 ♔c1 ♘d5 26 ♖e1 c3

Black's main task is to penetrate to the second rank with his rooks.

27 ♖a3 ♘b4

Black couldn't play 27...♖b2 on account of 28 ♖xc3. Now, however, the threat is 28...♘xc2 29 ♔xc2 ♖b2+.

28 ♖e2 ♖d8 29 e4

White can do nothing active; 29 ♗b3 would be met by 29...c2 30 ♗xc2 ♖dc8.

29...♖c6

Decisive. The rook here is protected by the knight, so that after 30...♖d2 31 ♖xc3 Black can play 31...♖xe2. White has no defence against the invasion by the rook.

30 ♖e3 ♖d2 31 ♖exc3 ♖xc2+ 32 ♖xc2 ♖xc2+

At this point Capablanca brushed the pieces aside (as a gesture of resignation) and went on to the next board. The look on his face was not exactly amiable. I am therefore sceptical when eye-witnesses say that Capablanca expressed praise for my chess abilities.

0-1

This episode, incidentally, was only the first in a number of exhibitions in which Chess Kings faced future successors to the throne. In 1963, for example, Botvinnik gave a display with clocks in which pupils of his chess school took part. Among them was the 12-year-old candidate master Anatoly Karpov.

The players' comments on that game are interesting. "In a won position I gave away my queen, but still managed to draw," said Botvinnik. "In actual fact, when I saw that the Grandmaster had blundered his queen away, I turned to the master who was Botvinnik's assistant and asked him to suggest that the simultaneous player should take his move back. The ex-World Champion declined to do so, and since I didn't want to score a point by 'illegitimate' means, I deliberately made a mistake in reply, which led to a draw." Thus, Karpov.

Things by no means always turned out so well for the young talents. In 1975 the 12-year-old Garry Kasparov, still a candidate master, played the following game against Vasily Smyslov in a 'clock simul' within the context of the 'Tournament of Grandmasters and Pioneers'. (This was the unofficial name given to the extremely popular and very useful team competition of the Palaces of Young Pioneers in the USSR.)

Kasparov – Smyslov
Ruy Lopez [C60]

1 e4 e5 2 ♘f3 ♘c6 3 ♗b5 g6 4 d4 exd4 5 ♘xd4 ♗g7 6 ♗e3 ♘f6 7 ♘c3 0-0 8 0-0 ♖e8 9 f3 ♘e5 10 h3 a6 11 ♗e2 d5 12 f4 ♘c4 13 ♗xc4 dxc4 14 ♕f3 c5 15 ♘de2 ♗d7 16 e5 ♗c6 17 ♕f2 ♘d7

18 ♗xc5 ♘xc5 19 ♕xc5 ♖c8 20 ♖ad1 ♕h4 21 ♕e3 g5 22 ♘d5 gxf4 23 ♖xf4 ♕g5 24 ♘f6+ ♔h8 25 ♕f2 ♖xe5 26 ♘d4 ♗xf6 27 ♖xf6 ♗xg2 28 ♔h2 ♖e3 29 ♕xg2 ♕xf6 30 ♕xb7 ♕f4+ 0-1

During the same event Kasparov played in an exhibition against Anatoly Karpov. Eleven years later, as World Champion, he himself gave a display against pupils of the Botvinnik-Kasparov correspondence school, which had assembled in the little Lithuanian town of Druskininka for one of its periodic sessions. There among the youngsters was the 11-year-old candidate master Vladimir Kramnik. Neither of them suspected that their match in London in the autumn of 1900 would bring about a 'change of dynasty' in the chess kingdom.

But let us return to the increasing size of individual simultaneous displays.

As we know, mathematics recognizes no ultimate number; nor do the ambitious endeavours of simultaneous players. Following Marshall, Andrei Lilienthal played 155 games in Moscow in 1935 –

this was the largest 'simul' to be given by one person on Soviet territory! International Master George Koltanowski played on 271 boards at San Francisco in 1949, but the quality of opposition was frankly low – the score of +251 -3 =17 merely bears this out. A few months later in 1950, Grandmaster Miguel Najdorf played a more serious selection of opponents on 250 boards and won 226 games while losing 10 and drawing 14. The Swede Ulf Andersson performed brilliantly in a small town in his homeland on 6-7 January 1996, losing only two games from a display on 310 boards.

Anyway, here is the record to date. The Yugoslav Grandmaster Bojan Kurajica, World Junior Champion for 1965, chose to give a display on the biblical number of 666 boards – the number of the Beast in the Apocalypse. The event took place in Sarajevo and lasted 26 hours and a few minutes. A total of 237,481 moves were made (an average of 35½ per game), and the simultaneous player made the outstanding final score of +570 -13 =83, that is nearly 92 per cent!

However, the little-known Canadian master George Berner might also claim the status of a record-holder. Admittedly the display he gave in Toronto in 1960 was only against 30 opponents. On the other hand, after every trip round all the boards, he would either dance, or read verses in a variety or languages, or sing operatic arias and folk songs – or else play the mouth organ, or even

the shepherd's pipe! A Jack of all trades – enough said!

Unfortunately nothing is new. When Johannes Zukertort arrived in what is now the State of Wyoming during one of his tours in 1883-4, it turned out that a simultaneous display could not take place because of the lack of people in the town who could play chess. Nothing daunted, the maestro walked up to the piano that was standing in the room, and began a concert. Zukertort was, after all, a superb pianist as well as a chess master; he was a pupil of the outstanding 19th-century teacher Ignaz Moscheles.

The display that involved more 'running about' than any other was probably the one given by the Dutch master Van der Scheeren in the summer of 1984 in the Eindhoven football stadium before the annual match for the national championship. Each of the 10 boards measured 10x10 metres, so that to make, for example, the opening move e2-e4 on all of them, the simultaneous player would have to walk 120 metres or so; then the move 2 ♘f3 could only be carried out after something like 350 metres! If there were 30 or 40 moves to be played like this, the distance in kilometres would be getting on for a marathon!

Still, what about the *quality* of simultaneous games? Here is just one example which Mikhail Tal used to recollect with delight; as we all know, his serious tournament games were similarly replete with beautiful combinations.

Tal – NN
Berlin 1974

NN – Rossolimo
Paris 1944

14 ♗g5
Now on 14...♗xg5, the stock sacrifice 15 ♗xh7+ works, so to speak, in its pure form: 15...♔xh7 16 ♘xg5+ ♔g6 17 ♘xf7!. However....
14...♘xe5
"To be absolutely honest I had missed this capture, but (in my defence!) it may have been because my intuition hinted to me that this kind of play in the opening would not do. I had to find a way to prove that this move was bad. And I did." (Tal)
15 ♗xe7 ♘xf3 16 ♖xf3 ♕xe7 17 ♗xh7+ ♔xh7 18 ♖h3+ ♔g8
"Now the hackneyed 19 ♕h5 gives White nothing after the no less hackneyed 19...f6. But White succeeds in introducing a new motif into the age-old combination." (Tal)
19 ♘f5 ♕g5 20 ♕h5!
"Black resigned. He is mated after either 20...♕xh5 21 ♘e7+ etc., or 20...f6 21 ♘e7." (Tal)
1-0

And what does the following simultaneous game lack in brilliance?

The pressure that Black has organized against f2 is at present half concealed. He now robs that point of its protection with an exceptionally spectacular stroke.
1...♖d1!!
However strange it may seem, White could resign at once! Capturing with 2 ♕xb5 or 2 ♖fxd1 would allow mate in two.
2 ♗xb7+ ♔b8 3 c4 ♖xf2!
This is much quicker than 3...♗xf2+ 4 ♕xf2 ♖xf2 5 ♖fxd1 ♕c5 6 ♗d5+ ♔c8 7 ♔h2, although even then, after 7...♖f6, Black would finish the game with a mating attack.
4 ♕xb5 ♖fxf1+ 5 ♔h2 ♖h1 mate

Unconventional displays

There are a great many of these, and they are just as varied as the human capacity to dream them up and implement them technically. A patent piece of exoticism, for instance, was a simultaneous display given in 1929 by Savielly Tartakower – a Grandmaster, the king of chess journalism at the time, and amazingly adventurous. He was playing from an aeroplane! Three years later Alekhine did the same. In those days the flight from Los Angeles to San Francisco took 3½ hours, and the World Champion contended by radio with 7 opponents in both those cities. Unfortunately not all the games were finished.

The ingenuity of David Bronstein went further still. In 1978 he played a four-board mutual simultaneous match against Rafael Vaganian, and in 1982 he played Mikhail Tal on eight boards. "At first I felt uneasy about playing eight Bronsteins at once, but then I consoled myself with the thought that David would be fighting against eight Tals," was the ex-World Champion's comment on this episode. He won 5:3 (+4 -2 =2). The games were first-rate; the following is just one example.

Tal – Bronstein
Queen's Indian Defence [E12]

1 d4 ♘f6 2 c4 e6 3 ♘f3 b6 4 a3 d5 5 ♘c3 ♗e7 6 cxd5 exd5 7 ♗f4 0-0 8 e3 c5 9 ♘e5 ♗b7 10 ♗d3 ♘bd7 11 ♕f3 ♖e8 12 0-0 a6 13 ♕h3 ♘f8 14 ♗g5 cxd4 15 exd4 ♘e4?

This allows White to transfer his pressure to a less well defended point in the Black position: f7.

16 ♘xe4 dxe4

After 16...♗xg5 17 ♘xf7! ♔xf7 18 ♕h5+, White emerges with an extra pawn and a continuing attack.

17 ♗c4 ♗d5 18 ♕b3 ♗xc4 19 ♕xc4 ♘e6 20 ♘c6

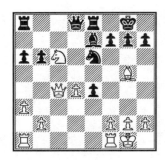

With this White acquires a material plus, and the game might seem to be entering its technical stage.

20...b5!? 21 ♕a2 ♕d7 22 ♘xe7+ ♔h8!?

The technical stage? Not a bit of it! The extremely sharp struggle carries on.

23 ♗h4 g5 24 ♘d5!? gxh4 25 ♘b6 ♕b7 26 ♘xa8 ♘f4 27 b4

Bringing the queen into play.

27...♖g8 28 d5!

After 28 g3 e3! Black would have a strong attack. Now the white queen threatens to reach e5 in a couple of jumps.

28...♖xg2+ 29 ♔h1 ♕d7

The impudent white knight has survived. All that remains is to reduce to an ending....

30 ♕b2+ ♔g8 31 ♕b3

Killing two birds with one stone: The black queen can reach neither d5 nor h3.

31...♘d3 32 ♖g1

Just in time; Black won't mate by 32...♘xf2+.

32...♖g4 33 ♕c2 ♔f8 34 f3! ♖xg1+ 35 ♖xg1 ♕f5 36 ♖f1 e3 37 ♘b6

With this striking move (threatening a check on c8), the knight heads for the epicentre of the battle.

37...h3
Black is extracting everything he can from the position. For the moment, 38 ♕c8+ ♕xc8 39 ♘xc8 is bad on account of 39...e2.
38 d6!
Renewing the threat.
38...♘f2+ 39 ♖xf2 exf2 40 ♕xf2 ♕d3 41 ♘d7+ ♔e8 42 ♘f6+ ♔f8 43 ♘d7+ ♔e8 44 ♘e5 ♕xd6 45 ♕e2 ♕e6 46 ♕e4 1-0

This was surely the record achievement under the heading of 'mutual exhibitions', and yet it had antecedents that began more than six decades earlier in a situation that was also 'record-breaking'.

At a chess gathering in Petrograd (the Slavonic name given to St Petersburg after the outbreak of the First World War), a display was being conducted by Fyodor Dus-Chotimirsky. In the Chigorin Memorial (St Petersburg 1909) he had beaten both of the tournament winners – World Champion Emanuel Lasker and Akiba Rubinstein! In the 'All-Russian Amateur Tournament' at the same time and place, the young Alexander Alekhine had come first and gained the master title. Alekhine was now a Grandmaster and made no secret of his World Championship dreams. When he chanced to turn up in the hall where Dus-Chotimirsky was striding back and forth in front of the tables, someone facetiously suggested that he should join in the 'simul'.

And lo and behold, he agreed – there has been nothing else like it in chess history! The Grandmaster, however, asked to play on two boards. He took the games seriously, and yet lost one of them – to a mere master, playing simultaneously! Eye-witnesses testified that Alekhine was extremely mortified by his 1:1 score and left the scene of battle forthwith.

Two contests in 1932 made a more natural impression. First, Alekhine in New York played on 50 boards, each of which had four consulting players sitting at it. They offered worthy resistance to the World Champion: his score was +30 -6 =14. Shortly afterwards in Havana, at a display by Capablanca, each of 66 boards was manned by a full five 'consultants', but they came off none the better for it; he scored +46 -4 =16!

As for so-called 'tandem displays' (in which two exhibitors make alternate moves – without always understanding each other), an event in Berlin in 1909 came way ahead of all others. The German masters Curt von Bardeleben and Wilhelm Cohn were playing on 21 boards, 'blindfold'! For increased effect they played against each other at the same time, and this too was without sight of the board! Unfortunately nothing good came of it, and when Bardeleben, who was a little younger but much more experienced, took Cohn to task for some blunders during the play, the latter in his embarrassment began making excuses: "Everything got so mixed up in my head that I started losing track of when you were my partner and when you were an opponent." So Napoleon seems to have been right: "If only the Lord rids me of allies, I will deal with my enemies myself!" And yet as a chessplayer the Emperor was very, very mediocre.

However, the Berlin exhibition had an antecedent four decades earlier, which had attracted a good deal of comment from the world's press, especially in England. This occurred in 1868, at a gathering of the British Chess Association at St James's Hall in London. Wilhelm Steinitz, who was to become the first official World Champion 20 years on, was pitted against his constant rival Joseph Henry Blackburne. They had chosen a method of combat which was completely unusual at that time: they were playing 'blindfold' against the same five opponents and also against each other. The game between the masters ended in a draw, but against the participants in the exhibition Steinitz scored only 2 points while Blackburne scored 3½. Up until the Berlin event, then, the record for this chess format belonged to these luminaries from the second half of the 19th century.

An event in 1981 possesses record status for its unconvention-ality among other things. This was a display given by the then World Champion Anatoly Karpov, the ex-Champion Boris Spassky, and Germany's strongest Grandmasters of the day: Robert Hübner and Wolfgang Unzicker. They faced only 100 opponents in all – but these were computers, equipped of course with various chess programs. Without undue effort, the masters made a 100% score! Well,

electronic chess was then still in 'short trousers', whereas now, even in one-to-one combat, World Champions playing a computer sometimes suffer a fiasco.

For over a century, in fact, the simultaneous player was a good deal more than head and shoulders above his opponents, whereas today, more and more frequently, the role of the amateurs is taken over by players with high or even the highest chess titles! Thirty years ago, a display against masters and Grandmasters would clearly still have been something from the realm of unscientific fantasy. The exceptions could easily be counted on the fingers of one hand. Thus in 1949, Paul Keres gave a display – with clocks, of course – against eight top players from Bulgaria. In effect they were the country's national team, though no one called them that at the time. The simultaneous player performed brilliantly to win every game! Still, this was held to be in the nature of things; the Bulgarian masters of those days, frankly, were still fairly weak. Alexander Tsvetkov, several times national champion, was the clear tail-ender in the 1947 Chigorin Memorial Tournament in Moscow, managing only 4 draws from 15 games. The future Bulgarian Grandmasters who made their mark – Milko Bobotsov, Nikola Padevsky, Georgi Tringov – were still mere youths when Keres gave his display.

Still, that event did leave a trace, at least for Paul himself. The Bulgarians presented him with a commemorative cup – twenty years later!

And then in 1974, ex-World Champion Mikhail Tal took on the Australian team. This unusual encounter made a strong impression worldwide (whereas Keres's display had gone largely unnoticed), and was essentially the first event of its particular kind. I reported on it in the Riga magazine *Shakhmaty*. The title of my article alludes to the tournament regulations of those years; a clause familiar to everyone stipulated the time control of "40 moves in 2½ hours and 16 moves per hour thereafter, with accumulation of unused time" – which by now belongs to history.

One and a half cups of coffee per hour, with accumulation of sugar

The USSR Central Chess Club on Gogol Boulevard, Moscow, is used to switching off its lights at half past eleven. Just occasionally this has been prevented by extraordinary happenings such as meetings between chessplayers and cosmonauts, or Grandmaster blitz tournaments – when those present have left the club by one in the morning. Yet during its existence of more than a decade and a half, the club has never seen an event like this one. All through the night the great tournament hall was lit up by the chandeliers, and you could hear the characteristic click of chess clocks being pressed. What's more, it was round about six o'clock in the morning when the positions on the eight boards aroused the greatest interest amongst the Grandmasters, arbiters and representatives of the press who were present in the hall.

There is not one word of exaggeration in this account. The contest was truly out of the ordinary. Ex-World Champion Mikhail Tal was playing a match by telephone and telex against the best chessplayers of the continent most distant from us: Australia. The Australians had politely requested the privilege of not turning their night into their day – which in full accordance with the laws of nature transformed Tal automatically into a 'nocturnal' simultaneous player. True to his principle of being willing to 'try anything' (which once, as is well known, landed him in a bullring), Tal consented to the experiment.

So there he was in the tournament hall with a cup of coffee in his hand, walking to and fro between the tables behind which his invisible opponents were facing him – the Canberra Champion Kraske, the New South Wales Champion MacLaurin, the former Australian Champion Hamilton, and other masters from Adelaide, Perth, Brisbane, Melbourne and Sydney. I may add that less than a month later, the participants in this match were to take part in the jubilee Olympiad in Nice, and that the match itself created an unprecedented upsurge of interest in chess in Australia. It was broadcast there on television, and demonstration

243

boards were set up in shop windows in the cities from which the players had been delegated. Indeed, it was precisely with the aim of propagandizing chess in this way that the Australians had elicited the peculiar 'odds' of playing in the daytime. The session lasted 9 hours! Only four of the games ended within that time. Then an arbitration team of Grandmasters Yuri Averbakh and Salo Flohr, whose decision the Australians accepted without demur, adjudicated the unfinished games. In the end, the ex-World Champion made the score of 5½:2½ with 4 wins, 3 draws and one loss.

To be honest, when play ended at 11 o'clock in the morning, Tal's outward appearance was less than radiant. I therefore didn't have the heart to conduct a lengthier interview with him than the one I now reproduce.

"Did you enjoy playing 'blind' like that?"

"Well, how shall I put it? At the end of the day it's better playing with 'visible' opponents, though of course matches like this are worthwhile too – especially as they're sometimes the only answer to the problem of distance."

"Are you satisfied with the results of the exhibition, in terms of points scored and the quality of the games?"

"I'm not at all convinced I would have played differently face-to-face, either better or worse. All the same, it's more usual – again I'm not saying better or worse, just more usual – to be able take a look at your opponent now and then during the game."

"When you say usual, isn't this connected with something that's been known for a long time – that you hypnotize your opponents in some way?"

"Perhaps there *is* a connection, though if the latest results are anything to go by, I'm a *retired* hypnotist. But to come back to the games – they were fairly interesting, they contained all sorts of plans. Besides that, they set me a new problem – that of the ninth hour of play, when I made some serious mistakes."

"One last question: how many cups of coffee helped you to play all through the night in that Central Chess Club tournament hall?"

"Let me see now ... about one and a half cups per hour, with accumulation of unused sugar!"

In conclusion, here is one game that did finish before adjudication time. Tal caught his opponent in an elegant trap in an outwardly simple position, although the ending was worse for Black in any case.

Tal – Jordan
Sicilian Defence [E70]

1 e4 c5 2 ♘f3 ♘c6 3 d4 cxd4 4 ♘xd4 ♘f6 5 ♘c3 e5 6 ♘db5 d6 7 ♗g5 a6 8 ♘a3 ♗e6 9 ♘c4 ♖c8 10 ♘d5

White avoids the well-known continuation 10 ♗xf6 gxf6 11 ♘e3 ♘d4 which keeps his opening advantage. Instead, over-the-board, he discovers a pawn sacrifice leading by force to the more pleasant ending.

10...♗xd5 11 exd5 ♘e7 12 ♕d3 ♘exd5

More or less obligatory, as 12...h6 13 ♗xf6 gxf6 14 ♘e3 leads to a total blockade of the light squares in Black's camp.

13 0-0-0 ♗e7 14 ♗xf6 ♘xf6 15 ♘xd6+ ♕xd6 16 ♕xd6 ♗xd6 17 ♖xd6 ♔e7 18 ♖d2 ♖hd8 19 ♗d3 ♖c5 20 ♖e1 ♖d4

He should probably have removed his king from the line of fire by 20...♔f8.

21 c3 ♔d6

Continuing to play with fire.

22 ♔c2 ♘d5 23 ♔b1!

Black can't unravel his knot of pieces without destroying their co-ordination. White's advantage becomes palpable.

23...♖h4 24 ♗e4 ♔e6 25 c4 ♘b4?

The decisive mistake. The least of the evils was 25...♘c7, and if 26 ♗xb7 then 26...♖hxc4. Now the rook on c5 unexpectedly turns out to be trapped.

26 a3 ♘c6 27 g3

Black would be glad to settle for 27 b4 ♖xc4 28 ♗d5+, which costs him the exchange for a pawn. White justifiably demands more.

27...♖g4

Black loses a rook after 27...♖xh2 28 b4.

28 h3 ♖xe4 29 ♖xe4 f5 30 ♖h4 1-0

Then began the incredible 'Kasparov era' of 'clock simuls' against immensely strong teams. Each of these events took the record to new heights.

December 1985: a full eight-board encounter with the 'Hamburg' club team headed by the English Grandmaster Murray Chandler. Kasparov started play two hours after landing in Hamburg. Moreover, before the start of the event, to the astonishment and delight of his opponents, he offered them the white pieces in half the games. All this taken together led to Kasparov's first relative failure as a simultaneous player – and to date, his only one. He scored 3½:4½, although some of the games were outstanding.

Behrhorst – Kasparov
Grünfeld Defence [D82]
(notes by Kasparov)

1 d4 ♘f6 2 c4 g6 3 ♘c3 d5 4 ♘f3 ♗g7 5 ♗f4 0-0 6 e3 c5 7 dxc5 ♘e4 8 ♕b3 ♘a6 9 cxd5 ♘axc5 10 ♕c4 b5!! 11 ♘xb5

11...♗xb2!

Of course not 11...♕a5+? because of 12 b4!. For that reason it may not be obvious why I give an exclamation mark to the move played. It looks as if Black solves his opening problems easily. However...

12 ♗c7!

What is Black to do after this intermediate move?

12...a6!!

A fantastic resource! It was impossible to calculate all the variations following this queen sacrifice; in such situations the best thing is to rely on intuition.

13 ♗xd8 axb5 14 ♕c2

I will give one of the possible variations following the capture of the pawn: 14 ♕xb5 ♗c3+ 15 ♔d1 ♖xd8 16 ♖c1 ♖xd5+ 17 ♔c2 ♗f5

18 g4 ♖xa2+ 19 ♔b1 ♖a1+ 20 ♔c2 ♘d6+ 21 gxf5 ♖xc1+ 22 ♔xc1 ♘xb5 23 ♗xb5 ♖xf5, and Black should win the ending.

14...♗c3+ 15 ♕xc3

A king move would lose at once (15 ♔d1 ♖xd8), but giving back the queen that White has just won looks very strong....

15...♘xc3 16 ♗xe7

16...♘b3!!

A combinative stroke calculated in advance, of a kind rarely seen in simultaneous play.

17 ♖d1

Not 17 ♗xf8 ♘xa1 18 ♗c5, on account of 18...♘e4!.

17...♖xa2! 18 ♗xf8 ♔xf8 19 ♘d4 ♘xd1 20 ♘xb3 ♘xf2 21 ♖g1 ♘g4 22 d6 ♘xe3 23 ♘c5 ♗g4 24 h3 ♖c2! 25 ♘a6 ♗e6

The rest is elementary, though Black still needs to be careful and accurate.

26 ♗e2

Of course 26 ♗xb5 is bad in view of 26...♘xg2+.

26...♗c4 27 ♗f3 ♘f5 28 d7 ♔e7 29 ♘b8 ♖c1+ 30 ♔f2 ♖xg1 31 ♔xg1 ♘d4 32 ♗e4 f5 33 ♗b1 ♗e6 34 ♔f2 ♗xd7 35 ♔e3 ♘c6 36 ♘xd7 ♔xd7 37 g4 fxg4 38 hxg4 ♔e6 39 ♔f4 ♔d5 40 ♗a2+ ♔d4 41 ♔g5 ♘e5 42 ♗g8 b4 43 ♗xh7

b3 44 ♗g8 b2 45 ♗a2 ♔c3 46 ♗b1
♔d2 47 ♔f4 ♔c1 48 ♗e4 ♘c4
49 ♗xg6 ♘a3 50 g5 ♘c2 0-1

May 1986: Karpov faced the West German junior team, whom as a matter of fact he did not greatly surpass in age. The team included the future famous Grandmasters Wahls, Lutz and Brunner, but the result was nonetheless 6½:1½ to the youngest World Chess Champion in history.

A year later, revenge was exacted from the 'Hamburg' club, which this time had two International Masters, four FIDE Masters and two national masters playing for it. Kasparov's score of +6 -0 =2 speaks for itself. In the next display, the honour of Switzerland was defended only by six International Masters, to whom Kasparov 'dropped' one half point! There followed victories against the teams of France, Argentina – and Germany. The last-named was the first all-Grandmaster simultaneous display. Here is what Kasparov himself said about it:

The proposal to play on on a 'winner takes all' basis was an excellent publicity ploy. My 'impudence' disarmed my negotiating partners, and they immediately expressed their readiness to set about organizing the exhibition. The very format of the contest was a severe test of the World Champion's potential, and compelled my opponents to mobilize all their reserves in preparing for the match.

In the pre-match period one circumstance played into my hands. The point is that 1991 had been one of the least successful years of my chess career. It is not impossible that for this very reason the German team, deep down, were underestimating my chances, notwithstanding all the seriousness of their preparation. This included providing a reserve player, appointing Grandmaster Klaus Darga as a special coach, and holding a special training session in Baden-Baden. In addition, the drawing of lots, which was done in my absence, apportioned the colours in the way most favorable to my opponents: Vlastimil Hort and Matthias Wahls were given Black, while Eric Lobron and Gerald Hertneck had White.

In brief, the Germans believed that the new BMW model, dark green in colour, which stood in the playing hall, would be theirs without trouble. Now that the score of 3:1 in my favour has gone down in history, the matter is easy to discuss. The game scores bear impartial witness to one thing: at no moment was there any 'risk' that the German team would win a single game, let alone the match....

I would like to give an example of a successful pre-match discovery which I employed in one of the games in this exhibition. It repeats an idea which I had previously used only once (in the 5th game of the 1990 World Championship match).

Lobron – Kasparov
Simultaneous match,
Baden-Baden 1992
King's Indian Defence [E94]
(notes by Kasparov)

1 d4 ♘f6 2 c4 g6 3 ♘c3 ♗g7 4 e4 d6 5 ♘f3 0-0 6 ♗e2 e5 7 0-0 ♘a6 8 ♗e3

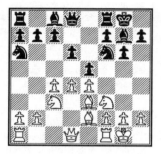

8...c6
I don't play this in ordinary tournaments, because after the strongest reply, involving a queen exchange, White acquires a small but stable plus in the ending – which is not at all what I want. An exhibition, however, is a different matter.

9 dxe5 dxe5
At this point, under the gaze of the immense television audience as well as the public who packed the spectators' hall to overflowing, Lobron in his indecision sank into thought for 50 minutes, thus freeing my hands to play more calmly and confidently on the other boards.

10 h3
Although Lobron understands the position perfectly well, he steers clear of complications and thereby relieves me of any opening problems and any possible surprises.

10...♕e7 11 ♕c2 ♘h5 12 ♖fe1 ♘c7 13 ♖ad1 ♘e6 14 c5 ♘hf4 15 b4 ♘xe2+ 16 ♘xe2 ♘c7 17 ♘c3 a5 18 a3 axb4 19 axb4 f6 20 b5 ♘xb5 21 ♘xb5 cxb5 22 ♕b3+ ♗e6 23 ♕xb5 ♖fd8 24 ♖xd8+ ♖xd8 25 ♖b1 ♖d7 26 ♕a5 ♗f8 27 ♕a4 ♖c7 28 ♖b6 ♔f7 29 ♘d2 ♖c6 30 ♖xc6 ♕d7 31 ♖a6 bxa6 32 c6 ♕d3 33 ♕a5 ♗e7 34 ♕c7 ♕c3 35 g4 h6 36 ♗xh6 ♕xh3 37 g5 fxg5 38 ♕xe5 ♕xh6 39 ♘f3 ♕h3 40 ♘d4 ♗f6 41 ♕c7+ ♗e7 42 ♕e5 ♗c4 43 c7 ♕g4+ 44 ♔h1 ♕h3+ 45 ♔g1 ♕g4+ 46 ♔h2 0-1

While Lobron was sitting immersed in thought I succeeded in putting a 'bind' on Wahls and afterwards never relaxed the pressure for a moment. He couldn't withstand the tension and eventually lost.

Kasparov – Wahls
Simultaneous match,
Baden-Baden 1992
King's Indian Defence [B07]

1 e4 d6 2 d4 ♘f6 3 f3 e5 4 d5 c6 5 c4 ♕b6 6 ♘c3 ♗e7 7 ♘ge2 0-0 8 ♘g3 cxd5 9 ♘a4 ♕c7 10 cxd5 ♗d7 11 ♗e3 ♖c8 12 ♘c3 ♘a6 13 ♗e2 ♗d8 14 0-0 ♕a5 15 ♔h1 ♘c5 16 ♗d2 ♘e8

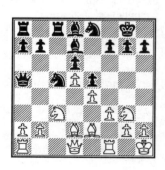

17 f4 exf4 18 ♗xf4 ♗f6 19 ♗g4
♕d8 20 ♗xd7 ♕xd7 21 ♕f3 ♖c7
22 ♘f5 ♗xc3 23 bxc3 ♘a4 24 ♕g3
♘xc3 25 ♖ae1 f6 26 ♗xd6 ♘xd6
27 ♘xd6 ♔h8 28 e5 ♘xd5 29 e6
♕c6 30 ♖d1 ♖f8 31 ♘f7+ ♔g8
32 ♖xd5 ♕xd5 33 ♕xc7 ♕xe6
34 ♘d6 ♕xa2 35 ♕xb7 ♕e2
36 ♕d5+ ♔h8 37 ♘f7+ 1-0

It might seem that the incredible had been achieved and that the record to end all records was established. An all-Grandmaster quartet had been defeated. One of its members had been one of the world's strongest players, though alas at an earlier date. His colleagues, on the other hand, had yet to climb to great heights on the ladder of world ratings. But then in 1998, Kasparov gave an exhibition against the Israeli team, which had gained the bronze medals in the world Olympiad! Its members – Boris Alterman, Ilya Smirin (with whom Kasparov had played 'one-against-one' in the star-studded USSR Championship of 1988), the future European Champion Emil Sutovsky, and Alexander Huzman – had ratings round about the 2600-mark, the boundary of the super-class. The result of the contest was staggering – 3:1 in the first round and 4:0 in the second. After this, Tommy Lapid, President of the Israeli Chess Federation and a nationally popular journalist and political commentator, gloomily declared: "In Tel-Aviv on the occasion of the 50th anniversary of the foundation of the state of Israel, Garry perpetrated a *pogrom*...."

With this, indeed, the record height had been reached, beyond which perhaps there would only be the theoretical possibility of exhibitions against the British and Russian teams at full strength....

For that reason there is little point in dwelling on Vladimir Kramnik's exhibitions against the teams of Switzerland and (again) Germany, or Kasparov's against the team of the Czech republic. Astounding though they are in themselves, these events cannot claim record status.

One other display, however, holds a record to this day. One Monday in June 1999, in New York, Garry Kasparov played 1 e4, and the move was projected on a giant illuminated screen. This began an encounter without precedent in chess history: 'Kasparov versus the whole world', via the worldwide Internet. But let him explain it himself:

An enormous participating audience is expected. There are normally 5 million people in the Microsoft Gaming Zone. The organizers are making provision for millions of people to get online and take part in this game. Realistically, however, I think that 200-300 thousand will play.

Here is how it will work. I have 12 hours in which to make my move with White. I send the move via the Internet to the Microsoft headquarters in Seattle. From there it will be communicated to four experts whom the company has selected. They too will have 12 hours at their disposal (or perhaps more, if I play faster). The experts assess the situation

249

on the board, and each one suggests a move in reply. In so doing, as far as possible, they should supply an explanation in popular terms as to why they are proposing this or that move. Then all the suggestions will be posted and presented to the Internet public by the English Grandmaster Daniel King. Over the next 18 hours the world considers which of the suggested moves to select. Then, during 6 hours, voting takes place. In this way, the complete cycle – my move, the deliberation, the voting, and the reply – is meant to take 48 hours. We have estimated the possible duration of the game, and I hope we can manage within two or three months or so.

Four juniors under the age of 20 have been invited to be the expert consultants. At first it was assumed that some famous Grandmasters would fill this role, but that idea was abandoned, since there was the risk that players could fall victim to the 'hypnosis' of the big names. Microsoft came down in favour of Irina Krush, the US Women's Champion; Florin Felecan, the highest-rated American junior; Étienne Bacrot, the French Grandmaster who has recently won a strong tournament of young Grandmasters in Switzerland; and the German girl Elisabeth Pähtz, with whom I played an exhibition game in Frankfurt not so long ago. She already has quite a good feel for handling the position, although her

rating, to date, is not high. On the other hand her Grandmaster father will always be there for her. Moreover she has the backing of ChessBase, and I suspect that she will also be helped in her decisions by that firm's product Fritz 5.32. In principle, any Internet user can send his own suggested move to the Microsoft website, and Danny King will communicate it to the rest. In any event the majority vote will have the final say.

As in an election, the move chosen will be announced, followed by the voting figures. That way, no one's vote will be influenced by the ongoing count. It seems to me that the voting procedure may prove no less exciting than the play itself. There is much here that is very interesting! For the first time, for example, the extent of the potential chess public will be measured right down to the last person. Even during my match with Deep Blue these data could not be obtained, since you couldn't tell why someone had visited the website – perhaps they just did, or perhaps they were interested in the game score. Here it is a different matter. If someone votes for a move, they are actually playing!

If I don't succeed in perplexing my opponents right at the start, through an opening innovation, then the chances in an extended struggle will be roughly equal. I won't be able to afford a moment's weakness! They won't make any blunders; everyone these days has the strongest chess programs on CD. The search for the best continuations will be professional; it will be narrowed down and confined to 2 or 3 lines. I imagine too that the experienced presenter Danny King will be able to guide the audience in the right direction.

Overall this event is immensely significant for the future of chess. The Internet will be able to help chess to compete with the most popular forms of sport. Just imagine that gigantic audience – hundreds of thousands of people all over the world will be playing chess at once. Isn't that impressive?

Without a chessboard

One of the most significant books in the history of mankind – perhaps coming next after the Bible, the Koran and the Talmud – is arguably the *Encyclopaedia, or Classified Dictionary of Sciences, Arts, and Trades*, produced in the second half of the 18th century through the efforts of the writer Denis Diderot and the mathematician Jean Le Rond d'Alembert. They assembled such an outstanding array of authors for this work that its 17 volumes of text and 11 volumes of illustrations succeeded in many ways in altering the system of views of the entire Old World, conservative as it was and wholly reluctant to evolve. The fuse was lit for the great French Revolution.

Well, in this encyclopaedia of the future, which cast doubt on absolute kingship and the indisputable nature of the divine, space was accorded to an amazing fact which in its way even defied understanding. François-André Danican Philidor – the brilliant composer of short comic operas that were performed in court theatres all over Europe, who was even more famous as a chessplayer – had played three games at once against different opponents, without having a single chessboard in front of him! Philidor was playing *blindfold*, dictating his moves to his opponents. Being used to the applause and goodwill of theatre audiences, he himself evidently held this 'exhibition' to be so significant that he had invited a thoroughly refined gathering to witness it.

In a word, this was a sensation! And yet – it was not the first time that claims had been made about the extraordinary nature of a chess game. In Kazan University Library there is a medieval manuscript which has become available for study 1250 years (!) after it was written. In restrained terms characteristic of the east, the author speaks of a certain Said ben Jubair who could "play chess with his back to the game, thanks to his skill and perspicacity". That was before the year 714, in the era of *shatranj*; Said later perished at the executioner's hands. The treatise 'The Fragrance of the Rose', by the eighth-century Arab philosopher and theologian Muhammad Sukaikir of Damascus, refers to one al-Ajami from Halab, who "plays chess without looking at the board, and even composes verses at the same time". And it would appear that he played on no less than 10 boards at once! In Europe, it is only in 1266 – that is 550 years later! – that we find a mention of "the Saracen Buzecca, playing against Italy's three best chessplayers simultaneously, without sight of two of the boards". This kind of play is sure to have made a powerful impact on the imagination of people at the time. When, after a further six centuries (!), the great Paul Morphy gave a simultaneous blindfold display on 8 boards in Birmingham (this too was in the presence of the entire chess *beau monde*) and scored +6 -1 =1, his record was considered to be positively out of this world: "Morphy is above Caesar, for he came and conquered without seeing!"

Those earliest 'blindfold' games of our predecessors have passed into oblivion, but since Philidor's time, some though not all of them have been preserved.

Brühl – Philidor
London (year unknown)
(notes by Neishtadt)

1 e4 ♘h6 2 d4 ♘f7
There is no cause for astonishment. Black was not only playing without looking at the board, he was giving his opponent *odds of the f7-pawn* too.
3 ♗c4 e6 4 ♗b3 d5 5 e5 c5 6 c3 ♘c6 7 f4 ♛b6 8 ♘f3 ♗e7 9 ♗c2 ♗d7 10 b3 cxd4 11 cxd4 ♗b4+ 12 ♔f2 g5!
Immediately exploiting the fact that the white king has incautiously placed itself on the same diagonal

as the black queen, Philidor breaks up his opponent's pawn chain. At this point the least of the evils would be 13 g3 g4, when Black wins the d4-pawn to secure material equality. However, the brilliant Frenchman's opponents were still quite largely incapable of thinking on such lines. White's reply allows Black to open up the f-file for his attack.
13 ♗e3 gxf4 14 ♗xf4 ♖f8 15 ♗e3 h6 16 h4 (forestalling 16...♘g5) **16...0-0-0 17 a3 ♗e7 18 ♛d3 ♖g8 19 ♘bd2 ♖df8 20 ♛c3 ♔b8**
Philidor declines to win a pawn at once, as he probably doesn't want to simplify. However, after 20...♘fxe5 21 dxe5 d4 22 ♗xd4 ♛xd4+ 23 ♛xd4 ♘xd4, Black could work up a strong attack even without queens: 24 ♗d3 ♗c5 25 ♔f1 ♗c6, and White has no way of defending f3; thus 26 ♖h3 loses to multiple exchanges on f3 followed by a check on g1. The attempt to block the dangerous diagonal by 24 ♗e4 doesn't help either; Black still continues 24...♗c5, and if 25 ♔f1 then 25...♗b5+ and wins.
21 ♖h3 ♘fxe5 22 dxe5 d4

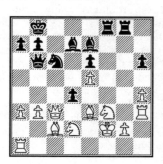

23 ♘c4

Philidor evidently played the preliminary king move to b8 so as to answer 23 ♗xd4 not with 23...♛xd4+ but with 23...♞xd4. Then how could White defend against the discovered check?

(a) 24 ♔f1 would be met by 24...♗b5+ 25 ♞c4 ♞xf3 26 ♖xf3 (or 26 gxf3 ♖g1+ 27 ♔e2 ♖g2+ and wins) 26...♖xf3+ 27 gxf3 (or 27 ♛xf3 ♖f8) 27...♖g1+ 28 ♔e2 ♖g2+, forcing resignation.

(b) White would therefore have to reply 24 ♞c4. It would be hard to claim that Philidor, playing blindfold, had precisely calculated all the possible variations in such a complicated position. The important thing, however, is that his intuition didn't fail him. Thus, the calm retreat 24...♛c7 would maintain Black's winning attack. The knight can't be taken because of 25...♗c5, and on top of everything else Black threatens 25...b5.

23...dxe3+ 24 ♞xe3 ♗c5 25 b4

Black would keep up a fearsome attack after 25 ♖e1 ♗d4. Now the game comes to an end.

25...♗xe3+ 26 ♛xe3 ♖xg2+ 27 ♔xg2 ♛xe3

In the old days they didn't like to resign, and White carried on playing without his queen. Philidor delivered mate on the 33rd move **(0-1)**.

In the following strictly positional encounter, Black stakes everything on a superior, and later winning, endgame. This treatment would be endorsed by leading masters in our own day.

Brühl – Philidor
Blindfold display on 3 boards,
London 1783
Bishop's Opening [C23]

1 e4 e5 2 ♗c4 c6 3 ♛e2 d6 4 c3 f5 5 d3 ♞f6 6 exf5 ♗xf5 7 d4 e4 8 ♗g5 d5 9 ♗b3 ♗d6 10 ♞d2 ♞bd7 11 h3 h6 12 ♗e3 ♛e7 13 f4 h5 14 c4 a6 15 cxd5 cxd5 16 ♛f2 0-0 17 ♞e2 b5 18 0-0 ♞b6 19 ♞g3 g6 20 ♖ac1 ♞c4 21 ♞xf5 gxf5 22 ♛g3+ ♛g7 23 ♛xg7+ ♔xg7 24 ♗xc4 bxc4 25 g3

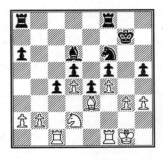

25...♖ab8 26 b3 ♗a3 27 ♖c2 cxb3 28 axb3 ♖bc8 29 ♖xc8 ♖xc8 30 ♖a1 ♗b4 31 ♖xa6 ♖c3 32 ♔f2 ♖d3 33 ♖a2 ♗xd2 34 ♖xd2 ♖xb3 35 ♖c2 h4 36 ♖c7+ ♔g6 37 gxh4 ♞h5 38 ♖d7 ♞xf4 39 ♗xf4 ♖f3+ 40 ♔g2 ♖xf4 41 ♖xd5 ♖f3 42 ♖d8 ♖d3 43 d5 f4 44 d6 ♖d2+ 45 ♔f1 ♔f7 46 h5 e3 47 h6 f3 0-1

A year earlier, incidentally, Diderot had written a letter warning Philidor against blindfold chess: "I was talking to Monsieur de Légal, and he said, 'When I was young I once tried playing a game blindfold. At the end of the game I had such a headache that I never performed any such tricks again.' It is madness to ignore danger out of vanity, and if you dissipate your talent, you are surely not hoping that the English will provide support for your family."

The following game is from Morphy's display already mentioned.

Morphy – Littleton
Birmingham 1858
King's Gambit [C39]

1 e4 e5 2 f4 exf4 3 ♘f3 g5 4 h4 g4 5 ♘e5 d6 6 ♘xg4 ♗e7 7 d4 ♗xh4+ 8 ♘f2 ♗xf2+

Not an obligatory decision; a better choice is 8...♕g5 9 ♕f3 ♗g3 10 ♘c3 ♘f6.

9 ♔xf2 ♘f6 10 ♘c3 ♕e7 11 ♗xf4

White's lead in development is indisputable; his opponent seeks his chances in material gains.

11...♘xe4+? 12 ♘xe4 ♕xe4 13 ♗b5+! ♔f8

There is nothing else; if 13...♔d8, then 14 ♗g5+.

14 ♗h6+ ♔g8 15 ♖h5 ♗f5 16 ♕d2 ♗g6 17 ♖e1 1-0

"It is easier to go diving and bring back pearls than to play like that."

This was the comment on Morphy's exhibition by the player whom Europe unanimously called 'the northern Philidor' – the strongest player in the still enigmatic Russia, Alexander Petrov. It was after another century – a century of striving, cruelty, and a vast increase in knowledge – that a young Hungarian, who was not yet even a master, wrote some lines in an exercise book that were originally addressed only to himself. (He didn't learn chess at all until very late, at the age of 16 – though within a year he was the national junior champion.)

Blindfold play arouses admiration and amazement. And yet the matter's so simple! What does a chessplayer do? He calculates variations many moves ahead, without moving the pieces about. He sees the board and at the same time he doesn't see it, because the end position of a variation is quite unlike its starting position. He moves the pieces in his mind, and not even on a flat surface but in space, sensing their mutual relations as something self-evident. So there is nothing supernatural in the fact that many chessplayers can play blindfold.

Next comes the succession of record-breaking displays that were known to this young man:

In 1878, Johannes Zukertort played 16 opponents without looking at the board. It was not until twenty-five years later that this achievement was surpassed by the American Harry Nelson Pillsbury. On tour in Moscow in 1902, he gave a blindfold display on 22 boards (+17 -1 =4)!

In 1919 Richard Réti took the record to 24 boards. There was one amusing episode. During the display a respectable lady came into the room where Réti was, watched him for a long time, and then exclaimed, "This is a swindle! I can tell perfectly well that his eyesight's in order!"

Some blindfold displays were also given by Alexander Alekhine. *[We shall speak of these shortly.]*

In 1937, the American George Koltanowski added another two boards to Alekhine's record, making it 34.

And finally, in 1947 in Sao Paulo, the Argentine Grandmaster Miguel Najdorf achieved the seemingly impossible: he conducted a blindfold exhibition against 45 opponents!

This account leaves one or two things out, and some points need elaboration. Thus for example on 27 July 1902, Pillsbury gave a display on 21 boards in wholly unique and truly record-breaking circumstances. For one thing, this was a rest day during the great international tournament at Hanover; the next round was on the following day, and Harry was in contention for first place. Secondly, his opponents in the display had the right to consult each other and to move the pieces while analysing. The event lasted nearly twelve

hours – with a short break – and finished with the score of +3 -7 =11.

Pillsbury's next exhibition broke records again – by its exotic and eclectic nature. The Grandmaster played twenty games of chess, six of checkers, and a blindfold game of whist too! How he could succeed in such a triathlon defies comprehension. But he did!

Pillsbury – Blumenfeld
Moscow 1902
French Defence [C00]

1 e4 b6 2 d4 e6 3 ♗d3 ♗b7 4 ♘e2 ♘f6 5 ♘g3 c5 6 c3 cxd4 7 cxd4 ♘c6 8 ♗e3 ♘b4 9 ♘c3 ♘g4 10 ♗b1 ♕h4 11 a3 ♘a6 12 ♕e2 ♗e7 13 ♗d3 ♘c7 14 ♖c1 0-0 15 ♗d2 f5 16 ♘d1 ♖ac8

17 ♔f1 f4 18 ♔g1 ♘xf2 19 ♘xf2 fxg3 20 hxg3 ♕xg3 21 ♖h3 ♕xf2+ 22 ♕xf2 ♖xf2 23 ♔xf2, and the position was adjudicated a win for White (**1-0**).

In 1904 the record fell to Vladimir Ostrogorsky, a first-category player from Moscow who was known only in Russia, and in nothing like all of Russia either. In a tournament on the Baltic, he had shared victory with the future master Bernhard Gregory – who likewise never counted for much, either in Russia or in Germany where he settled after the Revolution. Without in any way wishing to slight the participants in that record-breaking blindfold display on 23 (!) boards, I will venture to recall the famous words from Griboyedov: "A little more in number, a little cheaper in value."

In chess lore, that episode of the perspicacious lady who exposed the 'blind' Grandmaster Réti is sometimes transferred to an exhibition by Alexander Alekhine. (Or were ladies who hung around chess events basically all alike?) Aspiring to a match for the crown, and creating the image of himself as an exceptional player (which he plainly *was*, even without any advertising 'stunts'), the future World Champion followed up the New York tournament of 1924 by breaking the world record with a blindfold exhibition on 26 boards, scoring +16 -5 =5. In this case there were some first-rate contestants: the future Grandmasters Isaac Kashdan, Herman Steiner and Alexander Kevitz.

Later, on 1 February 1925 in Paris, Alekhine did battle with 27 opponents, losing only 3 games and drawing 2.

In Chicago in 1933, by now the World Champion, he raised the record to 32 boards.

Alekhine – Anderson
Scotch Game [C45]

1 e4 e5 2 ⵞf3 ⵞc6 3 d4 exd4 4 ⵞxd4 ⵚc5 5 ⵚe3 ⵞxd4 6 ⵚxd4 ⵚxd4 7 ⵛxd4 ⵛg5 8 ⵞc3 c6 9 h4 ⵛh6 10 g4 ⵛf6 11 e5 ⵛe6 12 0-0-0 ⵞh6 13 ⵚh3 b6 14 g5 ⵞf5 15 ⵛf4 g6 16 ⵞe4 0-0 17 ⵞd6 ⵛxa2 18 ⵚxf5 gxf5 19 h5 ⵚa6 20 g6 ⵛa1+ 21 ⵠd2 ⵛxb2 22 gxh7+ ⵠh8 23 ⵤhg1 c5

Here Alekhine announced mate in 5 moves. Black checked through the variations with full sight of the board, and agreed.
24 ⵤg8+ ⵠxh7
Or 24...ⵤxg8 25 ⵞxf7+ ⵠg7 26 ⵛh6+ ⵠxf7 27 ⵛf6+ ⵠe8 28 hxg8=ⵛ mate.
25 ⵛxf5+ ⵠxg8 26 ⵤg1+ ⵠh8 27 ⵛf6+ ⵠh7 28 ⵛg7 mate

And this was not long after Alekhine had written: "Despite holding the world record, I cannot consider myself an ardent supporter of this form of chess sport. I value blindfold chess merely as a means of propaganda."

On the following day he showed all the games of the display to the Czech Journalist Karel Opočensky!

After that, something occurred to astonish the chess world: the telegraph agencies reported from Saragossa that a completely unknown local player named Juncosa had outdone Alekhine by giving an exhibition on 33 boards, winning 32 games and losing one. Soon, however, the astonishment turned to laughter. It transpired that the crafty Spaniard had announced his exhibition in the newspaper, but only three people turned up for it. He duly beat two of these, while counting the 30 'defaults' as wins for himself!

Still, perhaps there is some point in regarding this as a personal record for Señor Juncosa. After all, playing three games blindfold – that was what Philidor had done nearly a century and a half earlier.

All this was perfectly well known to the young employee of the Budapest fuel resources centre who loved swimming and spoke fluent German, French and Russian. Leafing through that exercise book from earlier years, he said out loud to himself, "*I'm* going to play on *fifty* boards!" Then he cut himself short: "But will I have time?"

Janos Flesch had every reason to be doubtful. Not that he was frightened. During three months in a tumour clinic, you can get used to anything. When the doctors gathered for their consultation, he already knew his sentence. The dark area in his lungs left him with no hope, or 'chances' as he thought to himself in chess language.

He walked through the streets of springtime Budapest. No, he was not thinking about death. Who *does* think about it at the age of twenty-five – even if their illness, according to the doctors, is incurable? Janos was thinking of life. How long did he have? One year, two? Perhaps more, if he was lucky....

At home, Janos sat for ages in front of his desk and looked at his chessboard. Since childhood he had distinguished himself by his imagination and outstanding abilities. He could perform the most complex mathematical calculations in his head, and after becoming keen on chess he liked to play without looking at the board. At twenty-two he became a chess master – a 'promising' one, as journalists added at the time.

Some lines published more than a quarter of a century ago in a Soviet newspaper enable any reader possessing some sympathy to experience the atmosphere of that even earlier time.

He succeeded, although it had taken two long years of preparation. What didn't he work at! Problems of psychology and the higher reactions of the nerves; the history and theory of chess. He trained indefatigably, playing more than a thousand games blindfold. He studied all the details of the record-breaking displays.

Then the day arrived when 52 chess tables were set out in one of the best halls in Budapest, and 52 chessplayers took their places at them. To an outsider it looked like a large but nonetheless conventional simultaneous exhibition. Yet the exhibitor was absent. The 27-year-old Hungarian master Janos Flesch was in a neighbouring room under the strict supervision of the arbiters, and was directing his chess armies through a messenger.

It was Sunday 16 October 1960. The exhibition lasted thirteen and a half hours, with three five-minute breaks. Four hours after the start of play, the messenger couldn't stand the nervous tension and fell down in a faint. But Janos didn't notice how time went by.

"The whole exhibition passed like one moment," he said afterwards.

But everything comes to an end. When the marathon was over the arbiters announced the result, which would have been a record even in a conventional display. Janos had won 31 games, drawn 18 and lost only 3. He had been facing 4 candidate masters, 12 players of the first category and others of the second and third. Flesch had played 40 games with White and 12 with Black.

Here is one of the games.

Flesch – Grumo
King's Gambit [C37]

1 e4 e5 2 f4 exf4 3 ♘f3 g5 4 d4 g4 5 ♗xf4 gxf3 6 ♕xf3 ♕f6 7 ♘c3 ♘e7 8 ♘b5 ♘a6 9 ♗xc7 ♗g7 10 ♘d6+ ♔f8 11 ♕xf6 ♗xf6 12 ♗xa6 bxa6 13 ♖f1 ♘g8 14 e5

Black resigned (**1-0**).

The exhibition was filmed by a Budapest documentary crew and shown in seventy countries. For thirteen and a half hours Janos Flesch became a chessplayer known to the entire world.

"Do you mind telling us, Janos – could you have demonstrated all the games of your record exhibition?"

"For half a year, I could have done. Now after fourteen years, I only remember the best ones."

"Did you use any special system for memorizing the games during play?"

"The only method I followed had to do with the opening stage. With White I began with 1 c4, 1 d4, 1 e4 and 1 ♘f3 (from left to right, in other words), then I repeated the series. Apart from that, I aimed for sharp, combinative variations, and not only because they're individiual and easy to distinguish. I had to get the fight against the weaker opponents over as quickly as I could, or get positions with clear-cut plans against the stronger ones. Otherwise I relied on nothing but my memory. I held all the positions in my head."

"How did you feel during the exhibition?"

"I didn't feel anything; I only thought. I could tell it was all going normally, because the doctors watching me were keeping calm.

"I knew that performances like that were dangerous to your health. But that side of things didn't bother me at the time, although I took all the precautions at the doctors' insistence. Alekhine artificially sustained his nervous system with black coffee during his displays, but he was complaining about his heart for some months afterwards. When Pillsbury was playing blindfold he smoked one cigarette after another. *I* limited my rations to two bars of chocolate, two glasses of lemon juice and three raw eggs.

"There was one other danger, which Grandmaster Miguel Najdorf warned me of. After his display in South America he was laid up for about a month with a spasm of the brain vessels. I avoided that danger by some special exercises.

"Generally speaking everything passed off happily, except that I lost six kilos of weight in one day."

"What happened afterwards?"

"For a long time afterwards I couldn't play 'normal' chess. It was only three years later that our federation took the risk of including me in a big tournament. It was a good start

– I made an IM norm. But even now it's hard for me to get rid of the feeling that I play better without a board than with one."

"Janos, what was it that made you go in for something so dangerous?"

"My illness. When the doctors more or less condemned me to death, I decided I had to do something important and useful. It wasn't just the record I was after. I wanted to prove that the human brain can stand enormous strains and that we only use an insignificant part of its inexhaustible reserves.

"I'm convinced that any chess master can play blindfold on 20 boards at once, given a certain training. But it ought not to be done – the danger is too great. Didn't those great masters of the past, Zukertort and Pillsbury, hasten their end with those exhausting blindfold displays?"

"But how did you manage to recover from your illness?"

"That has remained a mystery. Most of the specialists presume that my lungs had some congenital irregularity which looked like a tumour when X-rayed. But some doctors think it's possible there was a spontaneous healing as a reaction of the organism to the tremendous overstraining."

Two decades after this exhibition, having won a couple of international tournaments and received prizes in some others, Janos Flesch obtained the Grandmaster title. He found time to write some books, but was killed in a car crash just three months after crossing the fifty-year threshold. His record simultaneous blindfold display, which no one so far has surpassed, allowed him to gain a quarter of a century of full and rewarding life.

In the Soviet Union, public blindfold displays were prohibited as early as the 1920s, on the grounds that the health of the 'blind' player could be seriously impaired. I can therefore offer only the fragmentary reminiscences of ex-World Champion Mikhail Tal, who rarely collided with the official barriers openly but always did what he considered necessary.

I must admit I don't have much personal experience in this field. I remember the Kiev film studio where they were shooting *Seven Steps beyond the Horizon*. They decided to include a blindfold chess display in one of the scenes. Unexpectedly (for me!), they invited Mikhail Tal to act the role of the blindfold player! Of course I *had* played blindfold before – when there was no chessboard to hand. This goes way back – a friend and I 'diverted' ourselves that way during college lectures. (Now I can say straight out that it was a *very* bad thing to do!) But one day I happened to give a blindfold display for a perfectly respectable reason. It was in the winter of 1962-3. I was in Moscow Hospital number 52, 'condemned' to undergo an operation. Petrosian and Botvinnik were busy preparing

for their match, but they were kind enough to find the time to visit me. Their visits became known to the hospital inmates and drew attention to me.

I had quite a peaceful night following the operation. In the morning I was woken by a knock at the door. Four figures in medical attire appeared in the ward, and I heard rather a strange greeting: "We're very pleased to see you here, dear Grandmaster! Couldn't you give us a little 'simul'?" The day before, that would have been physically possible, but now...! I couldn't walk, so it was decided I should play blindfold. It was a large room, and my four opponents (fortunately there were no more chess sets around than that!) set themselves up in the far corner. The Grandmaster called out "e2-e4", and play began. The exhibition lasted a full hour and and was cut short by the appearance of the doctor who had finally located his patient and was now inviting him to the operating theatre. The game still going on was adjudicated a loss for my opponent. I had already won the other three.

All the same, four years later when the people in Kiev invited me to give a display for the film, it took me unawares. However, the director F.Sobolev persuaded me. The ten-board blindfold display in the studio was complicated by the business of filming. Round about move six, the cameraman came to the end of his reel. Towards move ten, something happened to the sound. After move fifteen, the lighting technicians' work shift ended. By a gentlemen's agreement I didn't analyse the adjourned games, and the next day the encounter ended satisfactorily.

There is nothing supernatural about blindfold chess; it is all a matter of utilizing the player's professionally trained memory. After all, no one is astonished when a conductor conducts an orchestra without a glance at the score, or a pianist performs a highly complicated piece without looking at the notes. We are used to this, but something similar in chess appears to many people as 'black magic'.

The blindfold exhibitor has the most trouble with the first few moves, when the positions on the various boards are as like as the buildings on a modern housing estate. Later, when each game acquires its own theme, it all becomes a good deal simpler. Chess literature contains quite a large quantity of beautiful combinations created by players without sight of the board. Here is an example from a simultaneous blindfold display given by Alekhine in 1925.

Alekhine – Schwartz

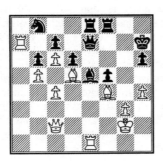

In this position the 'blind' Grandmaster exploited his advantage with the help of a spectacular combination, the idea of which emerges after ten moves:

34 c5! bxc5 35 b6 ♖c8 36 ♕c3! ♖fe8

Clearly 36...♗xc3 37 ♖xe7+ would be hopeless for Black.

37 ♗xe5 dxe5 38 ♕xe5!

Without this possibility the previous move would have been useless.

38...♕xe5 39 ♖xe5 ♖xe5 40 ♖xc7+ ♖xc7 41 bxc7 ♖e8 42 cxb8=♕ ♖xb8 43 ♗e6! (decisive) **43...♔g6 44 c7 ♖f8 45 c8=♕ ♖xc8 46 ♗xc8 c4 47 ♗a6 c3 48 ♗d3 ♔f6 49 ♔f3 ♔e5 50 ♔e3 h5 51 ♗c2 ♔f6 52 ♔f4 ♔g7 53 ♔xf5 ♔h6**

Hoping that White won't 'see' the stalemate resulting from 54 ♔f6.

54 ♔f4 1-0

"I consider this game to be one of my best achievements in blindfold chess." (Alekhine)

To quote Tal again: "The current world record of 52 boards, achieved by the Hungarian Janos Flesch, seems to me frankly abnormal; the burden is just too great. Naturally such a performance is impossible without special training in this specific type of play. And is it necessary? I would point out that blindfold play is also used as one of the forms of training for conventional matches. In particular, before our match in 1965, Boris Spassky conducted a blindfold simul against 8 or 10 players from Sochi, at the insistence of his coach Bondarevsky. I don't remember what the result was, but he won the match against me. All the same, I'm not a fan of blindfold play. Why? Simply because it's pleasanter with a chess set!"

One other blindfold display must be acknowledged as a record, even though it was played on no more than four boards. The point is that it was held under blitz conditions – ten seconds per move, for the blindfold player and his opponents. The former naturally had to make four moves within that time! The American Grandmaster Reuben Fine brought it off! It was in 1945. He inflicted defeat on all his opponents, one of whom was later to hold the Grandmaster title and be a contender for the world crown – Robert Byrne.

Five years later, the same Fine, who had practically given up active participation in chess, nonetheless played a match blindfold against another future Grandmaster! True, his opponent sitting at the board – Herman Pilnik, many times Champion of Argentina, who was soon to gain the highest chess title, the right to play in the Interzonal, then one of the coveted places in the World Championship Candidates Tournament – was victorious in this match, scoring 6½:3½.

In some cases, record status must be accorded not so much to the events as to the players – on account of their age. Thus, Pavel Ponkratov, a schoolboy from Chelyabinsk, started playing several opponents blindfold at the age of twelve! Within two years he had conducted 12 blindfold training sessions and 4 official displays. In the most recent of these, he faced twelve opponents – four men, six boys and two girls. This was in 2002, in Crete. The result was impressive: +6 -0 =6! Here is how Pavel concluded his fight against the 'grown-up' G.Popadopoulos:

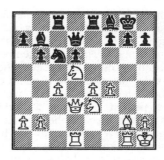

23 ♘f6+! gxf6 24 ♗h3+ 1-0

Then again, there was the American George Koltanowski's performance in 1985. He was still a mere master (the Grandmaster title was only awarded to him 2 years later, 'on the strength of his successes'), but already an ex-President of the US Chess Federation. In the Californian town of Belvedere he conceded only half a point in a blindfold display – against five opponents. A banality not worth the mention? Far from it! The point is that the grey-haired maestro had completed his eighty-second year! "At 28 I was going for the record, but at 82 I'm just exercising my memory," he commented. His 30-board display in 1931 in Amsterdam had indeed been a record; then in Edinburgh in 1937, George had faced 34 opponents without losing a single game.

Prizes and stakes – frivolous and serious

Of all living beings on this earth, man is the only one that gambles – even at times when there would seem to be plenty of other strong emotional stimuli. One gladiator or the other is destined to perish, but the Coliseum audience aren't content to see a sword plunged into his body; they make bets with each other to the tune of hundreds of thousands of sesterces, on whether the *retiarius* (net thrower) will vanquish or be vanquished.

Accordingly, chess, which arose as an instrument of single combat, could not have existed without stakes. The one major difference was that it was the players themselves, in the first place, who had to back up their ambitions with something very substantial. Contrary to a widespread adage, the stake was never higher than life, but history *does* know of cases where chess was played for a prize tantamount to life itself.

Abu-Jafar, a giant of a man, dragged a thick oak plank from below, pushed it between the handrail supports and fastened one end to the deck. The other end quivered above the blue of the sea, about nine yards out from the ship's side.

"This is how we'll play, *M'sieu* Leonardo," he said. "If you win, a hundred gold pieces are yours. If *I* win, you will stroll out to the end of this plank and jump off. There are no sharks here, you will die a peaceful death. Do you agree?"

True, these lines are not from a historical document but from a story by that excellent writer and strong chessplayer Evgeny Zagoriansky. (Muscovites are familiar with his ancestral home of Zagorianka, and I have never met a more 'blue-blooded' person than him.) The story, however, is based on the book by Alessandro Salvio, Doctor of Theology, which appeared in 1604. Moreover, one other legend is considered to be more or less authenticated; it involves Robespierre, virtually most tragic figure of the French Revolution, who regularly visited the famous chess café *La Régence* (its site is now occupied by the offices of a major airline). A short, thin young person approached him and proposed a game under the agreement that the winner would be granted a wish. The Incorruptible (that was Robespierre's sobriquet, remember?) agreed – and lost. Thereupon the young person removed her hat, from under which a cascade of hair tumbled down her back; and no longer disguising her high-pitched girlish voice, she asked Robespierre to spare her fiancé who was condemned to the guillotine. With an unfaltering hand the Incorruptible wrote out a suitable order to the commandant of the Conciergerie prison....

Another example takes us to Cajamarca, the legendary city of the Incas, at the beginning of 1533. Two Spanish conquistadores were bent over a table with a chessboard marked out on it, and pieces fashioned out of clay. Eventually the hand of one of them reached out towards his bishop, but at that moment a quiet voice was heard from among the crowd of onlookers: "No, no, captain, you must move your rook."

The astonished looks of those present turned towards the man who had spoken these words. He stood out from the rest by his attire and the colour of his skin. It was Atahuallpa, the captive Emperor of the Incas. From observing the game of his captors, he had quickly absorbed its rules and mastered its fine points. Captain de Soto followed his advice, and quickly defeated Riquelme – treasurer to the conqueror of Peru, Francisco Pizarro.

There was not long to wait before the loser took revenge, however. A few days later the Consultative Council of 24, in the presence of the King of Spain's representative, decided Atahuallpa's fate. Eleven votes were cast for his release, and twelve for his death. A 'draw' would have transferred the final decision to the King's court in Spain, but ... a thirteenth vote to execute the last Emperor of the Incas was cast by the treasurer Riquelme.

That was long ago. Round about 1970, I went to Kiev to interview Professsor Konstantinov, the deputy Director of the Meteorological Institute, about a game he had played at pistol-point. The story was for the 'Four Knights Club' television programme. It happened in 1944. He was not yet a doctor of physical and mathematical sciences, but merely a 20-year-old lieutenant of engineers and a

prisoner in a German concentration camp. Not a day passed when he was confident of seeing the morrow. Nonetheless he played chess with his comrades in misfortune. Here too (400 years on!), clay pieces were used. Konstantinov was the best player; his sessions with David Bronstein at the Kiev Palace of Pioneers inevitably took effect.

One day an SS officer came into the hut accompanied by some soldiers. He seated himself imperiously at the plank table and signalled to Konstantinov with his finger. "They say you're a good player, don't they? Sit down!" In a highly significant gesture he unfastened the holster of his pistol. "You can take White!"

They didn't play for long. If I remember rightly, it was around move 18 that Konstantinov suddenly saw an uncomplicated but most spectacular three-move combination which won immediately. A constant opponent from those innumerable prison-hut games noticed it too. He whispered, "Don't do it!" However (when Konstantinov recalled and demonstrated all this in front of the cinecamera, his lips resembled two white ribbons trembling in the wind), self-esteem prevailed, together with a wish to get the better of the enemy in a seemingly improbable place. The white rook sacrificed itself. One further blow, and....

In the deathly silence, the SS man slowly stood up. Was he affected by 'operation Bagration' which the Soviets had recently launched in

Belorussia? Did he feel some vestiges of sporting honour?

"Du hast Glück, Mensch" ("You're a lucky fellow"), he growled; then he did up his holster again and went out. The door had hardly shut behind the last soldier when Konstantinov's comrades rushed to embrace him.

All the same, chess has much more often been played for a stake less than life itself. Back in the 10th century, according to an Arabic *mansuba* (this was the the ancient name given to chess problems and endgame positions), a potentate's wife whom her husband had staked on a game cried out at the critical moment: "Give up your rooks, not me!"

She was beautiful, and the potentate had his wits about him. Thus it was that the 'Dilaram mate', named after the wife who had spotted the combination, went down in chess history for all time:

1 ♖h8+ ♔xh8 2 ♗f5+

Don't be astonished; this was the era of *shatranj*, from which modern chess developed. The elephant (the forerunner of the bishop) moved just like this – two squares along the diagonal, with the ability to jump over a piece of either colour.

2...♔g8 3 ♖h8+ ♔xh8 4 g7+ ♔g8 5 ♘h6 mate!

And that was in a position where Black to move could have mated in four different ways!

Later on, money made powerful inroads into life, excluding the romantic from many spheres of human intercourse. For instance, before their return match for the world crown, Lasker and Steinitz paid a deposit of 200 roubles each to the Moscow Chess Club as a guarantee that they would not pull out of the contest. For tournament prizes it became customary to award both the master title to the winner and, naturally, sums of money in the respective national currency.

Unfortunately there was only a slow growth in those official prizes offered by the organizing committees that used chess tournaments to advertise emerging health resorts like San Remo, Bled, Baden-Baden and Kemeri. There were, however, exceptions. Thus, at the start of the 20th century, a German wine and spirits magnate donated a sum of 1500 gold reichsmarks as a prize for one single game. But the game was played with special pieces. They were created by glass-blowing, and contained the most varied forms of liquor; and a captured piece had to be 'drunk up' on the spot!

For this show, they invited the World Champion Emanuel Lasker and an Austrian Grandmaster with a highly interesting style, Carl

Schlechter. The latter's eyes started out of his head when the Chess King began like a tyro: on move two he flung his queen all the way forward, as players do when they are going for the well-known Scholar's Mate.

But the Grandmaster's astonishment was even greater when Lasker answered 2...♘c6 with 3 ♕xf7+??!. Schlechter had some beautiful combinative attacks to his name, but what match was he for Lasker? Lasker the doctor of mathematics, the dramatist and, even more important, the doctor of psychology and world-class card player! At this point, following the rules of this unique game, Lasker drank about 8-10 grams of some liqueur out of the pawn. Schlechter had to drink from the queen, which contained something like 150 grams of the strongest vodka. Within five minutes the respectable, well-mannered Austrian was blind drunk, since food was prohibited by the rules! So even without his queen, by constantly avoiding eating enemy pieces from which he would have to drink, the World Champion brilliantly succeeded in mating the black king!

This curiosity is perhaps the most entertaining page in chess history. In general, over the past hundred years, those who have ventured to devote themselves entirely to the ancient game of the mind have repeatedly ended their lives destitute. Apart from that, some have worked as taxi drivers like Nicolas Rossolimo, or accountants like the famous American Sammy Reshevsky; some have taught in colleges, schools and universities; in our own day they travel the endless round of 'weekend tournaments' where good fortune is always deceptive and inconstant.

For a long time, to be sure, Soviet players were in a category apart. Spuriously registered as PT instructors or sometimes as factory metalworkers, they were paid a moderate allowance by the State Committee for Sport, while the particularly distinguished ones were permitted to buy an automobile without waiting their turn (more of that later), or to set up a *dacha* in a prestigious semi-governmental estate in the environs of Moscow. After winning one of his championship laurel wreaths, Botvinnik was even given a garage not far from his home – which was more *like* a champion's reward!

Putting aside the laughter amidst the tears, the fact remains that the originators of chess theory, the creators of chess beauty and the best players in the world have not felt abundantly secure.

There have been some rare exceptions, however. Thus for example José Raoul Capablanca y Graupera offered to 'defend' his chess crown for a prize fund of 10 thousand dollars, almost a fairytale figure by the standards of the mid-1920s. Without that sum, no claimant to the throne could even think of an audience with His Chess Majesty. "Capa has cut himself off from everyone by a wall of gold," the newspapers wrote at the time, and indeed the stake appeared incredibly high. As often in this life, however, it was a case of "Vengeance is mine; I will repay." When Alexander Alekhine *did* succeed in finding sponsors and wresting the crown, he agreed to give Capablanca a return match – on those same conditions of Capablanca's. The ex-Champion didn't manage to leap over his own golden barrier, and the inexorable march of time started working against him – even though Capa's wins in top-class events roughly a decade later, in the third Moscow tournament and at Nottingham 1936, brought him universal acclaim.

The level of chess prizes was raised in good earnest by Bobby Fischer, the god to whom all chess professionals to this day are prepared to pray. The hope of western chess, who had twice won World Championship Candidates matches by the fantastic, almost mythical score of 6:0, he refused to play his match with Boris Spassky for 125,000 dollars, an enormous sum for those days – so the English banker Slater doubled it in order to save the match! Incidentally the Communist Party Central Committee was seething with indignation that the 'socialist' Spassky had not only lost to the 'capitalist' Fischer but received so much money. Previously, however, the Grandmasters had not been deprived of the 'peanuts' they received as prizes; there was no hard-and-fast law about it; and this ex-World Champion with anti-Soviet sentiments made the best of it, refusing to hand over a single cent.

From then on, there was no way back for the organizers of tournaments and matches. Of course the stakes didn't always run into hundreds of thousands, but sometimes – in World Championship matches – they ran into millions. The prize fund was dramatically increased by the current FIDE President Kirsan Ilyumzhinov, who is also President of Kalmykia; he made a full 5 million available to the participants in the first World Championship under his own knockout system! At first, to be sure, he was counting on sponsors, but none presented themselves, so to keep his word he had to provide everything out of his own pocket. Well, all honour and praise to him. He publicly promised that the next Championship would take place in the following year (1998) with an overall prize fund of 10 million, but this figure was destined to 'shrink' somewhat. At Las Vegas in mid-1999, there were again 100 players (in principle there *cannot* be so many pretenders to the throne; Chess Kings, after all, are 'one-off' products, not articles from a conveyor belt); but only 3 million dollars were at stake – that is, roughly the same sum as in each of the last two top-level matches between Kasparov and Karpov.

On this subject, apart from the official prize money put up by Seville, New York and Lyon (cities extremely keen on holding the matches), I must mention the most original and precious chess prize I have ever seen: a gold and platinum crown, studded with more than a thousand white and black gems. It was created by the world-famous Cartier firm of jewellers, which was founded in the south of France by the Russian Shaposhnikov when he fled from the Bolsheviks. (I am proud to have been able to hold it in my own hands.)

Meteor-like, the crown made its fleeting appearance on the chess horizon. Immediately after the match Garry Kasparov put it in a perfectly ordinary travelling bag, covered over with a tracksuit in case the customs people grew too curious, and took it away from Lyon in France to nearby Geneva in Switzerland. There it was purchased by Kirsan Ilyumzhinov, not yet President of FIDE but already President of Kalmykia. The crown then descended into a bank safe until better days (or, heaven forbid, worse ones), securely protected by the age-old traditions and almost 200-year-long neutrality of Switzerland. The money obtained for it was given by Kasparov to Armenian refugees from his native Baku, when the indestructible amity of the peoples of the Soviet Union revealed itself once more amidst the bright glint of knives and daggers.

The fate of other prizes, notably some with the most exalted origins, is less clear. Thus, Franz Joseph, the Emperor of Austria-Hungary, donated the magnificent sculpture 'Victoria', made of pure silver and weighing 12 kilograms, to the winner of the 1896 Budapest tournament which was dedicated to the 1000-year existence of Hungary. First place, however, was shared – by the young Hungarian Rudolf Charousek and the highly experienced Mikhail Chigorin – and the organizers added a new clause to the regulations, stipulating a match between the two. Chigorin won 3:1, and received ... 2500 crowns. Charousek was given 2000 – while the sculpture remained with the tournament committee.

Afterwards, for nearly 20 years, it adorned the premises of the Budapest Chess Club – but after the First World War, it was lost. I wonder if the present owner of this sculpture knows what it was intended for, and what its history was.

Then there was the prize for the winner of the All-Russian Amateur Tournament, which took place together with the St Petersburg Master Tournament of 1909 (this was an international congress in memory of Chigorin). In the words of the tournament book, "His Imperial Majesty the Sovereign Emperor most graciously consented to donate a luxurious artistic vase (valued at 637 roubles) from the imperial Farfor factory, as a prize awarded in the name of His Imperial Majesty." The price was comparable to that of a herd of 20 cows, in other words not all that high. There is a well-known photograph of the young Alexander Alekhine, with this work of applied art standing next to him. As to what became of it, whether the fragile Farfor vase survived the conflagration of war and revolution – who knows?

Some prizes awarded at the famous St Petersburg 'Tournament of Champions' are similarly lost in the depths of the past. On 9 May 1914, the St Petersburg newspaper *Evening Time* reported: "A most convincing indication of the sympathies aroused by this event was something no one expected: a gift from the jeweller Fabergé to all the competitors, as a memento of the tournament. He donated 11 gold and enamel goblets and bowls, worked in the Russian style. Six of these were presented at once to the non-finalists." The remaining 5 Grandmasters had gone forward to the second stage of the contest. For some reason Doctor Siegbert Tarrasch, who published the tournament book with the organizers' permission, says not one word about these gifts.

The record for unexpectedness and originality can perhaps go to a prize which Garry Kasparov and Anatoly Karpov received from the organizers of the London half of the return World Championship match in 1986. It was for the best game played in those imposing surroundings of the Park Lane Hotel. The English national team, who were just preparing for the forthcoming Olympiad, played the role of judges. Frankly there was not a large choice. The struggle had been bitter and nerve-racking; both players' victories contained obvious mistakes, and anyway the English were clearly averse to giving preference to either one. In the end the prize was awarded for an extremely sharp draw, and each of the two 'Grandmaster K's' was presented on the stage with a little leather bag, mildewed and not pleasant to the touch – but containing golden guineas from the time of Queen Elizabeth I. They had lain in the vaults of the Bank of England for about a century and a half.

An utterly unique 'special prize' was donated by a certain German chessplayer and sent via Lasker to the organizers of a match that was in progress in Berlin between Siegbert Tarrasch and Jacques Mieses. It was in the autumn of 1916. The First World War was dragging on and causing considerable hunger in Germany, engaged in fighting on two fronts. Specifically, town dwellers were each allowed 5 grams (!) of margarine per day on their ration cards. But evidently that generous chess supporter had close links with agriculture or lived in the country himself, and his prize looked entirely fit for a king: it was half a pound of butter! Real butter, all out of the goodness of his heart!

Another 'edible prize' was no less original and of record weight, being 500 times heavier! The powers of sovereign Latvia, for all their verbal tributes to Mikhail Tal, had no wish to preserve his flat in Riga and turn it into a museum. His extremely rich collection of prizes was therefore transported to Moscow. It was there in the centre of the city, in some rooms of the Minsk Hotel, that a chess club named 'The Hussar from Riga' was opened by one of Tal's friends: the Yugoslav Ratko Knezević, a press photographer and a businessman at the same time. The 8th World Champion's trophies were arranged there in specially prepared glass cases. A most impressive blitz tournament was held in Tal's honour, and the winner was literally struck dumb by the prize, which was lifted onto the chess table with great difficulty. It was 100 kilograms of chocolates from Knezević's confectionery business!

We may presume that Grand-master Yuri Balashov's five children were satisfied when their father gained such a tasty success.

Alas, I must repeat that there is nothing new. In West Germany, a prize with exactly the same weight had been awarded to Leonhard Hanke after he won the decisive duel against Professor Rudolf Liebrich in the country's first post-war lightning championship. That's right, it was in 1948 – the country was still in ruins, and although America's Marshall Plan was in operation (the USSR, victorious but so hungry, had proudly refused such 'capitalist' aid!), no scrap of anything came amiss. So Hanke gave a satisfied smile when they showed him his prize – some sacks lying against the wall, containing 100 kilos of potatoes.

Now a small digression: 'provisions' had been offered as prizes to contestants even earlier. Thus for example, the winner of a Hull Chess Club tournament at the end of 1902 received a fattened goose as his prize, while the player coming second received a pineapple! But for one thing it was a handicap event, and secondly it was Christmas time; and a nice pleasant joke – evoking a pleasant, delicate smile, rather than an uproar of laughter – is something the English have always been good at.

Anyway, you will agree that this was better than Max Euwe's worn-out hat which he left behind in a South American chess club, and which was presented periodically as a prize there!

A much more amusing case was the top prize in the super-final of the Moscow speed chess championship (15 minutes per game), held in honour of the 70th birthday of that born-and-bred Muscovite, ex-World Champion Vasily Smyslov. Half the 56 competitors were Grandmasters, and to be honest, this was largely because the winner would have the right (!) to purchase an automobile with his own money. Like it or not, in the USSR cars weren't simply sold, they first had to be *allocated*, which meant that a scrap of paper stamped by the relevant organization was more precious than any other reward.

Anyway, what *would* have to happen was that the top four players finished with equal scores! They were Alexei Dreev and Yuri Razuvaev (Moscow), Rafael Vaganian (Erevan) and Evgeny Sveshnikov (Cheliabinsk). To acquire three more authorization coupons would have been an impossible task, so the advice given to the Grandmasters was obvious: to buy one wheel each! And the rest might as well be scrapped!

Or again they could club together to buy the car and then sell it for a black-market price and split the profit. In short, they could settle the whole matter by arithmetic!

The unexciting and concrete prize for brilliancy in this tournament went to the Odessa player Vladimir Tukmakov for his attack against Ilya Smirin of Minsk.

Tukmakov – Smirin

19 ♗xf7+! ♔xf7 20 ♘g5+ ♔f6
After 20...♔g8 21 ♕b3+ Black is faced with either a smothered mate or huge material losses.
21 ♘xh7+ ♔f7 22 ♕b3+ ♗e6 23 ♘g5+ ♔f6 24 ♘xe6 ♕c6
It emerges that after 24...♖xe6 25 ♕f3+! ♔g5, White has a pretty and unconventional mate with 26 ♗e3.
25 ♘xg7 ♔xg7 26 ♖ac1
And being 'three down', Black resigned **(1-0)**.

As for the most insulting prize, this was probably the one awarded to Aron Nimzowitsch for his superb game against the elder Johner brother (Paul) in the Dresden tournament of 1926. They handed him a case of 5000 excellent cigarettes of the Hilderhof brand. The Grandmaster turned bright red; he not only wasn't a smoker, he couldn't even stand a whiff of tobacco smoke.

As the most curious stake in modern chess practice, we should probably single out the one put up by Señor Luis Rentero for the match he organized between Vladimir Kramnik and Alexei Shirov in 1988. This match was meant to decide who would be Garry Kasparov's opponent in a contest for the title of the world's strongest chessplayer (a peculiar title, arising from the fact that Kasparov had broken with FIDE five years earlier and forfeited the official status of Champion, but remained undefeated and was, in reality, the best). The president of the newly begotten World Chess Union, which existed for about half a year and did nothing apart from arranging this match, solved the problem of the stake by going one further than that clear-cut classical formula, 'winner takes all'. In this case it was the *loser* who would receive everything, or more excactly, his due – while the winner's prize would be carried forward, so to speak, to the deciding match with Kasparov. Kramnik was wise beyond his years and almost in a state of shock at this weird arrangement; he was rightly considered the favourite and had every reason to count on winning the match. He nonetheless deferred to his friend Shirov – formerly from Riga and a pupil of the great Tal, but by now a 'fully qualified'

Spaniard – and duly began the contest.

Then a miracle occurred, which once again emphasized the proverb of not counting your chickens. Vladimir's play didn't come together; he was in a feverish state all the way. Despite that, all he needed to do was conduct the following won position to its logical conclusion....

Kramnik – Shirov
Linares 1998

13 d6!
By this stage White was in a pleasant situation – Shirov had spent more than an hour on the clock, Kramink much less.
13...♘f6
After 13...♖e8, Black would have to reckon with 14 ♘b5.
14 ♗g5
Renewing the threat of g2-g4.
14...♖e8
One plausible move was 14...♗e6!?, allowing the threat. However, up to this point Kramnik had been playing very quickly and confidently, and Shirov evidently wanted to take the game out of home analysis, whatever the means. Perhaps the reason for refraining from 14...♗e6 was not actually 15 g4, which the Spanish Grandmaster

may not have considered dangerous, but the manoeuvre 15 ♘h3. Then in order to prevent the consolidating move 16 ♘f2, Black would want to play 15...♗xh3, but that would involve a loss of tempo.
15 ♖d1!? ♗e6
If 15...♖e6, then 16 ♘h3 again proves unpleasant for Black. After 16...♗f8 17 ♘f2, he doesn't succeed in winning the pawn: 17...♖xd6 18 ♗xf6! ♕xf6 19 ♘fe4.
16 ♘h3 ♘c4
Not a fully justified decision. In the light of what follows, the preliminary 16...♖c8 was essential.
17 ♗xc4 ♗xc4 18 b3 ♗a6?!
Although White would be distinctly better after 18...♗e6 19 ♘f2, Black would still be fairly safe from any imminent advance of the d-pawn.

Now was Kramnik's last chance to level the score in the match. But one of the basic symptoms of bad form is a lack of discipline in analysis. So it was here. Kramnik started by studying the consequences of the move that looks most promising, 19 d7, and quickly concluded that it would give him a definite but not wholly decisive plus after 19...♕xd7 20 ♕xd7 ♘xd7 21 ♖xd7 e4 22 ♘xe4? f5. He immediately set about analysing other lines, but after (e.g.) 19 ♘f2 ♕d7 20 ♗xf6 ♗xf6 21 ♘d5 ♗d8 22 ♘e4 ♔g7 White has nothing. To his misfortune, Vladimir forgot to come back to 19 d7 at the end of it all. On a second examination he would easily have ascertained that against 21...e4 he could practically win by 22 ♘d5, as 22...exf3+ can be answered by either 23 ♔f2 or 23 ♘e7+. On 19 d7 Black would probably have to settle for the forlorn 19...♖f8; then after 20 ♘f2 White would have a huge advantage.

The move White chose was the result of his contradictory and inconsistent calculations:

19 ♘d5?

The stunning refutation was not long coming.

19...e4!!

Sacrificing a rook, Black unleashes a spectacular and irresistible attack.

20 ♘xf6+

Or 20 d7 exf3+! 21 dxe8=♕+ ♕xe8+ 22 ♕e3 ♘xd5 23 ♖xd5 ♕c6! 24 ♖d8+ ♖xd8 25 ♗xd8 ♕c2 26 ♕e8+ ♗f8, and again Black wins in all variations, as you can easily verify.

20...♗xf6   21   d7   ♕b6!! (beautiful!) **22 dxe8=♕+ ♖xe8 23 ♕e3**

Of course, 23 f4 loses even more quickly to 23...e3! followed by a diagonal check. Nor does 23 ♕f2 help, in view of 23...exf3+ 24 ♔d2 ♕xf2+ (or 24...♕b4+ 25 ♔c1 ♕c3+ 26 ♕c2 ♕a1+ 27 ♕b1 ♖c8+) 25 ♘xf2 ♖e2+.

23...♗xg5   24   ♕xb6   ♗xh4+ 25 ♔d2 axb6 26 fxe4 ♖xe4

You cannot hold out in positions like this.

27 ♔c2 ♖g4 28 ♖d2 ♗e7 29 ♖g1 ♔g7 30 ♘f2 ♖f4 31 ♘d3 ♖e4 32 ♖gd1 ♗b5 33 a4 ♗c6 34 ♖e1 ♖xe1 35 ♘xe1 ♗b4 (winning another pawn; the dénouement is near) **36 ♖e2 ♗xe1 37 ♖xe1 ♗xg2 38 ♔d2 h4 39 ♔e3 ♗d5 40 b4 h3 41 ♖e2 f5 42 ♖d2 ♗e4 43 ♔f4 ♗g2 44 ♖d7+ ♔f6 45 ♖h7 g5+ 46 ♔g3 f4+ 47 ♔g4 ♔e5 48 b5,** and White resigned without waiting for the reply **(0-1)**.

The result was that the match was lost, but the smaller portion of the prize fund was 'won' (though not in full; Señor Rentero couldn't resist the temptation to keep a bit of it back). As for the Kasparov-Shirov match, it was of interest to no one in the world, not even the authorities in the Spanish province of Andalusia who had virtually promised to arrange it. So it didn't take place, and in a word, the loser took all! All that was going, anyway.

One other novel prize – a chess knight mounted on a billiard ball, all in white jade – remained unawarded after an even more novel match between two World Champions: José Raoul Capablanca and Erich Hagenlohen. They met in Monte Carlo in September 1922. The Chess King had arrived from London where one week previously he had taken first prize in the very strong tournament, with the brilliant undefeated score of 13 out of 15. Alekhine had finished a point and a half behind; then came Vidmar, Rubinstein, Bogoljubow, Réti, Tartakower, Maroczy.... The King of Billiards had completed his customary professional tour. And each 'king' felt fairly at home within the other's 'realm'.

The proprietor of the hotel where these celebrities were staying was keen to make use of the occasion, and at a banquet held in their honour he stepped into the role of 'matchmaker'. The result was that on the following day, a 'billiards and chess summit match' began – in its way, an event for the record books. The first round saw the 'kings' with cue in hand; the winner would be the first to score 100 points, with José Raoul having 75 points' start and the privilege of playing first.

'Capa' had a good deal of success: he potted the balls for 19 points, taking his total to 94. Unfortunately Hagenlohen scored 23 with his 'opening move', then continued without a falter to collect his century without giving Capablanca another chance to play.

Then the time came for the chess battle, in which the Billiards King in his turn received odds – of queen's rook.

Capablanca – Hagenlohen

1 e4 e5 2 ♘c3 ♝c5 3 f4 exf4 4 d4 ♝b4 5 ♝xf4 ♝xc3+

Not the strongest, but then any exchanges are favourable to Black.

6 bxc3 d5 7 e5 ♝e6 8 ♝d3 ♘e7 9 ♝g5 h6 10 ♝h4 0-0

By preparing queenside castling with 10...♛d7, Black could have ensured his king a less troubled reign.

11 ♛h5

After 11 ♘f3 ♝g4, one more white piece would be exchanged off.

11...c6 12 ♘f3 ♛d7 13 h3 ♘f5 14 g4! g6?

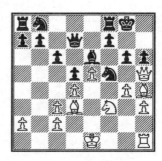

Black is enticed by the opportunity to trap the white queen, but....

15 gxf5!! gxh5 16 ♖g1+ ♚h8 17 ♝f6+ ♚h7 18 fxe6 mate

So the match score was 1:1, and the statuette remained in the hotel owner's possession. He didn't manage to bring the two kings together for a second match.

Hunting down the prizewinners

Suppose that by your own efforts or by the will of Caissa you have gained admittance to a tournament where, on an objective assessment of the strength of the opposition, you can scarcely count on victory or a high placing. What can you do to make the event memorable, both to yourself and to the admirers of your talent? The answer couldn't be simpler: either play the most brilliant game of the tournament, or else try to gun down the players who are going to win the prizes (more exactly, those who are most likely to).

Such things have occurrerd quite a few times, and it is possible to look for the record-holders in this form of hunting.

First, though, a reservation. We are not talking about the third or fourth prize winner outplaying the two or even three rivals who come above him in the tournament table; chess history knows plenty of such cases. Suffice it to recall, say, the 1925 USSR Championship, in which the master Boris Verlinsky most convincingly crushed all three players who finished ahead of him; they were 'only' Efim Bogoljubow, Grigory Levenfish and Ilya Rabinovich. Or Zagreb 1965, where Lajos Portisch did the same thing.

Nor are we talking about famous Grandmasters playing below par but showing their strength against none other than the tournament prizewinners. That, for instance, was how one of the Soviet Union's strongest women players, the future World Champion Liudmila Rudenko, performed in two events: the national championships of 1946/47 and 1951. Or take the tournaments at Mar del Plata 1982 and London 1984, where after 'settling down' in the very middle of the tournament table, Bent Larsen and Viktor Korchnoi used their claws against the winners. Or the 1973 Women's Interzonal on the island of Menorca, where one of the favourites, the Romanian Grandmaster Elizabeta Polihroniade, did very badly overall but beat Valentina Kozlovskaia, the first prize winner; while from her games against the players who shared second prize, she scored three

draws and a win against Nana Alexandria.

No – we are talking about results that were unpredictable in the highest degree.

As the first such case, we will take the Mikhail Chigorin Memorial at St Petersburg in 1909. There on 28 February, at the festive banquet that concluded the tournament, a special prize from the St Petersburg Chess Association, amounting to 25 roubles, was presented by Prince Peter Demidov to Fyodor Duz-Khotimirsky "for his wholly exceptional result against the first two prizewinners". Fyodor's overall performance, in the main international tournament, had been just middling; after 6 rounds he had 1½ points, after 11 rounds he had 3. He finished in 13th place with 8 out of 19. And yet – first Akiba Rubinstein and then the World Champion Emanuel Lasker, who shared first and second prizes, laid down their arms to him.

Duz-Khotimirsky – Lasker
(notes from the 1909 tournament book)

After losing two tempi in the opening by the excursion ♕d8-a5-

d8, Black has ended up in a position without obvious weaknesses but very cramped and passive.

20 ♘xd7!

Securing the two bishops, White reveals the correct approach to the position. He thereby consolidates his advantage in the long term.

20...♕xd7 21 h3 ♖ac8 22 ♕e2 ♖c7 23 f5 ♘h7 24 e5

Now 24...♘g5 will be met by 25 f6.

24...exf5 25 ♗xf5 ♕d8 26 ♖d1 g6 27 ♗c2 ♕c8 28 ♗b3 ♖c1 29 ♔h2 ♘g5 30 ♖fd3 ♖xd1 31 ♖xd1 ♗d8 32 h4 ♘e6

If 32...♘h7, then 33 e6.

33 d5 ♘f4 34 ♕e4 ♕g4

An attempt to swindle the opponent, since Black's position cannot be held without counterplay; White's two bishops and passed pawn are too powerful.

35 g3 ♗xh4 36 gxh4 ♖c8 37 ♖d3

The only defence, but a perfectly adequate one, against the threatened ♖c8-c3.

37...♖c1 38 ♕f3 ♕f5 39 ♖d4 g5 40 e6 ♕e5 41 ♖e4 ♕d6 42 e7 1-0

This record for 'hunting skill' lasted quite a long time – until the first post-war tournament (*two* world wars had come and gone) at Groningen in 1946.

This was a gathering of very strong chessplayers headed by ex-World Champion Max Euwe; the other Chess Kings up until then had all departed this life. It was, furthermore, the first international tournament for three of the five Soviet participants. Objectively, Alexander Kotov counted as the least experienced of them and, if I may say so, the least strong. Among

his 'superiors' were not only Euwe but the US Champion Arnold Denker, Miguel Najdorf who was already a seasoned warrior, and the strong Hungarian player Laszlo Szabo. The prognosis was borne out: Kotov was outdistanced by all of them, scoring only about half the possible points. But of these 9½, three were scored against the first four finishers. Kotov defeated both the tournament winner Mikhail Botvinnik and the second prize winner Max Euwe, while drawing with Vasily Smyslov and Miguel Najdorf. His record in hunting the top players had proved excellent.

Botvinnik – Kotov

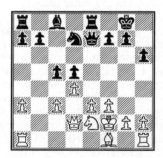

14 ♘f4?

This seeming gain of tempo is ineffective; the right move is 14 ♘g3. As the game goes, the knight is insecurely placed and doesn't defend the king.

14...♘f6 15 ♗d3 ♗d7 16 h3?

The leader of the tournament – and of Soviet chess – has plainly lost the thread of the game. At this point 16 ♖he1 was obligatory; White would answer 16...b6 with 17 ♘e2!, heading for g3 and preparing e3-e4.

16...♕d6 17 ♖hb1

Thinking of activity on the queenside if nowhere else.
17...b6 18 ♗f1 ♖e7 19 a4
White can't bring his knight to e5 by 19 ♘d3, in view of 19...♗f5, when 19 ♖e1 is simply essential.
19...♖ae8 20 ♖e1 c4!
The white knight is deprived of the d3-square; material losses are inevitable and the game cannot be saved.
21 g4 g5 22 ♘e2
On 22 ♘g2, Black plays 22...♕h2 23 ♗e2 ♖xe3!.
22...♖xe3 23 ♘g3
This allows the concluding stroke, but what else can White do? After 23 ♘g1 ♘e4+! he will lose his queen or be mated by the black queen on g3. On 23 ♕xe3, Black wins by 23...♕h2+ 24 ♗g2 ♖xe3 25 ♔xe3 ♕xg2 26 ♖h1 ♘e4! 27 fxe4 ♕xe4+.
23...♕xg3+! 24 ♔xg3 ♘e4+ 0-1

It is true that if we are looking for the best result against the prizewinners by a non-prizewinner, this honour is shared by two contestants other than Kotov, since he himself (finishing 10th-12th) 'latched on to' the last prize. On the other hand, he and Smyslov did receive special medals for beating the ex-World Champion.

Well, was the record for hunting the prizewinners established? Yes and no. Kotov did after all hold the title of Soviet Grandmaster; but in some tournaments which shortly followed, it was ordinary masters who created the sensations. In the All-Russian Chigorin Memorial Tournament in 1951, the Leningrader Konstantin Klaman, an officer in the fire service, drew with the tournament winner, the formidable Vasily Smyslov, and inflicted defeat on the players who shared 2nd-3rd places: Lev Aronin, the silver medallist from the USSR Championship, and Mark Taimanov who within a year was to be a candidate for the chess throne. And yet against the other 10 participants in the final, Klaman scored a mere 2½ points!

Moreover, seeing that four years earlier Klaman had brought up the rear in the USSR Championship despite beating the gold and bronze medallists Keres and Bondarevsky, the record as a 'hunter' is perhaps his. Still, the final choice in these matters is up to the individual – because in more than a thousand tournament tables I have studied, some other similar surprises may be found.

Thus, for instance, an immense impact was made by the sensational victories of the master Nikolai Kopylov, a graduate in technical sciences, in the 1951 USSR Championship. With Black in the first round, he defeated Tigran Petrosian – who went on to take second prize, and within a year would be a Grandmaster and a candidate for the world crown. In round two, Kopylov beat the eventual Championship winner, Grandmaster Paul Keres. Next, the World Champion Botvinnik succumbed too! After that, who remembered that the Leningrad engineer finished a modest eleventh? His wins were acknowledged with a special prize. Subsequently, owing to major work commitments, Kopylov switched mainly to correspondence chess, but still remained true to his style.

Petrosian – Kopylov
Moscow 1951
(notes from the tournament book)

Everything up to here has followed the 5th Botvinnik-Bronstein game from the recent World Championship match.
13 ♖e1 f4!
The exchange sacrifice is not correct, but leads to great complications.
14 ♗xf4 ♖xf4 15 gxf4 ♕xf4 16 d5 exd5 17 ♖xe7
Better 17 cxd5, threatening 18 ♖e4. With the move played, White gives his opponent an opportunity to develop his queen's knight with tempo and quickly bring his queen's rook across to attack the king.
17...♘c6 18 ♖e1 ♖f8 19 ♗e4!
A very difficult move to find over-the-board; you might call it a problem-move. White now repulses Black's attack.
19...dxe4 20 ♕d5+ ♔h8 21 ♕xe4 ♕f6!
Ingeniously sidestepping a queen exchange.
22 ♕xg4 ♘d8 23 ♕g3 ♗xf3 24 ♖ac1 ♘e6 25 ♘c3 ♘d4 26 ♖e3 ♗c6 27 ♘d5 ♕f7 28 ♖ce1 b5!

White had left this tactical stroke out of account.
29 ♖e7 ♕g8 30 ♔f1 bxc4 31 ♘e3 c3 32 ♖c1 c2
In time trouble Black misses his chance to win the exchange back by 32...♗b5+ 33 ♔e1 ♘e2.
33 ♘xc2? (the decisive mistake)
33...♕c4+ 34 ♔e1
If 34 ♔g1, then 34...♘f5 35 ♕g5 ♘xe7, and Black wins thanks to the defenceless position of the white king.
34...♘f3+
White lost on time **(0-1)**.

Eleven years later, International Master Vladas Mikenas made his return to the USSR Championship. Although his reminiscences included a win against the great Alekhine a quarter of a century earlier, the veteran was well past his prime as a chessplayer. Nonetheless his score line in the tournament table begins with victories against the gold and silver medallists, who on this occasion were Viktor Korchnoi and Mikhail Tal. The Leningrader was young enough to be Vladas's son, while the new ex-World Champion might have been his grandson – just.

Then in the international tournament at Rovinj-Zagreb in 1970, the results of Vladimir Kovacević created a tremendous stir. Though still only a master at the time, the future Grandmaster was not all that young (he was 28). No supernatural feats where expected of him, and yet they occurrred. With a respectable 50-per-cent score, he was one of a group of contestants who headed the lower half of the tournament table. Unlike the rest of them, however, he had avoided losing to the titans Smyslov and Gligorić who shared second prize, and sensationally defeated the tournament winner Bobby Fischer – who was heading towards the chess throne by leaps and bounds.

Fischer – Kovacevié
French Defence [C15]
(notes from *Chess*)

1 e4 e6 2 d4 d5 3 ♘c3 ♗b4 4 a3
This variation had hardly been played for some 20 years.
4...♗xc3+ 5 bxc3 dxe4 6 ♕g4 ♘f6 7 ♕xg7 ♖g8 8 ♕h6 ♘bd7
Fischer-Uhlmann in an earlier round went 8...♖g6 9 ♕e3 ♘c6 10 ♗b2, and Black eventually got into difficulties after 10...♕d6; however, he gets a good game after 10...♘e7 or even 10...e5.
The other major alternative at this juncture is 8...c5. The text move has not been played enough to allow a definite evaluation.
9 ♘e2 b6 10 ♗g5 ♕e7 11 ♕h4 ♗b7 12 ♘g3 h6! 13 ♗d2
If 13 ♕xh6? then 13...♘g4! and White loses a piece after 14 ♗xe7 ♘xh6 15 ♗h4 ♖g4 or 15 ♗b4 a5.
13...0-0-0 14 ♗e2 ♘f8 15 0-0 ♘g6 16 ♕xh6!?
This move may well be a blunder – at any rate it allows Black a dangerous attack – but 16 ♕h3 also leaves White in a defensive position: this at least provides some material solace!
16...♖h8 17 ♕g5 ♖dg8 18 f3

Hoping for 18...♘h4 19 fxe4! ♖xg4 20 ♗xg5, and all of a sudden White is forcing events.
18...e3!

19 ♗xe3
19 ♕xe3 loses quickly after 19...♘d5 20 ♕g5 (or 20 ♕f2 ♕h4 21 h3 ♘gf4) 20...f6 etc.
19...♘f8 20 ♕b5 ♘d5 21 ♔f2
The best defence: 21 ♗f2 (21 ♗d2 is even worse) 21... c6 22 ♕b3 ♕h4 wins quite straightforwardly.
21...a6! 22 ♕d3 ♖xh2 23 ♖h1 ♕h4 24 ♖xh2 ♕xh2 25 ♘f1 ♖xg2+ 26 ♔e1 ♕h4+ 27 ♔d2 ♘g6! 28 ♖e1 ♘gf4 29 ♗xf4 ♘xf4 30 ♕e3 ♖f2!

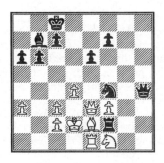

White resigns; he has no counter to 31...♘xe2, winning a piece **(0-1)**.

Among the women there have also been some contenders for the record. For example, the tournament tables of two successive USSR Championships had a rather unusual appearance. In 1971 a little-known first-category player from the Ukraine, Irina Spivak, whose appearance in the final was considered a freak and who duly finished in one of the last places, nonetheless defeated the first and second prize winners and avoided defeat against the third; these were, respectively, the future Grand-masters I.Levitina, M.Litinskaia and M.Ranniku. The following year Tatiana Belova, a first-category player from the Leningrad district, went one better: she literally crushed the champion Litinskaia as well as those who shared the silver medals: Levitina, V.Kozlovskaia and International Master O.Andreeva.

The list of claimants to the record in this sphere may be fittingly concluded with the name of Ludek Pachman. You could certainly not say he was little-known. He became a Grandmaster shortly after that international title was instituted; he won the championship of Czechoslovakia, a major chess-playing country, seven times running; and he ranked among the most prominent theoreticians. But when his country rebelled against regimented socialism and Soviet tanks suppressed the 'velvet revolution' in Prague, Pachman became one of the leaders of the freedom movement. He subsequently spent some years in prison, then emigrated. Chess of course remained the chief affair of his life, but even as a theorist he had fallen behind; the years passed, and his energy waned. When, therefore, at the Geneva tournament in 1977, the 53-year-old veteran suddenly crushed the first and second prize winners Bent Larsen and Ulf Andersson, without even losing a single game against the other players in the top half of the table – this was worth a great deal!

Terrible vengeance

In the rich history of humanity, the feeling for revenge has sometimes played a fateful role, leading to wars, changes of ruling dynasties and even the repartition of the world. And since chess is known to be an image of life, this scarcely noblest of human inclinations has constantly found embodiment in chess too – and still does!

The category of small-scale vengeance includes, for instance, the final session of the game Reshevsky-Geller from the 1953 Candidates Tournament in Switzerland. The game had been adjourned in a rook ending with two extra pawns for White, and Geller related afterwards that "on the day before resumption, Reshevsky even inquired whether I was going to resign without playing on. On entering the tournament hall he made much show of ordering a cup of coffee and beginning to stir it, clinking with his spoon as he did so."

However, a mere 12 moves after resumption, the following position was reached:

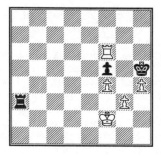

53...♖f3+!
"The bomb explodes. By taking the rook, either now or after 54 ♔g2 ♖xg3+, White would be giving stalemate! I admit that at this point I indulged in little a piece of revenge which has been pointedly described in chess literature. While a stunned Reshevsky was looking at the board, I ordered a glass of tea and began stirring the sugar just as thoroughly as he had done earlier." (Geller)

54 ♔e2 ♖xg3 55 ♖xf5+ ♔xh4
Now everything is clear. Both kings are cut off from the pawn, and if it advances independently, this will lead to full material equality. On the 60th move the players agreed a draw (½-½).

Revenge in chess on a *large* scale, reflected in a tournament table and clearly bidding for record status, had occurred much earlier, in Hamburg in 1910. When the list of names was assembled for the international tournament there, the venerable world-class master Siegbert Tarrasch protested with uncommon virulence, both orally and in print, against including the small, slim young Englishman Frederick Dewhurst Yates among the competitors. Generally speaking, Doctor Tarrasch did have some reasons on his side. It was only a year since Yates had entered the international arena; he had yet to become the strongest master in his island country; his two sensational victories against the great Alekhine were still in the distant future. In principle, the Hamburg tournament fully upheld Tarrasch's judgement. After being admitted after all, Yates won only one game and finished last. But that win was scored against Tarrasch. And with Black, too! And with what an attack! I may add that it cost the haughty doctor three places in the tournament table.

Tarrasch – Yates
Tarrasch Defence [D32]

1 d4 d5 2 ♘f3 ♘f6 3 c4 e6 4 e3 ♗e7 5 ♘c3 c5 6 ♗d3 ♘c6 7 0-0 0-0 8 b3 b6 9 ♗b2 ♗b7 10 ♖c1 ♖c8 11 cxd5 ♘xd5
Forced, because if 11...exd5 then 12 ♗f5 is unpleasant.

12 ♘e2
It was worth considering 12 dxc5! ♘xc3 (or 12...♗xc5 13 ♘e4 ♗e7 14 ♗b1!) 13 ♗xc3 ♗xc5 14 ♕e2.

12...cxd4 13 ♘exd4 ♘xd4 14 ♘xd4 ♖xc1 15 ♕xc1 ♗d6 16 ♘f3 ♕e7 17 ♕a1
Perhaps too artificial. A more active move was 17 ♕c4!?, to switch the queen to the kingside.

17...f6 18 ♘d4 f5
The initiative has clearly passed to Black.

19 ♖c1?
Does a rook always have to occupy an open file? There are exceptions to every rule!

19...♘xe3! 20 fxe3 ♕g5 21 ♔f2
Not so much defending the pawn on e3 as running from the burning house. After 21 ♗f1 ♕xe3+ 22 ♔h1 ♕f4 23 ♔g1 ♕xh2+ 24 ♔f2 ♕h4+, White could resign.
21...♕xg2+ 22 ♔e1 ♗xh2
Played not for material gain but to acquire the g3-square!
23 ♗e2 e5
An even quicker way was 23...f4! 24 e4 (or 24 exf4 ♗xf4 25 ♖c2 ♗e3, and mates) 24...♕g1+ 25 ♔d2 ♕e3+ 26 ♔d1 f3 27 ♘xf3 ♖xf3 28 ♖c3 ♕g1+.
24 ♘e6 ♗g3+ 25 ♔d1 ♗f3!
26 ♗xf3 ♕xf3+ 27 ♔c2 ♕e4+
28 ♔d2 ♕d5+ 29 ♘d4 exd4
30 ♗xd4 f4 31 e4 ♕xe4 32 ♖c4
♖d8 33 a4 ♗f2 0-1

The bitter taste of victory

This phrase is in the nature of an oxymoron, and yet such things do exist; the bitter taste of victory is familiar to many people, and perhaps to no one more than to Grandmaster Miguel Najdorf who carried it with him throughout his long life.

Following his 80-year jubilee which literally all the world's chessplayers had cause to celebrate, the witty and benign 'Don Miguel'

with his boundless love of chess was greeted everywhere with sincere delight. In one of his interviews Najdorf was asked about his most memorable games. He mentioned his wins against Mikhail Botvinnik in the first major post-war tournament at Groningen in 1946 and against Bobby Fischer at Santa Monica precisely 20 years later. He then singled out one other game, a practically unknown one, against a player who himself is unknown today.

"The game as such isn't interesting," Najdorf said. "I just remember it for its human consequences. At the beginning of 1939 Poland's strongest players took part in a tournament in Warsaw to decide who would be included in the national team for the coming Olympiad in Buenos Aires. Towards the end, two players were competing for the last vacant place: Teodor Regedzinski who was of Polish stock, and my close friend Isaak Appel, a talented master who was Jewish. You will see in a moment why I mention their ethnic origins. In the last round Appel had to play me, and only a win would guarantee him a place in the team and a voyage to Argentina. But the game was a fair fight, and I'm afraid I won. I say 'I'm afraid', because to this day I bitterly regret that win. Regedzinski got into the team and Appel stayed at home. During the Olympiad, as you know, Hitler invaded Poland, the Second World War began, and a good many chessplayers – Jews first and foremost – stayed on in Argentina. The Nazis drove Appel into the ghetto, where he perished. If he had been playing in the team and Regedzinski had stayed in Poland, I'm convinced that *he* would have stood a much better chance of surviving."

It would hardly be possible to find anything else to set beside these reminiscences reaching back 50 years.

Was that, then, the record for a bitter victory? Or does it have a rival in the death of Ibarek Ruy, which occurred at the chessboard? This chess enthusiast and veteran of the Moroccan army was married 12 times (a record?) and naturally possessed a numerous progeny. It was with his youngest son, who was already past 80, that Ruy the elder played that tragic game – during which the successor incautiously pointed out an attractive possibility that his progenitor had missed. Out of vexation, the latter expired on the spot – at the age of 148 years...

Fortunately, scenarios on similar lines don't always end so tragically. On the contrary – take one of the Championships of Australia at the beginning of the 1960s. The tournament leader was Cecil John Seddon Purdy, twice Champion of New Zealand, four times Australian Champion, Grandmaster of the International Correspondence Chess Association and winner of the first-ever World Championship at postal chess. In the penultimate round he faced his own son John, whose performance in the tournament had been decidedly mediocre. However, as often happens, youth prevailed, depriving the highly experienced maestro of his fifth victory in the Championship.

After the game the son looked very satisfied, while the father merely wiped the sweat from his brow.

A closely related topic is the record for dejection on a birthday. Your birthday is always supposed to make you happy, especially if the number of years is a round figure – but Tigran Petrosian's mood on his fortieth was far from elated. He had to go and resume the adjourned 23rd game of his World Championship match, or even resign it outright. Even the draw which Boris Spassky offered over the telephone was of no comfort; on his jubilee birthday Tigran lost his title as King of Chess.

But it was Milan Vidmar the elder, venerable Grandmaster and Professor, who felt especially pained by a win – against a child. His account of the incident is quoted in the book by Alexander Koblentz, the master who taught and coached Mikhail Tal.

In Vidmar's words, the appearance in Vienna of the six-year-old Sammy Reshevsky caused a veritable panic in the local chess club. To begin with, everyone admired the infant prodigy's play; they were touched by his first victories and his droll comments. But when the boy made short work of the club's strongest players, the committee members were well and truly alarmed. The 'good name' of the club was at stake! They resolved to 'silence' the little monster at any price, and invited the well-known Viennese master Siegfried Wolf to do so.

"Where *is* this kiddy, then?" asked the maestro when he had hardly set foot inside the club. *"I'll put a stop to this palaver!"*

Wolf sat down at the board and was soundly thrashed.

Then Vidmar himself agreed to play the role of examiner. The Yugoslav player conducted the opening a little carelessly and, in his own words, experienced his opponent's iron grip. It was only with great difficulty that Vidmar succeeded in freeing himself and then went on to win. He had no recollection of how many hours the gruelling contest had lasted under the anxious eyes of the Viennese chess fans. Eventually his young opponent turned his king over as a sign of resignation.

The boy had played the whole game kneeling on his chair; otherwise he wouldn't have been able to reach the pieces. Without altering this posture he leaned a little further forward, laid his head on the chessboard and began crying bitterly. An awkward silence ensued. Vidmar departed on the quiet. By his own admission, the victory had given him no pleasure.

A great sacrifice

Time and again we have to admit the elasticity of the criterion. Cascades of sacrifices in chess are numbered in their thousands – from the time of Adolf Anderssen to our own era of Garry Kasparov and Vladimir Kramnik. Cases in which nearly all the fighting units merely fuel the fire of the attack, so that the last one of them checkmates the enemy king, can be counted as the rule rather than the exception. Given the absolute impossibility of

an objective choice, there is a case for proposing that the record-breaking sacrifice was one that occurred in the autumn of 1902, in the course of a tour of the cities and towns of Europe by Harry Pillsbury, then at the height of his powers. In the 'simuls' and individual games he always played blindfold; and in the following encounter, at the chess club of the London Polytechnic Institute, 'living chess pieces' were used.

Pillsbury – Bowles

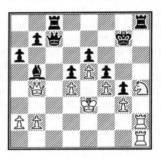

Possession of the open h-file promises nothing at the moment, so the American Grandmaster brilliantly seizes another avenue of attack – on the queenside.

37 Rc2!! Bc6

If Black captures the Trojan horse with 37...Wxc2, he is annihilated by 38 We7+ Kg8 39 Wxe6+ Kg7 (39...Kf8 allows mate in three: 40 Ng6+ Kg7 41 Wf6+) 40 Nxf5+ Wxf5 41 Wxf5. But now the pin on the c-file is decisive.

38 Wc5 Rh7 39 Rhc1 Wd8 40 b4 Rc7 41 a4 Rxh4 42 gxh4 Wxh4 43 b5 axb5 44 axb5 Wg3+ 45 Kd2 Wxf4+ 46 Kc3 b6 47 Wxb6 Rb7 48 Wxc6 We3+ 49 Kb2 Wxd4+ 50 Rc3 Wb4+ 51 Rb3 Wd2+

52 ♖c2 ♕d4+ 53 ♔c3 ♕d1 54 b6
d4 55 ♔c7+ ♖xc7 56 bxc7 d3
57 c8=♕ ♕xc2+ 58 ♕xc2 dxc2
59 ♔xc2 ♔g6 60 ♔d2 f4 61 ♖b8
♔f5 62 ♖g8 g3 63 ♔e2 ♔e4
64 ♖g4 g2 65 ♔f2 1-0

There might seem to be nothing unusual here; White realized his advantage accurately enough. But the point is that on move 55 he made a sacrifice, though temporary, of his queen – whose role in the 'live chess set' was played by his own young and passionately loved wife! And although a mere two moves later she reappeared on the chessboard, to be exchanged at once for the black queen (Bowles's wife!), who knows what words the famous but evidently careless husband would have had to listen to after the game?

A priceless book

Singling out an invaluable book from the immense bibliography of world chess literature would seem an impossible task. Anyway, what criteria would you apply? In terms of the money they would fetch, you would no doubt have to choose between the treatise of Alfonso the Wise (Europe's earliest manuscript on chess), the 'Paris manuscript' of Luis de Lucena, the works of Phillip Stamma or Gioachino Greco, perhaps the Persian manuscript preserved by the Royal English Asiatic Society under number 16856 in the catalogue, or first editions of Alessandro Salvio or the great François-André Danican Philidor. These are all famous works, hallowed by the centuries, and extant only in isolated copies

throughout the world. As to how informative chess books are, we cannot even discuss that criterion here. There is even less possibility of comparing the scope and usefulness of manuals on the opening, middlegame or endgame.

Nevertheless I will make so bold as to name one book as truly priceless. It is *A History of Chess*, the classic work by the English mathematician Harold James Ruthven Murray – but in a reprinted edition, rather than the original one of 1913. I am not speaking of the whole edition either, but one particular copy. In 1976, the American magazine *Funny, Funny World* told of a letter to Murray written by a policeman named Fergus Finch from the state of New Jersey. He related that while he was struggling with some robbers, a bullet fired by one of them "went into your superb book which was in my coat pocket, and got stuck about half way through chapter four." So *A History of Chess* saved a priceless human life, and is therefore itself priceless.

Alas, the distinguished chess historian was unable to read that letter. He had been dead for over 20 years!

(Work on the present book was practically finished when I came across Evgeny Gik's latest publication, entitled *Five Hundred Happy Chess Stories*. In among the fairly trivial tales and anecdotes, there is this very episode. We will put aside any moral questions of what there is happy about a bullet speeding towards the heart, and leave them to the conscience of the 'Master of Science, chess master and writer'. But according to Gik, it appears that Murray *did* receive the policeman's letter of thanks – in the other world, I presume! Ivan Andreyevich Krylolv's words had gone unheeded. He admonished one of the characters in his fables: "Lie by all means, but you have to know where to stop.")

As the chess book that took more reading time than any other in the world, we may smilingly name *Elements of the Game of Chess*, published in Boston in 1805. It was borrowed from the library of the small town of Harrisburg, Pennsylvania, then returned more than 120 years later. There is no reason to suppose that four generations of the Goodman family spent all their time studying this handbook for beginners, but when the 76-year-old Clyde sent the little volume to the astounded librarians in 1986, he wrote in his accompanying letter: "I do not know what prevented my great-great-grandfather from returning this book on time. Perhaps it was the Civil War of 1861-65, or perhaps the great flood of 1889. In any case you should be thankful for his forgetfulness, as this book is now rare and has been preserved for you complete and undamaged."

But let us return to the only means of comparison which the world accepts, that is, money. (The comparison is only relatively precise, as even the most stable currencies constantly fluctuate. The dollar at the end of the 19th century was a good deal 'fatter' than its 'namesake' decades later, while the rouble of the present and that of 1913 are like night and day!)

The highest price was paid at a Paris auction in the summer of 1991, for Lucena's 'Paris manuscript'. The original of this work had appeared no later than 1497; the manuscript up for auction was a French copy made by an Italian translator, on paper measuring 125x77 mm. It contains the rules for playing 11 openings, which Lucena presents as "the best I have seen in Rome and in all Italy, in France and Spain". There are also 28 chess problems ranging from two-movers to ten-movers, taken from the 150 in the original.

The manuscript had belonged to the French master André Muffang, who departed this life at the age of 93. Almost seven decades earlier (at Margate, 1923), he had shared 2nd-5th places with Alekhine, Bogoljubow and the Englishman Michell; although he lost to the first-named, he beat the second. Muffang had also been the owner of 'Royal Entertainments, or the Game of Chess, its Rules and Moral Worth' by the 12th-century poet and writer Abraham Ibn Ezra; *Chess, or the Royal Game* by Selenus, the earliest chess book to be printed in Germany; the first edition of Philidor's *Analyze* (1749); and very many other items.

The auction was attended by Boris Spassky, Lev Polugaevsky, Lubomir Kavalek and, of course, Lothar Schmid, the owner of a private chess library of record dimensions (about 30,000 editions!). The initial asking price for the 'Paris manuscript' was 60,000 French francs, which put many people off – but bids were soon running into six figures. The 'final duel' was conducted between an unknown person bidding by telephone and Monsieur Chamonal, the son of the well-known Paris bookseller. The 'on-the-spot' bidder proved stronger than the 'external' one, and at the sum of 295,000 francs, the auctioneer's hammer came down three times.

The most voluminous book on chess is *Kings of the Chess World* by Linder father and son, published in Russian in 2001. It contains 972 folio-sized pages, or in printer's terms, 150 sheets. In his whole lifetime Dostoevsky wrote about twice as much as that, and so did Pushkin – but Lermontov only wrote two-thirds as much.

Unfortunately this book established two additional records. One of them is for the number factual errors – they run into *hundreds*! The other is for a unanimous decision by the chief editors of all three Russian chess periodicals: they refused to publish reviews of it, in which these failings would naturally not have been passed over in silence. The editors in question were Alexander Roshal of *64: Chess Review*, an adept at under-cover intrigues; Alexander Kentler of *Petersburg Chess*, forthright and uncompromising in his words; and Vladimir Barsky, quite new to the job of editing *Chess Weekly*. Their ostensible reason for not reviewing the book was a noble wish to avoid offending I.M.Linder who had already celebrated his 80-year jubilee.

No one so much as thought about the offence to readers – and to history!

However, everything in this world is relative, and even the record held by the Linders' book is perhaps rivalled – however strange this may seem – by the 1998 *Guinness Book of Records*. Printed on environmentally friendly paper (as we learn from the publication data) and beautifully illustrated, it places chess in the games section rather than the sport section and accords it roughly 650 letters. Guinness Publishing Limited has evolved a detailed and painstaking system for ascertaining and checking records with maximum accuracy. (This again is according to the publication data page.) Despite this, the chess article contains over a dozen errors! Of course this isn't the same as the Linders' hundreds, but suppose we view it in percentage terms? The great Lasker's name is garbled (equating him with the well-known sexual adventuress from the film *Emmanuelle*). Other chess personalities named incorrectly are the strongest female player ever, the youngest of the Polgars; the genius Morphy, who is transformed into Murphy; and his contemporary Louis Paulsen, whose system in the Sicilian Defence is alive to this day although one-and-a-half centuries old. We are told that this last-named player once thought for 11 hours (!) over his 56th move. (The reference is to the well-known second game of Paulsen's match with Morphy in the final of the first All-American Chess Congress in 1857; the game was drawn after 15 hours, but featured neither 56 moves nor such endless thought. Paulsen really did once 'go to sleep over the position', but 'only' for 1 hour 15 minutes.)

Furthermore the English player Susan Arkell is said to have achieved a rating approaching 2700 at the age of 15. In short, the publishers' stern warning – that no part of the material may be reproduced by electronic, electrochemical, mechanical or any other means without permission – is patently superfluous. Who would pay genuine money for such a forgery?

We cannot conclude this tricky topic without a perfectly valid admission: there are not, never have been and never will be any factual books without errors. There is even an anecdote about the publishers of an encyclopaedia who set themselves the task of not allowing even the smallest misprint in it. When the proofs had been checked 5 or 10 times, they achieved their aim. Yet on the cover of the massive volume, the word *Encyclopudia* was printed in gold. Once again, then: "You have to know where to stop...."

* * *

So-called chess philately incorporates a whole range of mistakes, each more 'glaring' than the last. Over the past 30-40 years, the list of countries issuing postage stamps with chess themes has been increased by several states in Asia and, especially, Africa – where, strictly speaking, the the number of chessplayers can be numbered on the fingers, and a high level of chess culture has yet to materialize. This would evidently explain the incorrect placing of pieces in diagrams taken from actual historic games, the distorted names of champions beneath the diagrams, etc. etc.

Yet even in countries with long-established chess traditions, similar curiosities abound. For example, on one of the Yugoslav stamps commemorating the first post-war Olympiad (Dubrovnik, 1950) the artist portrayed a position from the famous Capablanca-Lasker game at the even more famous New York tournament of 1924.

On the stamp, however, the black bishop is for some reason converted from a light-squared one into a dark-squared one – it is transferred to f8. In that situation Lasker obviously wouldn't have prolonged his resistance for another dozen moves but would have resigned at once.

Now another curiosity. In Gdynia (Poland) in 1978, the regular dockers' and shipbuilders' Spartakiad took place, and for its chess section a special postmark was designed. But if you look at it carefully, you notice that the chessboard it depicts consists of 49 squares instead of the usual 64, as it only has 7 ranks and files. In the artist's view this was a perfectly legitimate variant....

288

As the record in this department, we may name a set of 4 postage stamps issued on 30 November 1979 in Mali. They are entitled 'Outstanding Chessplayers'. (Two years, one month and one day later, they were to be overprinted with a caption relating to Anatoly Karpov's victory in the World Championship match at Merano.)

In principle we all have our own views on whether this or that player belongs in the chess pantheon. No one is surprised to see Alexander Alekhine depicted on one of these four stamps. The choice of Efim Bogoljubow for the second stamp is a trifle controversial, while David Janowski on the third is rather more so. But the round-faced man aged about fifty who appears on the fourth stamp aroused nothing but astonishment. No one in the world had even heard of 'Grandmaster Schlage', and yet that was the name under which this 'outstanding chessplayer' appeared.

Still, every mystery is clarified sooner or later. It turned out that in the 1920s Willy Schlage, a national master, had twice taken the bronze medal in German Championships. He could not accept Hitler's rise to power, and after leaving his native country he settled in Africa where he worked in various places as a chess coach. It so happened that one of the postal officials who was involved in issuing these stamps had had dealings with Schlage way back in his youth; this was why he included him among the outstanding players and at the same time promoted him to Grandmaster rank.

Anyway, in his early years Schlage had produced some sparkling chess. In the chapter 'Vertical distances' we saw his game from which the 'Astronaut-Computer' encounter was copied.

* * *

In terms of straightforward annotations to moves, the record absurdity once occurred in the English magazine *Chess*. After **1 e4 e6**, the move **2 e5!??!** attracted comment.

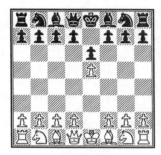

"Wilhelm Steinitz must be turning in his grave," the comment read. Actually this move was conceived by Steinitz himself, who employed it many times in the most serious competitions against the worthiest of opponents, such as Winawer (at Vienna 1882) and Blackburne (London 1883).... The first World Champion considered that after either 2...d5 3 exd6 ♗xd6 4 d4 or 2...c5 3 f4 ♘c6 4 ♘f3, White would preserve the advantage of the first move. Our wise chess predecessors should not be disturbed in vain.

In the opinion of *Chess Notes*, another English magazine, the record for incompetence could go to the author of a handbook for beginners, who 'taught' that "the game is drawn if one of the players repeats the same move three times within an hour." In a section on 'The Endgame', he advised his readers to advance their pawns to queen, if possible all in a bunch.

Peace, perfect peace?

In the matter of agreeing a draw, what records can there be? None, you would suppose. From one point of view this is right, but it isn't the end of the story. The most unusual clashes have more than once occurred during peace negotiations.

A 'dialogue' between Rashid Nezhmetdinov and Mikhail Tal during the USSR Spartakiad, Moscow 1959, has the most realistic claim to be the record for mutual incomprehension.

Nezhmetdinov – Tal

In the diagram position, the leader of the RSFSR side considered that he had no right whatever to take risks in the context of a team tournament, and after making his 16th move he offered a draw to the player who had won the

Soviet Championship twice and was soon to be World Champion. Tal made a movement with his lips, and Nezhmetdinov, whose hearing was not marvellous, took it that his peace offer had been accepted. At lightning speed, Rashid's hand reached out over the board and began switching the pieces from square to square, demonstrating equality in the variation 16...f5 17 ۞g5 ♗c5 18 ۞gf3.

Tal's amazement knew no bounds, for he hadn't spoken a word and was not thinking of a draw. The interests of his team required him to continue the fight, and anyway in this position Black has not yet exhausted his trumps. Therefore the pieces were put back, the battle was renewed, and Nezhmetdinov, somewhat piqued, felt an upsurge of pugnacity inside him.

16...a5

Of course this doesn't yet lose, but it does allow White to increase his lead in development. The black king is still in the centre, and it is no doubt too early to be thinking about counter-attacking against d3.

17 ♖ac1 ♗a6 18 ♖fe1 g6

In the event of 18...♗xd3? 19 f5 White has a very strong attack, but it turns out that this break can't be stopped anyway.

19 f5 ♗g7 20 f6!

By sacrificing a pawn White deflects the finely placed knight from the defence of c7 (20...♗xf6? 21 ۞xf6+ ۞xf6 22 ۞xe6 fxe6 23 ♖xe6+ ♔f7 24 ♖cc6) and puts a stop to the counterplay on the long black diagonal which his opponent has prepared.

20...♘xf6 21 ♘d6+ ♔e7

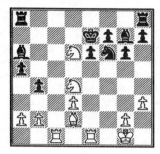

22 ♘xf7! ♔xf7 23 ♖c7+ ♔g8 24 ♘xe6 ♘e8 25 ♖d7 ♗f6?

Certainly the threat of 26 ♘xg7 ♘xg7 27 ♗f4 followed by ♗f4-e5 was only now that White obtains a won position. After 25...♗b5 26 ♖b7 ♗a6 or 25...♗c8 26 ♖d8 ♗b7, he would have to settle for repeating moves.

26 ♖f1!

With the sudden appearance of a mating net, the onslaught has reached the point where Black's game is beyond saving. The threat is 27 ♖xf6 ♘xf6 28 ♖g7 mate, besides which the f8-square must not be left unguarded. Black prolonged the fight by the only possible means:

26...♘g7 27 ♖xf6 ♘xe6 28 ♖xe6 ♗b5 29 ♖c7 h5 30 ♖xg6+ ♔f8

But once the time control was passed, he resigned, faced with unavoidable mate **(1-0)**.

As the record for a vehement reaction, we may take a retort made by the temperamental Miguel Najdorf during the third game of his match with Reuben Fine (New York, 1949). The American Grandmaster was a pawn down in a knight endgame. When he offered a draw for the second time, the Argentinian jumped up from his chair and shouted "two hundred dollars!" so that everyone in the hall could hear. In present-day terms, taking half a century of inflation into account, this price for half a point would come to about three thousand! An indignant Fine, in turn, naturally declined this proposal and continued playing, in a position that was by no means hopeless.

Fine – Najdorf
(notes by Levenfish)

58...f4+

Black can't do without this move, but it reduces his points of entry and with them his winning chances.

59 ♔f2 ♘d4 60 ♘d5 ♘c6 61 ♘c3 ♔h4 62 ♔g2 ♘e7 63 ♘e4 ♘f5 64 h3?

After 64 ♘f2 ♘e3+ 65 ♔g1 ♘c2 66 ♘d3 g5 67 ♔f2 Black would hardly be able to win.

64...♘e3+ 65 ♔h2 ♘c2 66 ♔g2 ♘e1+ 67 ♔f2 ♔xh3 68 ♔xe1 ♔g2 69 ♔e2 h5 70 ♘g5 h4 71 ♘e6 g5!

White resigned, as the pawn endgame after 72 ♘xg5 h3 73 ♘xh3 ♔xh3 is lost for him.

0-1

It was in a wholly amicable spirit, with no dialogue and just a smile, that the players signed the scoresheet after the third match game at Semmering in 1931, between Mir Sultan Khan, the Indian subject of the British crown, and Savielly Tartakower, the French citizen of Russian origin. There was nothing left on the board except a white king on e4 and a black king on e8. Yes, the Grandmasters had honourably followed the maxim laid down in the match regulations – to fight on to the very bitter end.

Boundless disrespect

Vladimir Mayakovsky, that great reformer of Russian poetry, wrote the lines: "A nail in my boot is more terrible than all the tragedies of Goethe." From a mundane point of view this rings true, and every chessplayer can complain of some crying injustice, some affront or incivility, that he has suffered at some time. For instance the ex-World champions Botvinnik and Karpov complained that during the 1994 Olympiad in Moscow they were not invited (which practically meant they were not admitted) to the FIDE Congress that was taking place at the same time. The English Ladies' Champion Mary Rudge, who won the first women's inter-national tournament in chess history at London in 1897, complained that "after losing a game, men often lose their temper and start behaving in an ill-mannered way. Once when I checkmated a certain gentleman, he swept the pieces off the board and called me a Texas cow." A century earlier, the London newspaper *World* had announced in a highly

frivolous tone that "last Monday the famous chessplayer Monsieur Philidor made his final move by departing for the other world."

In my view, though, all this pales beside a report by Stig Jonasson, working for the Swedish *Chess Journal*, who visited the city of New Orleans in the summer of 1988. In the house at 1113 Rue Charles, where the genius Paul Morphy was born, he discovered a museum – devoted to General Beauregard who commanded a Confederate army in the American Civil War, and the little-known mid-20th century novelist Francis Parkinson-Keyes! Of the great American who brought glory to his country, there was no mention at all! At 417 Royal Street, the house where Morphy lived and died, there was nothing either; a fashionable restaurant occupied the site.

At the baseball club which has been named after Morphy ever since 1859, not a single member knew who he was! Furthermore in the Saint Louis Cemetery, the grave of the strongest chessplayer of his time proved to be in a thoroughly neglected state. Even the inscription on the headstone was almost impossible to decipher. The ground all about was littered with rusty needles and broken syringes; drug addicts evidently found the spot congenial....

A Swedish record-breaker

The Swedish Grandmaster Anders Gideon Tom Stahlberg (usually called by his second forename) was in his own way a double record-holder. He lived for less than 60 years, in other words not too long, but proved to be the Olympic competitor of longest standing. He was a member of his country's team from 1928 to 1964, that is for 36 years, playing mainly on top board! In terms of both the time span and the number of Olympiads (13) in which he took part, Stahlberg surpassed Paul Keres (11 appearances in 29 years, for two national teams: Estonian and Soviet), the Dutchman Lodewijk Prins (12 Olympiads in 31 years), Miguel Najdorf (likewise 12, for the Polish and Argentinian teams, over the course of 35 years), and Erich Eliskases who played for three (!) countries – Austria, Germany and Argentina – in 8 Olympiads during a 30-year period.

In these events Stahlberg produced some first-rate play.

Stahlberg – Szabo
1st board, Helsinki Olympiad 1952

16 ♗e5!

By cutting off the black queen's route to the under-protected kingside, White practically compels his opponent to make a diversion on the opposite flank.

16...♗a4 17 c4! ♕d7

Or 17...♗xd1 18 ♗xh7+ ♔h8 (not 18 ♔xh7 19 ♕d3+ and

20 cxd5) 19 ♖xd1 ♕d7 (19...♕xc4 is met by 20 ♗d3 and 21 ♘g5) 20 ♗e4, and if 20...♖ac8? then 21 ♘g5.

18 ♖d2 ♘c6 19 d5! ♘xe5 20 ♘xe5 ♕d6 21 c5! bxc5 22 ♘xf7! ♖xf7 23 dxe6 ♔f8 24 exf7 ♖d8 25 ♖e1 ♖d7 26 ♕e4 ♕h6 27 ♖b2 1-0

The most gold medals in team tournaments were gained by Vasily Smyslov and Mikhail Tal, both World Champions at different times. As a member of the USSR team, Smyslov won the Olympic championship 10 times, the European Championship 5 times and the World Championship once. Tal was in the winning team in 8 Olympiads, 6 European Championships and 3 World Student Championships. Was Tal the record-holder, then? Perhaps not, because as a member of the Moscow team, Smyslov additionally won 2 USSR Team Championships, 2 Spartakiads of the Peoples of the USSR and one All-Union Chess Olympiad; while under the banner of the *Burevestnik* club he won two more USSR Team Championships as well as 2 USSR Cups and 2 European Club Cups. As for Tal, the teams of his native Latvia and the 'Daugava' Sporting Association (which practically amounted to the same thing) were unable to sustain him in the struggle for gold.

With his Olympiad performances, however, Tal did hold a record which persisted until the appearance of Garry Kasparov. He almost invariably gained the top score for his board, and three times (!) registered the absolute best result of any participant. He did this with wins in such scintillating style as the following.

Liebert – Tal
Skopje Olympiad 1972

22...♘de5! 23 fxe5 ♗xe5+ 24 ♔g1 ♕g3 25 ♘f3 ♘h4 26 ♘xh4 ♕h2+ 27 ♔f2 ♗g3+ 28 ♔f3 ♗xh4 29 ♗d4+ ♗f6 30 ♕f2 ♗e5! 31 ♖h1 ♕f4+ 32 ♔e2 ♕xd4 33 ♕xd4 ♗xd4 34 ♗f3 ♖g3! 35 b3 ♗c5 36 ♖ef1 ♖e7+ 37 ♔d2 ♖e3 38 ♗d1 ♖g2+ 39 ♔c1 ♖c3+ 40 ♔b1 ♗a3 0-1

Tal – Hecht
Varna Olympiad 1962
(notes by Tal)

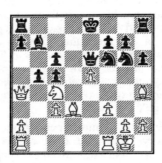

19 exf6!!
This move is reminiscent of the famous game Lilienthal-Capablanca, Hastings 1934/35, in which the young master quickly forced the ex-World Champion's capitulation. Hecht made his next move without thinking. Of course, any player of the Black side might feel very happy with the position after 19...0-0. No less than three white pieces would be *en prise*, and if the queen moved, Black would have nothing to fear after 20...♘xh4. Caution is required, however! On 19...0-0, White has the very powerful 20 ♖ae1!. If then 20...♕d5, there can follow 21 ♕c2 ♘xh4 22 ♘e5, with a very strong attack; while after 20...♕xe1 21 ♖xe1 bxa4 22 ♗xg6 fxg6 23 ♖e7, Black can't continue with 23...♖f7 on account of 24 ♘d6.

At this point, I was ... kissed, by the temperamental Najdorf who had been watching the game.

19...bxa4 20 fxg7 ♖g8

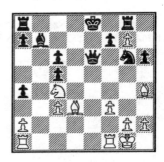

21 ♗f5!!
The climax of the combination! After 21...♕xc4 Black would have a whole (!) extra queen, but would lose to 22 ♖fe1+ ♕e6 23 ♖xe6+ fxe6 24 ♗xg6+ ♔d7 25 ♖d1+ ♔c7 26 ♗g3+ ♔b6 27 ♖b1+ ♔a6 28 ♗d3+ ♔a5 29 ♗c7 mate. Another try, 21...♕xf5, leads to a hopeless ending after 22 ♘d6+ ♔d7 23 ♘xf5 ♘xh4 24 ♖ad1+ ♔c7 25 ♘xh4 ♖xg7 26 ♖fe1; while the

variation 21...♘xh4 22 ♗xe6 fxe6 23 ♘d6+ and 24 ♘xb7 illustrates the 'dexterity' of the white knight.

Hecht selects the best defence, with a view to the counter-stroke on his next move.

21...♘xh4 22 ♗xe6 ♗a6

How can one of the pieces be saved?

23 ♘d6+ ♚e7 24 ♗c4!

The combination is concluded, giving White a distinct endgame advantage.

24...♖xg7 25 g3 ♚xd6

A mistake, as in this kind of position the bishop is stronger than the knight. Black could have preserved some saving chances with 25...♗xc4 26 ♘xc4 ♖d8.

26 ♗xa6 ♘f5 27 ♖ab1 f6 28 ♖fd1+ ♚e7 29 ♖e1+ ♚d6 30 ♚f2 c4

Creating a refuge for the king on c5. All the same, 30...h5, maintaining the knight on its important post for the present, was more tenacious.

31 g4 ♘e7 32 ♖b7 ♖ag8 33 ♗xc4 ♘d5 34 ♗xd5 cxd5 35 ♖b4 ♖c8

He should at least have exchanged the kingside pawns by 35...h5 36 h3 hxg4 37 hxg4 f5, though even that would hardly have saved the game. After the move played, which aims for 'mutual destruction', everything is clear.

36 ♖xa4 ♖xc3 37 ♖a6+ ♚c5 38 ♖xf6 h5 39 h3 hxg4 40 hxg4 ♖h7 41 g5 ♖h5 42 ♖f5 ♖c2+ 43 ♚g3 ♚c4 44 ♖ee5 d4 45 g6 ♖h1 46 ♖c5+ ♚d3 47 ♖xc2 ♚xc2 48 ♚f4 ♖g1 49 ♖g5

Black resigned in view of 49...♖xg5 50 ♚xg5 d3 51 g7 d2 52 g8=♕ d1=♕ 53 ♕b3+.

1-0

This game was acknowledged as the finest of the Olympiad, and as usual Tal made the best result for his board.

Tal – Petrosian
USSR Team Championship,
Moscow 1974

19 ♘eg5+! hxg5 20 ♘xg5+ ♚g8 21 ♕f4 ♘d7 22 ♖xd7! ♗xd7 23 ♗xf7+ 1-0

By taking first place on board 1, Tal outperformed Spassky, Smyslov, Petrosian, Bronstein, Geller....

But let us come back to Gideon Stahlberg's second record. He not only figured among the first batch of newly created International Grandmasters in 1950; he was also one of the first to be awarded the new title of International Arbiter a year later. So great was his authority that he acted as chief arbiter in 5 World Championship matches. It was during one of these that an incident occurred which in its way was unique.

The return match between Smyslov and Botvinnik in 1958 was going more than pleasantly for the challenger, that is the ex-Champion.

After 14 games Botvinnik held an overwhelming 4-point lead, and on top of this the 15th was adjourned in a forlorn position for White (Smyslov). On resumption, however, Black played some inaccurate moves, and in Botvinnik's own words he heaved a sigh of relief only when the queens were exchanged and the following position appeared on the board.

Smyslov – Botvinnik
Moscow 1958

Here Black sank into thought, working out a plan to exploit his large plus – two bishops in an endgame, with play on both wings! In so doing, he completely forgot about the clock. With each second, the look on the chief arbiter's face grew more strained; you could see this even from a distance. He didn't go away from the table; the flag on Black's clock crept upwards ... and then dropped. Botvinnik had still not made his 55th move when, to his genuine astonishment, Stahlberg's hand stopped the clock! I don't know if the word *record* can be applied to this situation, but such forgetfulness is definitely unique in matches for the crown.

And it fell to Stahlberg's lot to be officiating.

However, in the realm of refereeing, the Swedish Grandmaster did have one peer in Miroslav Filip from the former Czechoslovakia, who in addition to being a Grandmaster and International Arbiter was a candidate for the world crown. In playing the role of chief arbiter 5 times, his record was on a par with Stahlberg's, but there was one additional 'plus' which he held in common with the Dutch Grandmaster Jan Hein Donner. It was given to these two to look down somewhat on all and sundry, even on chessplayers with a build for basketball like Max Euwe, Vladimir Kramnik, Alexei Shirov and Yuri Averbakh – because they themselves (in the mornings at least) stood six feet six inches high.

Chess mysticism and reality

Anything great – whether historical personalities, inspired inventions or even monumental battles – always accumulates a rich stock of legends, conjectures and even testimonies; this no doubt is what gave birth to the immortal aphorism, "He's lying like an eyewitness."

Chess is not the least of human inventions, and it too, needless to say, has given rise to all conceivable types of story – both mythical and authentic – which have become part and parcel of its existence lasting for centuries and perhaps millennia. Here are one or two of them which may claim to be records.

* * *

Chessplayers, just like anyone else, have plenty of premonitions. There is no strictly scientific explanation for this; nerves, the workings of the subconscious, chance coincidences and perhaps some warnings or 'signs' from above – who knows? Those predictions which have precisely illuminated a chessplayer's career and future, years in advance, are equally inexplicable.

Boris Spassky used to tell the story of one of the 'games of his life' from the 1958 USSR Championship at Riga. In the final round he was playing Mikhail Tal and obtained a won position. A win would give Spassky the silver medal and a place in the World Championship Interzonal Tournament. A draw would give him bronze and a play-off match with Grandmaster Yuri Averbakh for the Interzonal place. But on resuming after the adjournment, Boris contrived to lose and was left with neither.

I was absolutely gutted. I walked along the street and wept – real proper tears, as you can imagine. Then I met the journalist David Ginzburg, a Draughts Master who spent eight years in Soviet labour camps. He came out, lived for a few years after that and then died.

"Boris", he said to me, "Are you crying? I'll just tell you what's going to happen – don't be upset. Tal will go on to win the Interzonal. Then he'll win the Candidates Tournament. After that he'll play a match

with Botvinnik, and he'll beat him. Then there'll be a return match and Botvinnik will win. *You've* got to keep playing and playing, and you'll achieve everything you want."

That, don't forget, was in 1958. David hit the nail on the head, he foretold everything like a Gipsy woman. I've never known such an amazing feel for prophecy.

These, you understand, are Spassky's own words.

* * *

And yet there is an even more astonishing case! What I regard as an absolute and scarcely repeatable record was set up in 1935 by the Austrian writer Elias Canetti.

The hero of the novel *Die Blendung* (The Glare), which he published in Vienna, is called Fischerl. He is a passionate devotee of chess. He dreams that he will become World Champion and emigrate to America where he will live the life of a recluse. Recounting his strange dream, he laments: "Not a single person in America could pronounce this stupid name of mine. Without exception they called me 'Mister Fisher'."

As we know, 8 years later in the USA the future Chess King was born....

Such a prophetic vision simply puts in the shade the American Grandmaster Robert Byrne's prognosis on the eve of the famous Spassky-Fischer match in 1972. Up until then the opponents had met five times, and the score stood at two draws and three wins to the current World Champion. Byrne nonetheless publicly proclaimed that the match would be over after the 21st game (the rules allowed for a maximum of 24) with a score of 12½:8½ to Fischer! The only pity is that the seer didn't place a bet on these figures at the bookmakers. He could have won just as much from the match as Fischer did!

* * *

The most extravagant reaction to a wholly mundane procedure was once produced by the German Grandmaster Robert Hübner. The players in a tournament had been given a questionnaire. After filling it in he signed it with four crosses, and explained:

"In former times our illiterate peasants would put three crosses in place of a signature. I do not understand very much about what is happening in today's world and am fully entitled to consider myself illiterate. I have appended the fourth cross because I am not merely illiterate but an illiterate Doctor of Philology...."

To this we should add that Professor Hübner has a command of about a dozen different languages (!), and that, for example, during the Chigorin Memorial Tournament in Sochi he could be seen on the beach with a little volume of Homer in his hands – in ancient Greek!

* * *

In general there is no lack of idiosyncrasies – or little super-stitions – among chessplayers of all ages and ranks. Thus, Grandmaster

Savielly Tartakower, a trenchant wit and at the same time the king of chess journalism in the 1920s and 30s, took a most unsightly old hat with him from tournament to tournament. He would only wear it on the day of the last round – and he would win. Notably, this hat did not guarantee him success in the casinos which he visited as though it were a job of work. The roulette table would regularly acquire both the Grandmaster's prizes and the numerous fees from his endless string of articles.

* * *

However, you might say that the ultimate record was attained at the very dawn of civilized chess. In 1642, in his tract on the healing power of religion, the English theologian Thomas Browne wrote that he had once tried conclusions at the chessboard with none other than the Prince of Darkness! "The devil gave me a pawn, but then he won my queen by a cunning manoeuvre," Browne recalled. He continued: "Offering up a prayer to the Lord, I succeeded in over-coming the enemy of mankind." Unfortunately this conqueror of the power of evil did not supplement his story by giving the scoresheet or even a printed score of this most important of games. Perhaps the trouble was that it would be another century before Phillip Stamma invented algebraic notation. Perhaps the devil's English adversary was already unable to tolerate that well-known descriptive system which his compatriots only grudgingly renounced in very recent times, in the last quarter of the twentieth century.

298

Index of Chapter Sections

Part One: Games

Part Two: People

Part Three: Tournaments, Matches, Events

Part Four: Around the Chequered Board

Index of Players